THE ELEMENTAL DIALECTIC OF LIGHT AND DARKNESS

ANALECTA HUSSERLIANA

THE YEARBOOK OF PHENOMENOLOGICAL RESEARCH

VOLUME XXXVIII

Editor-in-Chief

ANNA-TERESA TYMIENIECKA

The World Institute for Advanced Phenomenological Research and Learning
Belmont, Massachusetts

a sequel to:
Vol. IV   : Ingardeniana I
Vol. XXX   : Ingardeniana II
Vol. XXXIII : Ingardeniana III

as well as to the following volumes in philosophy and literature:
Vol. XII   : The Philosophical Reflection of Man in Literature
Vol. XVIII   : The Existential Coordinates of the Human Condition:
              Poetic — Epic — Tragic
Vol. XIX   : Poetics of the Elements in the Human Condition. Part 1:
              The Sea
Vol. XXIII   : Poetics of the Elements in the Human Condition. Part 2:
              The Airy Elements
Vol. XXVIII : The Elemental Passions of the Soul
Vol. XXXII : Phenomenology and Aesthetics, Approaches to Comparative Literature and Other Arts

THE ELEMENTAL DIALECTIC
OF LIGHT AND DARKNESS
The Passions of the Soul
in the Onto-Poiesis of Life

Edited by

ANNA-TERESA TYMIENIECKA

The World Phenomenology Institute

Published under the auspices of
The World Institute for Advanced Phenomenological Research and Learning
A-T. Tymieniecka, President

KLUWER ACADEMIC PUBLISHERS
DORDRECHT / BOSTON / LONDON

Library of Congress Cataloging-in-Publication Data

PN
47
.E43
1992

The elemental dialectic of light and darkness : the passions of the
soul in the onto-poiesis of life / edited by Anna-Teresa
Tymieniecka.
        p.   cm. -- (Analecta Husserliana ; v. 38)
    Includes index.
    ISBN 0-7923-1601-0 (HB : alk. paper)
    1. Literature--Philosophy. 2. Light in literature. 3. Darkness
in literature. 4. Dialectic in literature.   I. Tymieniecka, Anna
-Teresa. II. Series.
    B3279.H94A129 vol. 38
    [PN47]
    142'.7 s--dc20
    [809'.9336]   91-42956

ISBN 0-7923-1601-0

Published by Kluwer Academic Publishers,
P.O. Box 17, 3300 AA Dordrecht, The Netherlands.

Kluwer Academic Publishers incorporates the publishing programmes
of D. Reidel, Martinus Nijhoff, Dr W. Junk and MTP Press.

Sold and distributed in the U.S.A. and Canada
by Kluwer Academic Publishers,
101 Philip Drive, Norwell, MA 02061, U.S.A.

In all other countries, sold and distributed
by Kluwer Academic Publishers Group,
P.O. Box 322, 3300 AH Dordrecht, The Netherlands.

Printed on acid-free paper

Printed in the Netherlands.

TABLE OF CONTENTS

PART THREE

PART FOUR

PART FIVE

LIGHT AND DARKNESS:
THE PRIMEVAL DIALECTIC OF LIFE

When we refer in any way to light and/or darkness, their essential conjunction is necessarily surmised — conjunction and opposition. This very oppostion indicates a primal relationship: darkness without reference to light would have no degree in quality, no pitch, no intensity; in fact, it would have no qualitative endowment at all. This amounts to saying that there would be no meaning of "darkness." And the same holds true for light. It would at first seem that this type of intrinsic relatedness of light to darkness and the inverse holds for every pair of opposites. But where such pairs as straight and crooked, cold and warm, day and night certainly imply each other in their qualitative endowments, and the gradation to be measured in terms of "more and less," the dialectic exhausts itself in the nuances of their qualitative endowment and stops there. It does not touch their respective essential significant nuclei. As much as we may fancy a perpetual day, may we also envisage all lines being crooked in an infinite variety of ways. The situation becomes more puzzling with the opposites of warm and cold. This opposition seems to border on that of light and darkness. And, this for a good reason: they too acquire significance with their role in life. In fact, light and darkness are not only the primal fruits of *Imaginatio Creatrix* as this latter sets to work establishing a human significance of life, but they assume this role while being the primogenital moments of the construction of this gigantic, existential sphere of the living being which perpetually glimmers in qualitative variety. They play in a way a unique role with respect to all the other elemental factors. They emerge with the initial steps by which the human creative function establishes the main factors to become operative in the constitution of this specifically human sphere of life — the human world of life — but their entering into the constitutive functioning of the human being is fulfilling a unique role: the elements of light and darkness in their dialectics transmit into the human significance of life the basic existential operations of *life itself*. In their dialectical game, light and darkness bring together physis and psyche, natural growth and *techne*, the telic strivings promoting life with those spurning the spiritual unfolding, bios and

vii

ethos ... in an infinitely nuanced variating rainbow whose glimmering rays fulgurate, sparkle, expand, in an ever new play.

The dialectic of light and darkness appears then, as I have pointed out elsewhere,[1] as the essential element in the poiesis of life at large; playing in all its sectors: organic, vital, psychic, societal, spiritual and religious, a life-prompting and enhancing role on the one hand, and permeating them all, it unifies vital stirrings and moves with the specifically human experience.

Human language, artistic creativity, literary imagination and creation are so permeated by this dialectic that it needs a special and extensive analytic effort to disentangle from their tightly spun fabric the particular lines, threads, designs, and stitches through which light and darkness subtend and weave together its (this fabric's) living tissue.

This analytic work is the task of philosophy.

ANNA-TERESA TYMIENIECKA

NOTE

[1] Cf. by the present writer, *The Passions of the Soul and the Onto-poiesis of Culture* (Dordrecht: Kluwer, 1990).

ACKNOWLEDGEMENTS

Sincere thanks are due to my assistants Mark Olivere and Louis Houthakker for their help with the editing of this volume and the compilation of the Table of Contents; thanks are due too to Isabelle Houthakker for the proofreading of the text, and to Robert Wise for the preparation of the Index.

A-T. T.

Conference 1990: Sydney Feshbach, Hans Rudnick, Louis Houthakker.

Some participants in the 1990 seminar in aesthetics.

Some participants of the 1990 conference. From left to right, first row: Bruce Ross, Manuel Vázquez-Bigi, Jadwiga Smith, Rosemarie Kieffer, Marlies Kronegger, Lois Oppenheim. Second row: Bill Smith, Hans Rudnick, Kathryn McKinley.

The 1991 Conference. Cronkhite cafeteria: Maija Kule, Rosemarie Kieffer, A-T. Tymieniecka, Marlies Kronegger, Sarah and Jorge García Gómez.

Hans Rudnick (*right*), Louis Houthakker (*middle*) and Robert Wise (*left*).

Louis Houthakker preparing our book exhibit for the conference.

Hans Rudnick.

PART ONE

THOMAS RYBA

ELEMENTAL FORMS, CREATIVITY AND
THE TRANSFORMATIVE POWER OF LITERATURE
IN A-T. TYMIENIECKA'S *TRACTATUS BREVIS*

In 1977, the novelist John Gardner in his popular book, *On Moral Fiction*, described the once common premise behind the writing and criticism of literature:

It was once a quite common assumption that good books incline the reader to — in this wide and optimistic sense — morality. It seems no longer a common or even defensible assumption, at least in literate circles, no doubt partly because the moral effect of art can so easily be gotten wrong, as Plato got it wrong in the *Republic*. To Plato it seemed that if a poet showed a good man performing a bad act, the poet's effect was a corruption of the audience's morals. Aristotle agreed with Plato's notion that some things are moral and others not; agreed, too, that art should be moral; and went on to correct Plato's error. It's the total effect of an action that's moral or immoral, Aristotle pointed out. In other words, it's the *energeia* — the actualization of the potential which exists in character and situation — that gives us the poet's fix on good and evil; that is, dramatically demonstrates the moral laws, and the possibility of tragic waste, in the universe. It's a resoundingly clear answer, but it seems to have lost its currency.[1]

In her work the *Tractatus Brevis*, Anna-Teresa Tymieniecka re-affirms Gardner's approval of the essential rectitude of the Aristotelian characterization of literature's moral mission, but she does so in a way radically transformed by her philosophy of "beingness."[2] Though the *Tractatus Brevis* can best be described as containing the heart of her larger philosophical corpus, the heart it contains is three-ventricled, its new structure the result of Tymieniecka's original way of conceptualizing "human beingness" in relation to the three classical divisions of philosophy. In the span of some 141 pages, not only does she propose an original aesthetic theory — which is the major task she puts to herself — but she also outlines the metaphysics and ethics inseparably related to this new aesthetics.

In the present essay, I intend to discuss the *Tractatus Brevis* as a work which encapsulates, and yet transcends, the larger philosophy of A-T. Tymieniecka. More specifically, I intend to use it to contextualize her intriguing notion of the elemental form in literature, a notion which is, probably, her most original contribution to aesthetic theory and

3

A-T. Tymieniecka (ed.), Analecta Husserliana, Vol. XXXVIII, 3—26.
© 1992 *Kluwer Academic Publishers. Printed in the Netherlands.*

which in its development presupposes an ethics and metaphysics of literature. That such a contextualization is demanded is evident because of the grand panorama of Tymieniecka's interests. To isolate the notion of elemental form without giving an account of the larger philosophical context in which it nests is to ignore the richness of the notion; in short, it is to truncate its meaning. Such a contextualization has additional value in that it establishes the background for the other essays which follow in this volume and which, in one way or another, address the meaning of the elemental form of light.

THE TACIT STRUCTURE OF THE *TRACTATUS BREVIS*

The *Tractatus Brevis* contains a three-fold structure which mirrors A-T. Tymieniecka's conception of her task. Thus, in presenting her theory of literature she moves through a three-fold circuit, describing, first, the metaphysics presupposed by this theory, then the aesthetics of this theory and, third, her moral theory of literature. But, within her description of the first moment of this circuit (the metaphysics of literature), she repeats the categorical sequence by providing a brief phenomenology of those mental acts which play a constitutive role for culture, in general, and literature, in particular. Thus, *wonderment* corresponds to metaphysics, *fabulation* corresponds to aesthetics and *idealization* correspond to her moral theory. Her point, here, is an important one: no theory of literature which has a claim to profundity can shun questions about those constitutive acts of consciousness which give rise to — and, indeed are demanded by — the classical divisions of philosophy. Again, in the same discussion, she describes the three dimensions to human experience as intelligibility, beauty and morality. Finally, when she discusses the elemental forms, themselves, she implies that the elemental form of light corresponds to metaphysics because it "participates" the mental act of wonderment and is characteristically representative of intelligibility, the elemental form of the sea corresponds to ethics because it "participates" the mental act of idealization and is characteristically representative of morality but she leaves unclarified what corresponds to aesthetics. (Could it be the elemental form of the earth?)

The significance of this *triadomania* (to employ Peirce's neologism) is that it is founded upon distinctions at the core of human reality and is not a matter of mere philosophical construction. Simply put, the differences between the true/intelligible, the beautiful/meaningful and the good/ideal are metaphysical, and metaphysics is comprehensive of all human reality. Another way of describing the relationship between these triads is to see them as related to each other by an analogicity whose most obvious historical correlate is that analogicity possessed by the medieval notion of the scale of being. There is a significant difference between these two conceptions, however. Tymieniecka does not intend the analogicity which obtains between a disciplinary category and an elemental form as referring to some metaphysical *Ding an sich*. Rather, all of these metaphysical structures are analogical (in proper phenomenological style) only by virtue of the fact that they are constituted *within* human experience.[3] Moreover, the experience thus described is not simply experience as it is construed in Husserlian phenomenology — with its exaggerated sense of experience's fundamental rationality — but includes fundamentally irrational human acts, as well. In Tymieniecka's understanding, any phenomenology of experience worthy of the name must also entertain objects not susceptible to purely rational construction.

THE SUBLIMINAL FONT OF CREATIVITY AND THE IMAGINATIO CREATRIX

In the *Tractatus Brevis*, as in the first two earlier volumes of *Logos and Life*, Tymieniecka places the locus of creativity in those structures which are responsible for the unique form of existence she terms "human beingness." In the *Tractatus Brevis* two sectors of this complex have special explanatory significance: the Imaginatio Creatrix and the subliminal zone. Tymieniecka understands the subliminal zone as the zone which provides most of the grist for psychotherapy; it is the region which, if not restrained by structures of healthy consciousness, gives rise to the various forms of non-organic psychopathologies. Contrary to some psychoanalytic theories, however, Tymieniecka believes that the complete identification of the subliminal zone with the notions of the preconscious or the subconscious is a mistake. The primal zone represents a deeper stratum of human personality. It is improper to think of this zone in terms of consciousness at all, for as Tymieniecka explains "it does not partake . . . of the mind's light."[4] It can, however, come to the *awareness* of consciousness in one of two ways: through the psychopathology of the ego or through the creative process itself.

This zone which "comes first in the line of generation" comes "last in the line of discovery or apprehension."[5]

Psychopathologically, the subliminal zone erupts into consciousness when the deconstructed ego finds itself descending to "level of the pre(sub)-conscious."[6] There the ego finds that its remaining integral structures are consumed by primal forces; the bones of the psyche are, as it were, cracked in the teeth of the subliminal passions. The result is that the normal capacity of the ego to ignore the helter skelter associations which are typical of dream states and creative processes — a capacity which is based upon the healthy tendency of consciousness to screen and order reality — is broken and, as she puts it, "through the cracks of the dissolving structure comes the pull of the stygian vortices that drag [it] down into chaos, oblivion, unreason, anguish and fear."[7]

But though the subliminal zone might be compared to a vortex which draws down and smashes the disintegrating ego, in the healthy ego it — together with the Imaginatio Creatrix and various other subconscious zones — can be compared to a Catherine wheel. The very energy which when unbridled leads to destruction, when harnessed leads to creativity. The healthy ego reverses the direction of the energy and creative intentionalities and works are thrown off from the subliminal zone centripetally. Thus, it would be improper to characterize the subliminal zone in a purely negative fashion. The subliminal zone is also the realm of the psyche where the primordial passions originate, and the primordial passions are the motors for all human cultural achievement.

The way Tymieniecka conceptualizes these passions provides the rationale behind their fundamental ambiguity. Quantitatively, they can be characterized as having "pitch, force, power, etc." but qualitatively they can be described as "vehement, frantic, raging, indomitable, etc."[8] Both sets of descriptions are, until contextualized, value neutral. All, however, share a common structure, that of being "a sustained, all comprising, and purposefully oriented inner force that drives ... [humankind] onwards."[9] To call this an "instinct for survival" or the "life force," in a Bergsonian sense, is not far from the mark. However, what makes human "beingness" characteristically different from the forms of life of other creatures who share this brute animus is that, in psychologically healthy humans, the subliminal powers are under the direction of the will, intelligence and the creative imagination. Thus regulated, the subliminal passions are responsible for all creative works.

The faculty which operates instrumentally to shape the subliminal passions is the Imaginatio Creatrix. It operates on these raw materials in two different ways. The first of these is association. Association is the means by which the primal forces are "orchestrated" by means of culturally or experientially established "provisory schemes or 'views,'" and it is the result of the encounter between the experiencing ego and the socially constructed world around it.[10] But alone, association would result in bare *mimesis*; it could never aid in the production of entirely new cultural works. A second operation is demanded, as well, an operation which presupposes that association has already done its work. This operation is dissociation which concentrates on already preestablished coalescences in order to break them apart and reform them according to new possibilities or "provisional views."[11] Together, but under the guidance of the creative imagination, association and dissociation work dialectically and in tandem to generate new cultural forms and artifacts.

Although the Imaginatio Creatrix has almost unbridled freedom in transforming the raw materials of the subliminal passions, it is limited to three avenues of human concern which, in turn, are defined by three constitutive and indestructible intentionalities. The three avenues are the intellectual, the aesthetic and the moral and the constitutive intentionalities are wonder, objectification and idealization.

WONDER AS THE ORIGIN OF CREATIVITY

The starting point for Tymieniecka's discussion of the life significance of literature is the origin of metaphysical thinking. The source to which she returns is that source first described by Aristotle in Book A of the *Metaphysics*: the natural propensity of human beings to wonder. It is in wonder that philosophy finds the matrix from which it issues along with all of culture's creative endeavors. Extending the Aristolelian discovery, Tymieniecka describes wonder as the "essential stance" of humanity and she links it with a second form of intentionality which she calls "marveling." Wonder takes its objects conditioned by the concern to discover the reasons why they are and is directed toward beauty as a particular form of enchantment or entrancement. But this enchantment again necessarily implies a return to speculation about to why beauty leads to enchantment in the first place. Thus, wonder and marveling are related in an inseparable syzygy, a syzygy which in the energetic interpenetration of its components supplies one of culture's most important dynamos.

Tymieniecka describes the "marveling-wonderment coupling" as "the primogenital condition of the launching of the human spirit," and she argues that this is most easily proven with reference to the emergence of the consciousness of the sacred in primitive cultures.[12] The sacred (and its attendant complex of myth, rituals, sacraments and symbols) enters the awareness of primitive peoples not because of inquiries strictly germane to their survival — it is not a matter of the simple quest for mundane solutions — but, rather it is a matter of seeking the ultimate reasons for queries "beyond strictly practical interests."[13] It is in this quest that physical nature is impotent to provide satisfactory explanations, and so culture is initiated in the search for answers beyond the pale of the practical. Within culture, the process of inquiry is sustained not only by the institutions developed for this purpose but also by a triad of subjective, *inherent* drives: "natural curiosity, pure inquisitiveness and personal conjecturing."[14]

FABULATION AS THE OBJECTIFICATION OF CREATIVITY

But if the wonderment-marveling syzygy represents the first moment in the emergence of culture, it is followed quickly by a second moment which leads to the objectification of its speculative queries. This is the moment of creativity which always issues in objective representations. It can be described as having two species which lead to the grounds for the differentiation between philosophy and literature. The fabulae associated with literature are quite different in purpose than the creative works of philosophy both in structure and intent. The *Tractatus*, itself, as a work of philosophy (and more specifically metaphysics), has as its object the fabulation of literature. This means that in order to distinguish the functions of literature and philosophy, we must distinguish the kind of creativity which typifies each. In this differentiation, it is possible to find the answer to the question of how philosophy can take the fabulation of literature as its object and, indeed, what the "property rights" of literature and philosophy are.

The first form of creativity is peculiar to philosophy — and to the project of the *Tractatus*, in general. It is a form of creativity bent upon "discovering the positive truth about life, human existence and destiny and the universe" and results in textual objectifications written "in universal, objectively valid, rational language" and directed to the establishment of "rationally . . . schematic pattern[s] of descriptions, structures, and . . . laws" designed to explain "the definitive nature of reality."[15] Thus, philosophy — and more particularly metaphysics — is concerned about the way things are and their reasons for being as they are. The *Tractatus*, as an instantiation of philosophy, has as its purpose the disclosure of the fundamental structures and laws which underlie the forms of creativity of *both* literature and philosophy. In its peculiar self-reflexivity, the *Tractatus* has the upper hand over the literature it investigates because of its unique descriptive task. But by the same token, the *Tractatus* cannot claim to fulfill the task of literature, either.

The other species, fabulation, is the creative process which differentiates the arts from philosophy. Fabulation, unlike philosophical creativity, is not primarily directed to positive knowledge of being. "[O]n the contrary, it dismantles that state of affairs and recreates it . . . in order to convey the unique *personal* vision of life which the writer summons up."[16] Literature incarnates "vision[s] of life . . . in . . . deeply affective crystalization[s]" which intimately address the reader by means of their "life-situations, characters, intertwinings of events, etc." It expresses the "deepest feelings, emotions, strivings, and urges — stemming from . . . flesh and blood, and spirit."[17] This fabulation, Tymieniecka refers to as "the primordial function" of the creative orchestration "around which all the other sense-giving functions revolve."[18] It is the creative process by which works are produced in which the "human predicament" is interpreted from within the situations, aspirations and prospects of these works' authors. Fabulation gives rise to a multiplicity of Protean forms. "[R]itual, dance, mime, play acting, song, stories, the plastic arts, the organization of social life, laws, principles of distributive justice, etc." are no less than new paradigms of hope with respect to unrealized cultural possibilities.[19] Resultant are "prototypical models of human character, conduct, societal organization, visions of humanity," etc., which serve as the models for cultural style.[20]

Even if culture sustains general institutions for the purpose of investigations based upon wonder and marveling, the creative expression of their discoveries can neither be the product of social committees, the simple practical response to life-threatening facts nor a mere reflex of the *Zeitgeist*. Molded by the concern to understand ultimate meanings, the appreciation of beauty and the specific existential location of the

individual and his prospects, human experience becomes constructive
in a way not reducible to a mere survival response. The facts of life are
read in a new way and are clothed with a meaningfulness which does
not arise from mere practicality or expedience. Moreover, the very
expressions of fabulation are, in themselves, incapable of capturing the
process of fabulation in its intricacy, because fabulation is not only
about the expression of solutions but also about the constant invention
of solutions through the act of creation taken as an end in itself. The
construction of such "transcendent" meaningfulness is the business of
the second moment of cultural vivification, the moment of fabulation.

The creativity of fabulation is as much a deconstruction and reinterpretation of ossified experiential paradigms as it is the construction of
new paradigms. Tymieniecka makes this clear in her explication of the
process of fabulation:

Human fears, needs, dreams release the latent propensities of the subliminal soul, and
to respond to them the fabulating imagination sets to work. Opaque events, situations,
the people involved in them are imaginatively 'de-composed,' taken from their dense
factual interrelations and *conjecturally* transposed into transparent patterns of relations
and embroidered upon. It is in the interval between the decomposition and conjectural
transposition that the factual occurrences . . . direct the creative imagination to reach
into the conundrum of the life conditions . . . which are inherent to . . . the struggle for
survival.[21]

In fact, the creative act entailed by original fabulation is the means
by which it is possible "to unfold" a new metaphysics by which the
savant can reach "the ground of spirit."[22] That such a new metaphysics
is demanded arises from the present state of philosophy in which there
has been a shift from the structures of classical ontology in which being
was categorized as a static "and everywhere the same last principle that
. . . [maintains] whatever there is . . . in stasis or flux" to a "constitutive-
envisioning power of the human mind [i.e., the transcendental circuit of
human functioning]" as ultimate principle.[23] This shift signals the
predicament of modern man, the predicament of having the carpet of a
dependable reality pulled out from under him. Gone are the "millennial
preconceptions, dogmatic assumptions, . . . ontology and metaphysics
which [once] situated him within a frame assumed to be lasting and
within which all moves were cautious. . . . [N]o wonder that the alarm is
sounded over the 'death of man,' the 'end of metaphysics,' the 'rejection
of foundations.' "[24]

From these new conditions a new task devolves upon philosophy:

that of a return to the determination of ultimate principles but — this time — against the background of a *"full-fledged view of nature and the origins of life"* and at a new *"vertiginous level of 'origination and corruption' that the Great Philosopher barely tackled."*[25] Neither God nor the idea of metaphysics have died. Quite the contrary, both have merely been sleeping. Now it is possible for both to be resuscitated because of the new awareness that the supercession of the old metaphysics means that unlimited philosophical possibilities now exist for the exploration of the process of creativity, a process which is interlaced with every experienced reality. It is in the spirit of this new philosophical mission that the *Tractatus Brevis* presents its theory of the metaphysical, aesthetic and moral functions of literature. This new spirit is the source of its central discovery, as well. If a new metaphysic will see the light of day, it must find its vocabulary in the structures of human creativity. Thus, the fabulation which literature is provides the contemplative object for Tymieniecka's new first philosophy, but it exists, also, in its own right as the process by which the floodgates of creativity are opened and new cultural ideals enter the world.

IDEALIZATION AND THE PURPOSE OF GREAT LITERATURE

Although literature emerges from the propensity of humans to fabulate, great literature is distinguished from the simply banal by its moral character which is an aspect of its creative vision. Involved in the process of fabulation, itself, the moral animation of literature is essentially creative. This is not to say that the moral ideals contained in literature are purely new creations every time they occur. Indeed, Tymieniecka asserts that the moral function of literature is a matter of continuity and discontinuity. The greatness of literature is achieved when a sympathy is established between the reader and the author in the very context of this continuity and discontinuity. Put another way the greatness of literature is its ability to convey new moral insights which are unexpected, which address the existential situation of the reader and which are continuous (in some respect) with the culture from which they emerge.

One might well ask why the best literature must be moral literature and not simply creative literature of the highest order? The answer that Tymieniecka provides to this question is complex and is founded upon her conviction that culture itself presupposes a moral base for without such a base community could not exist. Yet this moral base does not have its origin within culture in any reductive sense but must issue from the subliminal zone of the psyche. For Tymieniecka the moral nature of literature is not a matter of established cultural standards existing externally and conditioning the artist. Certainly, much that is moral comes from outside us, but we should not suppose that this is the whole story. We must not conceive the development of moral values as a function of culture in some Bergerian sense as a matter simply of integration and then objectification.[26] In fact, Tymieniecka argues that the laws of society act on the individual ultimately to deaden his moral perception. Obedience to the laws of society means that:

... [W]e are woven into the web of the community of human interests, and through duty, responsibility, habit, the expressions of others, their attitudes toward us, and their appreciation, we are sustained by this web and acquire a secure feeling about ourselves. From our place and role in this web we draw a feeling of confidence, of 'belonging.'[27]

Thus, we begin to measure our value against the expectations of others and against the fulfillment of these expectations in community. Our identity becomes more and more bound to a communal locus.

We [begin to] ... live wrapped in the mantle of the trust ... our community places in us, believing ourselves to be naturally sincere, faithful, compassionate, honest, respectful and decent. To obey the rules and avoid friction, confrontation, awkwardness, unpleasantness, and conflict means, however, to remain on the established surface of things, to see only what is obvious to everybody. In conflict situations, however, the deep foundation of these rules, as well as out 'true' nature and inclinations, come to light.[28]

Liminal situations which dissolve the thin veneer of this societal control are useful for demonstrating how shallowly these values are founded. The breakdown of law and order or the existential alienation of the individual are boundary conditions that demonstrate the final foundation of morality cannot be societal consensus. Even Berger allows that general societal forms — no matter how tolerant of individuality — can be alienating.[29] To avoid the association of morality with cultural norms, Tymieniecka places the origin of moral literature beyond the structures of culture and locates it in the soul of the individual. In other words, though recognizing the often beneficial effect of societal standards on the individual, she opts not for a social explanation of morality but for an explanation which is essentially aretalogical. The origin of morality is to be found not in petty constraints imposed by culture from the outside in order to fulfill some function but in the composite of the subliminal passions, the will and the authenticity of the individual as these co-operate in some specific existential situation.

Tymieniecka is quick to point out, however, that this notion of morality is not aretalogical in the same sense as classical Greek ethics, nor is it habitual. Rather, it is aretalogical only in that it finds its roots in interiority and not in an externally imposed set of duties or strictures. It is not a matter of a simple collection of habits or virtues which are static or eternal and, thus, are to be universally inculcated. Indeed, she describes the distinguishing capacity of virtuous action to be that which "consists in an orchestrated shaping of our entire functioning and . . . 'virtue,' as this capacity, consists in *a dynamic thread uniting the subliminal moral ideal with the deliberative and prompting forces of the will and with those forces of our functioning that shape our conduct.*"[30] The moral capacity always addresses some situation and as such cannot easily be prepackaged for popular consumption. Yet, there are threads which unite all moral actions. Values must not be thought to be completely devoid of general descriptions or formulations. The threads which unite the values of the past and the values of the present are the general forms given to such notions as dedication, responsibility, faithfulness, reliability, courage, sincerity, integrity and, above all mercy — all lacking in the social existence of the postmodern America of the 1990s but still possessing lingering, meaningful referents.[31] In fact, general formulations are most appropriately called *ideals*, and the process for recreating them in unique historical situations and addressing them to unique audiences might be best termed *idealization*.

These general forms live on dimly in our postmodern consciousness, but what we lack in the present — and what has always been "the ground of the problematic" of morality — is a solution to "the discrepancy between . . . ideals and act; inner being and . . . overt action."[32] Neither ideals nor the process of idealization go to the ground of the problematic, because the morality or ethics of the philosopher do not usually contain the criteria of their application. The actor is often at a loss to explain how general moral principles — even generally agreed upon moral principles — are to be applied. This realization on Tymieniecka's part results in an essential reorientation of the study of morality away from abstract principles, societal constraints and *habita* in the direction of the morally exemplary individual (contextualized by all of the preceding, to be sure) but actually engaged in the process of making a moral decision. If one wants to know what morality is, Tymieniecka tells us, we must look to what characterizes a moral being which includes examining how a moral being acts in concrete situations.

In literature, moral being is best typified by characters such as Ahab of Melville's *Moby Dick*. In the qualities with which Melville invests him, Ahab represents supererogatory moral behavior at its finest. Above all, he is portrayed as a "commanding, independent, highly reflective personality" standing heads above common morality and living in revolt against it.[33] Recourse to Tymieniecka's description of Ahab makes clear the qualities which set him apart as an exemplary moral actor.

... [T]he recognition of the all-pervading forces of evil and their imaginative shaping into evil itself, occurs only when a full developed moral consciousness is coupled with independence of mind. With the realization of all wrong caused by human pettiness, comes awareness of human evil and this in turn insight into the overwhelming insidiousness and the inscrutability of its elusive motivations and a tragic sense of its unavoidable consequences. Evil's unpredictability and constant reoccurrence in varying disguises forms a barrier against which the human being of . . . [intrepid] spirit painfully butts. Within the soul's subliminal workshop, human pettiness, human evil, turns evil as such into a fate, a pursuing doom. Its taking shape within the human soul engenders a comparable passion to seek evil out, to meet it and break it, a passion which takes possession of the entire person. . . . Ahab is of this superior cast.[34]

Ahab possesses the dynamic confluence of qualities which makes him moral: he is passionate, he is willful and his actions originate from an interior authenticity which is lacking in many who may even possess the two previous characteristics. Tymieniecka recognizes *authenticity* as the distinguishing mark of the moral actor. What she intends by this word is an inner disposition "to be true to oneself," but this phrase is not to be taken in any banal sense which makes the focus of this disposition egocentricity as the only value.[35] Rather, it denotes a passion and will to forsake the "the natural lifeworld and to establish . . . a new field of life nourished by . . . mind . . . in which . . . [one] has to take all moral responsibility . . . while being understood only vaguely at best . . . ."[36] It is a state in which "an inner self whose habits, tendencies, principles, and conduct are not relative to the rules and regulations of . . . established societal order but are uniquely his own."[37] Without this peculiar form of authenticity, other moral passions would be stunted, shrivelled affairs. With it, the complete fulfillment of moral being occurs and other passions such as courage ("the most vertiginous deployment of the subliminal soul . . .; this is the courage of all heroes, all revolutionaries, reformers, protectors, pioneers, saints, [and] geniuses"), innocence (the "deepest generosity of heart that redeems what is good, loving, heart-felt, and honest in the human being in its purity and innocence of the world as if it were still the first day of creation") and the complex of mercy, contrition and magnanimity are vivified.[38]

The reorientation of the moral dimension of literature in the direction of the moral actor affords the writers of literature a unique opportunity, because literature provides a medium in which concrete moral dilemmas can be fabulated and in which the responses of morally superior actors can be imagined. Moral literature thus becomes the dry lab of moral casuistry. But better than this, literature provides a medium by which new moral teachings can emerge as responses to situations which resonate with those of the reader. Thus, the possibility that moral literature can inspire and teach becomes a live one. But for this to occur one requires not only characters with moral qualities *in potentia* but also situations in which such characters may be placed so that these qualities may emerge in act. In fact, the fabulation of great literature always makes character and circumstance — as well as morality and creativity — inseparable components. It is to this realization that A-T. Tymieniecka directs her ingenious notion of elemental forms, general forms which stand to fictional personalities as the scripts of circumstance which elicit behavior and, thus, make the moral character of these personalities evident.

THE GENERAL NOTION OF THE ELEMENTAL FORM

It is a bit misleading to single out the moral significance of elemental forms as though this exhausted their complete relevance to literature. Elemental forms have a much broader relevance to literature, but to say this is not, in any way, to diminish their paramount moral function.

According to Tymieniecka, the subliminal sphere contains certain "life promoters" which are "fundamental to the human universe" inasmuch as they quicken and structure the script of lived experience.[39] She terms these "elemental factors" (in contradistinction to "elementary" factors), because the former phrase suggests their ingression into experience as animating and integral forces without which life would have no meaning, while the latter suggests simple building blocks from which a greater whole can be mechanically constructed.[40] The elemental factors do not possess an efficacy which perfectly determines how the experience of the individual will be formed. Rather, they are, instrumentally, at everyone's disposal and appropriation once one has learned to master the elementary factors from which they are created. Even so, they retain a general character which founds their universal meaning, a universal meaning which makes them carriers of human culture. The process by which the elemental factors come into being is described by Tymieniecka as follows:

> ... [I]t is in our subliminal sphere ... that the living individual masters the elementary factors and appropriates them for his own needs. By drawing them through the networks of the Imaginatio Creatrix, he transmutes the wild numb strivings that blindly strike out when vitally provoked into aim-oriented, concentrated powers that imitate and actuate elevated human endeavor. These "passions of the soul" or "elemental passions" originate and carry human culture.[41]

Corresponding to the elemental passions (without being exhausted by them) are what Tymieniecka's calls the "elemental forms." These are grand metaphors, archetypes or logotypes which are emblematic of complexes of these passions and which function, when embodied in literature, to evoke them.[42]

These elemental forms are experienced in the world, first, as those things which comprise the staging against which our lives are led, but they are, also, internalized so they become the symbols and instruments by which the passions uniformly associated with particular stagings may be evoked over and over again. In literature, these elemental forms are employed to establish the horizon against which characters act out their destinies. As the background to literary action, they determine both possibilities as well as what Joyce has called the "ineluctable modalities" of the involved fictional characters, and their merest suggestion is enough to establish, for the reader, a particular set of anticipations even before any action has taken place. This latter follows from the fact that the elemental forms are elemental in another sense: they are linked to the elements which compose the physical world. Not elements in the sense of Selenium, Polonium, Iron or Magnesium, they are elements in the ancient sense, *alchemical* elements analogous to those of earth, air, fire, water and the aether. Elemental, in this sense, these forms are expressive of the opportunities, limitations, conditions and metamorphoses experienced in the internal and external lives of humans. Great literature is, thus, a part of "the continuous work of the creative imagination in making the crucial passage between nature without and nature within man."[43] As such, it is nothing less than an alchemical process by which the writer uses his imagination to transform the reader by exposing the reader to the elemental forms.[44] In the creation of great literature, the writer acts as alchemist working out the implications of the elemental forms so that he and his audience may transcend the preconstituted world of nature as well as the preconstituted worlds of all preceding works of imagination. Transcendence achieved, both writer and audience are morally changed.

ELEMENTAL LIGHT

Elemental light is the logotype of an extensive hierarchy of phenomena which are related analogously one to another. It is "first in the line of generation" because it provides the mediating term for three spheres of reality — "[c]osmos, nature and the human inner self" — but also because it is emblematic of the constitutive processes of human experience.[45] Light is the grand archetype under which we gather a vast array of phenomena all having genetic primacy with respect to the constitution of human existence, in its broadest sense. "Our language . . . is suffused with metaphors of light, and . . . empirical life is conducted with constant poetical reference to light."[46] Light is symbolic of warmth, generation, daylight. On the physical level, without the mechanics of light, material reality — as we know it — would be impossible. On the psychological level, light is symbolic of the inner gaze directed to the dark recesses of the soul; it "divides the moods and inner psychological dimensions of experience into the present and the past and . . . sets horizons for our mobility as well as our repose."[47] Perceptually, sight — light's associated sensory modality — is the most versatile; in comparison hearing, smell, touch, taste are all limited and more deceptive. Light enables sight to define a horizonal frame of reference which is centered on the physical individual and which moves according to the whims, interests and necessities of his ego. Light and sight thus provide a window on the world, a panorama, by which the whole is grasped as extending outward along lines which never seem to converge.[48] Because it is the same for all individuals possessing sight, light is responsible for the possibility of the intersubjectivity of perception inasmuch as it allows the various frames of reference to be coordinated *isochronically*.[49]

Light, owing to its primordiality as an elemental form, stands in a peculiar dialectic to darkness. It takes darkness as its compliment, as the very means by which it may be known as light. In its taking a compliment, elemental light is essentially quite different from the elemental sea, for example. (At least, Tymieniecka does not provide us with a hint about a compliment to the sea's elementality). The very characterization of light as a form in relationship to darkness suggests a, not so implicit, reference to the ancient ontological distinction between form over-and-against prime matter. The important thing to realize here, however, is that though light may be juxtaposed over-and-against darkness and may even presuppose darkness in order to be light; this does not mean that darkness necessarily has a similar status as an elemental form. The very notion of a form — as the ancients well knew — implies a principle of order and structure over and against a chaotic lack of structure; it implies an ordering principle which is fundamentally different from any variety of pure potency that awaits shaping and forming, like the potency one finds in the notion of prime matter.

In application to specific features of human existence, the dialectic between light and darkness is emblematic of the relationship between the Imaginatio Creatrix and the subliminal passions. Relative to the light of intelligibility, the subliminal zone is darkness. But a struggle between light and darkness of a different sort is already at work within the subliminal zone itself. Before the creative vision transforms the workings of this dialectic so that consciousness has access to it, it already preexists at the deepest level of human experience, at a level which is below consciousness, subconsciousness and the realm of the prepredicative.[50] At this level, light and darkness do not signify anything which is primarily intelligible, although it is the primary intention of the human creative quest to make them so. No, at the level of the subliminal zone is found the "source of ultimate significant principles" which in their constant polarizing productions "sustain in their tension the relatively stable platform of humanly projected existence."[51] It is from the prerational attempt of primitive peoples to give accounts of this struggle — which though not cognized was sharply felt — that mythologies were born.[52] The subliminal struggle between these forces gave rise to the mythological struggles between forces of light and forces of darkness, forces of abundant life and forces of annihilation and the forces of good and the forces of evil.[53] The dialectic between light and darkness thus became a logotype "of the relentless impetus of life and the opposing individualizing constructive tendencies which struggle to capture . . . [this impetus] in coherent structured operations . . . [to] channel its flux."[54] The intent of this primitive drive to bring coherence to the subliminal zone achieves its *telos* in modern man's attempt to make it intelligible.

Cognitively, memory, will and even the *Imaginatio Creatrix* itself would be worthless without the illumination the intellect provides. Through complicated processes by which it provides the criteria for direction, relevance and choice, the intellect engenders the purposes to which the other faculties are directed.[55] But this is not its only illuminative function. It is also possible for the intellect to turn its light reflexively inward, on itself, in order to examine its own conscious workings.[56] "To know thyself" thus becomes epigrammatic of the luminous clarity which the intellect achieves when turned inward, unblinking, at its ego's "conduct, motivations, hopes and projects."[57]

The penetrating illumination of the intellect throws the terrain of the external and internal worlds into stark relief, each selvedge and promontory being clearly marked out and classified. The intellect, thus, operates like a two-edged sword dividing the world into things, regions and categories, the same discrimination being called forth into expression in the form of a " 'sign symbol' " or word which is nothing less than "the incarnation of the meaningful construct."[58] The expression of the word represents the highest achievement in humankind's social existence and the "ultimate manifestation" of intellect because through it the complete coordination of the lifeworld is made possible; through it anything which can be experienced may be expressed. In eventually establishing a linkage between light and the word, Tymieniecka's discussion of illumination resonates sympathetically with passages from the prologue to the *Gospel of John* and the book of *Genesis*. The utterance of human words has an obvious theological correlate in the Trinitarian generation of the Λόγος and in God's creation of the cosmos, [for] in passing from light to the word, we cover the infinitesimal distance spanned when the cycle of life's genesis was completed."[59] Of course, the genetic passage in consciousness from light to word is the exact inverse of the order of generation and creation in the Christian cosmogeny. The Christian theology of creation begins with the eternal generation of the Λόγος as an event without precedent and, then, proceeds to the creation of light as an event within time. But if one takes light as emblematic of the wisdom and nature of God — as is done in the Nicene Creed, for example — then light is as primordially constitutive of the Trinity as is the generation of the Λόγος. In fact, they are united in an identical act of being. The significance of this analogy is that it opens the logotype of light in its application to at least one religious cosmogony which makes both light and word metaphysically primordial.[60]

The instantiations of Light as material reality, as the condition for visual perception, as intelligibility and as the intelligible word do not exhaust the possibilities of this elemental form. There is remaining the hyperluminous light of magical, religious and mystical experience. This is the notion of light which, too, is focused interiorily but not for a discursive purpose such as the production of dogmatic statements possessing eternal validity or for the production of practical guides to day-to-day behavior. Instead, hyperluminous light works to reveal the intelligibility of our inner development.[61] It makes us "transparent to ourselves" so that we come to some understanding of "the ultimate reasons of [our] ... very existence."[62] It is in this spiritual quest for existential understanding and in its accompanying personal scrutiny that the boundaries of the intelligible world are broken and through the fissures pours an "'unearthly' light" which manifests the presence of a realm beyond the natural, a realm with infinitely open horizons to which the discursive intellect responds with blindness. The final instantiation of elemental light — indeed, the kind of light where archetype and ectype merge — is that of the "Ultimate, the unearthly divine, the God that would bring light into the world."[63]

Woven into the fabulations of literature, elemental light awakens a set of distinct passions both in the constructed characters and in the experience of the reader. The theme of light works literarily to bring to the fore actions on the part of characters which express the fundamental striving to grow, to understand, to penetrate, to divine and to transcend. These are themes which typify all that is best in culture; they express "an all embracing vision of life" expressed "in the form of exemplary works of art, of thought, of reflection and technique."[64] They also determine the "occupation" the character will have based upon his stance toward them. Their positive embodiment in a role almost certainly assures that the character will be a "scholar, scientist, builder, . . . inventor" or, one might add, saint.[65]

THE ELEMENTAL SEA

In his book *The Sacred and the Profane,* Mircea Eliade tells us that aquatic symbolism in religious texts conveys something of the elemental significance of water.

The waters symbolize the universal sum of virtualities; they are the ... "spring and origin," the reservoir of all the possibilities of existence; they precede every form and *support* every creation. ... On the other hand, immersion in water signifies regression to the preformal, reincorporation into the undifferentiated mode of pre-existence. *E*mersion repeats the cosmogonic act of formal manifestation; *im*mersion is equivalent to the dissolution of forms. This is why the symbolism of waters implies both death and rebirth. Contact with water always brings a regeneration — on the one hand because dissolution is followed by a new birth, on the other because immersion fertilizes and multiplies the potential of life.[66]

In literary works, the use of water as symbolic of transformative baptism is well known, but the varieties of transformation associated with this element are most often expressed in relation to engulfment in it. Movement *toward* engulfment is often symbolic of movement from form to formlessness; movement *from* engulfment is often symbolic of movement from formlessness to form. The act of engulfment, itself, represents the liminal state in which the transformation which has taken place is ambiguous and without determinate result — a state of pure potentiality in which no feature is any longer actual, a state which is the most frightening because of its indeterminacy.

Although novels may use emersion or immersion as episodic symbols, novels never sustain all the action in a plot against the staging of water as a medium of baptism. A momentary entry or emergence is of too brief a duration to be staging for the complexity of most plots. When great works of literature employ water they usually do so as the backdrop of the sea, and — in so doing — some, but not all, of the symbolic characteristics of water are transferred. The significant differences between water as baptism of transformation and water as elemental sea are those of spatial location and duration. The fact that most novels of the sea take place on the surface of a watery medium dictates the style of the actions and revelations which will be played out by the crews of humans slowly traversing its surface.

The sea is a sublimely vast expanse of water. In its sublimity, it threatens; in its vastness, it divides and isolates — it separates a crew from the conventions and protection of human society; in its depths it signifies a chaos which cannot be fathomed. As water, it is expressive of the fundamental capriciousness and ambiguity of existence — it can dissolve and it can reform. As a font of possibility, the sea functions in a fabula to emphasize the tenuous nature of human powers and life. It provides the staging against which great dramas may be played out, dramas about the valor, strength and reliability of humans but always as a backdrop in which the unexpected may happen at any moment.[67] The sea forces people together and sunders them apart; it offers escape and contingent safety but also danger and eventual death.[68] The sea moves in "rhythmic cadences" and drives people toward climactic moments which aid in the discovery of personal truth and — in the case of literature — the unfolding of plot.[69]

Whatever the traits of the characters of a story, the placing of characters against the horizon of the ocean means that their deepest natures will eventually emerge. The sea both in its experiential reality and in its function as a literary device implies that the voyagers may well have to pass through a liminal state — a baptism of trials — which will eventually leave them revealed for what they truly are. But even so, the elemental sea is not primarily a staging which produces perfect metamorphoses in individuals — like baptismal water; instead, it functions as a staging in which the true, deepest individual vices and virtues are revealed. As such a literary device, it has a fundamentally moral purpose. As Tymieniecka puts it: "The sea ... offers unique opportunity ... for probing the ... the core of humanness, ... the 'true' state of moral selfhood."[70] It does this by evoking a great many moral truths which become visible only when men are submitted to the dangers and liminality of long times spent on its surface. Among the many truths — both good and bad — of human nature which are revealed by the elemental sea are the following: (1) the "congenital human pettiness unredeemed as yet by the soul's designs"; (2) "the crude rule of facts on the sea" which "severs the innumerable interconnections of life"; (3) an "unpredictable vengeance [which] mirrors the unpredictability of the element"; (4) "the over powering force of human pettiness"; (5) "moral man in revolt, the human moral passions on the rebound"; (6) "the helplessness of the individual in the machinery of the human community"; (7) "man's ignorance of himself"; (8) "man's instinctive conformism"; (9) "the human beings's capacity for inward moral transformation" and (10) "the human condition — generosity, nobility of heart, benevolence."[71]

CONCLUSION

What the elemental form of light does for the literary theme of the search for truth, the elemental form of the sea does for the literary theme of the demonstration of moral worth. Thus, the symmetry of A-T. Tymieniecka's Catherine wheel of creativity is established. In literature, creativity is always the dominant purpose and end for the constructed work. But in the literature of thematic light, the theme of wonder in the search for truth conditions this creativity. On the other hand, in the literature of the sea a different orientation is apparent. Idealization conditions the creativity. Even so, great literature has always had a moral dimension without necessarily being about the sea. It possesses a philosophical dimension, as well. In fact, none of these dimensions are found in perfect isolation in great literature. But all great literature is characterized by one or the other dimension being dominant.

Finally, on the basis of the hints which Tymieniecka provides us, it now becomes possible to describe the differences between the specific areas of philosophical, moral and literary composition by describing the moments which are primarily, secondarily and tertiarily important to each. Literature is distinct from philosophy and ethics by having creativity (The Beautiful) as its primary concern, idealization (The Good) as its secondary concern and wonder (the True) as its tertiary concern. Philosophy, on the other hand, is primarily conditioned by wonder (The True), secondarily by idealization (The Good) and tertiarily by creation (The Beautiful). Finally, ethics takes idealization (The Good) primarily, wonder (The True) secondarily and creation (The Beautiful) tertiarily. According to Tymieniecka's understanding, there is no realm of human creativity which is devoid of the intentionalities of wonder, creation and idealization, though each may have a different dominance relative to the end sought. [See the following diagram.]

Purdue University

NOTES

[1] John Gardner, *On Moral Fiction* (New York: Basic Books, 1978), p. 23.
[2] In characterizing her philosophy as a philosophy of "beingness," A-T. Tymieniecka

has not employed this somewhat cacophonous neologism without a clearcut purpose. She argues that the Copernican revolution in philosophy was one of movement from static conceptions of being and an excessive objectivism toward a conception which emphasized the "constitutive-envisioning power of the human mind" as ultimate point of reference. In her words, what is important is "the poiesis of life as a constructive process which establishes the relative stability of instants of what-there-is." Operative here no longer is the conception of static being but rather the *process* of "beingness," a process of individualization "through which, as through a vehicle, life expands." See: A-T. Tymieniecka, *Tractatus Brevis* (Dordrecht: Kluwer, 1990), p. 9.

[3] What is implied in this analogicity is not antithetical to the project of phenomenology by any means. Both James M. Edie and Aron Gurwitsch, before him, have proposed a reconstruction of the Aristotelian analogy of being along phenomenological lines, the terms of the analogy being guaranteed by the fact that they are constituted within consciousness. What distinguishes Tymieniecka's approach from those of Edie and Gurwitsch is her discovery of a new set of transcendentals — the elemental forms. In this, neither Edie nor Gurwitsch would likely follow. See: Aron Gurwitsch, *The Field of Consciousness* (Pittsburgh: Duquesne University Press, 1964), pp. 379 ff. and James M. Edie, *Edmund Husserl's Phenomenology: A Critical Commentary* (Bloomington: Indiana University Press, 1987), pp. 90—111.

[4] A-T. Tymieniecka, *Tractatus Brevis* (Dordrecht: Kluwer), p. 22.

[5] *Ibid.*, p. 23.

[6] *Ibid.*, p. 26.

[7] *Ibid.*, p. 26.

[8] *Ibid.*, p. 70.

[9] *Ibid.*, p. 70.

[10] *Ibid.*, pp. 29, 134.

[11] *Ibid.*, p. 29.

[12] *Ibid.*, p. 36.

[13] *Ibid.*, p. 37.

[14] *Ibid.*, pp. 36—37.

[15] *Ibid.*, pp. 18—19.

[16] *Ibid.*, pp. 18—19.

[17] *Ibid.*, p. 19.

[18] *Ibid.*, p. 29.

[19] *Ibid.*, p. 29.

[20] *Ibid.*, p. 39.

[21] *Ibid.*, p. 38.

[22] *Ibid.*, p. 39.

[23] *Ibid.*, p. 9.

[24] *Ibid.*, p. 98.

[25] *Ibid.*, p. 99.

[26] See: Peter Berger, *The Sacred Canopy* (New York: Doubleday, 1969), pp. 3—28.

[27] *Tractatus Brevis.*, p. 132.

[28] *Ibid.*, p. 132.

[29] *The Sacred Canopy*, pp. 81—101.

[30] *Tractatus Brevis*, p. 137.

[31] *Ibid.*, pp. 124—125, 139.

[32] *Ibid.*, pp. 135—136.
[33] *Ibid.*, p. 108.
[34] *Ibid.*, p. 108.
[35] *Ibid.*, p. 137.
[36] *Ibid.*, p. 115.
[37] *Ibid.*, p. 139.
[38] *Ibid.*, pp. 115, 120, 125.
[39] *Ibid.*, p. xi.
[40] *Ibid.*, p. xi.
[41] *Ibid.*, p. xi.
[42] Rudolf Otto in *The Idea of the Holy* (Oxford: Oxford University Press, 1976), pp. 60—71, employs the term 'ideogram' to describe the way the essentially transcendental numinous is expressed in human thought and language. His choice of this term is, presumably, predicated upon the fact that an ideogram is not read literally as meaning the object which the ideogram represents but only as suggesting an emotional or cognitive content which the represented object evokes. In this sense, Tymieniecka's notion of the elemental forms are something greater than any individual instantiation they "collect," but they do include every instantiation. The elemental forms are thus transcendentals characterized by an analogicity in their instantiations. Because of this, I prefer to use the word 'logotype' to describe them.
[43] *Tractatus Brevis*, p. 38.
[44] Alchemy here is, of course, a metaphor. But the similarities between the alchemist's quest and Tymieniecka's understanding of the transformative powers of literature are instructive. Both the alchemist and Tymieniecka believe that the macrocosm and microcosm mirror one another, or at least there is a grand analogicity between each realm. Both believe that specific "works" (alchemical practice/creativity & sympathetic reading) lead to personal transformation. Finally, both believe that "exposure" to objects (elements/elemental forms) is capable of inducing those "virtues" in the individual which already inhere in the object at a different level of being. To extend the comparison further, see: Francis Yates, *Giordano Bruno and the Hermetic Tradition* (Chicago: University of Chicago Press, 1977), pp. 44—45, D. P. Walker, *Spiritual and Demonic Magic from Ficino to Campanella* (Notre Dame: University of Notre Dame Press, 1975), pp. 12—14 and Arthur Versluis, *The Philosophy of Magic* (Boston: Routledge & Kegan Paul, 1986), pp. 105—119.
[45] *Tractatus Brevis*, pp. 77, 99.
[46] *Ibid.*, p. 77.
[47] *Ibid.*, pp. 78, 84.
[48] *Ibid.*, p. 79.
[49] On the phenomenological significance of the notion of an isochronisms and its relation to Johann Lambert's transcendental optics see: Thomas Ryba, *The Essence of Phenomenology and Its Meaning for the Scientific Study of Religion* (New York: Peter Lang, 1991) pp. 25—41.
[50] *Tractatus Brevis*, pp. 22—23.
[51] *Ibid.*, p. 31.
[52] *Ibid.*, p. 31.
[53] *Ibid.*, p. 89.
[54] *Ibid.*, p. 31.

[55] *Tractatus Brevis*, p. 83.
[56] *Ibid.*, p. 81.
[57] *Ibid.*, p. 81.
[58] *Ibid.*, p. 84.
[59] *Ibid.*, p. 85.
[60] For two old, but still very good, treatments of the significance of light as a theological symbol, see: Edwyn Bevan, *Symbolism and Belief* (Port Washington: Kennikat Press, 1968), pp. 125—150 and Vladimir Lossky, *In the Image and Likeness of God* (Crestwood: St. Vladimir's Seminary Press, 1985), pp. 31—69.
[61] *Tractatus Brevis*, p. 92.
[62] *Ibid.*, p. 93.
[63] *Ibid.*, p. 93.
[64] *Ibid.*, p. 87.
[65] *Ibid.*, p. 88.
[66] Mircea Eliade, *The Sacred and the Profane* (New York: Harcourt, Brace and World, 1959), p. 130.
[67] *Tractatus Brevis*, p. 126.
[68] *Ibid.*, pp. 56—58.
[69] *Ibid.*, p. 102.
[70] *Ibid.*, p. 126.
[71] *Ibid.*, p. 102.

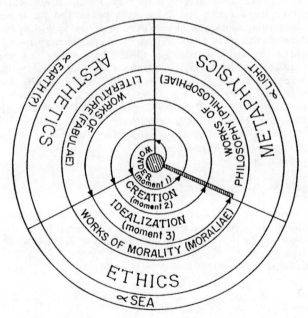

Tymieniecka's Catherine Wheel of Creativity

KRYSTYNA GORNIAK-KOCIKOWSKA

THE LIGHT, THE WORD, THE SEA, AND THE INNER MORAL SELF

Notes on the margins of Anna-Teresa Tymieniecka's Logos and Life, Book Three

Friedrich Nietzsche claimed the mistake made by all philosophers *before* him was they *first* accepted a certain system of values, mostly ethical, and only afterwards tried to *explain* the reality. This means people *first* make the decision about what is right and what wrong or what is good and bad, and only after this decision is made do they try to explore the reality — or rather that part of reality which they *first* *evaluated* as good, i.e., worthy of exploration (hence they claim their explanation, the research, to be right). According to Nietzsche, even if the philosophers declare that they search for the Truth (truth, by the way, *is a value*, too), their real goal is the "majestic building of morality".[1]

In *Logos and Life*, Book 3, Anna-Teresa Tymieniecka brings together the passions of the soul and the visions which we humans create and follow and what she calls the elements in the human condition — *light* and the *sea*. She also presents the role of the *word* in the structure she examines. Let me explore how she does it.

Tymieniecka places the genesis of culture within the critique of reason. In *Logos and Life*, Book 3, she continues what was the main subject in her two former books: the investigation of the genesis of the significance of *life* with respect to the role reason played in it. She pays special attention to the genesis of what she calls the "fountains of culture": ideals, virtues, sacralia, taboos. She shows how the creative forces of the human condition become crystallized through literature. Using literature as a model example, Tymieniecka examines the origin of cultural principles and ideas and states (as she already did in her previous books) that they emerge in the *twilight of consciousness*.[2] Tymieniecka advocates the view that the human being is a *totality* of body and mind. Within the sphere of the twilight of consciousness physiological functions interact with the so-called "higher" functions which develop in the crystallization process of the specific human

27

A-T. Tymieniecka (ed.), Analecta Husserliana, Vol. XXXVIII, 27—42.
© 1992 *Kluwer Academic Publishers. Printed in the Netherlands.*

condition. On this level, the human consciousness *in statu nascendi* learns how to react on stimuli, needs, etc. It does this already in its own, *human* way in which the *passions* and the *elements* play the basic role. The most important elements are, according to Tymieniecka, *light* (or the opposition of light and darkness) and the *sea*.

Claiming that *light* is one of the basic "onto-poietic factors in the great system of life"[3] (we may add that this is a basic notion for the culture of the West[4]), Tymieniecka takes part in the controversy over our human perception of the world. She is within the "Platonic" rather than the "Dionysian" tradition; for her, eye rather then ear, picture rather then sound, is the mediator between us and the world. This is important, since the choice and the *decision* about how we should perceive the world is a decision made by people "larger than life" (to use the expression used by Tymieniecka) who determined their — and consequently also our — vision of the world. Plato *saw* the world, but Luther *heard* it.[5] Nietzsche made of this "eye-ear" opposition a whole theory (as far as the expression "whole theory" can be applied to Nietzsche), Wagner wanted to reach a synthesis of both, and the writings of Heinrich and Thomas Mann are an example of specific rivalry between these two options in the field of literature.

Literature can be the field of such a rivalry because the substance of literature is the *word*. The word belongs to both spheres. If written, it is a picture; if spoken, it is a sound. The word is a meeting-place of both worlds: the world of pictures and the world of sounds. Consequently, it is no wonder that the Western culture is the culture of the word; it is the culture which bases itself on that specific type of communication combining pictures with sounds, the static with the dynamic.

According to contemporary science, motion (or energy) is the crucial attribute of the material world.[6] In her earlier writings, Tymieniecka stated that neither the variability, the mobility, nor the becoming and the vanishing of a being which is static in its nature are the object of our astonishment, but, rather, the persistence of a real thing among the waves of variability is what seems to puzzle us.[7]

In reference to the way in which living beings exist, motion is understood mainly as *action*, and *competition* is regarded as the basis for most of their activities. Therefore, the possibility of correct inter- pretation of the world is, and was, for human beings always tremen- dously important — sometimes the correct interpretation of the world is a question of life and death. More often it is the question of a possibly good life. As John Dewey used to claim, people do not think in order to find the truth, but to make life better.

People usually identify the good life with happiness,[8] and happiness is regarded as the goal for human life.[9] All human actions (and not human actions only, if we believe scholars like Lorenz or Popper) are the result of dissatisfaction with the present situation — a perfectly content individual does not do anything to change his/her situation.[10]

In order to act effectively, i.e., to reach a goal aimed at a certain minimal orientation of the conditions in which one acts, is indispensable. This orientation is nothing other than the image[11] of the world we possess — usually it is called "knowledge". The image (the knowledge) of the world we *believe* to be adequate to reality is the basis for the manner of our acting; the aim of our action is primarily the possibility of our existing at all, and secondly, it is making this existence as valuable (happy) as possible.

Human actions are mainly joint actions with other people. Effective cooperation requires an efficient communication system. With regard to human beings, language, speech, the use of words is the most perfect communication system of all systems that have been worked out so far.[12] Language serves best the purpose of transmitting thoughts which, in their essence, are the "images" of the world that we possess. In the process of communication, our image is compared with the images of the world that other people possess. If an action, based on my image of the world is more effective than an action based on image(s) of the world possessed by other people, then this proves the superiority of my image of the world over the others; simultaneously, it allows me to gain specific advantage over other people in collective action. The needs of that collective action necessitated work division which aims at the possible most effective utilization of the capabilities of such a team's members. In "my" case this would mean that my task consists in a further enriching of the image of the world worked out by me from the point of view of the community's possibilities for activity effective in the achievement of intended goals.

Work division also leads to *lesser* interest in the creation of genuine images of the world on the part of those members of the group who have accepted the superiority of "my" image of the world over the ones which they have created. They accept, so to speak, a priori the image of the world which is presented to them by me. Thus, they are ready to *believe* in what I *know* or what *I believe in*. In both cases their faith stems from trust they bestowed on me, which results from the initial proven superiority of "my" image of the world over the one proposed by others. "They" *believe* that "I" *know better*.

According to Friedrich Nietzsche, the consequence of social life — in any of its forms — is that people are divided into those (the few) who give orders and those numerous who take orders and are obliged to be obedient. Nietzsche, however, claimed that the efforts of all persons and institutions qualified to cultivate people are directed in modern times to the development in humans of the "instinct of obedience", which is made the highest virtue to such an extent that the "instinct of ordering" is killed even in those whose *duty* it is to order — who then try to give the impression that they do so out of obedience (to God, people, duty, personal conscience, etc.). Humans create gods, or ideas, or a "categorical imperative" for themselves so that they have something to which they *need* to be obedient. Such features as courage, pride, lawlessness and strength, which were the signs of greatness and of the goods of human beings in ancient (i.e., pre-Socratic) times, vanish, claims Nietzsche.

An artist of genius or a ruler in a feudal state most closely approaches the "superman" ("overman") for Nietzsche. Comparing Nietzsche's concept of the "superman" with Jaspers' "higher man", Leonard Ehrlich wrote:

Nietzsche measures man as he is against the Übermensch, "superman". Nietzsche does not doubt the coming of the superman. But superman (. . .) is not a model for man, and man a mere "bridge" on the way to the coming of superman. The coming of superman is not a matter of man reaching his measure; man cannot become a superman. The purpose of man, even of "higher man", is to pave the way for the coming of superman. It is different in Jaspers. When he says that man is finite and imperfectible, he does not mean that what we propose as the measure of man exceeds man in such a way that he is condemned to be and must content himself with being the mere bridge to such a higher realization of freedom. Jaspers means rather that when it comes to the tasks of freedom we can never set man's goal so high that it exceeds his possibility, nor is man's actualization so profound that no higher goals are possible.[13]

Both the "superman" of Nietzsche and the "higher man" of Jaspers are entitled to the greatest freedom; yet they themselves restrict it, taking upon themselves the responsibility for "the weak", "the masses", "the crowd".

However, despite all his contempt for "the weak", Nietzsche thought that it is the task of an *artist of genius* to create for the weak individuals a protective barrier against threatening reality. Art, being a *conscious and purposeful lie* about reality, is to be this barrier. Yet art is a lie but a lie which would let people live in a Dionysian way (i.e., in the fullness of life and the fullness of humanity).

The "weak" do not need to feel responsible. Nietzsche treats them as too "poor" to make such demands. In principle, he keeps the classic division into "masters" and "slaves". "Masters" are free and responsible only to themselves (in Nietzsche there is no responsibility to God), and "slaves" compensate for their lack of freedom with a lack of responsibility. But in contrast to Sartre and Fromm, Nietzsche does not think that the "masses" are, in fact, happy, having the possibility to "escape" from freedom and responsibility.

The problem from Nietzsche's perspective is that the "slaves" do not see and do not accept what their proper place is. They *assume that they are both able to be free and able to take responsibility*. This is why their resentment against the "masters" is so dangerous — the "slaves" *are able* to devastate the "masters". They are, however, *unable to be real masters*. This means that they are able to hinder the realization of the only really valuable goal of human beings: the coming of the "superman"; hence ultimately they are able to devastate the whole human species.

The above, however, is not the only problem. Analyzing *Lord Jim* by Joseph Conrad, a book which can be read an agonizing dialogue with Nietzsche, Anna-Teresa Tymieniecka shows the other side of the situation presented above:

As Conrad presents it, primitive society is by no means an ideal state of natural relations guided by natural virtues. We have seen that, on the contrary, primitive man, incapable of protecting himself from the ruthless predations of unscrupulous men, struggles in vain to acquire some stability for himself and his family — for whose security he trembles. The rule of the stronger and the more cunning keeps ordinary people in constant fear. They submit to an arbitrary rule. The primitives spontaneously seek the stability of a reliable ruler, and they will entrust themselves unconditionally to the judgement of people who prove themselves either stronger, or more cunning, or more just. Yet with the development of culture, that is, with the development of the human capacity for reflection and the estimation of situations and with the organization of the societal order according to stable rules which grant the individual a role in the general pattern of society's functioning, the person does develop a core sense of personal responsibility and self-reliance along with an estimation and his/her own role and prerogatives.[14]

Faith and reason, trust and knowledge became the moving powers of the human species during the very early stage of its existence. The problem is that through the large part of the history of that species, it was *alternatively* faith or reason, trust or knowledge. Humans swung constantly between these.

In a sense, one could say that whereas the developed communication system (language), as well as abstract thinking (group memory and ability to foresee) gave the human species superiority over other living organisms, on the one hand, they caused, on the other hand, tremendous inequality and stratification within the human species, such as is unknown elsewhere.[15] But these abilities allowed groups of people to create *visions* of what they understood *as* their happiness, not of what *is* but of what *should be*. They could project a common vision and act commonly towards its realization.

I said: vision.[16] Vision and perception are the two cornerstones of our relationship with the world. They are interrelated in such a way that neither of them has meaning without the other. Without perception no vision is possible. However, our perception of the world depends upon the vision we follow. *This is the sense of the statement Nietzsche cited at the beginning of this paper.*

Our perception of the world is subordinated to the vision we accept. Our vision is based on *what* do we perceive and *how* do we do this. Our perception is selective. We pay attention to some of the factors of reality, and disregard others. We claim some of them to be important and/or meaningful, and some of them not.[17] We do so, because of the vision we already possess. This is why it is so difficult — if not impossible at all — to realize the postulate of the act of knowledge which would exclude any premise, and pre-judgement. Therefore, the "pure" act of knowledge, be it in Nietzschean,[18] Husserlian, or other, must remain more or less an idealistic postulate as long as the human being is an *acting* being, i.e., a being following visions. If *enlightenment* in that form known in Zen Buddhism can be claimed to be the type of pure knowledge I have in mind here, then it is an example which supports my opinion — because that enlightenment is a total lack of any action and any "timeness".[19]

The human being becomes truly human, when he or she has a vision, is able to *create* this vision, and aims its realization. The vision makes our life worth living. Aiming the vision determines the way in which we deal with reality and how we function within it. To be able to create a vision and to share it with others is what makes our life valuable.

Tymieniecka claims: "It is in the aesthetic engagement of the human being in the arts, but particularly in the fabulating creativity of literature, that the specifically human life-significance originates and unfolds".[20]

Tymieniecka pays more attention to *light*, to the *picture* or *image* of the world than to sound (although one of the basic terms she uses in her philosophical language is that of "orchestration"). The picture, the image, is *static*. For Plato, who claimed the supremacy of lack of movement over movement, the concept of *mirroring* reality, of building *pictures* of it was an adequate one. But Tymieniecka advocates the dynamic character of reality. Such a reality cannot be understood as a set of static pictures only. And yet, she has the right to connect light with her dynamic vision of reality — light in our time does more than make it possible to mirror reality. Today "light" also means: "*energy*". In Tymieniecka's dynamic vision of reality, light has a proper place, as do the word and the sea. She, in fact, focuses her consideration on this dynamic meaning of light.[21] Claiming light to be "present at the origin of elementary life and omnipresent within it",[22] Tymieniecka chooses literature (i.e., the art that has the strongest links with words), and especially novels about the sea (i.e., about the factor of the material world that within Western culture has traditionally been associated with life and dynamism) in order to present her view on the problem of the human condition, on the relationship between different human individuals as well as between humans and the non-human world. She does so purposefully.

The sea *is* the picture *and* the sound. The sea is also movement, the permanent movement, or, rather, it is the world in which movement is the constant, "stable", substantial factor, one impossible to overlook. Being both stable *and* in motion, the sea is probably one of the most astonishing things in the real world with which we are confronted, maybe even as astonishing as the *phenomenon of life*. The art of the West often presents the sea as a *living being*, and it does so not because of the countless living organisms which inhabit it, but because of its own properties. Again, it is no wonder that Tymieniecka, whose field is phenomenology of life[23] chose the literature of the sea as the object of her investigation.

The sea, with all its movement, is the proper partner for the human being, whose main feature is acting. One may say that the same could be said about wind or fire. I do not think so. Both fire and wind need an object outside of them to exercise their power, to exist. They come and go. They arise and vanish. The sea is eternal (in the sense in which our Planet is eternal). It is always there, and at the same time it is a world on its own.

The sea is part of the same world that we are also part of. The sea is then part of our world. No. The sea *is not* part of our world.[24] We are not part of the sea (we *do* recognize ourselves as part of the earth — at least within the tradition of the Bible), neither is the sea part of ourselves. In its exclusiveness, and *because* of its "activity", the sea is our *partner*, responding to our actions, challenging them. In contact with the sea, we are strangers, "visitors", who *must* leave the sea sooner or later.

Tymieniecka writes:

The sea is a field on which awareness is heightened of the human situation of being at the verge of existence, of living from one moment to the next; entrusting oneself to a fragile vessel and being irremediably unshored facilitates the revelation of this truth and the laying bare of the deepest zones of the soul.[25]

The sea was the first big challenge for humans' conquering, adventurous nature; it was humans' first big source of experience in dealing with the unknown *active* world. The exploration of space is a very new event compared with the exploration of the sea. Hence, the sea plays still a much more important role than space in the history of our species and our culture.

Nietzsche thought it bad that people's knowledge is based upon values because he thought that values, once accepted, make the human being unable to be free. Nietzsche was against the *acceptance* of values *imposed* on people from outside. He wanted humans to be *creators* of values. Only such human beings as were creators deserved in his eyes to be called "humans", only those, who are not afraid of taking the risk of following their own vision, and of justifying it by their own will, knowing that everything they have, everything they *are*, is constantly at stake. Life, as Nietzsche saw it, does not differ very much from the sea as Tymieniecka presents it:

The sea, in offering man only the absolutely unstable and shaky platform of a boat, brings out the utmost fragility of his entire beingness; it allows the human being to be tried as to his/her strength, valor, reliability in radical either/or, life/death situations that cannot be postponed, evaded, or conjured away. It offers him/her unique opportunities for probing the very core of humanness, that is, the "true" state of moral selfhood.[26]

According to Nietzsche, people who search for happiness, who act for it, and in this acting follow trustfully those who "know better", are not worthy of being regarded as fully human any longer. As opposed to what has often been said about Nietzsche, I do not think that he totally negated the need for morality. He thought that morality was a necessity in people's struggle against the "beast in them", as well as against Nature.[27] Only as victors in these struggles can people call themselves "free". Morality was for Nietzsche a very important factor of *culture* (culture understood as a human-world or world created by humans). As was mentioned above, Nietzsche thought that people need morality to emerge from the level of animals and to reach power over Nature. The next step is to use this power in order to make themselves free according to their own will to power.[28] In that moment the new differentiation into "weak" and "strong", "slave" and "free" arises — according to the "quantum" of the will to power they possess. Then starts the process of the creation of the human-world, with all those new tensions about which Nietzsche wrote.

Nietzsche wanted weak individuals to accept their slavery. Morality gives them the *false feeling* of being *free* (i.e., responsible, too) which makes them active in their struggle against the strong Single ones who are closer than they are to the superman — that ideal for humans, that next stage in the development of the human species. In this way, the traditional morality impedes, in Nietzsche's opinion, the coming of the overman. Hence, Nietzsche in his criticism of morality is concerned with that phase in the history of humankind in which the coming of the superman is already possible. He regards morality before this phase as a rather positive phenomenon. However, *when morality starts to hinder the coming of superman, one must fight against it*, because the highest goal of humanity is to rise to the threshold of the era of the superman. After the superman comes, people will not need any morality, since they will have no need to feel either responsible or free.

Only those who have overcome the moral phase may be seen as *having the right to make promises.* They *may* promise because they are truly free, i.e., they are truly responsible for their thinking and acting. Their *will* is independent and so is *truly free* (as opposed to the traditional concept of the "free will" criticized by Nietzsche). Such people are exceptional and have the right to create values and to act according to those values.

The proud knowledge of the exceptional privilege of responsibility, the consciousness of the rare freedom, this power over themselves and over fate which enters their very deep self and becomes an instinct, the dominant instinct — how would he call this dominant instinct, assuming that he himself needs a word for it? There can be no doubt: this independent man calls it his *conscience* . . .[29]

Other people, the "slaves" do not have any right to give promises nor to feel responsible, since they are not free (i.e., not *strong enough*) and, therefore, cannot be sure that they will be able to keep their word.

Captain Ahab in Melville's *Moby Dick* — an object of Tymieniecka's investigation — can serve as an example of the exceptional truly free individual of whom Nietzsche dreamed. Ahab has also another quality Nietzsche thought to be a basic feature of the human being outranging the masses — courage:

The courage to tear himself from the natural life-world and to establish for himself a new field of life nourished by his mind, one in which he has to take all responsibility, indeed, everything, upon himself, while being understood only vaguely at best, is COURAGE which only the most vertiginous deployment of the subliminal soul can generate; this is the courage of all heroes, all revolutionaries, reformers, protectors, pioneers, saints, geniuses . . .[30]

Ahab, this exceptional human being who acts according to norms resulting from his inner passion and established by himself, saves the life of another human being who is on the opposite side of the spectrum of humankind, a boy, whom "all the white members of which live comfortably convinced of being good Christians"[31] consider to be less than a human being. In this active doing good despite the others' judgement, Ahab is very "Nietzschean" too.

Not easy pity or compassion, but the innermost passion of the soul, that of *human communion*, springs forth in Ahab's being; this is an encounter involving the deepest of ties at the "inmost center" between two human beings denuded of all the petty paraphernalia of worldly life-conventions and hypocritical morality, the tie of the purest of solicitudes.[32]

Karl Jaspers transformed Nietzschean "classic" aristocratic descent into aristocratic descent of the spirit as realized in the conditions of democracy. The problem which appeared was that people, accustomed to obedience and slavery, generally do not want to make use of their freedom. Jaspers, in fact, agreed with both Sartre and Fromm when he wrote of people:

They want only slogans and obedience. (. . .) How shall we talk with people who will not go where others probe and think, where men seek independence in insight and conviction?[33]

This seems to be one of the major problems of contemporary societies. Theoretically, people are entitled and have a right to much more freedom then ever before. Probably never before in the history of human civilization has freedom been praised as highly as it is now. And yet, we still do not know which attitude people really prefer: the static, passive attitude of mirroring others' views and/or values, or the dynamic, active attitude of creating ideas, values and worlds. From her recent book one can follow that Tymieniecka advocates the latter option. The crucial point of her investigation is to show how what we call (*falsely* simplifying it, as she claims) "reason" diversifies in infinite rational streamlets of significant facts and moments which carry on life's business ordering it in an intelligible way. "Reason" means for Tymieniecka, as it meant for Jaspers, much more than the function of mind. It cannot be *identified* with human's intellect alone. Tymieniecka, like Jaspers, opposes the break between the intellect and imagination, emotions, sensations, feelings, passions, etc. The human being is, according to her — and, as we know, according to growing conviction of not only philosophers, but of scientists too — a *totality*. From that point of view, the cultural formations of life are the work of the entire "creative orchestration" of all of the human being's capacities.

In the analysis of *Lord Jim* Tymieniecka repeatedly pointed out that Jim was a "better sort" of man. He was better because he wanted to "be true to himself", to his *moral* self. He did not simply follow what people expected him to do — his criteria and standards were far higher than those of the people who surrounded him. Analyzing his behavior and his motives, Tymieniecka arrives the conclusion that virtues:

are neither an inner principle (*arete*), as was believed in classical philosophies, nor a deeply rooted habit, disposition, or quality of our psyche. We have seen, in fact, that first the capacity to act according to our moral principles (. . .) consists in an orchestrated shaping of our entire functioning and that, second, "virtue", as the exercise of capacity, consists in a dynamic thread uniting the subliminal moral ideal with the deliberative and prompting forces of the will and with those forces of our functioning that shape our conduct.[34]

Did Tymieniecka find the solution to the old dilemma? Would she escape Nietzsche's criticism presented at the beginning of this paper? Has the situation Nietzsche was confronted with changed much since his times? Tymieniecka writes:

To describe postmodern humanity at large in the terms of our study, there is no radical break between the high moral ideals of the great humanistic periods of Occidental culture and our times. We might today by and large ignore the high elevations of the spirit that were expressed in the ideals, virtues, and feelings of the classical and neo-classical periods of our literature/culture. The very notion of "ideals" and "virtues" might have lost their appeal and might seem to be replaced by more down to the earth "values" of all sorts. Nevertheless, in describing the practice of the highly developed culture of Occidental postmodernity, we have enumerated some basic civic virtues that are actively assumed: dedication, responsibility, faithfulness, reliability, courage, sincerity, integrity, etc. These are all expected of the citizen. And in contrast to the classical period, these virtues are set forth as ideals not for people who are "larger than life" and who are of the cultural elite but for average ordinary people. The running of our societies is grounded in the realization of these common virtues by the great majority of people, and their concretization is considered an accomplished fact. Should we not consider them as variations of the ideals and virtues exalted in past cultural periods?[35]

Doing so, she has made her recent text a rich source of questions about the Western philosophical tradition. At the same time, it is an invitation to a new, probably long and difficult journey. She ends her work optimistically, finding the "Occidental man's quest for 'being true to himself' (. . .) more alive than ever".[36] However, in the foregoing part of the same sentence she states: "sometimes the passion to be true to oneself degenerates into a soul-searching quest for one's 'identity' or for 'authenticity', that goes in futile directions".[37] The question still seems to be open. Not only the sea, not only life, but the human being, too, still remains one of the most astonishing phenomena in the Universe. What do we know about who we are and what our future will be? And what if, for example, Konrad Lorenz was right when he claimed in his *On Aggresion* that we are only the "missing part of the chain", the part linking the living world with the true humanity? What new *visions* could we build on such a statement! . . . Will the work ever end? It seems already to have begun.

Adam Mickiewicz University, Poznan, Poland
Temple University, Philadelphia, U.S.A.

NOTES

[1] Friedrich Nietzsche, *Werke*, Vol. 2, ed. by Karl Schlechta, (Ullstein GmbH Frankfurt am Main-Berlin-Vienna: 1972), p. 13.
[2] This very useful and inspiring term does not mean the same as Roman Ingarden's "gate of consciousness", although it would be interesting to investigate how far Tymieniecka was inspired by Ingarden at that point.

³ Anna-Teresa Tymieniecka, *Logos and Life*. Book 3: *The Passions of the Soul and the Elements in the Onto-Poiesis of Culture*. "The Life-Significance of Literature", in: A-T. Tymieniecka (ed.), *Analecta Husserliana*, Vol. XXVIII, (Dordrecht: Kluwer Academic Publishers, 1990), p. 10.

⁴ It is too bad that Tymieniecka concentrated on the Western tradition only, although it is obvious that the inclusion of the Oriental symbolic of light and sea would change significantly the direction of her consideration. I hope that she will continue her writing on this subject. Her familiarity with the philosophies of the East allows us to expect some interesting conclusions, e.g., about en*light*enment or about symbolic and poetic on the sea in Zen Buddhism.

⁵ I do not want to examine here the often enough discussed issue of the influence both of them had on the development of art, and, of course, on the concept of proper epistemological procedures.

⁶ This has a long tradition within Western culture. Heraclitus, and Plato too, claimed already the same (although Plato by no means appreciated this changing character of the material world). In the case of Tymieniecka we have to deal with an interesting relation between the role played in her thought by the *static picture* emerging from "eye-knowledge", which she advocates when writing about the importance of light, and her acknowledgement that the basic character of reality is *motion* (for which the sea is the best expression).

⁷ See: Anna-Teresa Tymieniecka, "Trzy wymiary fenomenologii — ontologiczny, transcendentalny, kosmiczny — rola Romana Ingardena". Translated from English into Polish by B. Chwedenczuk in: *Fenomenologia Romana Ingardena* (Warsaw: Wydanie specjalne Studiow Filozoficznych, 1972), p. 203.

⁸ In the history of Western philosophical and religious thought both directions were explored: (a) To be happy means to be good, (b) To be good means to be happy. Generally speaking, it was accepted that: (a) A bad person cannot be *really* happy, (b) A happy person cannot be *really* bad. The problem of happiness is regarded here in a different way than it is in Durkheim's *The Division of Labor in the Society*, esp. pp. 179—184 (Emile Durkheim, *The Division of Labor in the Society*. With an introduction by Lewis A. Coser. Translated by W. D. Halls [New York: The Free Press A Division of Macmillan, 1984]). Durkheim identifies happiness almost exclusively with pleasure and is interested, first of all, in the problem of the durability and intensity of happiness as well as the problem of the relationship between happiness and the development of civilization. In his opinion people can feel happy at different stages of civilization and, therefore, the search for happiness cannot be seen as the goal which is the base for people's activities and the cause of "progress". Durkheim is here similar in his views to Herbert Spencer and to Stanislaw Brzozowski, a Polish philosopher of the beginning of the 20th century influenced by Spencer. Opposing the moral validity of such an understanding of happiness, Brzozowski, in turn, advocated for that very reason the "*heroic*" model of human existence, which brought him close to Kant and Nietzsche. What I mean here, however, in writing of people's search for happiness, is expressed better by Goethe in his *Faust* and is closer to the ancient Greek and Roman understanding of the problem.

⁹ Maybe happiness is the goal not only of *human* life, but of all forms of life, of life "as such". According to Karl Popper: "Life looks for a better world. Each living individual thing tries to find a better world, at least in order to survive or to swim a bit easier there. This is characteristic of all life, from the amoeba up to man. It is ever our wish,

our hope, and our utopia to find an ideal world." Karl Raimund Popper & Konrad Lorenz, *Die Zukunft ist offen* (Munich: 1985), p. 17.

[10] This is, of course, an abstract, model example. The assumption here is, first of all, that the given individual analyses constantly his/her situation, asking at every second whether he/she is totally content or not. In reality all individuals act very often without any consideration of their feelings or even without thinking about what they are currently doing and what can be the result of their actions. Nevertheless, the situation of lack of *any discomfort*, the situation in which everybody is absolutely happy, is the situation in which no action, no change, no movement is reasonable — therefore, if human beings are "*thinking* animals", no movement will happen. *This* is, in my opinion, Hegel's concept of the end of history. (In German, the word for "history" is "Geschichte". The word "Geschichte" comes from "geschehen" — to happen. The end of history is the end of any happenings.) History will have no end as long as at least one human being will feel even the smallest discomfort, will have the will to change his/her situation and will be able to try to do so. Changing anything in his/her own situation, this individual will change directly or indirectly the situation of at least one other individual making this other individual feel some discomfort, which will cause the next action, etc., etc. Usually, *below* a certain level of discomfort, there is no active attempt to change the situation. That does not mean, however, that the *desire* for change is not there — psychological or physical (e.g., the body tries to make its situation as comfortable as possible in order to survive).

[11] I use the word "image" purposefully — despite the reservation expressed previously. The point here is that we think traditionally about ourselves as *having images* of the reality in our heads. Because of the influence of Plato's philosophy over such a long period of the Western history, our language reflects the worldview imposed by him. One of the valuable attempts of post-modern thinkers (although I have doubts whether they will be really successful in this) is the deconstruction of the language, understood here as the deconstruction of the traditional patterns of links between words, their meaning, and the reality with which they are connected.

[12] Karl Popper claims: "Human being is first of all language. What is it that makes the development of culture possible? Critique. Through language and through critique we have developed culture". Popper in Popper-Lorenz, *op. cit.*, p. 39.

[13] Leonard H. Ehrlich, *Karl Jaspers: Philosophy as Faith* (Amherst: The University of Massachusetts Press, 1975), p. 228.

[14] Tymieniecka, *Logos and Life. Book 3, op. cit.*, p. 138.

[15] And yet, as Tymieniecka points out, using Melville's *Moby Dick* as an example, there are still links even "between two human beings as radically different by human worldly standards as they only could be: here, a young bell boy, an 'idiot' by all accounts, helpless, weak and life-forlorn, and, there, a powerful, strong educated ship commander". (Tymieniecka, *Logos and Life, op. cit.*, p. 117) These links are "not easy pity or compassion, but the innermost passion of the soul, that of *human communion*". (*Ibidem*, p. 116) They became recognized on the "*verge of existence*", which is somewhat similar to what Karl Jaspers called the "boundary situation". Jaspers wrote: "The basic condition is a mode of the boundary situations — that is to say, of human situations that are immutable, unlike situations in the world. We can neither avoid nor transcend them, but their shattering impact brings us to ourselves as possible Existenz.

What becomes of man in boundary situations makes out his greatness, and without considering these conditions of greatness we cannot truthfully love the nobility in it. The inevitability of struggle, of suffering, of death, of coincidence — these are what we call boundary situations." (Karl Jaspers, *Philosophical Faith and Revelation*, trans. by E. B. Ashton [New York: Harper and Row, 1967], p. 210.)

[16] What I mean here, is rather a "vision of the future" that is closer to Tymieniecka's term "Imaginatio Creatrix", whereas, if I understood her correctly, Tymieniecka uses "vision" not only in that sense, but also in a sense of "better seeing", "seeing through" or "being illuminated". (See Tymieniecka, *Logos and Life, op. cit.*, esp. pp. 81f., 94ff.)

[17] Tymieniecka writes: "Joseph Conrad, shows rightly (. . .) that "facts have no meaning". Without imagination and reflection, they simply remain meaningless. We otherwise do not "think" about them; when confronted with them we simply take instinctively the most expedient course of action that we are capable of. "We endow the brute facts of life with significance only as our mind moves from marveling to wonderment to fabulation." (Tymieniecka, *Logos and Life, op. cit.*, p. 37)

[18] Nietzsche was aware of this. Hence, he did not postulate the establishment of any "pure" or "non-biased" knowledge — he protested against the restrictive character of morality in the process of scientific and/or philosophical investigation of the world if moral norms are accepted in the manner of slavery, as something imposed from outside, and are not established by the act of will of the given individual. Nietzsche wanted us to have the courage to say that in the act of "knowledge" we are, in fact, the *creators*. We create the world claiming that it is as we *want* to see it, which means, as we want it to be.

[19] Nietzsche, and Jaspers too, knew that action and theoretical investigation of reality do *exclude* each other.

[20] Tymieniecka, *Logos and Life, op. cit.*, pp. 10f.

[21] ". . . In the previous stages of Occidental culture, the focus was on nature, as the ground for man and his life-world, and creation aimed at depicting it, mirroring it, imitating it. With the advent of the modern age which came to its culmination in our century, steps were prepared for the turn toward *man's own forces and powers*. This is precisely the period in which *these steps brought about a radical change in the creative vision itself* that the human being held about his universe of life that marks the advent of a new era. The focus of the creative vision of man with respect to the human province of existence is now deliberately on *his own powers and forces*, that is, *upon the forces, energies, mechanisms, and mysteries of the great fluctuations in the universal scheme* of life so that he may penetrate and command them". (Tymieniecka, *Logos and Life, op. cit.*, p. 97.)

[22] *Ibid.*, p. 10.

[23] *Ibid.*

[24] ". . . the sea is not in man's nature. On the sea man enjoys a merely provisional status, he not being an aquatic animal. He is absolutely dependent on his vessel and its condition". *Ibid.*, p. 135.

[25] *Ibid.*, p. 117.

[26] *Ibid.*, p. 126.

[27] See Nietzsche, *op. cit.*, Vol. 4, p. 450.

[28] *Ibid.*

[29] Nietzsche, *op. cit.*, Vol. 3, p. 247.
[30] Tymieniecka, *Logos and Life, op. cit.*, p. 115.
[31] *Ibid.*, p. 116.
[32] *Ibid.*
[33] Karl Jaspers, *The Question of German Guilt*, trans. from German by E. B. Ashton (New York: 1961), pp. 22f.
[34] Tymieniecka, *Logos and Life, op. cit.*, p. 137.
[35] *Ibid.*, pp. 138f.
[36] *Ibid.*, p. 140.
[37] *Ibid.*

LOIS OPPENHEIM

"NO MATTER HOW NO MATTER WHERE": THE UNLIT IN SAMUEL BECKETT'S *NOT I* AND *STIRRINGS STILL*

In the preface to Volume XIX of the *Analecta Husserliana*, Anna-Teresa Tymieniecka defines the purpose of our investigation of the Elements and clarifies the distinction to be made between the notion of the Elements that originated with the pre-Socratic philosophic tradition and that with which we are presently concerned: She defines the former as "the metaphysico-physicalistic principles of the composition of objective reality" and the latter as the "complexes of vital forces of Nature" operative within the human imagination.[1] In her preface to the companion volume of the series (Volume XXIII), she alludes to our delving into the "locus where human genius reveals itself in the interplay of life-forces"[2] and to our effort to open "a new access to the meaningfulness of the literary work by focusing upon its creation in this subliminal sphere in which the metamorphosis of the neutral order of Nature into life — into the felt resounding voice of human existence — takes place in the human creative act."[3]

It is significant, though not surprising, that Tymieniecka's vocabulary — like that of the practitioners of what she terms "the manipulative methods of structuralism, semanticism, linguistics, and hermeneutics," those methods that, she claims, cloud "the understanding of literature"[4] — is a *spatial* vocabulary and that the analogies she offers for the apprehension of the poetic are spatial as well. Need we be reminded that the major notions of the metalinguistic critical orientations of formalist inspiration — from *meta*phor to *extra*- and *intra*diagetic narrative, from *internal* and *external* diachronics to focalization — are also fundamentally *spatial* concepts and that the recent efforts to come to terms with narrative perspective, narrative function and narrative voice are all grounded in the spatial configuration of linguistic/metalinguistic exchange?[5] Tymieniecka's vocabulary, however, in choosing to ignore this opposition, in focusing, rather, on the *perceptual* foundation of literary creativity, brings into play a spatial dimension that extends *outside* the text, beyond the textual closure postulated by formalists and, despite themselves, deconstructionists alike — the latter

43

A-T. Tymieniecka (ed.), Analecta Husserliana, Vol. XXXVIII, 43—53.
© 1992 *Kluwer Academic Publishers. Printed in the Netherlands.*

calling into question the origins of figurative language only to further entrench it within the confines of an idealistic, as non-empirical, epistemological game of hide and seek. And it is *this* spatial dimension — one that has been shown by Tymieniecka to unfold on the horizon of the Human Condition disparate forces united in their challenge to the creative imagination — which "shelters" (to borrow a term from Heidegger) the ontology of language mediating thereby the relation between reader, writer and world.

An analysis of this space, this locus wherein creative function may be said to fuse with the interplay of elemental forces, reveals that it is, at once, both *irreducible to the visual* and *negatively productive*.[6] This is to say that the site of the writer's experience with language is neither *full* nor *representable* and that — only to the extent that it *opens onto* the facticity of the world (in accordance with the ex-static temporal constitution of all literary creation), only to the extent that it appropriates (in the sense of Heidegger's *Ereignis*) the opacity of the world to disperse it imagistically in the constitution of a *new* world — is it originary, creative of the world that the text achieves.[7] This is a site that has been characterized by Reiner Schürmann, in the context of the poetry of René Char, as "a locus, still too novel to think of, a place beyond representations and beyond that threshold where the overcoming of metaphysics is still the dominant problem."[8] It is a site that has been variously described by Michel Collot and Jean-Claude Mathieu as a "non-lieu," by Claude Esteban as a "lieu hors de tout lieu," by Michel Deguy as a "utopie dans le topos."[9] Its originary or creative function has been further described by Henri Maldiney as "L'espace [qui] s'espacie en tant que la forme se forme,"[10] by Jacques Garelli as "un foyer de surgissement."[11] It is perhaps best approached, however, through the dialectic of its negative productivity wherein the "non-lieu . . . donne lieu"[12] and absence is understood as the *potential for*, as opposed to a lack of, meaning.

The somewhat impressionistic if extravagant description — both our own and that of the authors just cited — of the topology of creative expression and, specifically, of the point of juncture of imaginative function with elemental forces owes its imprecision, in part, to the insufficiency of philosophic discourse to account for the poetic appropriation of the existentials analyzed by Heidegger, for one, as the *Da* of Dasein, Being-in-the-World, disclosedness and clearing.[13] Were it not ever thus, poetry would not be poetry and philosophy philosophy.

Indeed, it is this insufficiency of discursive thought that is endemic to the critical and philosophical (pre- or post-Socratic) preoccupations with topology and to the effort to define the truths of Being, whatever their manifestations (literary or other), as *localizable* phenomena.

This topological imperative is not, however, proper to philosophic or critical ideation, for creative expression, that passionate exposure of pre-cognition, is likewise insufficient as a full accounting for human experience. What allows us to speak in terms of "situating" the work of art and to raise the question of the *place* of its origin are not only the recurrent linguistic motifs and the variety of rhetorical devices whose analyses have led in recent years to a privileging of the production of textual reference, but a fundamental paradox of artistic expression, one uncovered, to be sure, in the *spatial* configuration of the poetic *Aufhebung* — the *elevation* or "surrealization" of the world that is the achievement of the work of art: An opening onto the world, the text — as a parable of creation — reflects nothing other than its own process of revelation.[14] And it is precisely this paradox, the very measure of the poetic function of art, that provides access, over and above thematic and rhetorical considerations, to the site that interests us here, that of the grounding of the creative imagination by the elemental forces of nature.

We will turn now to a writer whose work, in focusing on a dialectical interplay of light and dark, sets in a sort of metaphorical *mise en abyme* this paradox of poetic expression, this *enlightenment* or *illumination* of artistic process by the illumination of the world onto which it is said to open. In considering the late works of Samuel Beckett, primarily *Not I* and *Stirrings Still*, we will attempt to establish the continuity of this focus and to illustrate the negative productivity that originates from within it and is characteristic of the locus of elemental and imaginative fusion referred to above.

In recent years Beckett has written a number of plays and a single narrative in which the creative process is the focus of the literary endeavor. This is to say that the recent works not only theatricalize the ontological reality — that which is the *sine qua non* of all Beckett's work — and thus contribute to the corpus of literary equivalencies for the theses developed in Heidegger's *Being and Time*, Sartre's *Being and Nothingness* and Hegel's *Phenomenology of Mind*,[15] but that they theatricalize the creative process itself. Among the most effective means of establishing dramatic correlatives of the creative experience is the play with light that serves as the primary metaphor of the creative effort. It must immediately be said, however, that the parables of creative activity that emerge within those of ontological reality are inaugurated *not only* by the illumination of character or scene, but at least as often by the *absence of illumination* or *the fading of light*, both of which are negatively productive.

Let us take, for example, the eruption of Mouth onto the darkened stage at the beginning of *Not I*. Here, perhaps more than in any other Beckett text, there is a convergence of the visual and aural stimuli with the subject of the monologue itself: That from the first words of Beckett's disembodied organ of speech — "... out ... into this world ... this world ... tiny little thing ... before its time ... in a godfor- ... what? ... girl? ... yes ... tiny little girl ... into this ... out into this ... before her time ... godforsaken hole called ..."[16] and so on — that from these first words emerges an image, at once, of the fathomless expanse of our world *and* of that very orifice whose presence is the *dramatis persona* herself of the text is due to the absence of any light on the stage except for a spot that allows us to perceive the reddened lips of Mouth. The absence of light is precisely what *disanthropomorphizes* the fictive world and obliges the spectator to creatively fill the void of the unlit. The image of Mouth is constituted both theatrically and thematically, as opposed to symbolically or metonymically, by the congruence of a verbal irruption of "something" — namely, sound and meaning — *and* its opposite, "nothing" — ellipsis, lacuna.[17] Though the reader of *Not I* loses out on the visual horizon negatively or inversely produced by the blackened stage, he or she benefits (where the spectator does not) from the ellipses that precede (and continually intrude upon thereafter) the text. The effect is ultimately the same, however, for the impression is that of a linguistic pulverizing of any reality *outside* that of the monologue, a reality whose positing in ordinary discourse is the measure of communication.

It is also to be noted that the reference to "a ray of light [that] came and went ... came and went ... such as the moon might cast ... drifting ... in and out of cloud ... ,"[18] repeated, like the reference to a "sudden flash," intermittently throughout the text *is*, in fact, the very ray of light on Mouth that allows her to be seen in the dark. Here again, the convergence of the visual with the semantic deconstructs the *I* of *Not I* — the individuation of one who refuses to don any but the third person pronoun "she" — to the *eye* of Bishop Berkeley's *Esse est percipi* that is the premise for Beckett's work *Film* (originally entitled *The Eye*).[19] This, of course, is reminiscent of Beckett's *Rockaby*, as well, where the twice repeated "Stop her eyes"[20] puts an end to perception, synonomous with Being, in turn synonomous with Time and with language as the metaphoric correlate of existence.

It is precisely when we consider the play in the light (no pun intended) of the poetic *Aufhebung* — the process of dialectical negation and reconstitution through which the world is negated in its limited individuality, preserved in its essential being and elevated, in the imagistic or metaphoric use of language, to a higher reality, a "sur-reality" — that we perceive its dramatic functioning as a *textual redoubling*, a reflection of nothing other than its *own process of revelation*.

Insight into this process might be gleaned from the congruence of narrative and metanarrative that is achieved in *Not I* within the temporalization of the fictional language. The endless repetition of Mouth's tale of that April morning "when suddenly . . . gradually . . . all went out . . . all that early April morning light . . . [when] she found herself in the — what? . . . who? . . . no! . . . she! . . . [. . .] found herself in the dark . . ."[21] implies not a temporality conceived as a passage from past to present and present to future, but as the lived time of an eternal present — *ours*, in fact, as spectators (in the dark) of a play (also in the dark) — to the extent that Mouth's tale *is the actuality of our perception of Beckett's drama*. This is to say that the "then" of Mouth's narration is contemporaneous with the "now" of her metanarration provoking a deliberate confusion of text and reality that opens onto the poetic process of the *textual unveiling of text* as prerequisite to the *textual unveiling of world*.

Additional evidence of the simultaneity of Mouth's temporality with that of her spectators is to be found in the dimly lit interlocutor who stands downstage right[22] of the disembodied voice. Here again, it is the lack of light that prevents us from discerning more than the "simple sideways raising of arms from [his or her] sides and their falling back, in a gesture of helpless compassion."[23] Our difficulty in seeing provokes us to ask, with Enoch Brater, just what exactly Auditor does "to elicit Mouth's reactive 'what?'" and to wonder whether "this 'what?' [is] reactive after all? Is the monologue perhaps a soliloquy, and the respondent yet another fiction in the story Mouth unfolds?"[24] If we cannot see to know, neither can Mouth whose difficulties are compounded by the lack of ears with which to hear whatever it is the respondent says or does.

We have shown elsewhere[25] numerous possibilities for the interpretation of Mouth's discourse and its disembodiment in the context of recent feminist and psychoanalytic critical thinking. Such interpretation may focus on the circumscription of absence, on Mouth as the personnification of female genitalia inhabited by a non-ego, a "not I," or it may center on Mouth's linguistic transmutation of a male paradigm, on her marginalization as a figure of incompletion, her deformation of the male prototype. It may instead confirm Mouth as "a secondary object lacking autonomy"[26] — one seeking outside herself, in the third person pronominal expression, confirmation of her proper identity — an exemplification of a tradition of the reification of women. Such analyses, however, while not without value, appear to insufficiently account for the *theatricalization* of the fiction: Allowing the text "to come to closure in a total structure of relationships between signs and signifieds,"[27] as Eugene Kaelin does in his otherwise interesting study of Beckett, *The Unhappy Consciousness*, fails to consider that, to quote Tymieniecka, "drama 'plays' . . . at the borderline of two worlds: the fictitious one it presents, and the real one, which it breaks into."[28] On the stage, *Not I* becomes a segment of the real world, that which brings "the natural forces of real life in their evocative power"[29] into play with the fictitious world giving rise to the dramatization, the parabolization both of *human experience* (what Tymieniecka has called "the very heart of the universal human struggle for survival"[30] and I have referred to here as the "ontological reality") and of our *creative quest*. Only in this perspective can the darkened stage be said *to open onto the cosmic structure precisely to illuminate* (1) the spatiotemporal dimensions of the world and (2) the intentional structure of our perception of them.

Illumination is again a focus of the 1982 play, *Catastrophe* as it was of the short interlude, *Breath*, written in 1967. In *Breath*, whose title is perhaps an "amalgam of "birth" and "death","[31] a faint light is timed to increase and decrease in direct proportion to the inspiration and expiration of a single breath separating two cries of a newborn. Here no words are needed to embellish this vision of the facticity of human life, for the synchronization of light and breath "says" it all. The stage is lit to illuminate that topology which Heidegger claims, in "The Thinker as Poet", "tells Being the whereabouts of its actual presence"[32] and we could come no closer to the dimly lit recesses of the ontico-ontological experience.

Catastrophe, on the other hand — in the highly charged context of political repression (the play is dedicated to Vaclav Havel and premiered to protest Havel's imprisonment by Czech authorities) — explores directly (thematically) theatrical method: The question posed is that of how best, through the technique of lighting — specifically, the spot that fades — to distill in a final visual image the dramatic point. The significance of the question of lighting as a means of distillation takes us beyond the parable of birth and death witnessed in *Breath*: In dramatizing the play of light, the creative effort is made to reveal, as an objectivation of it, the genesis of the world. The play's manifest political overtones notwithstanding — and I refer here to the collaborative effort that *is* work in the theater as set against the powerful role played by the theatrical director — in going from *Breath* to *Catastrophe*, from ontology to cosmology, Beckett traces an evolution in and of itself as political as the textual allegory: From the catastrophe of life to the catastrophe of world — for the spot that enlightens and must ultimately fade is a metaphorical generative and degenerative force — to "play" becomes a mimicry of the *de*humanizing tendency that is our tragic flaw.

The remainder of our discussion of the play of light in Beckett will be devoted to *Stirrings Still* where references to light are unrelated to the mechanics of theatricalization. Central to this narrative, as to the plays, is the light symbolism, but here, unlike in the theater, words must replace the actuality of the visual effect. Unlike in Beckett's 1979 play *A Piece of Monologue*, for example, where light recedes as life and language are (as one) extinguished, light in *Stirrings Still* is limited to a purely linguistic function that which implies a temporal flux, and hence a time consciousness, that theatrical lighting is able to suspend. This is to say that the congruence of narrative and metanarrative temporality, such as is supported in *Not I* by the interplay of light and articulation, is unrealizable in narrative that removes the play of light from the experiential mode. Nevertheless, the verbal treatment of the light and darkness interplay fulfills the same affirming/negating, presencing/ab-sencing function.

The fear of darkness, like the desire for it, is evident in all Beckett's work where a fear of the end that invisibility implies gives rise to a

compulsion to be seen.[33] It is in this perspective that the objectivation
of self that constitutes the thematic structure of *Stirrings Still* is to be
interpreted. The doubling of character, like Mouth's denial of the first
person "I" and the old woman's quest, in *Rockaby*, "for another/
another like herself/another creature like herself"[34] appears, in the
context of this preoccupation with being visible, to falsify what is all too
often put forth as an appropriate critical framework in which to view
the psychosocial insufficiencies exemplified by Beckett's characters —
namely, the dissolution of the ego. To the extent that the world is
always that of one's perception as an individual within it and to the
extent that one can be fully conscious of one's Self as an individual only
to the degree that one is conscious of one's relation to the world, any
possibility for a truly integrated identification of the Self apart from its
relation to the Other is immediately negated. And it is this that is at the
origin of the dialectical interplay of anonymity and individuation that,
we would argue, is the single most significant thematic and structural
unifying force of Beckett's work, one that validates the splitting of
subjectivity manifested in the bifurcated expression of real and taped
voice in *Rockaby* and *Krapp's Last Tape* as in the character's viewing
of himself, in *Stirrings Still*, as one who disappears only to reappear
again and again at another place.

Reminiscent of *Waiting for Godot*, *Stirrings Still* takes place in a sort
of no man's land where one watches oneself "rise and go," "then go"[35]
to again be seen "in another where never,"[36] but here, unlike in *Godot*,
it is light, specifically a fading light (first artificial then natural), that, as
a recurrent thematic motif, provides a clue to the simultaneous fear and
desire to be done with it all. Indeed, it is the objectivation of Self — the
projected visibility of Self — that is the confirmation of existence
against the dreaded fading light of life. So too, however, is the refusal to
look outside, to profit from the window light when his own light was no
more, a reluctance to prolong precisely what in this character is
"stirring still."

Stirrings Still cannot be reduced, any more than any other Beckett
text, to the representation of an *a priori* notion of reality. That Beckett's
character is unable to locate, in this the penultimate stage of his life, any
orientational spatial or temporal points of reference that would allow
for a cohesive identification reflects both the incomprehensibility of
world and that of self and points to the illusory nature of memory and
the source of fictive creation. The fading of light — first the "outer light"

then "his own" — ironically leads not to the dark as end, but as the starting point for more. Another place, another appearance, another tale: such is the negative productivity that prevents conclusion and circumscribes the very limits of meaning. "No more no less. No less. Less to die. Ever less. Like light at nightfall,"[37] Beckett tells us in *A Piece of Monologue*. "Out of dark. A window. Looking west. Sun long sunk behind the larches. Light dying. Soon none left to die. No. No such thing as no light."[38]

From what precedes we may conclude that the negative productivity of the absence or fading of light in Beckett's mid-to-late texts constitutes a paradoxical reversal illustrative of two others: first, that of the revelation of the text's own poetic function through the revelation of an opening out onto the world and, second, that of the expanding ontological vision born of minimization. The recent dramatic and narrative discourse of Beckett achieves a degree of poetization unparalleled in contemporary prose and pays vital testimony to the "paradox of poetic activity that is the measure of its condition."[39] That these texts move away from a full semantic closure toward a syntactic fragmentation, a paradigmatic deformation is precisely what allows for their increasingly expressive potential and, thereby, their inauguration of a new genre that Brater defines as a "performance poem." From *Not I* to *Stirrings Still*, each Beckett work, to paraphrase a remark of the late director, Alan Schneider, "contains the whole of Beckett." One might go even further to conclude that each Beckett work, *enacting the irreducibility of the conundrum of human existence to conceptualization*, contains the whole of our ontological plight.

Montclair State College, New Jersey

NOTES

[1] Anna-Teresa Tymieniecka, "The Theme: Poetics of the 'Elements' in the Human Condition" in *Analecta Husserliana*, Vol. XIX (Dordrecht: D. Reidel, 1985), p. xi.
[2] Anna-Teresa Tymieniecka, "The Theme: The Plurivocal Poiesis of the Airy Element" in *Analecta Husserliana*, Vol. XXIII (Dordrecht: D. Reidel, 1988), p. x.
[3] *Ibid.*, p. x.
[4] *Ibid.*, p. ix.
[5] Cf. Michel Collot & Jean-Claude Mathieu, "Présentation" in *Espace et Poésie* (Paris: Presses de l'Ecole Normale Supérieure, 1987), p. 9.
[6] *Ibid.*

7 Cf. Reiner Schürmann, "Situating René Char: Hölderlin, Heidegger, Char and the 'There Is'" in *Martin Heidegger and the Question of Literature* (Bloomington: Indiana University Press, 1976), p. 178.

8 *Ibid.*, p. 186.

9 Collot & Mathieu, *op. cit.*, p. 8.

10 Henri Maldiney, "Espace et Poésie" in *Espace et Poésie, op. cit.*, p. 91.

11 Jacques Garelli, "L'Acte poétique, Instauration d'un Lieu Pensant" in *Espace et Poésie, op. cit.*, p. 30.

12 Collot & Mathieu, *op. cit.*, p. 9.

13 Cf. John Sallis, "On Heidegger/Derrida — Presence," paper presented at the Modern Language Association.

14 This paradox has been brilliantly articulated by Jacques Garelli in *La Gravitation poétique* (Paris: Mercure de France, 1966), p. 9.

15 Lance St. John Butler has written an excellent study that explores Beckett's work in the light of these theses: *Samuel Beckett and the Meaning of Being* (New York: St. Martin's Press, 1984).

16 Samuel Beckett, *Not I* in *The Collected Shorter Plays of Samuel Beckett* (New York: Grove Press, 1984), p. 216.

17 See our "Anonymity and Individuation: The Interrelation of Two Linguistic Functions in *Not I* and *Rockaby*" in *Make Sense Who May*, ed. Robin J. Davis & Lance St. John Butler (Totowa, New Jersey: Barnes & Noble, 1989), p. 40.

18 Beckett, *Not I*, p. 217.

19 Enoch Brater, *Beyond Minimalism* (New York & Oxford: Oxford University Press, 1987), p. 76.

20 Samuel Beckett, *Rockaby* in *The Collected Shorter Plays of Samuel Beckett, op. cit.*, p. 282.

21 Beckett, *Not I*, pp. 216–217.

22 Downstage audience left.

23 Beckett, *Not I*, p. 215.

24 Brater, *op. cit.*, p. 33.

25 In an essay entitled "Female Subjectivity in *Not I* and *Rockaby*" forthcoming in *Women in Beckett: Gender and Genre*, ed. Linda Ben-Zvi by the University of Illinois Press.

26 Susan Gubar, "The 'Blank Page' and Female Creativity" in *Feminist Criticism*, ed. Elaine Showalter (New York: Pantheon, 1985), p. 295.

27 Eugene F. Kaelin, "*The Unhappy Consciousness*," *Analecta Husserliana*, Vol. XIII (Dordrecht: D. Reidel, 1981), 8.

28 Anna-Teresa Tymieniecka, "Poetica Nova: Part I, The Poetics of Literature" in *The Philosophical Reflection of Man in Literature* (Dordrecht: D. Reidel, 1982), p. 55.

29 *Ibid.*, p. 56.

30 *Ibid.*

31 Butler, *op. cit.*, p. 51.

32 Martin Heidegger, "The Thinker as Poet," in *Poetry, Language, Thought*, transl. Albert Hofstadter (New York: Harper & Raw, 1971), p. 12.

33 Cf. James Knowlson, *Light and Darkness in the Theater of Samuel Beckett* (London: Turnet Books, 1972), p. 37.

[34] Beckett, *Rockaby, op. cit.*, p. 275.
[35] Beckett, *Stirrings Still* (London: John Calder, 1988), pp. 2—3.
[36] *Ibid.*, p. 10.
[37] Beckett, *A Piece of Monologue* in *The Collected Shorter Plays of Samuel Beckett, op. cit.*, p. 266.
[38] *Ibid.*, p. 267.
[39] Jacques Garelli, *La Gravitation poétique, op. cit.*, p. 9.

SIDNEY FESHBACH

THE LIGHT AT THE END OF THE TUNNEL
IS COMING RIGHT AT ME, OR, THE DIALECTIC
OF ELEMENTAL LIGHT AND ELEMENTAL DARK

(for Milton and Etta Ehrlich:
so much depends)

I. A PREFACE TO ATTITUDES AND METHODS

Under a gentle imperative to consider phenomenologically a physical element in literature, we are compelled to wander about, gather, consolidate, rethink, and re-experience mentally and sensually the mode of that element. This is true for several elements at once, such as the four classical elements.[1] In an introductory attitude I want to consider some aspects of the dialectic of elemental light and elemental dark; I believe it important to present very briefly something of my method of preparation because it influences the organization of that re-experience in this essay. My approach in several studies in the phenomenology of the elements has followed a vaguely pre-determined sequence of mental acts and research activities.[2] First, I review what I recall quickly of the element in literature, myths, religious texts, philosophy, natural philosophy, and physical sciences. Then I compare and sort out the experiences of the element along with the recollected textual evidence. Third, I seek a renewal of contact with the element as it is active in my emotional life as well. Lastly, I begin at this point to write something and, simultaneously, to initiate further research into texts, histories, commentaries, novels, poetry, and scientific works. Over the subsequent months, this project evolves into heavy files. The first phase should be emphasized: this is with the evidence in and of memory, hence, continued in and expressed from the mind, a human-istic prerequisite of all phenomenological studies. The presentation later at a lecture retains something of the spontaneity of a questioning still very much in motion; and the essay readied for publication is a con-solidation and, in the fashion of Husserl's titles, is always introductory.

Similarly, the order of this paper is, first, a quick semi-systematic, epitomizing inventory of related terms, and categories. This is followed

55

A-T. Tymieniecka (ed.), Analecta Husserliana, Vol. XXXVIII, 55—84.
© 1992 *Kluwer Academic Publishers. Printed in the Netherlands.*

by consideration of an exoteric religious text, *Genesis*, a philosophical text, Plato's *Republic*, and an esoteric religious text, *The Zohar*, each chosen not for its particular religion or philosophy, but for its centrality in European and European-influenced traditions. Inquiry into presentation of the dialectic of elemental light and elemental dark in *Genesis* 1.1—2.3 generated the concept of "primordiality"; the dialectic in the philosophical text, Plato's "The Myth of the Cave," from *The Republic* VI, restates the dialectic of primordial light and primordial dark in the terms of an epistemology. When surveying the information recalled and collected, I found that over the epochs of culture considered even slightly two large-scale cultural changes appeared to recur in my (and many others') thinking and to be influencing my attitude to the point of occluding fresh re-experiencing: the main change to be considered here is from the familiar cultural worldviews usually associated with the ancient-medieval European epoch to the renaissance-modern. I have personified these two cultural periods as two kinds of Adam, Naming Adam and Numbering Adam. After considering the texts from *Genesis*, *The Republic*, and *The Zohar* as differentiating between primordial light and dark and everyday light and dark, and summing up a related tradition, I turn to the cusp period of these cultural changes to consider one of Galileo's earlier scientific texts in which he makes a subtle shift in the terms he uses from those of a Naming Adam to a Numbering Adam. Then, I wonder about a relation of primordial light and primordial dark to infinite light and infinite dark, and to ideas of infinity embodied in the use in scientific writing of the verb forms of the infinitive, the constant present, and imperative instructions. Lastly, I consider briefly Hermann Broch's *The Unknown Quantity* and the relation of science and emotions and *The Death of Virgil*, with comments about its literary lineage and its intention to present a meditation at an extreme of the primordial light and primordial dark, where, perhaps, mathematics and poetry are the same.

I should add as a postscript to this preface what I am not considering here. I am not considering details of light: as a facilitator, the vehicle of the instrument of seeing things, or as an agency of change, even though both areas are extremely important; or darkness as an inhibitor or, by contrast, an inspirer; or the reverse, of light as distracting or blinding and dark as having its own productivity. I do not consider the enormous variety of lights stated in terms of the source of light, i.e., the differences of light from the sun, from the wood fire, from the burning wax of the candle, from the coal fire, from the kerosene, from incandescent, neon, fluorescent, and electric lights, from the television screen, even from the digital clock at 3:33 a.m. Or their concomitant darks. It is obvious and truly unavoidable that a phenomenology of light involves corollaries regarding the eyes: just as a study of the element earth must consider touch and the pull of gravity as made palpable in the fatigue of the muscles; just as a consideration of the element of water must include, in the ocean, the movement of the tides and currents tugging at the body, or, in the stream, the gentler brushing and pulling at the surface of the body; so light and dark are felt in degrees of visual strength, clarity, eye-fatigue, perspectives, vertigo, headaches, and so forth. What of light and dark in a bedroom, in the street, in the theater? In short, there is much omitted from this essay, but not forgotten.

II. A QUICK EPITOMIZING INVENTORY OF YIN AND YANG

In this section, I mention a range of terms, and even when not so noted, for every light there is in mind a dark. I intend a dialectical event in which the term used is only one of several terms: everyday light, everynight dark; daylight: sunlight, brilliant and varying, shadows, the edges of light and shadows, sharp and fuzzy; nightlight; moonlight and moon in phases of changing; starlight and the idea that the stars were believed to be permanent and never changing and ever exploding; reflecting planets, burning comets; sun spots; aurora borealis; mixtures of light and dark; clouds, mists, overcast glare; blue shadows of haystacks; chiaroscuro; obscurities, occlusions, and opacities. Then there are light and dark near the shore, with high degrees of transforming humidity, brilliant light and dark in the dry air of the desert, sudden appearances of sunlight and equally sudden appearances of dark in the mountains and valleys; constant glittering, blinding and colorful, reflections from planes of snow. There are those terrible images in the photographs of nuclear explosions and the sidewalks in Hiroshima bleached so intensely that, seemingly, people left their shadows burned into the surface. What of light-responsive materials: photographic materials, plants, animals, humans, sensory organs, the eyes; other organs are light sensitive, as is the pineal gland in birds, possibly in humans? What of the large complex circadian, seasonal, biological rhythms, the ecological dance in which micro-organisms, inducing dust and humans, and macro-organisms, including forests and oceans, participate? The ranges of the phenomena of the dialectic of elemental light and elemental dark are, need I say, thick and infrathin beyond words.

What of the simplifying myths and narratives of light and dark? The familiar constellations of astrology are such simplifications. The astrological patterns of ancient Assyria that are repeated as Leo and Taurus are mimed so often in artefact and art, with a lion on the back of a bull, claws digging into the flesh, teeth buried into the back. The Zoroastrian battles of Ahura-Mazda (or in descent, Spenta Mainyu) and Ahriman (or Angra Mainyu) refer to a cultural archetype that is found also in the earlier Sumerian stories of Gilgamesh and Humbaba, in Egyptian stories of Isis, Osiris, Anu, Mardu, and others, and in century-spanning thematic dualisms, such as Gnosticism, Manichaeism, and Kabbalism. The biblical Samson, his very name deriving from the Hebrew for "sun" and his career going from sight to blindness, from open field to dark dungeon, appears based on the career of the daylight sun and dark night. Then there are the caves of Altamira with their animals immersed in darkest cave and the probable magic-rituals of hunting and rites of passage, distant cousins of Delphic epiphanies and theophanies. Beowulf swimming in from overseas in a shining hero and amphibious Grendel attacks at midnight. We could add the Celtic Druid circles, megaliths open like Stonehenge in England or closed over by tons of earth and shining stones such as the Grange hill in Ireland; in these, people aligned the heaviest earth and stones with the motions of the constantly moving sun and with the constancies of precise moments for midwinter and midsummer. Certain moments of light are impressionistic moments of processes that are given special privilege in myth and poetry, such as the mixtures for beginning's dawn and ending's dusk and for high noon and midnight, that signify more than precise moments but entire attitudes in which appear highly charged epiphenomena. Paul Valery stressed dawn and noon, William Butler Yeats twilight, Edgar Allen Poe night and midnight; in Poe's "Fall of the House of Usher," Roderick Usher protects his eyes from the natural light and his ears from natural sound only to be forced to hear and see the uncanny. F. Scott Fitzgerald said that 4 a.m. is the midnight of the soul. Then John of the Cross wrote so brilliantly of "the dark night of the soul," which emerges from the *Cloud of Unknowing* and all the illuminations along the *via negativa*. Albert Camus emphasized the conflict of light and dark, Mediterranean and Central European worlds.

James Joyce revised radically Aquinas's concept of *claritas* to account at first for the kind of light that is necessary to aesthetic apprehension and creation, then for the contrast of the dark fallen world and the radiant renovated world of art. Ezra Pound's translation of Confucius's as *The Unwobbling Pivot* blends Plotinean light, ethics, and fascism and ends by obscuring the text by omitting its final section.[3] As in the story of Oedipus, blinding is punishment and may be the pre-condition for becoming one who sees the truth, a seer. Out of this brief semi-chaotic semi-cosmic inventory, randomly thickening and thinning, of the dialectic of elemental light and elemental dark, it is appropriate to turn to the first text, the text with the myth of creating out of chaos, of creating light and of creating light and dark.

III. GENESIS 1.1—2.3

The creation of light in *Genesis* is one expression of the constant of light in Mediterranean and European religions. The biblical text is so rich in meanings in itself, but centuries of interpretation have enriched it further, making its potential meanings more accessible and by inserting into it new potentials, like modifying the DNA of its cultural code. Because the text is so important and because I give attention to aspects not usually discussed, I present it in its entirety, with comments.

The word for "creating" is used only for God and never used for the work of "making" by humans. The creation, from *Genesis* 1.1 to 1.10, establishes distinctive, or differentiated, areas, or spaces (heaven, earth, waters, firmament), each with its own qualities and functions, and the "let there be light," or *y-he ohr* in Hebrew and *fiat lux*, the existential predication so relevant to this essay:

1.1. In the beginning God created the heavens and the earth. 2. Now the earth was unformed and void, and darkness was upon the face of the deep; and the spirit of God hovered over the face of the waters. 3. And God said: 'Let there be light.' And there was light. 4. And God saw the light, and it was good; and God divided the light from the darkness. 5. And God called the light Day, and the darkness He called Night. And there was evening and there was morning, one day. 6. And God said: 'Let there be a firmament in the midst of the waters, and let it divide the waters from the water.' 7. And God made the firmament, and divided the waters which were under the firmament from the waters which were above the firmament; and it was so. 8. And God called the firmament Heaven. And there was evening and there was morning, a second day. 9. And God said: 'Let the waters under the heaven be gathered together unto one place, and let the dry land appear.' And it was so. 10. And God called the dry land Earth, and the gathering together of the waters called He Seas; and God saw it was good.

From *Genesis* 1.11 to 1.13 the different areas have their appropriate lives and activities, which, I wish to stress are stated in terms of groups, species, not individuals, and the first set is related to elemental earth:

11. And God said: 'Let the earth put forth grass, herb yielding seed, and fruit-tree bearing fruit after its kind, wherein is the seed thereof, upon the earth.' And it was so. 12. And the earth brought forth grass, herb yielding seed after its kind, and tree bearing fruit, wherein is the seed thereof, after its kind; and God saw that it was good. 13. And there was evening and there was morning, a third day.

1.14—19 has stars, sun, and moon, or the elemental fire:

14. And God said: 'Let there be lights in the firmament of the heaven to divide the day from the night; and let them be for signs, and for seasons, and for days and years; 15. and let them be for lights in the firmament of the heaven to give light upon the earth.' And it was so. 16. And God made the two great lights: the greater light to rule the day, and the lesser light to rule the night; and the stars. 17. And God set them in the firmament of the heaven to give light upon the earth, 18. and to rule over the day and over the night, and to divide the light from the darkness; and God saw that it was good. 19. And there was evening and there was morning, a fourth day.

1.20—25 has the elemental water and elemental air as different spaces and within each the appropriate species:

20. And God said: 'Let the waters swarm with swarms of living creatures, and let fowl fly above the earth in the open firmament of heaven.' 21. And God created the great sea-monsters, and every living creature that creepeth, wherewith the waters swarmed, after its kind, and every winged fowl after its kind; and God saw that it was good. 22. And God blessed them, saying: 'Be fruitful, and multiply, and fill the waters in the seas, and let fowl multiply in the earth.' 23. And there was evening and there was morning, a fifth day. 24. And God said: 'Let the earth bring forth the living creature after its kind, cattle, and creeping thing, and beast of the earth after its kind.' And it was so. 25. And God made the beast of the earth after its kind, and the cattle after their kind, and every thing that creepeth upon the ground; and God saw that it was good.

Thus, in the two sections, 1.1—10 and 1.11—23, occur, first, spatiation and, second, speciation, along with the four classical elements and light. In 1.26—31, there occur hierarchization of species and human empowerment. That is to say, Elohim (Hebrew, a plural noun that takes a singular verb) has prepared the world for the creation of humans as well as of and for human acts. This also completed the first six days:

26. And God said: 'Let us make man in our image, after our likeness; and let them have dominion over the fish of the sea, and over the fowl of the air, and over the cattle, and over all the earth, and over every creeping thing that creepeth upon the earth.' 27. And God created man in His own image, in the image of God created he him; male and female created He them. 28. And God blessed them; and God said unto them: 'Be fruitful, and multiply, and replenish the earth, and subdue it; and have dominion over the fish of the sea, and over the fowl of the air, and over every living thing that creepeth upon the earth.' 29. And God said: 'Behold, I have given you every herb yielding seed, which is upon the face of all the earth, and every tree, in which is the fruit of a tree yielding seed — to you it shall be for food; 30. and to every beast of the earth, and to every fowl of the air, and to every thing there is a living soul, [I have given] every green herb for food.' And it was so.

This system finishes with sight and light, evening and morning. "31. And God saw every thing that He had made, and, behold, it was very good. And there was evening and there was morning, the sixth day." On the seventh day is created a new category, "rest," that is of necessity a reinterpretation of what came before, an indication and an iteration of notions of "acting," "working," "finishing," and "blessing" and "hallowing," to conclude with the startling distinction of "creating" and "making."

2.1. And the heavens and the earth were finished, and all the host of them. 2. And on the seventh day God finished His work which He had made; and He rested on the seventh day from all His work with He had made. 3. And God blessed the seventh day, and hallowed it; because that in it He rested from all His work which God in creating had made.

After God, or *Elohim*, says let there be light, certain events take place within its universal illumination — namely, creation of day and night, and so on. The light itself is created in dialectical opposition to the dense confusion of chaos and the prior cosmic dark. Because the sun and moon are not yet created (1.14—18), I see this light as primordial natural light, the alternative to which is not dark as such, but the prior chaos, chaos that at its thickest is primordial dark, and, later slightly less thick may be called wilderness. Spaces and species are "created" within or as illuminated by the primordial light. It is as though chaos (primordial dark) itself is being transformed by the process of differentiation permitted by the presence of light. And this process in turn is inseparable from the word-magic of naming, predicating, and sentence structures: God commands and states events, and they are created; He names them — one even is called "Day" and another is called "Night." These omnipowerful activities find their analogues in the endowment of humans with dominion over these spaces and lives contained therein and in Adam's being charged with naming of the other creatures (*Genesis* 2.19, which is not included in this section and is part of a different kind of narration): "Whatsoever the man would call every living creature, that was the name thereof." That is, there is a correlation of the divine activities in human's stating, naming, and power. Adam is given the task and the authority to name the animals. I take this as prime figure of the Naming Adam. (Another feature of this passage that I return to later is the text's stating that this light was "the first day," then there was "the second day," etc.; numbering, an act as important as naming, that differentiates and coordinates events must be and will be separately considered. As mentioned, I suggest a different Adam for this numbering, a Numbering Adam.) In *Genesis*, we see the creation of light and, indeed, the creation of different lights. One kind of elemental natural light is primordial natural light, the *ohr, lux*, of this first *y-he, fiat*. A second order, or secondary, natural light is produced by the sun, moon, and stars. These forms of elemental lights are different in degree or kind. Primordial light and the secondary light become associated with creativity and virtue, individual, mystical, and divine, and opposed to chaotic darkness. In the biblical dialectic of elemental light and elemental dark, perennial returns of darks occur within the subpatterns of the entire narrative calling forth new terms, such as wilderness, flood, desert, Babel, Valley of Death, and salty ocean, which are related to the "*sheol*, the Hebrew word for the infernal otherworld. [. . .] *Sheol* bequeathed to [Christian] Purgatory (and to [Christian] Hell) its characteristic darkness (from which souls in Purgatory eventually emerge into the light), a darkness that penetrates every recess of the subterranean world of the dead."[4] Such darks have their dialectical swing into new lights, rainbows, and mountain tops of revelation.

This primordial natural light is the analogue, indeed, the phenomenological objective correlative, for certain kind of light intended in epistemological passages of the philosophers when writing about those mutual activities of "presentation to the mind" and "representation," when they contrast conceiving with perceiving. This distinction is carefully drawn by Plato in *The Republic*, in "The Myth of the Cave" (and "The Divided Line"). This familiar passage is a conversation in which Socrates is conducting the exposition and Glaucon makes brief responses; without indicating any of the cuts, I have altered this easily available text.

IV. PLATO, *THE REPUBLIC* VII.514—520, "THE MYTH OF THE CAVE"

This passage makes use of a careful depiction of the changes of the eye when moving from light to bright light, and from light to dark, from adaption to the shadows, to the bright light, as well as the meaning of these experiences when transposed from the physical to the philosophical, the social, and the moral. Throughout, dialectically set against an elemental darkness as co-function, illusions seen obscure truths not seen, truths seen energize the seer to help others to see.

And now, I said, let me show in a figure how far our nature is enlightened or unenlightened: — Behold! human beings living in an underground den, which has a mouth open towards the light and reaching all along the den. They see only shadows, which the fire throws on the opposite wall of the cave. Would they not suppose that they were naming what was actually before them? At first, when any of them is liberated and compelled suddenly to stand up and turn his neck round and walk and look towards the light, he will suffer sharp pains; the glare will distress him, and he will be unable to see the realities of which in his former state he had seen the shadows. He will require to grow accustomed to the sight of the upper world. And first he will see the shadows best, next the reflections of men and other objects in the water, and then the objects themselves; then he will gaze upon the light of the moon and the stars and the spangled heaven; and he will see the sky and the stars by night better than the sun or the light of the sun by day. Last of all he will be able to see the sun, and not mere reflections of him in the water, but he will see him in his own proper place, and not in another; and he will contemplate him as he is. He will then proceed to argue that this is he who gives the season and the years, and is the guardian of all that is in the visible world, and in a certain way the cause of all things which he and his fellows have been accustomed to behold. And when he remembered his old habitation, and the wisdom of the den and his fellow-prisoners, do you not suppose that he would felicitate himself on the change, and pity them.

Throughout, Plato presents and transposes dramatically the experiences of perceiving that are all analogous to the process of learning, i.e., epistemology.

But, whether true or false, my opinion is that in the world of knowledge the idea of good appears last of all, and is seen only with an effort; and, when seen, is also inferred to be the universal author of all things beautiful and right, parent of light and of the lord of light in this visible world, and the immediate source of reason and truth in the intellectual; and that this is the power upon which he would act rationally either in public or private life must have his eye fixed. Whereas, our argument shows that the power and capacity of learning exists in the soul already; and that just as the eye was unable to turn from darkness to light without the whole body, so too the instrument of knowledge can only by the movement of the whole soul be turned from the world of becoming into that of being, and learn by degrees to endure the sight of being, and of the brightest and best of being, or in other words, of the good. And whereas the other so-called virtues of the soul seem to be akin to bodily qualities, for even when they are not originally innate they can be implanted later by habit and exercise, the virtue of wisdom more than anything else contains a divine element which always remains, and by this conversion is rendered useful and profitable; or, on the other hand, hurtful and useless. Did you never observe the narrow intelligence flashing from the keen eye of a clever rogue — how eager he is, how clearly his paltry soul sees the way to his end; he is the reverse of blind, but his keen eyesight is forced into the service of evil, and he is mischievous in proportion to his cleverness?

The experiential activities of "The Myth of the Cave" are explained in the brilliant simplicity of the epistemology of "The Divided Line," beginning at the bottom, which is comparable to the bottom of the cave, with *phantasia* and mounting with *pistis* and *dianoia* and concluding with the ill-defined *episteme* and *nous*. At the summit, *nous* is higher than the sun, divine, and I propose, filled with a primordial mental light.

Broadly defined, these primordial mental lights and darks invoke an enormous variety of philosophers, from, of course, Plato's combination of creation, cosmology, and numbering in the *Timaeus*, through Plotinus's *Enneads*, Augustine's concept of "the interior light," the complex, indeed, baroque elaboration on light and angels by Pseudo-Dionysius the Areopagite, and Descartes's light of the mind. Kant compared his sweeping enlightenment of the mind with the cosmic astronomical work of Copernicus. Hegel's owl of philosophy flies at dusk and the darkness appears in the writings of Sartre as opacity, nausea, negation of the light, and annihilation. John Stuart Mill "protested against those who supposed that for seeing the possession of an eye is a necessity";[5] Mill writes out of a tradition and an arrogance that presumes the mature and perfect human is the middle-class bureaucrat of the 19th-century who, eyeless, still sees the light. Obscurity throughout European culture is the motivation for perpetual, infinite self-perfection and social progress.

An interesting non-European text is Henry Corbin's *Man of Light*.[6] While Plato and Platonism are everywhere in his study, this text from the Gospel of Matthew, not quoted by him, seems particularly germane, "If thy eye be sound, thy whole body will be full of light." (Mat 6.22)

Corbin uses a term for what I have been calling a primordial mental or spiritual light: an "imaginal light." And the person on a spiritual quest searches for a suprasensory orient, which is objectively a spiritual orient and subjectively an orientation of the spirit. Interestingly, it is a "north" that is above, in the sky, a vertical north. As Copernicus's starry sky is the correlative of Kant's mental domain, so this "northern" sky is the correlative of the spiritual domain. In this view, the aurora borealis is the earth-light that is returning heavenward, as the soul yearns to do. Thus, Corbin recounts a "Night of light, the dark Noontide, the black Light," and he joins this with the Greek and Iranian concepts found in neo-Zoroastrian Platonism, to describe "the man of light," called *Phos* (Light) or Adam.[7]

A text that derives directly from the *Genesis* passage and indirectly through a complex tradition that seems, like Corbin's, to include a mixture of Gnostic and Plotinian traditions is the *The Zohar: The Book of Light, or Splendor.*[8] This text has, from one perspective, an enormous number of contradictions and conflicts. There is no question or desire here of eliminating them, because first of all, at one level of interpretation the text is clearly an amalgam of many traditions. At another level or in another perspective, and I believe this the more important level, it works with definitions and logic that are capable of assimilating widely different and contradictory approaches, as an infinity may be construed to assimilate different and mutually contradictory finite number-systems. There is no desire to homogenize the collection, but to allow it to encompass the thoughts of the believers. Or to put this in the terms just used: *The Zohar* operates within the logic of the primordial mental and natural lights, *nous* and *ohr*. Light and dark are in the title and throughout; this particular passage requires no commentary; obviously, it is a continuation, an extraordinary transformation, and an intense reminder of the potentials of the original text, *Genesis*. I have noticed that *The Zohar*, or more generally Kabbalistic literature, is used, as with alchemical texts in connection with gaining and expressing power, as a source of myths and rituals to produce the effects desired. This intention for *The Zohar* as a text of power is consonant with the opening passages of *Genesis*. As mentioned before, the primordial natural light (*ohr*) and primordial natural dark of these texts are a correlative of primordial mental powers.

V. THE ZOHAR: THE BOOK OF LIGHT, OR SPLENDOR

At the outset the decision of the King made a tracing in the supernal effulgence, a lamp of scintillation, and there issued within the impenetrable recesses of the mysterious limit a shapeless nucleus enclosed in a ring, neither white nor black nor red nor green nor of any colour at all. When he took measurements, he fashioned colours to show within, and within the lamp there issued a certain effluence from which colours were imprinted below. The most mysterious Power enshrouded in the limitless cave, as it were, without cleaving its void, remaining wholly unknowable until from the force of the strokes there shone forth a supernal and mysterious point. Beyond that point there is no knowable, and therefore it is called *Reshith* (beginning), the creative utterance which is the starting-point of all.

It is written: *And the intelligent shall shine like the brightness of the firmament, and they that turn many to righteousness like the stars for ever and ever* (Dan. XII.3). There was indeed a 'brightness' (*Zohar*). The Most Mysterious struck its void, and caused this point to shine. This "beginning" then extended, and made for itself a place for its honour and glory. There it sowed a sacred seed which was to generate for the benefit of the universe, and to which may be applied Scriptural words "the holy seed is the stock thereof" (Iss. VI.13). And there was *Zohar* [splendor], in that it sowed a seed for its glory, just as the silkworm encloses itself, as it were, in a palace of its own production which is both useful and beautiful. Thus by means of this "beginning" the Mysterious Unknown made this palace. This palace is called *Elohim*, and this doctrine is contained in the words, "By means of a beginning (it) created *Elohim*." The *Zohar* is that from which were created all the creative utterances through the extension of the point of this mysterious brightness. Nor need we be surprised at the use of the word "created" in this connection, seeing that [63] we read further on, "And God created man in his image" (Gen I.27). A further esoteric interpretation of the word *bereshith* is as follows. The name of the starting-point of all is *Ehyeh* (I shall be). The holy name when inscribed at its side is *Elohim*, but when inscribed by circumscription is *Asher*, the hidden and recondite temple, the source of that is mystically called *Reshith*. The word *Asher* (i.e. the letter, *Aleph, Shin, Resh* from the word *bereshith*) is anagrammatically *Rosh* (head), the beginning which issues from *Reshith*. So when the point and the temper were firmly established together, then *bereshith* combined the supernal Beginning with Wisdom. Afterwards the character of that temple was changed, and it was called "house" (*bayith*). The combination of this with the supernal point which is called *rosh* gives *bereshith*, which is the name used so long as the house was uninhabited. When, however, it was sown with seed to make it habitable, it was called *Elohim*, hidden and mysterious. The *Zohar* was hidden and withdrawn so long as the building was within and yet to bring forth, and the house was extended only so far as to find room for the holy seed. Before it had conceived and had extended sufficiently to be habitable, it was not called *Elohim*, but all was till included in the term *Bereshith*. After it had acquired the name of *Elohim*, it brought forth offspring from the seed that had been implanted in it.

What is this seed? It consists of the graven letters, the secret source of the Torah, which issued from the first point. This point sowed in the palace certain three vowel-points, *holem, shureq*, and *hireq*, which combined with one another and formed one entity, to wit, the Voice which issued through their union. When this Voice issued, there issued with it its mate which comprises all the letters; hence it is written *Eth hashammaim* (the heavens), to wit, the Voice and its mate.

Now I wish to summarize these comments about these several central examples of dialectic of elemental light and elemental dark as they lead from religion and philosophy into mysticism and then to consider another extension, this time toward mathematics and physical science.

VI. TWO LIGHTS OF PRIMORDINATION

A. *Nature*: *Genesis* 1.1 has "In the beginning God created the heaven and the earth." 1.2 has the earth was chaotic. 1.3 has the *lux fiat*. "In the beginning" signifies a primordial natural numbering and a potential ordinal numbering sequence. "The heaven and the earth" signifies primordial spaciation and a potential subdividing of spaces. Chaos signifies a primordial confusion and, anticipating 1.3, a primordial dark; it has in potential subsequent wanderings, errors, confusions, darks, and disintegration. "Let there be light" signifies a primordial natural light and a potential for the lights of the sun, moon, and stars and correct actions, judgments, creativity, and integration. In the subsequent verses of 1.4—2.3, primordial time, space, numbering, and light actualize some of these potentials in an existence that is between the primordial and the everyday, to be called here "aeonic." With the "fall" of Adam and Eve, the primordial and the aeonic are present as text and memories for, in Kierkegaard's sense, recollection and repetition.[9] (I am not now engaging the question Bonaventure asked, if an eternity and an infinity existed before the creation of *Genesis*.) *Genesis* 1.1—2.3 can be read, without much strain, as a nearly-Aristotelian expression of the Great Chain of Being, which, in the history of that idea by Arthur O. Lovejoy,[10] begins with the notion of creation as the overflowing of the plenitudinous sun.

B. *Mind*: Plato's "Myth of the Cave" indicates a memory of the sun, the open-air, and sun-lit knowledge in contrast to fire, the cave, and shadowy errors. His "Divided Line" implies an analogue of sunlit knowledge with *nous* and *episteme* and fire-lit errors with *phantasia*. I suggested before that Plato was providing a schematic analysis of the subjective correlative for objective living in the world and objective correlative for the subjective processes in knowing and the cultural products thereof, such as the sciences. For example, the elemental natural light, such as is generated by the sun in the open air, is analogous to the mental operations called *nous* and *episteme*, and the fire in the cave is analogous to the mental operations called *phantasia*. Between the two are *dianoia* (scientific knowledge) and *pistis* (experience-based opinion).

C. Extrapolating from the texts of *Genesis* and *The Republic*, we can suggest that the biblical primordial natural light, *ohr*, which is created before the secondary natural light, is analogous to a primordial mental light, *nous*; and that the narrator of the biblical text is projecting the mental operations of complete literary creativity, or acts of the imagination, which are called omnipotence and omniscience, or, in Corbin's phrase, "imaginal light." Biblical primordial natural activities and Platonic primordial mental activities are both prior to other activities and are co-functional. Because the activity of a primordial natural light in *Genesis* 1.1 is the objective correlative for the subjective primordial mental activity, it projects the process of seeing infinitely clearly, and there occurs a spatialization and speciation that is comparable to the "objects" or products of Plato's epistemological processes as in the spatializations of both "The Myth of the Cave" and "The Divided Line." That is, primordial mental operations are synonymous with projecting universal light as *fiat lux* or, restated more modestly, as Adam's naming. The individual mind transcends its own power not by seeking a still higher level of power, but by renaming concretized existence.

In Genesis 1.1–2.3, there is also a primordial time in the experienced sense of time that is different in kind or degree. In many works, Mircea Eliade compares the religious functions of this primordial time in many cultures; in every case he cites and interprets, primordial time is consonant with the idea of creative powers that are used to re-create an original time and place for the collectivity or the individual. This primordial time and primordial space have corollaries in the development of the classical sciences, e.g., the classical *quadrivium* of astronomy, arithmetic, geometry, and music. That is, each of these sciences appears to begin with a primordial time and primordial space in which subdivisions occur, just as *Genesis* begins with the primordial and subdivides into times, spaces, and species. More precisely, each of these sciences appear within the aeonic in the biblical sequence and within Plato's *dianoia* (in "The Divided Line"). The activities of the aeonic/

dianoic presumes the primordial acts of *ohr/nous*. Proclus provides a clue to this condition. His *Commentary on the First Book of Euclid's Elements*[11] implies an infinitizing of Euclid's geometry that is also epistemological, with the *nous* able to perceive a boundlessness which, if placed lowest on the Platonic scale of knowledge, *phantasia*, would be a confusing indeterminate chaos. That is, prior to the practice of each of the sciences is an attitude of totalizing, enclosing, and subdividing primordial light.[12] Primordial light provides an evenly distributed light that is presumed for the sciences, that is mental experience as an imaginal light. Thus, the sciences of optics, catoptrics (or reflection), refraction, and, later, radiation in alpha-rays and in television are developed using geometry which itself uses primordial light to illumine, so to speak, the surface of plane geometry! The languages of light and geometry are found in rays, minutes, radius, etc. Technological application extends the many theoretical measurements of light that are seen within the glow of primordial mental and natural light into the domains of the lit-up "laboratory" operating in the kitchen, studio, or, later the university, and then into everyday activities.

VII. ON THE CUSP OF THE MEDIEVAL AND THE RENAISSANCE PERIODS

Let us now explore the mutual applications of geometry and light. According to very shaky tradition, European geometry grew out of the work of Thales in Egypt and the legendary Pythagoras, and it is never far from moral, mystical, and philosophical interests, naming, metaphors, and analogies; that is to say, within the personifications mentioned earlier, Naming Adam dominates European culture until the Renaissance, when Numbering Adam appears within the different developments of secular culture, norms of quantification, and technological application. Numbering and secularization appear co-functions. During the period of Leonardo da Vinci (1452—1519) and Galileo Galilei (1564—1642) occurred the undoubted cultural shifting from ancient to modern, medieval to renaissance attitudes within social groups that were controlling the economic life, influencing the intellectual life, and producing the newest technology. For the transition from naming to numbering, consider the contrast of Leonardo's engineering and Galileo's.[13] Leonardo's is close to the experiential (looking and understanding, and analyzing and constructing), while, a hundred years later, Galileo is also experiential, indeed, arguing polemically for the empirical. Leonardo's extraordinarily inventive technology occurs within the epoch of the Naming Adam,[14] but is mainly brilliant innovations with materials used for centuries. Galileo's thought is deeply integrated with the technology of the telescope and the microscope, which use new materials and old in radically new ways, and with brilliant rhetorical skills that slide into the language of Numbering Adam by silent exchanges of naming for numbering. Note the metaphors related to light, but used polemically: Galileo wrote in a letter, "in science, the authority embodied in the opinion of thousands is not worth a spark of reason in one man." That spark is nourished by 'love of the Divine Artificer [. . .] the source of light and truth.' "[15] Galileo was working with the recently "rediscovered" text of Lucretius, *De Rerum Naturae* (*On the Nature of Things*) and Lucretius's renewed use of Democritus's concept of "atoms."[16] With the terms and implications of Lucretian "atoms" and a "corpuscular hypothesis," he began his translation of naming into numbering. He used a new set of metaphors and new hypotheses for the composition of matter too small for observation with the senses. More importantly, in the "solution" to the problem of the source of the light of the barium sulphur he introduced a new set of terms, drawn not from everyday spoken, written languages, and metaphoric syntax, but from a language so-to-speak that has its own syntax, that is, from geometry and mathematics. Redondi calls this "mathematical phenomenism," which is to attach to the phenomenal world the terms and operations of mathematics. It is important to note that of the *quadrivium* and the *trivium*, Galileo was proficient and expert in music, which he performed, mathematics, geometry, and astronomy, and rhetoric. He was a professor of mathematics, which, in practice, meant applications of mathematics (Euclidean geometry) to problems of astronomy, optics, and operations, which in sum were based on a worldview of a theory of mechanics. Galileo works most often in the science of astronomy and, therefore, most of his discussions are directly or indirectly about light and technology.

The first anecdote about Galileo can show in small what a shift in terms and rhetoric can do. He sought to provide a theory of the light from the stone, barium sulphur, which the alchemists called "sunlight sponge" ("*spongia solis*"). Galileo knew only the traditional name.[17] By dealing with a "sunlight sponge," a material on earth that by earlier accounts absorbed the light from the sun, Galileo began his revaluation of the place of the earth in the solar system.

The second anecdote is also about light. Comets obviously do not conform to the *a priori* perfect circles of planets and spheres. Why do they have their own curves and at what level of the "aether" do they soar? In this study the two sciences, astronomy and geometry, were joined as they were traditionally, but for Galileo and European culture, for they also continue the transition into Numbering Adam. Galileo did not like the implications of Tycho Brahe's analyses of the curves of the comets that made a line within the darkness of the sky and rather than admitting any loopholes into the astronomical theories of Copernicus he argued that the curves were illusions, "subjective optical meteors, 'apparent simulations.' [. . .] Galileo proposed to explain the comet as a luminous reflection on the atmospheric exhalations raised beyond the cone of terrestrial shadow, like an aurora borealis. The diminition of the size and speed of the phenomenon became plausible when one admitted that these vapors moved with a rectilinear motion, in a radial direction with respect to the surface of the earth: a solution identical to the one Galileo had proposed in 1604 for the new star."[18] His essay on the trajectory of comets is mainly polemical, figuring in the arena of lectures, sermons, rumors, gossip, new science, and old theology, an arena that as the life of Giordano Bruno attests, is dangerous.

More important for both its content and its impact on the cultural world is *The Dialogue Concerning the Two Chief World Systems.*[19] About the crucial rhetorical transformation in this work, Redondi writes, "The conceptual substitution takes place before the reader's eyes, but it is almost imperceptible, like an adept card trick — 'with your kind permission, my gentle Philosophers' — performed before the eyes of the readers of the *Discourses.* Galileo, through Salviati's mouth, speaks of points, spaces, and lines. The reader listens, fascinated by that audacious infinitesimal solution of a difficult geometric paradox — then he realizes that Salviati has begun to speak of particles instead of points, of voids instead of spaces, of bodies instead of lines, and that for every pair the terms are synonymous. [. . .] Now Galileo presents in the *Discourses* a mathematical theory of matter. Its constituents are 'unmeasurable parts,' that is, parts without extension and therefore 'indivisible,' lacking dimension and shape. He calls them 'atoms without measure, or non-quantum atoms,' but in truth they are mathematical points: we are in the world of mathematical abstraction, no longer in the material world of physics."[20] Later, Redondi calls this "mathematical phenomenology," a "phenomenist mathematical epistemology,"[21] and "a purely mathematical theory of the structure of matter, its methodology-of-choice being a prudent mathematical phenomenism."[22] It should be noted that the geometry Galileo is using is related to a particular philosophical-mathematical tradition, that of Plato, NeoPlatonism, Proclus, and Pseudo-Dionysus the Areopagite, and we might think that therefore he is continuing the language of the Naming Adam; but he is not. He may be the first in the modern epoch to engage astronomy, chemistry, and physics with the problems of what is sometimes called "Platonic realism," a Platonism that persists until the 20th century art of the abstractions of Kandinsky and Mondrian, the Analytic Cubism of Picasso, and the profoundly Conceptual art of Duchamp. The main concept that serves to indicate his was a radical cultural change is his use of the term "infinity:" it is the Trojan horse that, outwardly, appears familiar and from within traditional notions, but inwardly contains an army of concepts that will overcome the garrison of traditional dogmas.[23] It is this insinuation of new terms into intellectual argument, this exchange that I want to emphasize as an intellectual moment that fits in with the cultural developments of mathematization, quantification, and mathematical operations rather than with those of verbal syntax. The new numbering, or mathematical and quantitative, attachment and adequation to the physical world, has its own philosophical (and in Galileo's time, theological and political) problems that are analogous to those found in the early naming, metaphors, and analogies. Now, Aristotle is accused of "mere nominalism," and the easy, highly conventional identification of the verbal with the physical world is rejected. Redondi asked himself, "Could not Galileo's final methodological propositions have a value of truth beyond language? Could they not be dependent on a reality other than that which they enunciated?"[24] Names for objects were one truth, to be left to theology; a "truth beyond language" is simply numbers for objects. "Galileo denounces Aristotelian physics, accusing it of pure nominalism, and appropriates for the first time the slogan of 'the book of nature' counterposed to the books of Aristotle and his commentators, as if 'nature had not written this great book of the world to be read by others besides Aristotle.' Aristotle's texts are described as a prison of reason. Thus, hostilities with official Jesuit philosophy begin."[25] Because Aristotelian science had become subordinate to Christian (Jesuit) theology, conflicts with Aristotelian science were also conflicts with Christian theology or theologians. In the decree by the Roman Catholic Church of March 5, 1616, the Congregation of the Index banned Copernicus's *De revolutionibus orbium coelestium* because it defended "the Pythagorean doctrine concerning the mobility of the earth and the immobility of the sun."[26] Thus, the content-battle of astronomy with the Bible was also a formal-battle of quantification against qualitation and numbering against naming. To which charge, Tommaso Campanella in his *Apology for Galileo* responded by saying Pythagoras got this information from the Hebrews. His *Apology* contains "proposals for a renewed Scriptural hermeneutic and its Augustinian theses on nature as God's book in correspondence to the Bible. The new philosophy is the very ancient one of Pythagoras, Hebraic in origin; the Mosaic astronomy and physics are more orthodox than those of the pagan Aristotle."[27] The complaints by the various figures of the Roman Church all speak of the conflict of "mathematics" and "theology." In short, the battle lines were drawn confronting naming and numbering, traditional logic and the speculative constructions and mathematical logic and experimental constructions, and naming Aristotelian materialism and the numbering Platonic realism. With Galileo, we begin clearly the modern epoch of the Numbering Adam and technology.

Just as Plato felt compelled to present his epistemology in terms of the space of a "divided line," so in the midst of the language of geometry (and ultimately the model for all scientific discussions) are indicated the properties of numbering, natural sciences, and technology, and, ultimately, Numbering Adam. The language of Euclid in the *Elements* uses definitions, infinitives, givens, the present tense, and commands to construct. This lifts the *Elements* from its immersion in the history of Athens to the discourses of space and of simultaneity. Everything of Athenian culture remains, but consider definitions that the prediction in the verb "to be" allows only a constant present tense; this intends a meaning of an "eternal" present: "1. A point is that which has no part." "2. A line is breadthless length." "3. The extremities of a line are points." "4. A straight line is a line which lies evenly with the points on itself."[28] Consider the Postulates, e.g., Postulate 1, in which the instruction is comparable to the line in *Genesis*, "Let there be light." Here it is: "Let the following be postulated [. . .]." This is followed by the infinitive of the verb — an instruction as a permanent act, recapturable at will at any time: "to draw a straight line from any point to any point." Proposition 1: "On a given finite straight line to construct an equilateral triangle." Or Postulate 2: "To produce a finite straight line continuously in a straight line." Understood phenomenologically, it is not surprising that the study of light and dark, or optics, and reflections, or catoptrics, combines both the consideration of light and the *Elements* of Euclid. (The most recent example of this is the spatialization of nuclear events of light, of electrons and such, by Richard Feynman, by applying vector analysis.) Even though ancient Greek attitudes tended toward both a totalizing begun by Aristotle, whose work after centuries of use and redefinings had come to signify "the physics of the continuum and the qualitative principles of the science embraced by 'philosophizing' Peripatetics"[29] and a mystification of the notion of infinity as they did with the allegedly "irrational" concepts, I suggest that the grammar is such that within the geometrical system of space and simultaneity, the temporal is restated grammatically as notions of infinities, as eternal presents, as subdivisions of infinity, all as subject to absolute will. *Genesis* moves towards history and the fullness of time; *The Zohar* tells stories drawing history into the infinite. It is relevant that parts of the texts of *Genesis* and *The Republic* have certain affinities with that of Euclid or that there is a tradition of interpretation in which Proclus interprets both Plotinus and Euclid and in which geometry is understood as the exoteric surface of esoteric secrets.

VIII. MOVING BEYOND THE CUSP

Galileo's use of the telescope and the microscope led people to applaud him as "divine": "Johannes Faber, a prominent member of the *Accademia dei Lincei* reported to Federico Cesi, the *Principe* of the *Accademia*. 'I was astonished, and said to Signor Galileo that he was another Creator since he made things appear that until now were not known to have been created.' "[30] The next philosopher to enter this area and mode of interests was Descartes (1596—1650) with his geometric spirit and his epistemology of the light of the mind. He internalized the problems of that geometry that was used in Galilean physics and that internalization initiates the mathematization of the mental mode, with the argument of the separation of mind and body. Descartes's so-called "geometric spirit" and his influence inspired Jacques Maritain to speak of this as the "second fall of Adam," or, as I suggest, the creation of

Numbering Adam. John Locke (1632—1704) makes Descartes's geometric spirit and inner light more empirical by an epistemology of associationism, which facilitated quantification of the operations of minds and implied the thoroughness of mathematics.

We can advance swiftly this survey of Numbering Adam and the dialectic of elemental light and darkness to this century by merely listing some outstanding people in modern physics, which, it seems to me, is the history of the physics of light: Isaac Newton (1642—1727), a corpuscular theory, James Clerk Maxwell (1831—79), an electromagnetic theory, W. K. Roentgen (1845—1923), x-rays, A. H. Becquerel (1852—1908), natural radioactivity, Marie Curie (1867—1934) and Pierre Curie (1859—1906), disintegrating of "highest atomic weight" materials such as uranium and radium, which led to the analysis of structure of atoms, photons, electricity, electrons, Albert Einstein (1879—1955), a theory of relativity, including the speed and direction of light, Erwin Schrödinger (1887—1961) a wave theory, and Niels Bohr (1885—1962), a particle theory; and Richard Feynman (1918—88), developing a field called quantum electrodynamics (QED). Remove the study of elemental light and dark from the history of science and twentieth-century physics would disappear from the computer screen as would the screen itself.

In sum, with regard to the dialectic of elemental light and dark, a Ptolemaic Christian geocentric universe holds at the center, by definition, dark, the devil, and illusion, and the daytime sky, with its residual lights at night, an enveloping light of truth and divinity. A Copernican heliocentric universe holds, by definition, the sun in the center, i.e., light in the center and dark elsewhere. A non-heliocentric, galactic and beyond, universe places dark everywhere and light anywhere but in radically new ways. More recently, mathematicians and astrophysicists have generated the hypothesis of "black holes," which are light producers from which no light escapes, and light-strings, which carry and hide not Euclid's three dimensions or Einstein's four, but nine and ten dimensions. Clearly, it is time to consider a third Adam, or a New Eve.

IX. HERMANN BROCH

Hermann Broch's *The Unknown Quantity*[31] begins with a scene set in a physics classroom; the attendant is washing the blackboard of its

equations. The image of white chalk on the blackslate evokes the stars
in the nightsky, the correlation of the actual dark night sky with these
equations of astrophysics, and pleasures of watching the slate being
washed clean. The novel proceeds on the discoveries of the uncer-
tainties of quantum physics of 1927—29 and the irrationalities of the
main character's, Richard Heick's, emotions. Heick's family structure is
modeled, as it were, on the idea of a constellation made up of C. G.
Jung's personality types. At one point in the novel is mentioned, appropriate to this unity of mind and sky, Kant's equivalence of his work on
consciousness and reason, enlightenment, as his Copernican revolution.
However, Broch's *The Death of Virgil* is the masterwork that should be
considered in detail in a discussion such as this. First, I want to note
here several of the influences on its origins because they are directly
concerned with the dialectic of elemental darkness and therefore
elemental light. In England, in the eighteenth century a new school of
poetry developed two related lines, the "graveyard school," in which
poets meditated in or beside a graveyard, and the "school of night," in
which they considered the so-called "dark" side of existence, the
emotions.[32] Both schools tended to present sentiments and sentimen-
tality, especially after the literature of the Enlightenment, for they were
turning from official witty masks to personal emotional sincerity.[33] The
chief work of this "school of night" was Edward Young's "The Com-
plaint; or, Night Thoughts." He counterposes his individual sleep with
Genesis's dark chaos and his waking with the creation of the sun.

Night I. On Life, Death, and Immortality

Tir'd Nature's sweet restorer, balmy sleep!
He, like the world, his ready visit pays
Where fortune smiles; the wretched he forsakes;
Swift on his downy pinion flies from woe,
And lights on lids unsullied with a tear.
    From short (as usual) an disturb'd repose,
I wake: how happy they, who wake no more!
Yet that were vain, if dreams infest the grave.
I wake, emerging from a sea of dreams
Tumultuous; where my wreck'd desponding thought,
From wave to wave of fancied misery,
At random drove, her helm of reason lost.
Tho' now restor'd, 'tis only change of pain,
(A bitter change!) severer for severe.
The day too short for my distress; and night,

Ev'n in the zenith of her dark domain,
Is sunshine to the colour of my fate.
    Night, sable goddess! from her ebon throne,
In rayless majesty, now stretches forth
Her leaden sceptre o'er a slumb'ring world.
Silence, how dead! and darkness, how profound!
Nor eye, nor list'ning ear, an object finds;
Creation sleeps. 'Tis as the gen'ral pulse
Of life stood still, and nature made a pause;
An awful pause! prophetic of her end.
And let her prophecy be soon fulfill'd;
Fate! drop the curtain; I can lose no more.
    Silence and darkness! solemn sisters! twins
From ancient night, who nurse the tender thought
To reason, and on reason build resolve,
(That column of true majesty in man,)
Assist me: I will thank you in the grave;
The grave, your kingdom: there this frame shall fall
A victim sacred to your dreary shrine.
But what are you? —
    Thou, who didst put to flight
Primeval silence, when the morning stars,
Exulting, shouted o'er the rising ball;
O Thou, whose word from solid darkness struck
That spark, the sun; strike wisdom from my soul;
My soul, which flies to Thee, her trust, her treasure,
As misers to their gold, while others rest.
    Thro' this opaque of nature, and of soul,
This double night, transmit one pitying ray,
To lighten, and to cheer. O lead my mind,
(A mind that fain would wander from its woe,)
Lead it thro' various scenes of life and death;
And from each scene, the noblest truths inspire.
Nor less inspire my conduct, than my song;
Teach my best reason, reason; my best will
Teach rectitude; and fix my firm resolve
Wisdom to wed, and pay her long arrear:
Nor let the phial of thy vengeance, pour'd
On this devoted head, be pour'd in vain.
    The bell strikes one. We take no note of time
But from its loss. To give it then a tongue
Is wise in man. As if an angel spoke,
I feel the solemn sound. If heard aright,
It is the knell of my departed hours:
Where are they? With the years beyond the flood.[34]

Young's poem had an important influence on the German poet

Friedrich von Hardenberg, that is, Novalis (1772—1804). A description of his works by a critic, Eric A. Blackall, is instantly transferable to Broch. "Most of his poems are mystical in character, for his was a deeply religious nature [. . .]; and many of them are concerned with the transfiguration that comes through death, the return of the individuated self to the primal unity, the confluence of the finite with the infinite."[35] In the Night, Novalis finds his queen, with whom we should compare Mozart's Queen of Night in *The Magic Flute*.

I

What living being gifted with feeling, bestows not his love on the all-joyful light? Loves it before all of the wonders spreads out before him through regions of space — light undulating, color-filled, raying its mild omnipresence by day? As life's inmost soul it is breathed by the giant world of restless stars who swim in its blue ocean, by the sparkling stone, the peaceful plant, by the creatures' many-fashioned ever-moving life. It is breathed by the clouds many-hued, by the zephyrs, and, above all, by the glorious strangers, with the thoughtful eyes, the swinging gait, and the sounding lips. As a king it summons each power of terrestrial nature to numberless changes, and alone doth its presence reveal the full splendor of earth. Downward wend I my way to Night, holy, inexpressible, secret-filled — far away lies the world, sunk in deep vault; how dreary, forlorn her abode! Deep melancholy stirs in the chords of the breast, far-off memories, wishes of youth, dreams of childhood, short-lived joys and vain hopes of the long-endured life come in gray garments, like evening mists after sunset. Far off lies the world with its motley of pleasures. Elsewhere doth the light pitch its airy encampment. What if it never returned to its faithful children, to its gardens in its glorious house? Yet what flows so cool, so refreshing, so full of hid tidings to our hearts, And absorbs the soft air of melancholy? Hast thou too a human heart, O dark Night? What holdest thou under thy mantle which steals unseen upon my soul, giving it strength? Thou seemest but fearful — precious balm drops from thy hand, from the bundle of poppies. In sweet intoxication thou unfoldest the soul's heavy wings, and givest us joys dark, inexpressible, secret, joys which are promise of heaven. How poor and childish meseemeth the light with its varied affairs. How joyful and bless'd the departure of day. It is but because Night withdraws those who serve thee that thou sowest in the wide realms of space shining spheres, to proclaim in the times of thine absence thine omnipotence, thy returning again. More heavenly than those flashing stars in those wide spaces, seem to us the infinite eyes which the Night in us opens. Farther see they than the palest of that numberless host. Unneedful of light, they look through the depths of a love-enfilled heart which fills with unspeakable joy a loftier space. Praise to the world's Queen! to the lofty proclaimer of holy world, to the nurturer of blissful love. Thou comest, beloved . . . The Night is here — rapt away is my soul — finished the earthly way, once more art thou mine. I gaze into the depths of thy dark eyes, see naught but love and blissfulness therein; we sink upon night's alter, softest couch — The veil is shed, and kindled by the warm impress there glows the pure flame of the sweet sacrifice.

II

Must ever the morning return? Endeth never the thraldom of earth? Unhallowed affairs swallow up the heavenly coming of Night? Will never love's offering burn eternal and hid? To the light was appointed its time, A time to its watching — but timeless the rule of the Night; without end the duration of sleep. Holy Sleep![36]

"In fragments written down in 1798 [Novalis] developed the concept of the 'transcendental' artist who re-creates the world in himself and himself in the world by individual combinatory activity, thereby 'expanding his existence into infinity,' joining up in meaningful combination what is individual and accidental with the necessary and absolute whole, and thereby creating 'the most intimate community of finite and infinite.' He speaks also of this 'transcendental' poetry as being concerned with the '*symbolic* construction of the transcendental world,' and the novel as the form best suited to fulfill this ideal. 'The epic continues, the novel grows — arithmetical progression in the former, geometric in the latter.' Life itself becomes a novel made by the poet, and novel-writing a path toward knowledge of self and the world. The novel represents life but its mimesis is a poetic mimesis, 'masked events and personages which, stripped of these (poetic) masks, are events and persons well known (to us).' It does not present finite propositions or conclusions, it is the tangible realization of an idea, and an idea is an 'infinite series of propositions — an irrational quantity, unpositable, incommensurable,' but with an establishable law of progression. Hence for Novalis the events and personages of a novel are allotropes of an idea, a series of variations on an idea. It structure is a progression, but it should be a geometrical, not an arithmetical progression." [37] These words are directly applicable to Broch's epic lyric meditation, *The Death of Virgil* except in one major point. Goethe's *Wilhelm Meisters Lehrjahre,* for example, has a *Lehrjahre* of a person, but Novalis was concerned with the "*Lehrjahre* of a nation.":[38] this approach is extended by Broch in a fusion of an individual (Virgil) and two cultural periods, the Mediterranean-classical from Genesis and Homer to Virgil, and, in a leap, the European crisis in the twentieth century. Novalis is the crucial mediator from Goethe, to Broch, each a poet deeply committed to science and mathematics. Broch adapted the prose-poetry of Novalis, the associative meditation that extends itself constantly, referring at first to the world but soon reflecting on itself in such manner that there is a lyrical flight of the mind. Broch expresses his mind's exploring the primordial space, time, light, and dark in a dialectic which like that in *The Zohar: Book of Splendor* allows everything and all contradictions to coexist within its aura of infinity, its imaginal light.

"Fire: The Descent"

Now the world lay still before him, after all the previously endured pandemonium amazingly still, and it appeared to be late in the night, apparently past its middle; the stars glowed greatly in their courses, comforting and strong and quietly a-shimmer with reassuring recognition although disquietingly overcast despite the complete absence of clouds, as if a so-to-speak unyielding and impenetrable, cloudily-crystal dome through which the glance could barely pass were stretched midway between the starry spaces and that of the world below; and it almost seemed to him as if the demonic partition into zones to which he had been subjected during his recumbent listening and his listening recumbency had been carried here to the outside world and that here it had become sharper and more extensive than when it had been imposed on himself. The earthly space was so cut off and insulated from the heavenly ones that nothing more could be felt of that longed-for wind blowing between the worlds, and not even the hunger for air was appeased, even this pain was not lessened because the fumes, which earlier had enshrouded the city and which had been sundered but could not be blown away by the evening breeze, had changed to a sort of feverish transparency, thickened under the burden of world-segregation to a dark jelly which floated in the air, unmoving and immovable, hotter than the air and impossible to breathe that it was almost as oppressive as the stuffiness within the room. Ruthlessly that which could be breathed was separated from that which could not, ruthlessly, impenetrably, the crystal shell was spanned darkly overhead, a hard, opaque partition barring off the fore-court of the universe in which he stood, set upright by the iron hand, supported by it; and whereas formerly, ensconced in the earth's surface and stretched out over the Saturnian meadows, he had constituted the boundary between the above and below, in immediate contact with both regions and involved with both, now he towered up through them as an individual soul, predestined to her growing, who, lonely and single, knew that if she wished to hearken into the depths above and those below she had to hearken to herself: immediate participation in the greatness of the spheres was not granted to one who stood in the midst of earthly time and earthly-human growth, endowed again with both; only with his glance, only with his knowledge might he penetrate the infinite detachment of the spheres, enabled to grasp and hold them only with his questioning glance, enabled to restore the simultaneous unity of the universe in all of its spheres by his questioning knowledge alone, achieving only in the streaming orbit of the question the vital immediacy of his own soul, her innermost NECESSITY, the task of perception laid on her from the very beginning.

Time flowed above, time flowed below, the hidden time of night flowing back into his arteries, flowing back into the pathway of the stars, second bound spacelessly to second, the re-given, re-awakened time beyond the bonds of fate, abolishing chance, the unalterable law of time absolved from lapsing, the everlasting now into which he was being held:

> Law and time,
> born from each other,

annulling, yet always giving birth to each other anew,
reflecting each other and·perceptible in this way alone,
chain of images and counter-images,
noosing time, noosing the arch-image,
neither wholly captured, yet for all that
become more and more timeless
until, in their last echoing unison,
in a final symbol,
the image of death unites with the image of life,
portraying the reality of the soul,
her homestead, her timeless now, the law
made manifest in her, and hence
her necessity.[39]

In the last section of *The Death of Virgil*, Virgil's death is synonymous with a decreation of the universe: the seven days of creation are
reversed, the species disappear, the grass and spatial differences dissolve, and the primordial light is absorbed into the primordial dark.

CONCLUSION

This presentation of ideas and examples and interpretations about a
phenomenology of the dialectic of elemental light and elemental dark
began with an ontologic instance, that of primordial light and a prior
primordial dark in *Genesis*. A transition to an epistemologic instance,
that of the primordial light and primordial dark of the mind in Plato's
"Myth of the Cave," suggested that despite their distinct differences
between these texts and their primordial entities and the light of everyday experience, they could usefully bē seen as correlatives, each the
object and subject to the other. Summed, as it were, they gave content
to the concept of "imaginal light." Although, the cultural period was
personified as the Naming Adam. The rhetoric of Galileo when study-
ing the operations of lights as embodied in chemicals (*spongia solis*), in
outer space as perceived it from the earth and re-conceived it on earth
in geometric terms, was such as to make a radical shift from the
language of the "art" of everyday "naming" to that of the "science" of
"numbering." His transition is in the use and identification of physical
events in geometric and mathematical terms. Galileo's work indicates
the origin of a Numbering Adam. I discussed some of the implications
of the terms and syntax of Euclid's *Elements* for elaboration of the
imaginal light, whether primordial or aeonic. Hermann Broch believed
that the modern era is to be characterized not by philosophy and art,

but mathematics and science, i.e., art is subordinate to the Numbering Adam. He used the physics lecture-room in *The Unknown Quantity* as the space where the life of mathematics and emotions are intermingled. In his *The Death of Virgil*, we saw the dialectic of the elemental light and dark that occurs in most serious lyrical meditation. We noted in passing Edward Young's collocation of sleep and waking in terms of the light and dark *Genesis* 1.1–2.3; and Novalis's interest in science even as he wrote a "Hymn to the Night." After this wide-ranging and very abstract argument the essay concludes with the light-filled poem of William Carlos Williams, "the red wheelbarrow."[40] In this, there is no sun-, or moon-, or starlight; this image is the presence of an object in the mind, an image that like a circle of red resides, perhaps, in an ultimate fusion of the mode of primordial light, natural and mental, and the everyday light:

> so much depends
> upon
>
> a red wheel
> barrow
>
> glazed with rain
> water
>
> besides the white
> chickens

City College, CUNY

NOTES

[1] S. Feshbach, "Empedocles: The Phenomenology of the Four Elements in Literature," in *Analecta Husserliana*, Vol. XXIII, ed. A-T. Tymieniecka (Dordrecht: Kluwer Academic Publishers, 1988).

[2] S. Feshbach, water: "Literal/Littoral/Littorananima: The Figure on the Shore in the Works of James Joyce," in *Analecta Husserliana*, Vol. XIX, ed. A-T. Tymieniecka (Dordrecht: Kluwer Academic Publishers, 1987); air: "The hundredlettered Name," in *Analecta Husserliana*, Vol. XXXVII, ed. A-T. Tymieniecka (Dordrecht: Kluwer Academic Publishers, 1991).

[3] See Mary P. Cheadle, "The Vision of Light in Ezra Pound's *The Unwobbling Pivot*," *Twentieth Century Literature* 35/2 (Summer 1989), 113–30, 113, 121.

[4] Jacques Le Goff, *The Birth of Purgatory*, trans. Arthur Goldhammer (Chicago: University of Chicago Press, 1984), p. 26.

[5] Quoted by C. S. Sherrington, *Biological Basis of the Mind* (London: Cambridge University Press, 1947), p. 4.

[6] Henry Corbin, *Man of Light in Iranian Sufism*, trans. Nancy Pearson (Boulder: Shambhala, 1978).

[7] Corbin, pp. 2, 5, 6, 15.

[8] *The Zohar*, "Bereshith 1.1—6.8," trans. Harry Sperling, Maurice Simon, introd. J. Abelson (London: Soncino Press, 1931—34), Vol. I, pp. 63—4.

[9] Soren Kierkegaard, *Fear and Trembling and Repetition*, trans. Howard V. Hong and Edna H. Hong (Princeton: Princeton University Press, 1983).

[10] Arthur O. Lovejoy, *The Great Chain of Being* (Cambridge, Massachusetts: Harvard University Press, 1942).

[11] Proclus Diadochus, *Commentary on the First Book of Euclid's Elements*, trans., intro., not., Glenn R. Morrow (Princeton: Princeton University Press, 1970).

[12] This is discussed most pertinently by Ernst Cassirer's *magnus opus*, *The Philosophy of Symbolic Forms*, trans. Ralph Manheim, pref., intro. Charles W. Hendel (New Haven: Yale University Press, 1955). Thomas Kuhn's *Structure of Scientific Revolutions* (Chicago: University of Chicago, 1970), points out that such totalizings cause exclusions as "anomalies" that become the basis for the "revolution." The work of Michel Foucault and Jacques Derrida is to point the extent of the totalizing process, its weaknesses, and it moral dangers, for it renders "anomalies" "Others" and therefore judges, condemns, and punishes only through the exercise of power.

[13] Information about Galileo drawn from P. Redondi, *Galileo Heretic*, trans. Raymond Rosenthal (Princeton: Princeton University Press, 1987), and Richard S. Westfall, *Essays on the Trial of Galileo, Special Series: Studi Galileiani* (Vatican Observatory Publications, 1989). Westfall has an essay criticizing several of Redondi's theses. To make a clarifying distinction: I am not here taking from Redondi his discussion of atomism and the eucharist, with which Westfall disagrees, but his underscoring Galileo's rhetorical and semantic shifts in terms.

[14] See Leonardo da Vinci's *Notebooks* ed. Irma Richter (New York: Oxford University Press, 1985) and Kenneth Clark, Leonardo da Vinci: An Account of His Development as an Artist (Baltimore: Penguin Publ., 1963).

[15] Redondi, p. 37. Stillman Drake translates the Latin differently, but I believe "Divine Artificer" echoes properly Plato's "divine artificer" in the *Timaeus*.

[16] The importance of Lucretius's *De Rerum Naturae* cannot be discussed here, but it is central to the intellectual transformation from the ancient-medieval world to the renaissance-modern world. Its dynamics of nature, with atomism, combined with the poetics of light in Plotinus's *Enneads* provides an interesting start to a history of modern physics.

[17] Re-naming is part of the process of secularization and re-appropriation of the world within new questions. The term "*spongia solis*" names a process in its names and limits that process and the term "barium sulphur" names two chemicals, which locates the matter in a system of chemicals, viz., the Periodic Table, and yet does not limit the process but leaves open questioning regarding a process of fusion: that is, *spongia solis* explains too much and barium sulphur points at but does not yet explain.

[18] Redondi, p. 32.

[19] Galileo, *Dialogue Concerning the Two Chief World Systems*, trans. Stillman Drake, forw. Albert Einstein (Berkeley: University of California Press, 1967), rev.

[20] Redondi, p. 19.

[21] Redondi, p. 23.

[22] Redondi, p. 26.

[23] For this reason, Galileo's Lucretian atomism is seen by Redondi as in conflict with the Roman Church's theology of the Eucharist.

[24] Redondi, p. 27.

[25] Redondi, p. 37.

[26] Quoted in Westfall, p. 1.

[27] Redondi, p. 40.

[28] Euclid, *The Thirteen Books of Elements*, trans. Thomas L. Heath (New York: Dover, 1956).

[29] Redondi, p. 22.

[30] Westfall, p. 35.

[31] Hermann Broch, *The Unknown Quantity* trans. Willa and Edwin Muit, afterw. S. Feshbach (Marlboro: Marlboro Press, 1988).

[32] Interestingly, another "school of night" of nearly two centuries earlier, supposedly including Christopher Marlowe, also turned to metaphors displaced by orthodoxy, of the occult.

[33] For an anthology of the poetry of the night: see Charles Peake, *Poetry of the Landscape and the Night: Two Eighteenth Century Traditions* (Columbia: University of South Carolina Press, 1970).

[34] Edward Young, *Poetical Works* (Boston: Little, Brown, 1854).

[35] Eric A. Blackall, *The Novels of the German Romantics* (Ithaca: Cornell University Press, 1983), p. 107.

[36] Novalis, *Hymns to Night*, trans. Mabel Cotterell, New York: 1960, Library of Liberal Arts, pp. 3ff.

[37] Blackall, p. 109.

[38] Blackall, p. 108.

[39] Broch, *Death of Virgil*, trans. Jean Starr Untermeyer (San Francisco: North Point Press, 1983), pp. 96—7.

[40] Wiliam Carlos Williams, *Collected Poems*, eds. A. Walton Litz and Christopher MacGowan (Norwalk: New Directions, 1986), Vol. I, p. 224.

ELDON N. VAN LIERE

MONET'S REVEALING LIGHT:
EVOLUTION AND DEVOLUTION

> "I *must* before I die, find *some* way to say the
> essential thing that is in me, that I have never said yet
> — a thing that is not love or hate or pity or scorn, but
> the very breath of life, fierce and coming from far
> away, bringing into human life the vastness and
> fearful passionless force of non-human things."
>
> Bertrand Russell[1]

Light is ephemeral and elusive in itself and yet it is revealing and defining. As such it has served as a manifestation of Divinity, as the first thing created and as creative force itself. It is a symbol, then, of life and of truth as well as goodness. Yet as with all things it is more fully comprehended with in opposition to something, and nature has given us darkness with its aspects of primordial chaos, destruction and death. Light's opposite is not as negative as this suggests for light emerges from darkness; germination and creation take place in darkness, and while life seeks light it ultimately returns to darkness. The opposition of one to the other is essential to both light and dark.

Light and visual perception are inseparable, for while light does not need our eyes for its existence our eyes would be useless without it. The eye is, as Plato described it, "the most solar of instruments". Light and vision cannot be separated, and as vision is at the heart of painting it is an aspect of this that will be my focus. Great painters feel and even reason in terms of what they see, and this has nothing to do with words. Verbally formulated philosophies or causes, like technical tricks, can and often do prevent an artist from seeing with the mind's eye. The power of seeing decides both the emotional and intellectual elements in paintings of significance. Ledoux's *Eye Reflecting the Interior of the Theater of Besançon* (1804) presents an intellectualized play between that which is observed and the mind's eye.[2] The eye here is that of an actor standing on the stage of the theater designed by Ledoux and reflected in it is the auditorium while projecting out of the eye from under the lid are rays of light. The eye is presented here as both

85

A-T. Tymieniecka (ed.), Analecta Husserliana, Vol. XXXVIII, 85–99.
© 1992 *Kluwer Academic Publishers. Printed in the Netherlands.*

receptor and as the mind's eye which has the power to emit a light from within suggesting enlightenment.

The Impressionist painter Claude Monet (1840—1926) can, with more than a little justice, be called the painter of light. His vision with its emphasis on light resulted in a formidable body of work which is strikingly colorful and redolent with what appears to be a most positivistic view of life. His art is one that throws light into the darkness of shadow and thereby removes much of its mystery and terror. Yet in Monet's long career of looking with a brush in his hand he slowly and surely transformed his vision of light from its role as an essential element in his representation of modern life to something far more elemental and mysterious.

Early in his career (1866) Monet sought to paint a large picture which when exhibited would stand out from its neighbors.[3] The goal of his *Women in the Garden*, depicting four women in contemporary costume, was to paint modern life directly in the out-of-doors. To this end he dug a trench in the garden of his rented house in the suburbs of Paris and rigged a pulley system which allowed him to raise and lower the large canvas so he could work on the painting entirely *en plein-air* and reach all parts of it. A painter friend of Monet's who witnessed this devotion to the direct experience of outdoor light thought he was mad to go to such inconvenient lengths when he might work in his studio with far greater ease.[4] That Monet would seek to paint the whole of a major canvas out-of-doors without depending on small preparatory sketches which were more easily manipulated outside the studio in order to be faithful to the effects of sunlight reveals that early in his career he saw natural light as a dynamic elemental force and one that would prove to be a key ingredient in his development.

Monet's commitment to painting contemporary life reflected the influence of the work of Edouard Manet (1832—1883). As with the paintings of his older contemporary, Monet avoided storytelling and historical subjects and concentrated on a people oriented urban exist-ence painted with a blunt patchwork of light and dark.[5] While Monet's *Women in the Garden* fits into this point of view, Monet, unlike his mentor, started his career as a *plein-air* landscape painter (Manet's few landscapes were painted while either on holiday or while convalescing) working on the Normandy coast where light was an ever changing and determining factor in how and what one saw. This direct and immediate experience of painting before nature he here brings to the modern urban subject.

What Monet achieved is best seen by juxtaposing his painting with a work by Auguste Toulmouche (1829—1890) who was a distant relative of Monet's (by marriage). His *In the Library* shows that he, too, was interested in subjects drawn from contemporary life, but unlike Monet he painted in a traditional manner where light is used to model form and to reveal informational detail. This traditionalism in conjunction with the painter's taste for the anecdotal (for the young girls in the library are clearly seeking out some forbidden book) and the fact that he painted on a fairly small scale served to make Toulmouche popular, for his works were easy to accept and comprehend. Monet's painting was over ten times the size so on that basis alone it could not be seen as a charming keepsake or a bibelot. Brightly painted with relatively unmodeled colors it avoids telling any story or anecdote leaving the fresh brightness of light playing over these women as the dominant subject. Yet these women are engrossed in flowers; in fact, this appears to be their *raison d'etre*. In this painting Monet makes an association for the first time between women and flowers which was to dominate his subsequent figurative painting. Superficially an image of women in a garden is an innocuous subject or even a non-subject. Yet it is one that echoes a wide variety of themes that pervade ancient myth and Christian iconography alike. By self-consciously avoiding the past Monet hit upon the archetypal relationship of women and flowers and thereby becomes a part of a long standing association. The goddess Flora or the Madonna of the Rose Garden are not alluded to in this painting, but, by the fact that one of these women's dress spreads out to exist metaphorically as a giant blossom with a bouquet of smaller ones framed within it while her parasol could be said bloom above her and every one of the women looks intently at flowers or even lunges for them, they become part of their company. Charles Blanc who was a contemporary of Monet's and a much read art critic and theorist noted that color was a feminine element in painting for it depended upon instinct.[6] This echoes in still another way the association, for the colorist Monet is here delighted by these colorful blossoms that reach for the light and reflect it giving color to life.

The fact that Monet dug a trench in this garden to paint this canvas of women and flowers was a significant premonition of the gardener that Monet was to become. In so doing he was to create environments of burgeoning flower beds in which women and only women (with very rare exception) move about as if in some sacred life-giving precinct. The sunny day that fills this image with light was as essential to Monet's conception of it as it was to the growth and well-being of the flowers depicted. Bright sunny days would be the light of choice for Monet when painting his gardens.

Once Monet had settled in Argenteuil (1872) he took up transforming the garden of his rented house and exploring themes of suburban leisure as he developed fully the style we now call Impressionism with its concentration on light as a subject and not only a tool in the service of other concerns. To study the translation of light into paint to such a degree as to come to realize that what the eye sees are reflections and that these change constantly, is to think about objects that might be the subjects of painting less as solid three dimensional forms than as surfaces far more ephemeral than they had ever been thought to be before. To capture this on canvas meant exploiting color as never before. For Monet light came to mean color and color light. To mix black into a color or use it at all was to deny color and light, for black is the absence of light. So even shadows are full of color being painted with rich greens, blues and crimsons. As a result Monet's paintings such as *Argenteuil Basin* (1874) appear to be full of light.[7] In this painting the image is created by color loosely brushed in without sharp edges so objects seem to interact with surroundings and hold within them the potential for change. Contemporary leisurely activity was sought where people could experience refreshing air and water while always in sight of the shore and close to social amenities such as the restaurant we see in the background embraced by the trees. Monet's quick and sure painting style with its touches of fresh pure color to achieve the equivalence of a quality of outdoor light and immediacy was ultimately appropriate for the depiction of the present. This concentration on color which is the most emotional and positive aspect of painting along with the simultaneous banishment of a black based darkness with its attendant obscurity from painting would seem to have denied mystery altogether; yet Monet would within ten years self-consciously seek out qualities of mystery through continued investigation of this most positive of styles.

In the ensuing years Monet was at his easel which was placed out and about in all kinds of weather, and thereby he confronted all the seasons and the times of day. He may have centered himself in a suburban playground, but in painting its sailboats, promenades and gardens he immersed himself in nature with light and its endlessly varied manifestations a primary concern.

In 1873 Monet painted *The Bench* in the intimacy of his own garden.[8] Monet does not make us aware of it as we look at this painting, but the setting in which these figures are placed was of Monet's own making. With a degree of permanence in his life he planned, cultivated and nurtured his flower garden. in doing so he involved himself, in still another way, with the cycles of nature and with the vital qualities of growth and their intimate relationship with light. All of this would ultimately affect his art in profound ways. What dominates still is the quotidian, for in the foreground there are two large figures. This is a unique work as it is one of the rare occasions that Monet gives a male not only a presence but dominance in his garden paintings, and it is, too, one of the last times that he would make such an extensive use of black. The women and flowers juxtaposition is here also, but with the inclusion of the male presence there seems to be an irresistible need on Monet's part to give it a sense of drama. This too is unique. The pose of the male figure appears rather casual as he leans on the back of the bench, but his insistent blackness and the reaction of his delicate companion who has no thought for the bouquet beside her suggest something more ominous. The unsettling tension that dominates the foreground and takes place in shadow could be read simply as the most comfortable place to be on a hot sunny day, but given their emotional state, this would no longer be a concern and the shadow becomes a darkening which contributes to the brooding mood. Beyond, in full sunlight, is a massive flower bed and a demure young woman glowingly positive. It is as though not only shadows disappear in full sunlight, but so, too, does human drama. Male and female, light and dark, abundance and austerity are all used as foils one against the other with striking effect. However, Monet was not at all comfortable with such interpersonal situations, and his impatience with it may well be signified by its being unfinished. This excursion into enigmatic tensions is something he will seek means to avoid, and it could also be seen as the start of his slow process of purging the human form from his work altogether. One of his solutions was to distance himself from the figurative element as in his 1876 *Gladioli* in which the elements that served for the background in *The Bench* seem to have become the dominant light filled and trouble free subject.[9] Nothing threatens the positive coloristic mood here. Even butterflies dance about the blossoming profusion catching light and thereby adding to the sense of the ephemeral. The identification of woman with flowers is as intimate as ever if not more so. In the same year he painted *In the Field* where the female figure is literally buried in a flowery fecundity.[10]

As productive and as innovative as the five years were that Monet spent at Argenteuil he became dissatisfied with the suburban world of leisure. This can be seen in one of the very few paintings he produced in his last year there. In the *Flowering Bank, Argenteuil* (1877) the gardener in Monet focuses at what is at his feet, and as a result the flowers upstage the river beyond which had been a favored subject previously.[11] Like the female figure the landscape sinks into a profusion of nature which seems to draw light into it. While this was a premonition of things to come the artist was not ready for what this had to offer and went to Paris to seek out a motif that would allow him to deal with something quite different from leisure — power.

In choosing to paint a group of paintings dealing with the Gare Saint-Lazare Monet reveals his continuing tenacious desire to deal with contemporary life.[12] As modern as this station was Monet distanced himself from the people that utilized it to focus on an environment of light and atmosphere that melded together all the complexities of the place. Here under the great glass and iron shed of the railroad station he paints the comings and goings of these mighty creations of modern industrialization which embody speed and the contraction of space. These trains and this station in particular were commonplace in Monet's life, for he arrived at or departed from here when travelling to and from Paris. Yet what he presents us with is not a commonplace for this is not what the traveller intent on catching his train would notice. Looking down the tracks along the length of the shed with a steam engine puffing towards him, Monet created an aspect of visual drama which is enriched by the exploitation of the pervasive and transformative power of light. The roof with its section of glass allows for the penetration of light into this covered space creating not only a glowing bright patch of light on the pavement below, but a fascinating alteration of ephemeral steam and smoke as it passes unseen through space. Hovering in this space some of these "clouds" are lit up white by sunlight as it is drawn into them while those in the shade take on a cool blue tint. The shaded solid forms in the foreground are richly warm in color while those things not in the shade are bright and golden. The atmospheric steam and smoke, on the other hand, do not take on these hues suggesting a painting of opposites. Light, then, is absorbed, reflected and transformed in a richly complex way. By positioning himself beneath the shed Monet gives it a compositional importance for in enfolding and containing that which is fleeting one senses the important role it plays in the transformation. Oddly fragile and even delicate it contains not only the hulking, screeching and earth shaking engines but intangibles that appear, float and disappear in air. Its formality of structure and its shape serve to make it an echo of the cathedral in modern terms. The revelation of weightlessness, colored light and power are all now secular and yet can be glorified and recognized as wonderful.

Monet's excursion into industrial/urban power was ended by his financial difficulties which resulted in his moving into the country well away from Paris. Shortly thereafter his wife died which marked a turning point in his career, for he then began a decade of travels seeking out unique and even spectacular sites in nature. One of the most spectacular of these was the popular resort of Etretat on the Normandy coast where the chalk cliffs have been eroded to form three striking natural arches. This coast with its fascinating light was a place of renewal for Monet for he had started his career here, lived at Etretat for some months in 1868, painted here again in 1872 and returned to it often during the 1880s with the purpose of exploring this site. It was on one of these campaigns (1883) that he painted *The Manneport, Etretat, I* (Ill. no. 1).[13] Literally turning his back on the manifestations of the quotidian in the form of the tourists who flocked to the site and the social amenities that had been constructed for their comfort, Monet closed in on and confronted these magnificent natural formations and in so doing took a major step toward dealing with the richness of the elemental. To paint the great stone arch of *The Manneport* Monet positioned himself in a narrow bay with cliffs rising on three sides of him and far enough away from the great arch so that the sea was just visible within its frame. The dynamics of the composition are in its very fragmentary nature. Had he walked closer the arch would have loomed over him and the sea would have dropped out of sight. In looking at this painting one cannot complete the scene in the mind without having been there. There is, however, a completeness of idea, and this has nothing to do with the picturesque aspect of this site. Reduction rejects

Ill. no. 1 — Monet *The Manneport, Etretat, I*, 1883. The Metropolitan Museum of Art, Bequest of William Church Osborn, 1951 (51.30.5)

the picturesque and emphasizes a sign-like character. Monet clearly looked hard at what gives this monumental shape its life and in so doing imbues it with some of his own. His powers of concentration in painting this on the site had to have been formidable, for here clouds sweep in from the ocean, often with great speed shifting and changing all the while. The mood of the sea would have been equally fickle and at times threatening, for Monet, along with his painting gear, was once swept into the sea by a wave as he worked. It is light that creates the sense of temporal flux as it plays across the irregular surfaces of this stately mass from the sky above and from the shattered reflections from the water below. Here, then, in a secluded spot with waves pounding at the feet of the cliffs and winds swirling about him Monet confronted this great shape with a fascination and pugnaciousness that gave him an uncanny sensitivity and strength to do battle and not be overwhelmed. The light and color that fill the Manneport give it a sense of joy and happiness. This is the result of a near mystical resistance and conquest, for Monet is at the heart of a place where primal elements and forces do battle and in doing so have left a great stoical sign behind to be read. In painting this he was seeking new meanings, and this great shape and the others at this site which were created by eons of buffeting and then survived them was something Monet could clearly empathize with. Light and coloristic atmosphere which continued to be a fascination are now wedded to a striking shape giving it a sense of pulsating life rather than dissolution. Monet's preoccupation with the fugitive and the attendant loose brushwork of Impressionist technique was not a destructive force as some interpreted it to be. This vision is one that did not probe beneath the surface of such a subject to discover meanings as a scientist might. Instead he sensed that the soul of nature resides upon the surface and is associated with the lights and shadows that flicker across surfaces. This is where the energy is found rather than in some anatomical structure or subterranean energy seething within. Like a true lover of nature Monet was preoccupied with appearances, for it is in these that nature reveals its poignant reality as a living, moving truth, and this is evidenced by Monet's ever enriched understanding which results in giving a painting such as this symbolic significance. Monet expressed this himself in a later conversation; "I am simply expending my efforts upon a maximum of appearances in close correlation with unknown realities. When one is on the plane of concordant appearances one cannot be far from reality, or at least from what we know of it . . . Your error is to wish to reduce the world to your measure, whereas, by enlarging your knowledge of things, you will find yourself enlarged."[14]

The time in between his travels in the 1880's to seek out and paint dramatic sites such as those at Etretat, Monet spent at Giverny with his extended family cultivating his gardens which spread down a slope from the house to the south with the sun backlighting the flowers planted there. While creating a garden paradise in these years he was not ready to see it as a subject for his painting. Even though he made one last excursion into figure painting he did not choose to place his models in the garden but rather in sunlit flowering fields or in small boats. These paintings were to mark the end of his painting modern life as manifested in the human form. The rejections and returns that Monet makes

in the course of his career are interlockings of innovations and ideas
with light ever present as a revealing and a transformative factor. Taken
as a whole this can be seen as a progressive enrichment that leads
towards a primal beginning.

The 1890's saw Monet develop the notion of series. Through a
number of paintings of the same subject he sought to present a collection of moments. Grain stacks near his home or the cathedral at Rouen
were painted while he concentrated on what he termed the *"enveloppe"*.
This was the elusive intangible ambience of light and atmosphere which
existed between himself and the object beyond. After exploring this
idea throughout the decade he finally turned to his own garden and
began in 1899 a series dealing with the "Japanese" footbridge over the
water-lily pond he had created (Ill. no 2).[15] In speaking to Marc Elder
Monet said; "It took me some time to understand my water-lilies. I had
planted them for pleasure, I cultivated them without thinking of painting them. A landscape does not sink into you all at once. And, then,
suddenly, I had the revelation of the magic of my pond."[16]

This is not a great stone arch but a modest and domestic decorative
footbridge that implies people, and many of the photographs taken of
the bridge included friends and family. But Monet was no longer a
painter of modern life, and in the nearly forty years of lonely contemplation of light and color, time and space since he painted *Women in
the Garden* there occurred a deepening richness of the everyday joy
found in a lonely vision of nature — intimate and awesome at once. The
visual confrontation with the elemental powers of nature as revealed to
the eye by an active ever changing light in the 1880's resulted in an
absorption of those things into the elemental self that allowed him to
touch the mystery of creative force. This is what the aging painter
brought to bear as he focused on his domestic domain, the character of
which had been carefully created by Monet satisfying his second
passion, gardening. In this more modest setting he began to seek the
mysterious and make it graspable.

Isolated and without root the bridge hovers while being specific
enough to serve as a spacial anchor for an amorphous space. The arch
of the bridge is reflected below creating a curiously eye-shaped form
that contains the water-lilies. This may well not have been intended to
be seen as eye-like, but as sight itself is so much a part of Monet's
concern the shape carries meaning intended or not. While the bridge
does not reach either bank it is still read as a means by which one

Ill. no. 2. — Monet *Bridge Over a Pool of Water Lilies, 1899* The Metropolitan Museum of Art, Bequest of Mrs. H. O. Havemeyer, 1929. The H. O. Havemeyer Collection (29.100.113)

reaches something. In this case it is not by passing across it but through it. The unanchored bridge sweeps over the water-lilies that in turn look up at it and the sun beyond as if they were the last manifestations of the women who were in the past so intimately associated with flowers or of those who more recently stood on this bridge looking down and then, having passed on, leave behind lingering reflections. The notion of penetration that looking through the arch indicates will be even more significant when the gardener in Monet turns his eyes downward and looks at the pond free of bridge and even banks as he does in subsequent paintings. The bridge would seem, too, to have been a means by which to reach this last and most elemental stage of Monet's career.

Once he does so the surface of the water becomes the subject and our expectations are set adrift.[17] The world is upside-down, and as a result of this and its amorphousness fascinating possibilities opened up for Monet to deal with a new and suggestive merging of elements and meanings. Atmosphere, that airborne moisture that Monet had concentrated on and saw absorbing light and transforming objects, is now effectively eliminated for water itself. With its dual aspects of transparency and reflection associations can be seen as destroyed or disguised yet, on the other hand, enriched. Within this pond at his feet he discovered the world in microcosm. These images are not stamped by the materialist's hand; instead it is a matter of sensation, feeling and idea. In limiting his vision to this pond and finding there reflections of sky is to suggestively merge the two infinities of aerial space and aqueous depths. It is the intangible of light that binds these two infinities. The earth of rock and soil plays no role here. It is as if by some mysterious chemical reaction of these intangibles a fragile and yet potent symbol of life emerges. The waterlilies poised between the two become the evanescence of life. The pads and blooms we know to be tangible, but they are fragile and transitory. Drawn to the light and reflecting in its blossoms the life-giving powers that brought them into existence, they shimmer on the reflective surface of the pond, all of which masks the gloomy depths in which the mystery of birth took place. The cycle of life is not depicted through images of seasonal shift, for he never paints this pond ice covered nor do autumn leaves float about. Having as a landscape painter and a gardener dealt with this seasonal cycle he discovered the cycle of life and death within the swamp-like nature of his pond. Beneath the shimmering veil of reflected light the presence of a world of dank decay is suggested. It was up from this murky depth that the blossoms rose toward the light, and it is into it that they will sink into decay. These clusters of waterlilies have a character that echoes the bouquet on Camille's lap in his early *Women in the Garden* and the mounded flower beds in his garden at Argenteuil. Women, the footbridge and even the seasons were no longer necessary, but they all served as means by which Monet reached this point, and their implications echo after them in these waterlily paintings. What has been constant throughout has been light and its handmaiden, reflection. One looks down to see the sky, clouds, treetops, flowering plants and in the shadows hints of death. The mystery Monet discovered here was a primeval one where water is the medium that embraces all the elements and life and death as well. The fascination with changing moments and fugitive effects has been wedded to the timeless, for the beginning has met the end and the elemental cycle is complete.

I initiated this discussion with an image of an eye which reflected in its iris the outside world, while at the same time it projected rays like some mystic source of light. Investigation and contemplation of what the eye sees can result, as we have seen, in a richly complex understanding. Impressionism was not and often still is not seen as a style as dense in its implications as I have presented it. Odilon Redon (1840— 1916) who was a contemporary of Monet's referred to Impressionism as being "too low ceilinged" for him. The superficials were there to be seen, but the implications were not comprehended; yet he, too, was fascinated with the study of nature. Unlike Monet, however, he also had a deep faith in the power of the imagination which he pursued in his art. In 1883 he produced an image for a set of lithographs titled *Origines* which he called "The Vision of the First Flower". In this anthropomorphic image a primeval fern uncoils in a dark world and wrapped in its coil is a human eye that like the plant itself aspires to reach upward toward the light and the heavens. By bracketing Monet between two symbolic images of the human eye, I have sought to reinforce the importance of this "most solar of instruments" in relation to light. Monet would not have accepted such symbolism; yet his eye aspired, and his mind's eye radiated upon what he saw while taking it all in. His early discovery of light and his investigations of its related phenomena led him in the course of his sixty year career to paint images that present his perceptions about light and open our eyes but also prove him to have been profoundly reflective, exploring more and more the metaphorical possibilities in a progressively elemental view of nature. As Cezanne is reported to have said of Monet: "He is only an eye, but what an eye."[18]

Michigan State University

NOTES

[1] From a 1918 letter to Constance Malleson in *My Philosophical Development* (London: 1959), p. 261.

[2] The French architect Claude-Nicolas Ledoux (1736—1806) published his five folio volumes *L'Architecture considerée sous le rapport de l'art, des moeurs et de la legislation* in 1804. While this formidable production reviewed his career as an architect, describing projects like the Theater at Besançon (built between 1775 and 1784 and still standing today) by the means of very specific plans and elevations, there is a fantastic aspect to this publication which the *Eye* indicates reflecting Ledoux's involvement with a Masonic-like secret society.

[3] *Women in the Garden*, (1866), Oil on canvas, 2,56 × 1.2,08, Musée d'Orsay, Paris.

[4] Gustave Courbet (1819—1877) visited Monet several times at his rented house at Ville d'Avray in 1866. For an account of these visits see: Duc de Trevise, 'Le Pèlerinage de Giverny', *La Revue de l'art* (January—February, 1927) and G. Geffroy, *Claude Monet, sa vie, son oeuvre* (Paris: 1922), v. I, ch. VIII.

[5] Manet's *Le Déjeuner sur l'herbe* of 1863 exemplifies this style of painting. The poet/critic Charles Baudelaire, who was a friend of both Manet and Courbet, no doubt influenced them as to the value of the depiction of modern life and through them and others was an influence on Monet. Baudelaire's ideas on this subject were published in *Figaro* on November 26, 28 and December 3 of 1863 and can be most readily found in *The Painter of Modern Life and other Essays*, Jonathan Mayne, trans. and ed., (London: 1964).

[6] Charles Blanc, *The Grammar of Painting and Engraving*, trans. Kate N. Doggett, (New York: 1874), p. 146.

[7] Oil on canvas, 0,54 × 1.0,73; Rhode Island School of Design Museum of Art, Providence.

[8] Oil on canvas, 0,60 × 1.0,80; Anneberg Collection, U.S.A.

[9] Oil on canvas, 0,60 × 1.0,815; The Detroit Institute of Arts.

[10] Oil on canvas, 0,60 × 1.0,82; Private collection.

[11] Oil on canvas, 0,54 × 1.0,65; Private collection.

[12] *Gare Saint-Lazare* (1877) oil on canvas, 0,75 × 1.1,00; Musée d'Orsay, Paris.

[13] Oil on canvas, 0.65 × 1.0,81; The Metropolitan Museum of Art, New York, Bequest of William Church Osborn, 1951 (51.30,5).

[14] Georges Clemenceau, *Claude Monet: The Water Lilies* (New York: 1930) p. 154f.

[15] Oil on canvas, 92.7 × 73.7; The Metropolitan Museum of Art, Bequest of Mrs. H. O. Havemeyer, 1929. The H. O. Havemeyer Collection (29.100.113).

[16] Marc Elder, *Chez Claude Monet à Giverny* (Paris, 1924) p. 12.

[17] *The Waterlily Pond* (1919) Oil on canvas, 2,00 × 1.6,00; Carnegie Institute, Pittsburgh.

[18] The evolutionary aspect of Monet's career that led him from the depiction of contemporary life to a primal elementalism can just as easily be seen as a process of devolution as my title indicated. It is interesting to note the parallel this forms with Michelangelo's Sistine Chapel frescoes. Those of the ceiling start with the depiction of the *Drunkenness of Noah*, which emphasizes the world of the flesh, and then progresses backwards in time to culminate with the most abstract scene in the series which depicts

the most elemental act of God, *The Separation of Light and Darkness*. This elemental beginning is situated directly above Michelangelo's later fresco, *The Last Judgment*. This Christian iconographical program establishes a cycle where beginnings meet endings and endings denote a new existence. Monet, for his part, rejected organized religion along with its rich tradition of visual images spending a lifetime in active contemplation of nature. His constant questioning of what he observed in his pursuit of light was the key to his discovery of the artistic means by which he could depict the essential cyclic mystery of the elemental in nature.

SITANSU RAY

TAGORE ON THE DIALECTICS OF
LIGHT AND DARKNESS

Continuing Research on Elements of the Human Condition

The vast span of Rabindranath Tagore's (1961—1941) works abounds
with various moments of the dialectic of light and darkness. In this
paper, I shall treat only a few selections.

I

Let us first come to the famous poem *"Nirjharer Swapna-bhanga"* (i.e.,
the awakening of a fountain from dream),[1] compiled in the poetical
work *Prabhat-Sangit*[2] (1290 B.S., 1883). *Prabhat-Sangit* means the
morning-songs. Tagore was only twenty two years of age when he
published *Prabhat-Sangit*. It is surprising to note that just the previous
year his *Sandhya-Sangit*,[3] which means the evening-songs, was published. While the pensive aspects of post-adolescent phase were expressed in *Sandhya-Sangit*, the first-felt luminous and dynamic aspects
of the blooming youth were expressed in the poems of *Prabhat-Sangit*,
i.e., the Morning-Songs. The poems of *Sandhya-Sangit* were the outcome of Tagore's introverted mood. The poems of *Prabhat-Sangit*
reveal that the poet comes out of the cave of his heart to the outer
world, lustrous with morning light. In another sense, the outer world
entered into his heart and illuminated it. The poem entitled *Nirjharer
Swapna-bhanga* is one of the key-poems of the whole work.

Quite in later years, Tagore recollected his marvellous experience of
composing the key-poems of *Prabhat-Sangit*. This recollection is found
in Tagore's prose-work *Jiban-Smriti* (the reminiscences). The title of
the relevant chapter is also *"Prabhat-Sangit"*.[4]

For the time being he moved from Jarasanko Tagore-palace to 10
Sudder Street, where his elder brother Jyotirindranath Tagore resided
for a period. From the verandah, he could view the garden of the free
school, situated on the eastern side. One fine morning, he viewed the
rising sun through the trees of the garden. The fact may be apparently
quite usual. But, while viewing the rising sun, he all of a sudden felt that

A-T. Tymieniecka (ed.), Analecta Husserliana, Vol. XXXVIII, 101—107.
© 1992 *Kluwer Academic Publishers. Printed in the Netherlands.*

a curtain was removed, as it were from his vision. He experienced waves of joy, beauty, bliss and glory. He said,

"From my childhood, I have been seeing with the eyes only, from today I started to see with the whole of my consciousness"[5] (translated). The morning light made him realize the cosmic joy as well as the abundance of the joy of the human and animal world. The charm of the movement of the human body charmed him anew, again and again, from moment to moment. As he saw a cow, fondly licking the body of another cow, he realized some immeasurable aspect of the infinite joy and beauty of creation.

II

Darkness has other kinds of effects. But, darkness does not necessarily mean the darker side of life, though very often it is depicted in literature in that way. It is also generally argued that darkness has its value since light is light only in contrast to darkness, just as joy is contrary to sorrow. Furthermore, darkness facilitates closeness and affords privacy, which may be marred in light.

Another role of darkness is found in Tagore's symbolic drama *Raja*[6] (1910), i.e., *The King* or *The King of the Dark Chamber*. The king meets her queen Sudarshana only in darkness. Sudarshana is eager to see him in light but the king will not expose himself in light in front of the Queen. Outwardly the king is ugly. To avoid the queen's repulsion, the king does not appear before her in light. That is why a mysterious and mystic darkness is rather necessary. This truth applies to ordinary human life also. Sudarshana represents such an ordinary human life. The king symbolizes himself as Reality, which is very often awesome. Light exposes that awe. Once that is exposed, man faces the Reality. Man may attain fulfilment through his eradication of error and endurance. The Reality brings forth ultimate bliss at last. Light wins over darkness only after an unavoidable course of ups and downs. This is the gist of the drama, though I am not going to give the details of it. Tagore also produced a somewhat shorter version of the same drama under a newer title *Arupratan*[7] (1920), which means a gem symbolizing Truth and Reality alike. It is interesting to note that Surangama, the royal maid is much more enlightened and prudent than Sudarshana. The maid's contribution to the Queen's spiritual evolution from ignorance to enlightenment charges the drama with romantic fervour. As the sun rises, it is Surangama who sings —

Bhor holo bibhabari, path holo abasan.
Shuno oi loko loke uthe alokeri gan.[8]

That means, — with the dawn, the path ends; listen to the music of light throughout the world.

III

Now, let us come to Tagore's essay *"Din O Ratri"* (1904),[9] i.e., day and night. Day and night produce a rhythmic flow in man's outer and inner life. Daylight shows the distinctness and differentiation of things. Night provides phenomenological closeness. Day is the time for activity and night is the time for repose. That is why our dynamic energy is centrifugal in our day time chores and centripetal during nocturnal repose and love. Yet, that does not mean that night is associated with utter seclusion. Daylight overpowers all the other luminaries of the sky. Night on the surface of the earth directs our glance towards countless heavenly bodies shining in the sky. In this sense, our consciousness is centrifugal at night also. The vastness of the cosmic world, and our placement within it, are better realized at night.

IV

Sight and sound are two vital aspects of our relationship with the world. Tagore delivered two great lectures on them at the temple of Santiniketan. Those two lectures are *Dekha*[10] (seeing) and *Shona*[11] (hearing). Tagore deeply felt a close relationship between seeing and hearing. Inter-relationship among our senses is called synaesthesia in the modern discipline of experimental psychology. Tagore's realization is more or less intuitive in nature. Seeing, most often, inspired music in him. In the lecture *Shona* as well as in various songs, stars are metaphorized as tunes of the *veena* (Indian musical instrument). In Tagore's songs, stars are associated with nocturnal *ragas* and *raginis* (Indian melodies), and the sunlight is associated with daytime *ragas* and *raginis*. On the whole, light in these cases plays the role of musical

tunes[12] in Tagore's creative consciousness. The Pythagorian concept of
cosmic music is comparable. Tagore declared in Pythagorean style —

It is not a poetic phantasy, nor is it a rhetorical utterance — music is being played day
and night abounding in the infinite sky and endless time[13] (translated).

In a personal letter to his niece Indira Debi, Tagore wrote —

Could we try attentively, we would have been able to translate the grand harmony of all
the light and colourfulness of the world into a great piece of music.[14]

The colourfulness of visual things are products of light, and Tagore's
reactions to them were musical. Fragrance also is concomitant with
them. As Tagore says in one song —

Come to my life in newer and newer entities. Do come as fragrance, as hue and as
music.[15]

V

Moonlight, being the reflected light of the sun, is soft, misty and
romantic to the poets. It is a mild light, but without any heat. Supernatural tales have been associated with the moon, perhaps in every
culture of the world. I am not going to treat them. Nor am I going to
develop how the moon or the moonlit night has been a favorite theme
of modern Bengali songs and poems. But it is surprising to notice that
all the six of the fullmoon nights of the year are set aside for some
festival or other in Hindu culture, in Indian culture in a broader sense.
At least three of them are associated with the love-making ceremony of
Lord Krishna and his lady-love Radha, for example, *Jhulan-Purnima*, a
night for frolicksome swinging in the fullmoon night that occurs around
August, *Ras-Purnima*, a night for the love-dance in the full-moon night
that occurs around October-November, and *Dol-Purnima* a night for
sprinkling coloured powder or water on each other which occurs during
the fullmoon day and night in the spring season, around March. Tagore
transcended the rituatislic orthodoxies associated with these nights as
he explored and utilized their aesthetic sides. Quite a number of
Tagore's songs are there meant for singing on various fullmoon nights.
Even today boys and girls along with their teachers sing those songs in
chorus while moving slowly through the light and shadows along the
avenues of Santiniketan in the style of a slow procession.

VI

Now, let us come to a particular portion of the first poem of the poetical work *Patraput*[16] (1935—36). In this poem we visualize two simultaneous picturesque scenes, one of the setting sun and the other of the rising full moon at the same moment. The poet is, as it were, in Darjeeling (a beautiful hill-town on the Himalayas). There are a group of jolly youths accompanying him as it is a pleasure-trip. All are enjoying the natural surroundings. By chance it happens to be the time of sunset. The golden rays of the setting sun have deluged not only the western sky, but also the valley, the hill-tops and far away river-courses. On the whole, the scenery is extremely beautiful to look at. The poet and all others have stopped merry-making. Silently they are gazing at the western region. All of a sudden the poet turns back and the full moon over the eastern horizon is in his sight, as, by chance, it happens to be a fullmoon day. This sort of experience is unforeseen, most rare and unexpectedly thrilling. The poet metaphorizes the sunbeams as the tune of the golden string and the silvery light of the moon as the reasonance of the silver string of a *veena*. The synchronization of these two tunes brings forth a unique and rare experience to the poet. Synaesthetic shift of different shades and colours of light to the realm of sonorous tunes may be counted as an extra-ordinary aspect of the phenomenology of light.

VII

The phenomenon of *Akash-Pradip* (the sky-lamp) must be high-lighted in this paper. *Akash-Pradip* is a lamp suspended at the top of a pole erected on the roof or house-top. It is set up and lit every evening by the Hindus during the Bengali month of *Kartik* (mid-October to mid-November) in reverence to Gods and bygone forefathers. Tagore's mind was free from such customary rites, but he could not discard the ethos associated with *Akash-Pradip*. *Akash-Pradip*[17] (1939) is also the title of one of his poetical works written at the last phase of his life. He was perhaps conscious of the evening coming down in his life. The hidden semiosis of the rhetoric of *Akash-Pradip* signifies this.

VIII

Dipavali is the celebrated illumination-ceremony observed at the post-autumn last darkest night of the dark fortnight. The Goddess *Kali* is worshipped at that night. Tagore did not care for such a Goddess. But he could not deny the supra-religious ethos of the illumination-ceremony, symbol of shining lives eradicating darkness.

There is a beautiful Tagore-song for this *Dipavali* ceremony.[18] The purport of the song is that, as the mist has covered the starry sky, we have to light numerous lamps of our own to illuminate our houses and the earth to do away with all the gloom and darkness.

IX

Light and darkness influence human conditions to a great extent, as sound and silence also do. But the nature of those influences cannot be generalized. It varies from person to person. Each and every case is unique. Detailed explorations will be interesting no doubt, but arriving at any conclusion or formulation of any law is quite difficult, perhaps impossible. That is why, from the vast span of Tagore's works I have selected only a few important portions to show Tagore's dialectics and phenomenological reflections of light and darkness. I cannot claim that this paper is be-all and end-all on the topic, but this much I can say, that I have not missed any significant facet. Further discussion in the form of question and answer will clarify the points more and more.

Visva-Bharati University

NOTES

[1] *Rabindra-Rachanabali* (Tagore's Works), Birth Centenary Edition (Government of West Bengal, 1961), Vol. I, pp. 44—48. (Henceforth *RR*. The following number will be that of volume.)
[2] *Ibid.*, pp. 37—78.
[3] *Ibid.*, pp. 1—36.
[4] *R.R.* 10, pp. 99—105.
[5] *Ibid.*, p. 107.
[6] *R.R.* 6, pp. 303—361.
[7] *R.R.* 6, pp. 521—560.
[8] *Ibid.*, p. 559.
[9] *R.R.* 12, *Dharma* (religion), pp. 9—14.

[10] *R.R.* 12, *Santiniketan* (Lectures delivered at Santiniketan temple), pp. 124—126.
[11] *Ibid.*, pp. 126—128.
[12] Some such songs may be sung while presenting the paper.
[13] *Shona, op. cit., R.R.* 12, p. 127.
[14] *Chhinna-patrabali* (stray letters), letter no. 73, *R.R.* 11, p. 82.
[15] *Gitabitan* (Tagore's song-book), *R.R.* 4, p. 58.
[16] *R.R.* 3, pp. 347—384; *Patraput* means a leafy pot.
[17] *R.R.* 3, pp. 631—673.
[18] *Gitabitan, R.R.* 4, p. 381.

PART TWO

THEODORE LITMAN

THE SUBLIME AS A SOURCE OF LIGHT
IN THE WORKS OF NICOLAS BOILEAU

Nicolas Despréaux, better known as Boileau is by far the greatest rhetorician France has ever produced. Like his Greek and Latin predecessors, Aristotle and Horace, he managed to impose on his contemporaries the aesthetic rules that he believed should be applied to every genre that existed in literature. In his *Art Poétique* (1674) which is itself a perfect model of how poetry should be composed, Boileau imposed himself as a critic of infallible taste. He did not hesitate to condemn the works of writers who used pompous and extravagant language such as the members of the "precious" school of thought. At the same time he had the taste and the sensitivity which enabled him to recognize the genius of such great authors as Corneille, Molière, La Fontaine and Racine. More than three hundred years after he died, Boileau is still admired today as a man of impeccable taste. Except for scholars who specialize in 17th century French literature, the authors he condemned for their poor artistic achievements are totally unknown today but those he lavished with praise are still beloved in France and throughout the world.

Boileau's rules were all based on the conviction that anyone who deals with literature must at all times be guided by reason and everything he writes must be the product of sound and logical judgment, good sense and normal mental powers. Thus, as far as the theater was concerned, for example, the rules of reason dictated that the plot of each play should never extend beyond a period of twenty four hours, that the entire action of the play should take place in only one location and that all the events that are depicted in the play should be directly related to only one central theme. The most important rule was the one of verisimilitude which demands that regardless of what literary genre an author may be dealing with, everything he writes must give the appearance of being reasonable, truthful and acceptable by any reader's common sense. Boileau's enemies regarded him as a tyrant who had assigned himself the position of supreme judge who ruled in the name of reason.

However, the amazing thing that occurred is that the same year the

A-T. Tymieniecka (ed.), Analecta Husserliana, Vol. XXXVIII, 111–119.
© 1992 *Kluwer Academic Publishers. Printed in the Netherlands.*

poet published his *Art Poétique*, he also published a book called *Le Traité du Sublime* and his *Réflexions sur le Sublime* which created a furor in all literary circles because these works completely contradicted the ideas he had formulated in his famous poem. The concept of the sublime was first introduced in literature by an obscure Greek author of the first century A.D. known as Longinus. In his free translation of Longinus' work on the sublime, Boileau declares unequivocally that the sublime is the highest form of literary expression that man can possibly create. No rules of any kind can be prescribed for the creation of such an extraordinary utterance of the human soul. Furthermore, the sublime is so ineffable that it cannot be grasped by reason and can only be recognized by the powerful effects it has in the heart and soul of those who are exposed to it.

Since Boileau was totally unable to define the sublime he had no other recourse than to offer examples of this mysterious force which, according to him, any normal human being can experience at once when he encounters it in literature. The sublime is extremely rare and except for a few examples he found in Greek and Latin literature and in some of Pierre Corneille's tragedies, Boileau offered as the greatest example of the sublime the astonishing Latin rendition of the creation of light by God as it is described in the first book of Genesis: "Fiat Lux." The translation of these two simple words loses some of its sublimity but for Boileau there was never any doubt that even when they are uttered in French or in English they constitute the greatest example of the sublime in the world: "And God said: 'Let there be light; and there was light.'" Boileau wanted to make sure that his readers do not confuse the sublime with the sublime style of writing and thus he wrote in his preface to *Le Traité du Sublime* the following passage which he gives us as his definition of the sublime: "Longinus does not mean what orators call the sublime style, but the extraordinary, the marvelous which overwhelms in the discourse and which makes it so that a work ravishes, delights and enraptures. The sublime style always requires big words; but the sublime can be found in one thought, one figure of speech, one expression. Something may be in the sublime style, and not be sublime, that is to say having nothing extraordinary nor astonishing. For example: "the sovereign ruler of nature with one word created light: this is in the sublime style, however it is not sublime, because there is nothing there that's very extraordinary and it can easily be found. But "God said: let there be light, and there was light", this extraordinary expression, which describes so well the obedience of the universe to the orders of the creator, is truly sublime, it possesses something divine. One must therefore understand by sublime, in Longinus, the extraordinary, the surprising and, as I have translated it, the marvelous in the discourse."[1] In his *Traité du Sublime*, Boileau insisted that the sublime be expressed in the most concise and simple manner possible,[2] that the most common people should be able to understand all the words that are used[3] and, most important, that it should produce the most powerful emotional reaction a human being can experience through its contact.[4]

There is no doubt that the sublime which rises beyond the intellectual boundaries of reason brings light to the heart and spirit of all those who are exposed to it. As a matter of fact it is this very light which flashes suddenly through a person's soul that Boileau considered to be the essence of the sublime and it is for this reason that he used the "Fiat Lux" as its primary example. God's creation of light provided Boileau with two basic arguments against his critics; first, he refers to it as the most beautiful example of the sublime in literature and declares that it cannot be elucidated by the powers of reason. Consequently, it rises above all the rules and cannot be considered as the product of Art. To support his argument he refers to Moses as follows: "The divine spirit which inspired him thought for him, and has made them (the rules of art) work for him with so much art that one does not notice that there is any art (in his discourse)."[5] Secondly, Boileau asserts that there is a definite link between light and the sublime which enables mankind to come out of the darkness in which he has lived for so long. These two arguments gave rise to the most notorious literary battle of the 17th and 18th century "La Querelle des Anciens et des Modernes." The "Modernes" who accepted Boileau's *Art Poétique* as a guide for their literary endeavors believed that like physics or medicine literature improves constantly with time and that consequently, the authors of the 17th century were far superior to those who had lived in an age of ignorance and darkness. On the other hand, the "Anciens" who were deeply moved by Boileau's concept of the sublime were convinced that those who had received divine inspiration when they composed the Old and the New Testaments as well as the Greek and Latin authors of antiquity were far greater than their contemporaries because they lived in an untamed world which provided them with a powerful affinity for the sublime, a source of light which brings humanity out of its obscurity.

This deep conviction became an obsession for Boileau who fought mercilessly against the "Modernes", using his concept of the sublime as a weapon, until he died in 1711.

His main argument against the "Modernes" such as Daniel Huet, Charles Perrault, Fontenelle and Houdar de la Motte was basically always the same: how can such learned men fail to be moved by the sublime which emanates such radiant light in the souls of all the common people who come in contact with this extraordinary literary force? Boileau cannot defend the sublime in any other way than to accuse his enemies of being insensitive or of being the victims of bad taste which prevents them from seeing the light that should illuminate their spirit. For example, Boileau attacks with great sarcasm Daniel Huet who was a Bishop for not recognizing the sublimity of the "Fiat Lux" and for failing to see, as a man of the Church, the light that Longinus, a pagan, had encountered when he read this marvelous phrase: "I have quoted the words from Genesis as the most proper expression to bring my thought to light, and I have used it with the greatest willingness because this expression is cited with praise by Longinus himself, who, in the mists of the darkness of paganism, did not fail to recognize the divine that existed in these words of the Scriptures. But what will we say about one of our most learned scholars of our century, who enlightened by the lights of the Gospel, did not notice the beauty of this passage; has dared, I say, argue in a book he has written as an apology of the Christian religion, that Longinus made a mistake when he thought that these words were sublime."[6] Boileau never stopped referring to the link that exists between his concept of the sublime and light. At first, he got entangled with the "Modernes" debating over minute literary details they would use as examples to show the superiority of such minor 17th century authors as Mme de Scudery, Chapelain, Saint-Amant and Quinault over the "Anciens" who had produced the great Greek tragedies and such writers as Homer, Pindar and Virgil. But in time, Boileau realized that he was wasting his time debating with men who were obsessed by "Modernism" and who, in his opinion, were incapable of seeing the light that emerges from the sublime. He then simply accused them of having corrupt tastes for literature and of being blind. Addressing a writer like Charles Perrault, the famous author of the fairy tales who was one the leaders of the "Modernes", Boileau states: "But when writers have been admired for a great number of centuries, and have been scorned by only some people of bizarre taste (for there are always some depraved tastes), then not only there is rashness but there is folly, to continue to doubt the merit of these writers. If you do not see the beauty of their writings, you should not conclude that they are not there, but that you are blind, and that you have no taste".[7]

Another powerful argument Boileau used is that just as light is undestructible the writings of the "Anciens" will live on forever while those which only possess a shining appearance in the present will be forgotten forever by the majority of the people. For Boileau the criterion of time is crucial to his concept of the sublime, for the light it produces in man's soul can never be destroyed. Thus he asserts unequivocally that "we must think about the judgment that all posterity will pass on our writings".[8] Boileau constantly reminds the "Modernes" that they should not confuse what might seem brilliant at the time with what will live on forever: "Whatever stir a writer may have created during his life, whatever praise he may have received, one cannot on this account undisputably conclude that his works are excellent. False brilliancy, the novelty of his style, a cast of thought which was in fashion, could have made them worthy of praise; and it may happen that during the following century people will open their eyes and that they will scorn what they had admired".[9] Finally Boileau condemns all those who are incapable of being moved by the sublime which is as eternal as the light God has created and advises them to abandon the world of literature once and for all: "It matters to know what this marvel the Anciens have made us admire for so many centuries consists of; and one must find a way of seeing it or to renounce literature for which you must believe you have neither taste nor genius, since you do not feel what all men have felt".[10]

What Boileau's enemies could not understand was the fact he was the rhetorician who had himself declared emphatically in his *Art Poétique* that the rules that are dictated by reason and logic must at all times be adhered to in all literary endeavors. How could this man contradict himself the way he was doing now by standing up for the concept of the sublime which cannot be clearly defined and the essence of which is a mysterious light that takes hold of the reader's soul? To the "Modernes" what Boileau called the sublime in the Scriptures, in Greek and Latin literature was the product of the disorder and confusion that existed at a time when men lived in a world of ignorance and darkness. But in two lines Boileau had included in his *Art Poétique*, the author had already announced, perhaps unconsciously, his affinity for the sublime. In order to defend the impulsiveness of a poetic genre, the ode, and particularly the works of the great Greek poet Pindar, Boileau had written:

> Its impetuous style, is often the product of chance;
> In it a beautiful disorder is a result of art.[11]

In his implacable war against the "Modernes" and to make the sublime triumph, Boileau used this argument time and time again, realizing full well that he was, in a way, contradicting the precepts he had set out to establish in his *Art Poétique*. But for Boileau, the champion of the rules and order, the sublime had to prevail at all cost. The author got to a point where he declared that at times it was preferable not to comply with the rules he had himself formulated for all literary genres. Again Boileau insisted that only men without taste are not able to understand this basic concept regarding Art:

Effectively, this precept, which gives us a rule not to obey at times the rules, is a mystery of art, which is not easy to make a man without taste understand, who believes that *Clélie* and our operas are models of the sublime style; who find Terence bland, Virgil cold and Homer devoid of judgment, and that a kind of oddness of mind makes him insensitive to what normally moves all men.[12]

This quote from Boileau's *Discours sur L'Ode* summarizes his position on the sublime perfectly. The sublime strikes all normal people like lightning and only critics who have no taste are unable to see and feel it in the works of the "Anciens" which have been a source of admiration by ordinary people for centuries.

Because of its link with the concept of light, the sublime became a key aesthetic and philosophical concern in the 18th century, commonly known as the age of enlightenment. Even though the philosophers considered reason the greatest attribute that man possesses, they nevertheless accepted and fought for the concept of the sublime. In England, for example, the great philosopher Edmund Burke published his famous essay *Philosophical Inquiry into the Origin of our Ideas of the Sublime and the Beautiful* in 1757. For Burke the sublime becomes a mode of aesthetic experience found in literature and far beyond it. Any object which excites the experience of producing the extraordinary light in man's soul Boileau had written about now becomes a source of the sublime. Thus, the sublime becomes a subject of psychological study for the philosophers. In his *Discours sur la Poésie Dramatique* published in 1758, the French philosopher Diderot wholeheartedly supports Boileau and the "Anciens" and uses language the classical rhetorician would certainly not have approved of to present his ideas:

In general, the more a people is civilized, polite, the less its morals are poetic; everything becomes weak as it becomes ornate. When does nature prepare models for art? It's when children tear out their hair around the bed of their dead father; when the mother displays her breast and beseeches her son to do her bidding by baring the breasts he has suckled, when a friend cuts his hair and spreads it over the body of his friend. . . .

Diderot comes to this remarkable conclusion about art: "Poetry demands something enormous, barbaric and savage."[13] Even Voltaire who had always been very critical of anything that reminded him of the fervor members of the clergy would sometimes display when they delivered their sermons and while practicing other clerical endeavors, could not ignore the power of the sublime in literature. In his article *"Enthousiasme"* in his *Dictionnaire Philosophique*, published in 1764, Voltaire warns that enthusiasm is like wine and that it can destroy reason but it can also stimulate the mind and give the brain a little more vitality. He offers a compromise between reason and the sublime and finally declares that a reasonable enthusiasm, as he puts it, is the gift of great poets.[14]

The concept of the sublime continued to preoccupy writers well into the 19th century and the Romantics were as fascinated by this phenomenon as much as their predecessors. Victor Hugo, for example, never stopped proclaiming, throughout his long life, his infinite admiration for Shakespeare whose works had been condemned during the Classical period because they did not obey the rules that had been set up for the theater. Even though Victor Hugo was a great poet and a great novelist, he did not possess the genius of the British author for the theater but he recognized, along with all the other Romantic writers of his time, that the plays of Shakespeare contain, as he put it, an extraordinary mixture of the sublime and the grotesque which makes this English poet the greatest playwright in the world. In conclusion, we can say that with the publication of his *Art Poétique*, his *Traité du Sublime* and his *Réflexions sur le Sublime*, Boileau unwittingly launched a philosophical issue of gigantic proportions into the history of literature and especially of French literature. In total opposition to the strict observance of the rules he wanted to impose on the authors of his time and which he had defined and formulated himself, Boileau spent his entire life fighting for the concept of the sublime which is not rooted in the logical processes of reason but in the experience of a mysterious and indefinable illumination of the human soul.

City College, CUNY

NOTES

Since there are no English translations of *Le Traité du Sublime* and *Les Réflexions sur le Sublime* I have translated the passages I have quoted from these works myself. The original French texts written by Boileau are given in the notes that follow:

[1] Login n'entend pas ce que les orateurs appellent le style sublime, cet extraordinaire et ce merveilleux qui frappe dans le discours, et qui fait qu'un ouvrage enlève, ravit, transporte. Le style sublime veut toujours de grands mots; mais le sublime se peut trouver dans une seule pensée, dans une seule figure, dans un seul tour de parole. Une chose peut être dans le style sublime, et n'être pourtant pas sublime, c'est à dire n'avoir rien d'extraordinaire ni de surprenant. Par exemple: le souverain arbitre de la nature d'une seule parole forma la lumière: voilà qui est dans le style sublime: cela n'est pas néanoins sublime, parce qu'il n'y a rien là de fort merveilleux et qu'on ne peut aisément trouver. Mais "Dieu dit: que la lumière se fasse; et la lumière se fit." ce tour extra-ordinaire d'expression, qui marque si bien l'obéissance de la créature aux ordres du créateur, est véritablement sublime, et a quelque chose de divin. Il faut donc entendre par sublime, dans Longin, l'extraordinaire, le surprenant, et, comme je l'ai traduit, le merveilleux dans le discours." (Boileau, *Oeuvres*, Tome II, *Le Traité du Sublime* (M. Amar. Ed. Firmin-Didot & Cie., 1878), p. 363.)

[2] Soyez simple avec art, Sublime sans orgeuil, agréable sans fard. (Boileau, *Ouvres*, Tome II, *L'Art Poétique* (M. Amar. Ed. Firmin Didot & Cie., 1878), p. 193.)

[3] Writing about another example of the sublime taken from Pierre Corneille's tragedy *Horace*, Boileau states: "Voilà de forts petites paroles; cependant il n'y a personne qui ne sente la grandeur héroïque qui est renfermée dans ce mot" qu'il mourût", qui est d'autant plus sublime, qu'il est simple et naturel, et que par là on voit que c'est du fond du coeur que parle ce vieux héros, et dans les transports d'une colère vraiment romaine." (Boileau, *Oeuvres*, Tome II, *Préface de 1701* (M. Amar. Ed. Firmin-Didot & Cie., 1878), p. 365.)

[4] A cela je pourrais vous répondre en général, sans entrer dans une grande discussion, que le sublime n'est pas proprement une chose qui se prouve et qui se démontre mais que c'est un merveilleux qui saisit qui frappe et qui se fait sentir." (Boileau, *Oeuvres*, Tome II, Réflexion X (M. Amar. Ed. Firmin-Didot & Cie., 1878), pp. 477—78.)

[5] "L'esprit divin qui l'inspirait y a pensé pour lui, et les (les agréments et les finesses de l'école) a mises en oeuvres avec d'autant plus d'art qu'on ne s'aperçoit point qu'il y ait aucun art . . . ." (Boileau, *Oeuvres*, Tome II, *Réflexion X* (M. Amar. Ed. Firmin-Didot & Cie., 1878), p. 485.)

[6] J'ai rapporté ces paroles de la Genèse comme l'expression la plus propre à mettre ma

pensée à jour, et je m'en suis servi d'autant plus volontiers que cette expression est citée avec éloge par Longin même, qui, au milieu des ténébres du paganisme, n'a pas laissé de reconnaître le divin qu'il y avait dans ces paroles de l'Ecriture. Mais que dirons-nous d'un des plus grands savants hommes de notre siècle, qui éclairé des lumièes de l'Evangile, ne s'est pas aperçu de la beauté de cet endroit, a osé dis-je avancer, dans un livre qu'il a fait pour démontrer la religion chrétienne, que Longin s'était trompé lorsqu'il a cru que ces paroles étaient sublimes?" (Boileau, *Oeuvres*, Tome II, *Le Traité du Sublime, Préface de 1682* (M. amar. Ed. Firmin-Didot & Cie., 1878), p. 363.)

[7] "Mais lorsque des écrivains ont été admirés durant un très grans nombres de siècles, et n'ont été méprisés que par quelques gens de goût bizarre (car il se trouve toujours des goûts dépravés), alors non seulement il y a de la témérité, mais il y a de la folie, à vouloir douter du mérite de ces écrivains. Que si vous ne voyez pas la beauté de leurs écrits, il ne pas pas conclure qu'elles n'y sont point, mais que vous étes aveugles, et que vous n'avez point de goût." (Boileau, *Oeuvres*, Tome II, *Reflexion X* (M. Amar. Ed. Firmin-Didot & Cie., 1878), p. 459.)

[8] "Il faut songer du jugement que toute postérité fera de nos écrits." (Boileau, *Oeuvres*, Tome II, *Reflexion X* (M. Amar. Ed. Firmin-Didot & Cie., 1878), p. 389.)

[9] "Quelque éclat ait fait un écrivain durant sa vie, quelques éloges il ait reçus, on ne peut pas pour cela infailliblement conclure que ses ouvrages sont excellents. De faux brillants, la nouveauté du style, un tour d'esprit qui était à la mode, peuvent les avoir fait valoir; et il arrivera peut-être que dans le siècle suivant on ouvrira les yeux, et que l'on méprisera ce qu'on a admiré." (Boileau, *Oeuvres*, Tome II, *Reflexion X* (M. Amar. Ed. Firmin-Didot & Cie., 1878), p. 458.)

[10] "Il s'agit de savoir en quoi consiste ce merveilleux que les Anciens ont fait admirer de tant de siècles; et il faut trouver moyen de le voir, ou renoncer aux belles lettres, auxquelles vous devez croire vous n'avez ni goût ni génie, puisque vous ne sentez pas ce qu'ont senti tous les homes." (Boileau, *Oeuvres*, Tome II, M. Amar. Ed. Firmin-Didot & Cie., 1878, p. 460.)

[11] "Son style impérieux souvent marche au hasard; Chez elle un beau désordre est un effet de l'art." (Boileau, *Oeuvres*, Tome II, *L'Art Poétique*, M. Amar. Ed. Firmin-Didot & Cie., 1878, p. 460.)

[12] "Ce précepte effectivement, qui donne pour règle de ne point garder quelquefois de règles, est un mystère de l'art, qui n'est point aisé de faire entendre à un homme sans aucun goût, qui croit que la *Clélie* et nos opéras sont des modèles du genre sublime, qui trouve Térence fade, Virgile froid, Homère de mauvais sens, et qu'une espèce de bizarrerie d'esprit rend insensible à tout ce qui frappe ordinairement les hommes." (Boileau, *Oeuvres*, Tome II, Ed. Lefèvre, MDCCCXXIV, p. 284.)

[13] "En général, plus un peuple est civilisé, poli, moins ses moeurs sont Poétiques; tout s'affaiblit en s'adornissant. Quand est-ce que la nature prépare des modèles de l'art? C'est au temps où les enfants s'arrachent les cheveux autour du lit d'un père moribond; où la mère découvre son sein et conjure son fils par les mammelles qui l'ont allaité ou un ami se coupe la chevelure, et la répand sur le cadavre de son ami . . . La poèsie veut quelque chose d'énorme, de barbare et de sauvage." (Diderot, Denis, *Oeuvres esthétiques*, Int. et Notes de Paul Vernière. Ex. Garnier frères, 1959, pp. 260–61.)

[14] "L'enthousisme raisonable est le partage des grands poétes . . ." (Voltaire, *Oeuvres, Dictionnaire Philosophique*, Ed. Moland, Tome 18 (Paris: Garnier frères, 1878), p. 556.)

PETER MORGAN

LIGHT IN WORDSWORTH ILLUSTRATED

In this paper I will examine the topic of light in Wordsworth, paying particular attention to his sonnet, "Composed upon Westminster Bridge, September 3, 1803." I will first present the sonnet (1); then I will place it in a sequence of relevant poetic and prose passages, influential on it and analogues to it. These will be found in writing in English from both before and after the time of Wordsworth, as well as contemporary with him. They will extend from the poets Milton (2) and Thomson (3), influential on him, through lesser-known, late eighteenth-century observers of the landscape. These demonstrate the visual climate in which he was working (4 and 5). The immediate contemporary is Wordsworth's own sister Dorothy who describes laconically in her journal the scene which he will present with poetic elaboration (6). The theme of light is omnipresent in Wordsworth's poetry, but I will have to move on chronologically beyond it. Also, Wordsworth's sonnet in particular belongs in a literary, specifically poetic, tradition descriptive of the atmospherics of the city of London. This tradition grew in strength towards the end of the nineteenth century. I will not examine it, because it has been well studied. Rather, I will present two prose texts of the century, the first a description from a forgotten novel by T. H. Lister (7). The final passage in this sequence is from the mid-century philologist and anthropologist Max Müller. I appreciate Müller's attempt to express the cultural significance of Wordsworth's modern poetic response (8).

My only reservation concerning Wordsworth's powerful evocation concerns that aspect of experience that he has excluded, in order to purify the presentation of the relation between God, the world and man. The personal is importantly present in the sonnet, but not in the individual shapes of the human beings with whom Wordsworth was psychically and materially involved: his beloved and loving sister Dorothy who as we have seen is actually with him as he composes the sonnet; his former lover and their daughter whom he and Dorothy are on their way to visit in France, before he will return in order to marry. These several sexual and familial preoccupations, involving anxiety I

121

A-T. Tymieniecka (ed.), Analecta Husserliana, Vol. XXXVIII, 121—129.
© 1992 *Kluwer Academic Publishers. Printed in the Netherlands.*

should say because of their complexity, Wordsworth elides, in order to achieve the poetic focus that he does. I think the biographical background of the poem is important, even as one considers it as a panegyric of light in a religious context. I represent this hidden dimension with two quotations which give pictures of Wordsworth's later life, first in the family and second as a distinguished public figure (9 and 10).

All this represents a glimpse into facets of the literary tradition, specifically of the celebration of light, in which Wordsworth's sonnet belongs. There is also a pictorial tradition. To illustrate this I would briefly evoke Guido Reni's painting "Aurora" which the poet admired (i): the art of Canaletto in the mid-eighteenth century in which the Thames scene is viewed with topographical exactness but as artistically as by Wordsworth (ii): the contemporary art of Turner who paints not only the sunrise in different locations (iii), but also a contrasting nocturnal scene of the burning of the Houses of Parliament at Westminster (iv). In the late nineteenth and early twentieth centuries not only painters such as Manet and Kokoshka but also photographers joined in the quest for representation of this particular scene: Frith realistically (v), Coburn impressionistically (v), and Brandt abstractly (vii). These all join the poet in making a contribution to the depiction of the London river, especially at Westminster, bathed by light. Finally, Oldenburg attempts an act of sabotage by scrawling a drawing of a toilet plunger over a picture postcard view of the scene (viii). He may deny the purity of the experience of light that our artists, especially Wordsworth, had insisted on and tried to identify, but he cannot erase it!

1. the sonnet —

Composed Upon
Westminster Bridge,
Sept. 3, 1803.

Earth has not any thing to show more fair:
Dull would he be of soul who could pass by
A sight so touching in it's majesty:
This City now doth like a garment wear
The beauty of the morning; silent, bare,   5
Ships, towers, domes, theatres, and temples lie
Open unto the fields, and to the sky;

> All bright and glittering in the smokeless air.
> Never did sun more beautifully steep
> In his first splendor valley, rock, or hill;   10
> Ne'er saw I, never felt, a calm so deep!
> The river glideth at his own sweet will;
> Dear God! the very houses seem asleep;
> And all that mighty heart is lying still!

Wordsworth hyperbolically presents his response to the beauty of the early morning light shining upon the tranquil city as he suddenly sees it at the beginning of his journey from London to France. The sense of tranquillity and freedom, however momentary, is greater than what the poet has experienced directly through nature, so he thanks God for it.

2. Wordsworth knew and admired Milton's passage in *Paradise Lost*.[1] The scene is broadly similar to that in his sonnet; however, Milton's observer is not the human being suppressing his evil proclivities, but Satan himself.

> (Satan looked down)
> with wonder at the sudden view
> Of all this World at once. As when a Scout
> Through dark and desert wayes with peril gone
> All night, at last by break of chearful dawne
> Obtains the brow of some high-climbing Hill,
> Which to his eye discovers unaware
> The goodly prospect of . . .
> . . . some renowed Metropolis
> With glistering Spires and Pinnacles adornd,
> Which now the Rising sun guilds with his beams
> (III. 542 ff).

3. Thomson celebrated light in a passage which would constitute a *locus classicus* for the theme in English poetry down from the date of its publication in *The Seasons* in 1727 through the nineteenth century.

> But yonder comes the powerful king of day
> Rejoicing in the east. The lessening cloud,
> The kindling azure, and the mountain's brow
> Illumed with fluid gold, his near approach
> Betoken glad. Lo! now, apparent all,
> Aslant the dew-bright earth and coloured air,

He looks in boundless majesty abroad
And sheds the shining day, that burnished plays
On rocks, and hills, and towers, and wandering streams
High-gleaming from afar. Prime cheerer, Light!
Of all material being first and best!
Efflux divine! Nature's resplendent robe,
Without whose vesting beauty all were wrapt
In unessential gloom; and thou, O Sun!
Soul of surrounding worlds! in whom best seen
Shines out thy Maker! may I sing of thee?
                                        ("Summer," 81ff).

Wordsworth in his sonnet answers Thomson's final question with an expression of idiosyncratic personal enthusiasm.

4. The sublime passages by Milton and Thomson not only anticipate Wordsworth's sonnet, but they also anticipate the theory of the aesthetic response to the world which will be developed in the late eighteenth century, producing the cultural climate which Wordsworth enjoyed. This is illustrated at a modest level by two further passages, from Whately on gardening, 1770, and Malton describing the scene at Westminster in 1792. Whately responds aesthetically to the beauty of the morning and he shows how human contrivance can contribute to enhance it. Wordsworth sees London as a great artefact in this spirit. Whately writes that "to every view belongs a light which shows it to advantage." He continues:

In a *morning*, the freshness of the air allays the force of the sun-beams, and their brightness is free from glare; the most splendid objects do not offend the eye; nor suggest the idea of heat in its extreme; but they correspond with the glitter of the dew which bespangles all the produce of the earth, and with the chearfulness diffused over the whole face of the creation. A variety of buildings may therefore be introduced to enliven the view; their colour may be the purest white, without danger of excess, though they face the eastern sun; and those which are in other aspects should be so contrived, that their turrets, their pinnacles, or other points, may catch glances of the rays, and contribute to illuminate the scene.[2]

Wordsworth is viewing *his* morning scene, its buildings bathed in the light of the sun, in the spirit of the connoisseur in this passage.

5. Malton, with other topographical observers close to Wordsworth's time, describes the particular scene at Westminster, using the plural personal pronoun "we." Like the poet, he is responsive to the aesthetics

of the scene as he participates in it. Westminster Bridge "rises boldy before the spectator . . . ennobled by a multitude of objects in motion . . . We eagerly ascend the summit of the Bridge, to enjoy the prospect which opens on every side," including "the towers and pinnacles of Westminster-Abbey . . . the steeple of St. Margaret's." Malton enlarges on this picture with detailed description of particular views on both sides of the river looking east:

From this station, on looking to the south, we command a view of about two miles of the river, terminated by the Surrey hills in the distance, with the Lambeth Church and the venerable Palace of the Archbishop of Canterbury on the east shore; and nearly opposite on the west, the four turrets of St. John's Church in Westminster . . . . On looking to the north down the river, which beautifully winds to the east towards Blackfriars Bridge, and here displays a great . . . breadth of water . . . we are presented with a prospect, perhaps not to be equalled by any view of the kind in Europe. Somerset Place, the chef d'oeuvre of Sir William Chambers, principally arrests the eye from the colour and magnitude of the building; and next the Adelphi, an elegant pile, erected from the designs of . . . Robert Adam . . . . The Temple buildings and gardens terminate the distance; over all majestically rises the upper story and dome of St. Paul's, with the roofs of many public buildings and a multiplicity of steeples, which combined with the busy moving scene beneath, form a most splendid and interesting picture; even the black octangular pyramid at York-buildings Water-works, by breaking the lines, adds considerably to its beauty.[3]

Here Malton provides all the details that Wordsworth occludes. His response is assimilated in the grandiose feeling of the poet. Dorothy Wordsworth, having experienced the scene in the company of her brother, describes it directly in a diary entry. The "troubles and disorders" to which she initially refers are absent from the sonnet. She is both more and less exact than William in her timing of the experience. Like him, she appreciates the beauty and the unique sublimity of the scene, seeing in it an affinity with such a scene in nature. She writes:

After various troubles and disasters we left London on Saturday morning at 1/2 past 5 or 6, the 31st of July (I have forgot which.) We mounted the Dover Coach at Charing Cross. It was a beautiful morning. The city, St. Paul's, with the River and a multitude of little Boats, made a most beautiful sight as we crossed Westminster Bridge. The houses were not overhung by their cloud of smoke and they were spread out endlessly, yet the sun shone so brightly with such a pure light, that there was even something like the purity of one of nature's own grand spectacles.[4]

7. Perhaps T. H. Lister, the author of *Granby*, 1826, read Wordsworth's sonnet and rehashed its themes in an awkward but still revealing way, noticing the city dawn's special effects of light and sound.

There is a sense of a muted echo in Lister's passage, but there is also the sense of an addition with a character of its own, as he combines the conventional personal with the general, and with a specificity of observation:

he left the ball, and sallied out into the fresh cool air of a summer-morning — suddenly passing from the red glare of lamplight, to the clear sober brightness of returning day . . . he viewed the town under an aspect in which it is alike presented to the late retiring votary of pleasure, and to the early rising sons of business . . . . Had it not been for the cool grey tint which slightly mingled with every object, the brightness was almost that of noon. But the life, the bustle, the busy din, the flowing tide of human existence, were all wanting to complete the similitude. All was hushed and silent; and this mighty receptacle of human beings, which a few short hours would wake into active energy and motion, seemed like a city of the dead . . . . No sounds were heard but the heavy creaking of a solitary waggon; the twittering of an occasional sparrow; the monotonous tone of the drowsy watchman; and the distant rattle of the retiring carriage.[5]

8. The final passage in this sequence, though there will be an addendum, is from the mid-nineteenth century philologist and anthropologist Max Müller. Max Müller writes eloquently of the dawn, but for him it is not an intensely meaningful personal experience. In its depth it is a primitive one which he observes from a distance and tries to recapture. It is noteworthy that as he makes this effort, he quotes Wordsworth, though not this particular poem. Müller presents his own age as an advanced epoch of rational science to which the dawn is "merely a beautiful sight." In his day the poet at best is a relic of a lost way of experiencing. In his passage Müller makes a marvellous attempt at bridging the gap between the ancient, primordial, poetic response and the modern, scientific, rational, prosaic one. He makes use of Wordsworth as he does so, but he does not recognise the persistence of the poetic power of response to a natural phenomenon which Wordsworth exemplifies. I myself in the late twentieth century accept the validity of the urgency of Wordsowrth's vision. This cannot be diminished by considering it as a merely historical phenomenon.

The dawn, which to us is merely a beautiful sight, was to the early gazer and thinker the problem of all problems. It was the unknown land from whence rose every day those bright emblems of a divine power which left in the mind of man the first impression and intimation of another world, of power above, of order and wisdom. What we simply call the sunrise, brought before their eyes every day the riddle of all riddles, the riddle of existence. The days of their life sprang from that dark abyss which every morning seemed instinct with light and life. Their youth, their manhood, their old age, all were to the Vedic bards the gift of that heavenly mother who appeared bright, young, unchanged, immortal every morning, while everything else seemed to grow old, to change, and droop, and at last to set, never to return . . . . The whole theogony and philosophy of the ancient world centred in the Dawn, the mother of the bright gods, of the sun in his various aspects, of the morn, the day, the spring; herself the brilliant image and visage of immortality.

It is of course impossible to enter fully into all the thoughts and feelings that passed through the minds of the early poets when they formed names for that far far East from whence even the early dawn, the sun, the day, their own life, seemed to spring. A new life flashed up every morning before their eyes, and the fresh breezes of the dawn reached them life greetings wafted across the golden threshold of the sky from the distant lands beyond the mountains, beyond the clouds, beyond the dawn, beyond "the immortal sea which brought us hither." The Dawn seemed to them to open golden gates for the sun to pass in triumph, and while those gates were open their eyes and their minds strove in their childish way to pierce beyond the limits of this finite world.[6]

9. My only reservation concerns the aspect of experience that Wordsworth has excluded from the purview of his sonnet, in order to purify his presentation of the relation between God, man and the world. The personal is significantly present here, in the efforts at personification and the direct address to God. But lacking is reference to the other human beings with whom Wordsworth was immediately involved: his beloved and loving sister Dorothy, actually sitting beside him as he composes the poem; his former mistress and their daughter in France whom he and Dorothy are on their way to visit, before his return in order to marry a third woman, Mary Hutchinson. These sexual and familial preoccupations, inducing anxiety I should say because of their complexity, Wordsworth elides, in order to achieve the particular poetic focus that he does. I think that the biographical background of the poem is important, though it is hard to identify because of the poet's reticence. However, it can be represented by two passages which throw light on Wordsworth's life, first in the family and secondly as a public figure.

The first passage presents a benign picture of the family situation late in Wordsworth's life which followed from the crucial decision made at the time when the sonnet was written. It illustrates a *ménage* of constraint which must have caused some psychic damage, particularly to Dorothy, the most vulnerable member of the group. Henry Crabb Robinson provides a background as he sums up Wordsworth's domestic situation, writing in his diary for 1835 of the "hopeless mental imbecility" of Dorothy. "She was fond of repeating the favourite small poems of her brother . . . and she could often be *tamed*, if I may say so, by being desired to repeat a poem." The daughter Dora, with a very similar name to Dorothy's as Robinson observes, "was the apple of her father's eye." Very sickly, "after this year there have succeeded marriage, travelling, death." The one reassuring feature in Robinson's account is provided by the tranquil image of Mary: yet, "because she is so admirable a person, there is little to say of her."[7]

This family situation is exemplified in the impressions of Harriet Martineau, conveyed to Elizabeth Barrett Browning as late as 1846:

> You know Wordsworth's affairs are most comfortable in his old age. His wife is perfectly charming & the very angel he shd have to tend him. His life is a most serene & happy one, on the whole, & while all goes *methodically*, he is happy & cheery & courteous & benevolent, — so that one could almost worship him. But to secure this, every body must be punctual, & the fire must burn bright, & all go orderly, — his angel takes care that everything shall, as far as depends on her. He goes every day to Miss Fenwick, (he always needs some such daily object, — & she is the worthiest possible) — gives her a smacking kiss, & sits down before the fire to open his mind. Think what she could tell, if she survives him![8]

10. The second passage also shows Wordsworth as the centre of attention, not too reluctantly basking in the admiration of a group of schoolboys. They write out and read the sonnet, commenting on it with critical diligence, seeking to give an explanation of a particular line. The hermeneutic tension of this exercise is relieved as the poet himself takes over, especially when he asks for the boys to be given a holiday and they burst into applause. The exultation here experienced momentarily between boys and poet is not utterly alien from that experienced by the poet in relation to the city, the world and God, as he experiences in the sonnet the light of the early morning. Wordsworth's son-in-law Edward Quillinan reminisces:

> After wine and cake we were ushered into the schoolroom . . . . The boys rose and bowed, sat and gazed; pencils and slates were brought out at word of command; pedagogue gave out, line by line, the Sonnet supposed to be written on Westminster Bridge. All the boys wrote it, one echoing the Master, as the clerk . . . does the clergyman. When finished, several boys in turn read it aloud: very well too. They were then called upon to explain the meaning of "the river glideth at its own sweet will." One boy, the biggest . . . made a dissertation on the influence of the moon on the tides etc etc and seemed rather inclined to be critical; another said there was no wind, another that there were no water breaks in the Thames to prevent its gliding as it pleased; another that the arches of the bridge had no locks to shut the water in and out: and so

forth. One boy said there were no boats — that was the nearest. Poet explained: was then called upon by Pedagogue to read his Sonnet himself; declined: Ped. entreated: Poet remonstrated: Ped. inexorable; Poet submitted. I never heard him read better. The Boys evidently felt it; a thunder of applause; Poet asked for a half-Holiday for them — granted — Thunders on Thunders . . . *Seriously speaking* the whole scene was indescribably animated and interesting.[9]

All this material represents a glimpse into different aspects of the literary tradition of the celebration of light to which Wordsworth's sonnet belongs. The coda is necessary because the praise of light has a psychic source which demands exploration of the inner, the psychological, as well as the outer, the natural, the social and the divine. Here the insight into the psychological comes in the form of anecdotal visual pictures.

University of Toronto

NOTES

[1] See *The Romantics on Milton*, ed. Wittreich, 1970, p. 104.
[2] Thos Whately, *Observations on Modern Gardening*, 1770, pp. 242, 245—46.
[3] Thos Malton, *Picturesque Tour through the Cities of London and Westminster*, 1792, p. 3.
[4] Dorothy Wordsworth, *Journals*, ed. Moorman, 1971, pp. 150f.
[5] T. H. Lister, *Granby*, 1826, I, pp. 297—99.
[6] F. Max Müller, *Lectures on the Science of Language*, 2nd series, 2nd ed., 1868, pp. 498—500.
[7] Henry Crabb Robinson, *On Books and Their Writers*, ed. Morley, II, 1938, pp. 474f.
[8] Robert Browning and Elizabeth Barrett Browning, *Letters*, ed. Kintner, 1969, p. 462.
[9] Wm Wordsworth, *Letters*, 2nd ed., V, ii, ed. Hill, (Oxford: 1979), p. 395.

COLETTE V. MICHAEL

LIGHT/DARKNESS AND THE
PHENOMENON OF CREATION IN VICTOR HUGO

In this paper we will show that the interpretation, which has long held the field, of an epic poem written by Victor Hugo lacks coherence; we will suggest a new paradigm and analyze the poem from this new vantage point.

"Dieu" is a long poem published in 1891, six years after the death of its author, Victor Hugo. The genesis of this poetic work is important. According to his daughter Adèle the section,[1] now titled "Dieu" (or "God"), first called SOLITUDINES COELI, was read by the author to his family at home on 2 May 1855. The question of why it was not published until 1891 has plagued the critics; some have seen this postponement as an indication that the poet was entertaining thoughts on the creation of his own metaphysical doctrine.[2] Reading reports, published by L. Barthou, of Hugo's correspondence with his editor, it is clear that such is not the case. Indeed Hugo requested of his publisher that the title be modified several times obviously with the publication intent; after SOLITUDINES COELI it was to be ASCENSION DANS LES TENEBRES, or "Ascent into darkness"; and on the 12 February 1856, Hugo suggests that the title be changed to DIEU (GOD) and that this lone word be written in big letters whereas his own name be printed in very small letters. The Journet and Robert edition of that work has a subtitle "L'Océan d'en haut" (or The Ocean of the Heights). (According to Wendy Greenberg it is also known as "La Voix du Gouffre" 1856—1857 no publisher, p. 96.). In March 1857, the publisher advise Hugo of the impossibility of publishing this text because the religious attitude prevalent under the strict imperial exigencies should make it unadvisable. In other words what prevented Hugo from publishing his text was plain censorship. Indeed Baudelaire's *les Fleurs du mal* were condemned a few months later.

Editors have also compounded the difficulties by taking liberties with Hugo's text which was originally written on sheets folded lengthwise; Hugo wrote the poem on the right side of the page, leaving the left side for additions or rare corrections. In the NE VARIETUR edition (Hetzel-Quantin, 1891)[3] there are no explanations about the choice

131

A-T. Tymieniecka (ed.), Analecta Husserliana, Vol. XXXVIII, 131—148.
© 1992 *Kluwer Academic Publishers. Printed in the Netherlands.*

made by the editor; sometimes the additions are included; at other times they are not, and all this, without any justification. Other editors have taken even more liberties with the text. The annotated edition compiled by Jacques Truchet and published in 1950 by Gallimard in the Pleiade Series includes not only the twenty one fragments entitled "VOICES" of the Ollendorf edition but an addition of four more "Voices". In a previous edition there were only eleven "voices." The manuscript is preceded by a section entitled "L'esprit humain" dated 26 April 1866; its writing would be by ten years posterior to the original text. Another change made by editors is the inclusion of titles and subtitles to the eight sections entitled "Dieu"; although an outline exists,[4] that outline is posterior to the composing of the poem, and according to Journet and Robert (p. 192) nowhere is there a justification that would authorize the publisher to add these formulas as title or epigraph in the different parts of the poem; nor are there any reasons to mention the assorted birds, a fact that has mislead the readers.[5] Therefore in this essay, we will restrict our analysis to Hugo's text such as it is published in the critical edition of Journet & Robert.[6]

* * *

This poem, often ignored, is rendered difficult not only by the symbolic world the author creates but also by what has been called the somewhat whimsical philosophical interpretations it presents. But this is a distorted reading since it attributes to the poet our own logical intentionality in our previous readings of philosophical systems. Indeed as pointed out by Michael Riffaterre

> The literary phenomenon is a dialectic between a text and its reader. If we are to formulate rules governing this dialectic, we must be certain that what we are describing is actually perceived by the reader; we shall have to know whether he is always obliged to see what he sees or if a certain freedom is allowed; and we must know how this perception takes place. It seems to me, adds Riffaterre, that in the vast field which is literature, poetry is especially inseparable from the concept of text. If we do not consider the poem as a close and finished entity we will not always be able to see the difference between poetic discourse and literary language.[7]

And the point is of course that we must see the difference between poetic discourse and philosophical language. There is no intention here of getting bogged down on what is philosophical except perhaps to say that in any philosophical system we expect some sort of coherence between metaphysics, epistemology and ethics. Here Victor Hugo makes no pretense at coherence within each system. Because the title is "GOD," a title termed "pretentious" by Charles Renouvier who thought a more modest and apt title should have been "the Idea of God";[8] because several religions are discussed, because the poem appears at first glance to be a search for an absolute, critics have held fast that Hugo was describing, and I quote "a narrator-hero who consults eight winged beings in order to learn the nature of God."[9] This has been the paradigm which has prevailed with editors and critics. Ever since the publication in 1900 of Charles Renouvier's book, *Victor Hugo* this is the cognitude attitude that has been applied to this particular poem; that "Dieu" was in poetic form Hugo's view of the idea of God has been assumed to be a given fact. That some of the metaphors under this paradigm lacked intelligibility was not questioned although the choice of winged beings lacked explanation. In other words THE PARADIGM has been the idea of God in some religions and in some philosophical systems; this was the code of reading underlying this whole interpretation. This code is so ingrained that it had lead critics to say:

In Hugo's universe, everything thinks, everything speaks; it is natural that, while ascending, the spirit would hear from birds an expose on the meaning of several religions and philosophies.[10]

I believe there is nothing natural in this context about the explanations given by these birds; why a griffin? why a vulture? how could light follow an angel in a series comprised of birds?

* * *

Now if we ignore this background and attempt to prove that a text can, as Robert Scholes puts it "survive the absence of its author, the absence of its addresses, the absence of its object, the absence of its context,"[11] and the absence of the code it has been normally attributed and if we start again by just looking at the text, then we arrive at a most interesting interpretation.

There are in this text two opposite, continually recurring paradigms: darkness and light, or if you will, evil and good, matter and spirit, hate and love. Darkness in the poem DIEU is synonymous to nothingness, gulf, gloom, depth, night, even tomb, and especially evil, both as receptacle and content. But from this nothingness, from this abyss comes forth some vibrant glimpses of the creative gestation in the mind of a poet.

* * *

All sections begins with the same verse: "Et je vis au-dessus de ma tête un point noir: (And I saw above my head a black spot). From this black spot will evolve numerous ideas about the world of the poet. This first encounter of the man is with a bat, a cave dweller, inhabitant of the dark depth, which shouts to the intruder: "Man, what is the meaning of the horrible adventure called universe?" In this somber abyss, there are no creator, only possibilities that are not sought, nor achieved:

> Noire ébauche que personne n'achève,
> L'univers est un monstre et le ciel est un rêve;
> Ni volonté, ni loi, ni poles, ni milieu;
> Un chaos composé de néants.[12] (108—110)

Although the world exists, although it is inhabited by the bat, a flying mammal, often associated with the witches's sabbath; although there is an encounter with man, it is a world of emptiness, a world devoid of spirit, a kind of Platonic cave where there are only shadows and illusions. If something, the germ of idea, in this universe is alive, "it is not yet born. It is in a total darkness; not having seen the light, it does not as yet have any sight; it is a world groping in its own nothingness." The bat, a cavern dweller, symbolizes a being stopped in a stage of evolution; a being blinded by light, ignorant of truth, a being devoid of spirit.[13]

"Le monde est à tatons dans son propre néant." (145) And it is impossible to express even in words the immense amazement of the sleeping darkness. (128) The world is mute.

* * *

In the second encounter, the dark spot turns out to be an owl, also a bird of night, symbol of sadness, of solitary retreat but an animal which played in ancient China an important role as a symbol of invention, and in a negative sense as a fabricator (of lies); it is also an emblem of thunder, thereby an announcement of light and of the blacksmith who builds; this bird of darkness is filled with doubt about the meaning of the black environment in which he lives and which, at first glance, appears to be without existence:

> Quel sens peut donc avoir
> Ce monde aveugle et sourde, cet édifice noir,

> Cette création ténébreuse et cloitrée
> Sans fenêtre, sans toit, sans porte, sans entrée,
> Sans issue, o terreur! (323—325)[14]

The owl does not cohabit the cave with the bat; he is out in the open, endless night; but the first ray of light appears when vaguely perceived are some investigators, researchers who in the darkness are so faintly recognizable as to be only dark shadows:

> Par moments des blancheurs
> Passent; on aperçoit vaguement des chercheurs.
> Sans savoir si ce sont réellement des êtres,
>   Et si tous ces sondeurs du gouffre, mages, prêtres,
> Eux-mêmes ne sont pas de l'ombre à qui les vents
> Donnent dans le brouillard des formes de vivants.

The very existence of these thinkers, prophets, djinns, demons and wizards, and poets are questioned; all of them in the somber enclosure are asking questions about the meaning of nature, of destiny, two aspects of one and the same entity; (352— 355)[15] The spector of life called man suffers, caught between the two tragic voices of Nature and Humanity; human anguish finds neither explanation nor solace in a universe without creation. But from the edge of the abyss can be perceived, up on the heights, some signs of life; gestation is in progress, sometimes amid some terrifying and unknown worlds; is all that enough to prove that somewhere an author exists, a "voyant" what has a broad knowledge spreading through good and evil? That this creator will endure the agony of birth? This is followed by a most important question: Is creation voluntary? Can man be justified in believing in the possibility of light in this infinite darkness? Man is helped in his search by the son of Zeus and Maia, the God Hermes who, in classical mythology, is the messenger of the Gods and himself God of science and invention. He is also the guardian of roads, boundaries, and commerce. Mediator between the divinity and men, he was a guide to souls in the kingdom of the dead. The Gods were so impressed by his talents that they gave him the power to see the light of truth and he became their messenger. Mediator Hermes was also the God who opened the way of strange roads, of organized disorder, i.e., to know is to be ignorant: "Savoir c'est ignorer." (535) But Hermes is also the God of disorder and master of deception; and it is thanks to his cunning that there is now on Mount Olympus place for a language of transgression.[16] It is thanks to Hermes that now is glimpsed the possibility of creation out of nothingness, out of the darkness:

> Il se peut qu'avec l'amas crépusculaire
> De ses grands bas-reliefs qu'un jour lugubre éclaire,
> Avec son bloc de nuit, de brume et de clarté,
>   La création soit, devant l'immensité,
> Un piedestal ayant le néant pour statue. (576—584).

* * *

Only in the third section of the poem does the opposition between light and darkness take shape on an equal footing and only then does this opposition becomes a confrontation between good and evil symbolized by a lone raven.

> Ils sont deux; l'un est l'hymne et l'autre est la huée.
> Ils sont deux; le linceul et l'être, la nuée
> Et le ciel, la paupière et l'oeil, l'ombre et le jour.
> La haine affreuse, noire, implacable, et l'amour.
> Ils sont deux combattants.
> Le combat c'est le monde. (763—767)

In Genesis, (8, 7) the raven is a symbol of hope for, at the end of forty days, "Noah opened the window of the ark which he had built and he set forth a raven, which went forth to and fro, until the waters were dried up from the earth." As such the raven suggests a new beginning. When despair covers the entire universe with darkness, a new dawn blooms with an immense smile. In Greece, the raven was consecrated to Apollo and had a prophetic function. According to Guy de Tervarent in *Attributs et symboles dans l'art profane*, the raven is also a symbol of loneliness, and voluntary solitude of the one who had chosen to live on a superior plane; this would apply in particular to the lonely world of the creator, here the poet. The two fighters are alone. Nothing above them. At each other they throw winter and spring, flash of lightning as well as ray of sunshine; they are the frightening duel of creation. (857). In turn each of these giants emerges the winner;

> l'homme semble un dieu de sagesse vêtu,
> Et tout grandit en grâce, en puissance, en vertu,

Ou dans le flot du mal tout naufrage et tout sombre,
Selon que le hasard, roi de la lutte sombre,
Precipite Arimane ou voile Ormus terni,
Et fait pencher, au fond du livide infini,
L'un ou l'autre plateau de la balance énorme. (894—900)

A romantic world filled with birds, flowers and flowing springs (889) is replaced by turmoil and chaos. According to a legend in Tite-live, Curtius, dedicating himself to the Gods Manes, hurled himself down the open gulf formed during an earthquake in the Forum. As for the Virgil formula, QUISQUE SUOS PATIMUR MANES, "each of us endure our Manes"; This was interpreted by a Virgil's commentator, Servius, as meaning that at birth two genies await us, one that pushes us toward goodness, the other toward evil; after death, there are the witness of our destiny, freedom or reincarnation. Here is the first indication of the belief in Hugo of the possibility of metempsychosis; the transmigration of soul is a reoccurring topic.

* * *

In part IV the reader is introduced to the vulture, entrails eater, also considered an agent regenerator of vital forces contained in organic decomposition; in other words the vulture is also a purificatory of sorts, a magician who insures a cycle of renewal by transmuting death into new life. For the same reasons, the vulture is associated with celestial fairs, themselves purificatory and fecund. This fertility is sometimes translated as an aspect of wealth: vital, material and spiritual wealth. (Chevalier and Gheerbrant, vol. iv, p. 361). The vulture was eating Prometheus when appeared Orpheus. (949). Distracted by the enchanted voice, the vulture, "stupid, followed and thus was Prometheus delivered." (955) Changing the legend here V. Hugo does not bring Eurydice out of the hell she was confined. Prometheus, helped by Orpheus thus teaches the vulture to listen to the spirit. The teaching is all about the many gods that reign on Mount Olympus as well as on earth. From Venus to Hecate and Destiny, all in nature belongs to the three goddesses: "le sort est tigre, Hecate est sphynx, Venus est femme." (992) In this immense caryatid, the gods perform their bacchanals guided by Cybele, the primordial source of all fecundity. She directs, masters and commands vital power. Of all the deities she is the most productive; she is the Magna Mater. Although she is often pictured as a beautiful women, ornamented with flowers, sitting below the tree of life, surrounded by lions, a sign of power, she shares some of the gifts credited symbolically to the vulture: she has strange powers of regeneration, of revitalization. Under her influence and that of Bacchus and the help of the faithful Isis, all the passions are unleashed; all the appetites are satisfied; in a superb rendering of poetic dementia, V. Hugo described the bacchanals of the Gods:

> Toutes les passions et tous les appétits,
> S'accouplent, Evohé! rugissent, balbutient,
> Et sous l'oeil du destin calme et froid, associent
> Le râle et le baiser, la morsure et le chant,
> La cruauté joyeuse et le bonheur méchant,
> Et toutes les fureurs que la démence invente;
> Et célèbrent, devant l'esprit qui s'épouvante,
> Devant l'aube, devant l'astre, devant l'éclair,
>   Le mystère splendide et hideux de la chair;
> Et cherchant les lieux sourds, les rocs inabordables,
> Echevelés, pâmés, amoureux, formidables,
> Ivres, l'un qui s'échappe et l'autre qui poursuit,
> Dansent dans l'impudeur farouche de la nuit! (1062—1074)

In scabrous orgies, Géo, the earth, opened without respite to long embraces engulfs in her black flanks an entire world of lovers. It is a world where the plague are titans and the vices are Gods. (1174) Where man is left only with a question: How to escape? All repeat, why? why? None guess the obscure secret of the divine and infernal darkness. Is wanting to know enough to open the gates of this black laybrinth? Prometheus, alone, has willed to bring man out of darkness; he has labored, taught, civilized in order to make of the globe a living and radiant sphere; wishing to put man as the height of the gods, he has brought their wrath on him and he was punished. But man was left with some hope because he had, at last, the flame. All man had to do was wait. If he knew how to think, and enlighten something in himself:

> S'il se souvient qu'il peut, puisque l'idée a lui,
> Allumer quelque chose en lui de plus que lui,
> Qu'il doit lutter, que l'aube est une délivrance,
> Et qu'avoir le flambeau, c'est avoir l'espérance;

Car deux sacrés rayons composent la clarté,
Et l'un est la puissance, et l'autre est la beauté." (1358)

* * *

The poet continues his ascent toward the light; he again meets with a "black spot": an eagle. This majestic bird first reviews what has been said during the first four encounters. In the beginning there was only darkness and nothingness: no creator but progressively more and more light appeared until in this fifth encounter we witness Moses cry out and apostrophe to the sun:

O soleil! nourricier du monde, anachorète!

Has he brought the light out of darkness? The eagle sees the poet, an earthworm and asks more questions:

Es-tu quelque Etre à qui la clarté dit: Va-t-en!
Sorti du grand flanc sombre et triste de Satan? (1513—1514)

But the poet cannot, as yet, claim any achievements; he is only a weakling passing by, (1515) unaware even of what Job had achieved with patience. Man is an insignificant being constantly threatened by death; his days are numbered in the maze of obscure roads. Although at times he is master of wind and lightning he is but a dream. (1634) Still the poet needs some knowledge to understand what he witnesses for the "universe is an obscure text" (1430). Has the poet translated it into his own language? The poet is then challenged for his ignorance and his lack of creativity.

Fais-tu le froid, le chaud
La nuit, l'aube (1450)

Is he at the basis of any mystery? The eagle enumerates all the great actions not yet attempted by the poet. Could he be the speaker, one of the great discontented of the black immensity? (1500). On the bench of the accused, the poet is criticized for not being a creator, for having the ephemeral life of a plain man without tomorrow, a plain man unable to compete with the one who creates:

Fantômes! vous flottez sur les heures obscures

> Dans ce monde où l'on voit passer quelques figures!
> Hommes, qu'êtes-vous donc? Des Visages pensifs.
> . . . Vous souffrez à toute heure et de tous les côtés.
> A quoi bon? étant tous au néant emportés. (1653—1655)

By contrast, the creator is an eternal sower who, when opening his hand spreads in space the lights of the stars, a handful of golden fruitful grains; although, occasionally, even the creator is threatened by a leviathan, a monster of primitive chaos capable of swallowing the sun (Chevalier, Vol. III, p. 120). That Moses should be mentioned by the eagle, the bird of light and illumination, an image of the sun, appears to also have a significance; both man and bird had visions of the creator, both venturing (in the poem) on the heights of Mt Sinai.[17] According to tradition, this solar bird has also a piercing sight; he sees all from afar; he is in some ways omniscient; therefore, king of the heights, he symbolizes, not only transcendental power but spiritual ascent, having bonds with the heavens which have conferred upon him a special gift in order to allow him to remain on high in the unchartered heavens. (Chevalier, Vol. I. pp. 21—27).

* * *

With the beak of an eagle and the body of a lion, the griffon, the next winged being met during the poet's ascent, reflects both the symbolism of two natures, of earth and of the sky. He evokes the humane and the divine, participating in the terrestrial power of the lion and of the celestial energy of the eagle. Among the Greeks, reports Chevalier (pp. 389—390), the griffon was also a symbol of strength and vigilance, but at the same time represented an obstacle to be surmounted in order to reach the treasure or the goal to be achieved. This dual nature is also reflected in the sixth section of the poem "Dieu". Man is both mind and matter and because man is matter, he is responsible for evil in the world which has manifested itself since the fall of Adam:

> Et depuis ce jour-là, l'urne amère est remplie.
> Sous la faute d'Adam tout le genre humain plie. (1731—1732)

Follows a lengthy description of the horrors befalling man who has let his spirit be controlled by his flesh:

> Toute l'humanité tinte comme un beffroi.
> Partout l'horreur, le râle et le rire, et l'effroi.

Toute bouche est ulcère et toute faîte est cratère.
Un bruit si monstrueux sort de toute la terre
Que la nuit, veuve en deuil, dit au jour qui rougit:
C'est le tigre qui parle ou l'homme qui rugit. (1745—1750)

However, there is a redemption for the man whose spirit is the receptacle of a ray of light, in other words there is hope for the man who has felt the pangs of creation:

Mais le livre de vie est là, divin registre,
L'homme, c'est l'âme; l'homme est l'hôte d'un rayon,
Et la matière seule est la damnation. (1780—1781)

At this point the griffon, an eye on the firmament, staring at the infinite, as if intoxicated by the rays, lion because of his mane, eagle because of his wing, sings an hymn to the creator-poet who, with a word, created tangibles and mystery, everything that can be named and everything that must be suppressed (1929). Nowhere better than in the few lines that follow, the middle and turning point of the poem, is it clearer that the hymn being sung here is not to the gods of any religion but to the god creator, who will eventually be recognized by posterity with a burst of light:[18]

Dieu fait évanouir les gonds des villes fortes;
Entre ses doigts distraits il tord le pâle éclair;
Le grand serpent lui semble un cheveu dans la mer.
Il est le grand poète, il est le grand prophète (1930—1935)

* * *

The seventh section of the poem is nothing less than an hymn to progress and an ode to man's creative spirits. All the great accomplishments of erudites, researchers, investigators through the ages, of all countries, of all types, of all places are mentioned by an angel with a black wing (1978) which may be a reference to Corinthians II (11:14); the angel of light is one of the names of Satan; this is based on Paul's second letter stating "and no marvel for Satan himself is transformed into an angel of light." That this angel of light is Satan would fit much better into this poem than any other interpretations since creation comes out of darkness; in this section Hugo sees progress coming of evil; in other words, there is no vaccine against the plague until there is a plague. In a long series of scintillating eidetic reductions, Hugo brings out some of the gifts to humanity made by the great of mankind honoring, among many others, Columbus who "plucked a continent in the depth of the horizons"; Pythagoras who subjected a shadow to his scrutiny; Halley, of the comet, a bursting harbinger; Harvey, who said, "blood flows and man lives"; Franklin, who tamed lightning and of course, Gutenberg

> fait du jour, de l'amour, de la vie
> Avec le plomb fondu du vieux supplice humain; (2120—2121)

What better honors to printing that these two verses! Writers, Dante and Shakespeare are included in the listing of great inventors. Others like Diderot and Rousseau are not named but mentioned in the verses

> Ils sont tous dans le vrai, le beau et dans l'utile.
> Allez! Prenez la bêche et bêchez le jardin! (2132—33)

Let us note that the passage I just cited begins with Eve who dared to seek knowledge and ends with Adam who failed to investigate for himself. Revealed religions as it is pictured here are impediments and are neither salvation nor a road to truth.

Explaining all that has gone on before in the cavern inhabited in total darkness by the bat, in the owl sphere, in the dual field of the raven and up to his own etheral space, the angel states that each step obliterating darkness has been through a luminous verb:

> Car, sur chaque échelon de l'échelle où meurt l'ombre,
> Le verbe lumineux succéde au verbe sombre;
> On monte à la parole après le begaiement. (2019—2021)

and we are talking about progress which must necessarily come out of evil. Let us listen to Victor Hugo.[19] What is progress? A luminous disaster, dropping as a bomb and remaining as a star. In a flamboyant exhortation and incandescent rhetoric Hugo calls to arms:

> Allons, marche, esprit de l'homme! Avance.
> Accepte des flèaux l'énorme connivence!
> Marche! Oui, souvent, douteux pour qui l'a souhaité,
> Le progrès, effrayant à force de clarté,
> A, quand il vient broyer le faux, l'abject, l'horrible,
> Des apparitions de crinière terrible.

... Le progrès, qui poursuit ses vaincus haletants,
Qui veut qu'on soit, qu'on marche et qu'on creuse et qu'on taille,
Pousse ses légions d'azur dans la bataille,
Ses penseurs constellés, éthérés, spacieux
Tous ces olympiens vêtus d'un pan des cieux. (2187—2202)

Invention and creation are what make men divine; it is through creation that man reaches Mount Olympus, domain of the Gods. It is through inventions and creations that divine men, solar men crush evil and darkness:

Et ces hommes divins, et ces hommes solaires
Font marcher leurs bienfaits au pas de leurs colères.
Le bien saisit le mal et l'écrase à son tour.
Accepte l'incendie invincible du jour,
Homme! va! jette-toi dans ces gueules ouvertes
Qu'on nomme inventions, nouveautés, découvertes!
    L'esprit humain chercheur de Dieu, voit par moments
Les rayons s'irriter comme des flamboiements,
Quand poussant devant lui la foule coutumière,
    Il va de l'hydre d'ombre à l'hydre de lumière!
N'importe! ne crains pas le progrès rugissant
Pour le sage, le bon, le juste et l'innocent!
Ne crains pas le progrès dévorant les ténèbres! (2207—2219)

In this ascending movement progress is annihilating darkness and gloom.

* * *

Continuing his move upward, the poet meets a blinding light adorned with two white wings and he is told of a God creator who creates a world only because he has seen a void, an abyss. The "light" asks, adding a questionable attribute, how to show God, "this frightening formless" to the poet; however the question is more intended to mean how to be God than how to see God for then is discussed the birth of idea undone by words. How is one to visualize a God; how is one to grasp the englobing power of an omniscient creator? Is he Allah, Brahma, Pan, Jesus, or Jehovah? (3545) The inclusion, in this array of Gods, of Jesus, a man who created a religion but a man who has been seen, betrays the question. Anyone can be a creator; some with known faces, others will always remain an idea without embodiment although their spirit live on.

* * *

The poem ends with the birth of a new creation by the poet who then dies. This is perfectly consistent with a deconstructive interpretation. Once an author, an inventor has created a work or publicized an invention, that invention, that work, that poem no longer belongs to him but to the world. For the world in the majority of cases the author is dead, only the luminosity of the invention, of the poem, lives.

The first of the winged beings encountered was a bat which was supposed to represent atheism; the second an owl, describing skepticism; then came a bird of ill-omen, the raven, a spokesman of manichaeism; next the spirit was confronted by a vulture that was to explain paganism; the eagle followed as a representant of mosaism; the griffon talks of christianity; an angel told about rationalism; and lastly these winged beings were followed by light, or by "what does not as yet have a name" presumably, by what will tell about things to come.

In this epic are indeed examined some religions, not necessarily in their order of creation in the world but as progressive appearance of light out of an abyss of darkness, in a universe englobed in obscurity. That the religions are not given in chronological order is clearly an indication that the poet is not writing a history of religions; that some of the most important religions, or philosophical systems, are omitted, confucianism, buddhism, taoism, shintoism, islam, hinduism is also an important factor; that the form adopted to give that interpretation is poetry also indicates that Hugo is looking at a phenomenon — progress not religion — not as a philosopher but as a poet.

A "retroactive reading" a term used by Michel Riffaterre,[20] to explain a method of decoding double signs will also indicates that the different stages achieved by man in his search, his attempt at bringing progress, represent the creative act, a creation to come out of darkness. So that this interpretation is made from one point of view only; that of the ascent from darkness toward enlightenment, from ignorance to truth, from nothingness to creation, and in particular the creative act of the poet. This theme which is beyond the scope of this paper, reappears in numerous works of Victor Hugo, in *La légende des siècles*, in *Les Rayons et les ombres*, in *Promontorium Somnii* where he states that the work of a writer belongs to what does not exist; it is leveled by

From darkness to Creation in Hugo

IX — DAY	Spirit — creation total absence of darkness
VIII — LIGHT	Implies some darkness
VII — ANGEL	
VI — GRIFFON	
V — EAGLE	
IV — VULTURE	
III — RAVEN	
II — OWL	
I — BAT	Matter — Darkness total absence of light no creator

darkness with nothingness; a forbiding defiance of light weights on it. The vast iniquity of the gloom submerges it . . . until a burst of light brings it forth to the attention of posterity.[21]

Now, in conclusion, if we examine again the original medieval latin title, that is SOLITUDINES COELI, which roughly translated means The Loneliness (in the plural) of the Heaven or the Deserted Spheres of the Summit, again we see that this text is not about the idea of God or a history of some religions. It is about the loneliness of the creator of new ideas, a god in his own right, often jeered and ridiculed by society, but literally a man, a pseudo god, who has seen the light.

Northern Illinois University

NOTES

[1] This is the second section in the Gallimard Pléiade Edition, (1950) edited by Jacques Truchet, which includes "La Légende des siècles", "La Fin de Satan" and "Dieu." pp. 945—1143 and notes pp. 1281—1324. However, the critical edition (3740 verses) published in 1960 by René Journet et Guy Robert (Nizet, 1960) does not include the fragments that make up the bulk of the Pleiade Edition.

[2] Charles Renouvier, *Victor Hugo, le philosophe* (Paris: Armand Colin, 1900). Renouvier states (p. 311) "Une doctrine, c'est la conclusion que nous devons tirer . . . de l'hésitation que l'auteur mettait à se séparer de son oeuvre."

[3] As reported by Journet and Robert, p. 5.

[4] Inserted one below the other are the following mentions to be found, according to Journet & Robert, in the Folio 3: "L'athéisme nihil — le scepticisme quid? — le manichéisme duplex — le paganisme multiplex — le mosaisme unus — le christianisme triplex — le rationalisme homo — ce qui n'a pas encore de nom dies — ce qui n'a pas encore de nom deus." p. 191.

[5] Journet & Robert, p. 192: "Aucun oiseau n'est nommé en tête. Si les éditeurs de IN ont cependant cru bon de les faire figurer à cette place, c'est que chacune d'elles caractérise en gros le développement qu'on l'a fait précéder. Mais elle en laisse souvent échapper la véritable signification."

[6] This edition is the one used here. Numbers in parenthesis refers to the lines of the poem in that edition.

[7] Michel Riffaterre, *Sémiotique de la poésie* (Paris: Editions du Seuil, 1978), p. 12 (My translation).

[8] Ch. Renouvier, p. 310.

[9] Wendy Nicholas Greenberg, *The Power of Rhetoric: Hougo's Metaphor and Poetics* (New York: Peter Lang, 1985), p. 81.

[10] Journet & Robert, p. 194. "Dans l'univers de Hugo, tout songe, tout peut parler. Il est tout naturel qu'au cours de son ascension l'esprit s'entende exposer par des oiseaux le sens des philosophies et des religions."

[11] Robert Scholes, "Deconstruction and Communication", *Critical Inquiry* **14** (1988): 279.

[12] My translation: No one is here to complete this black sketch/ The universe is monstrous and light is but a dream;/ No will, no law, no poles, no medium;/ All is a chaos of nothingness.

[13] Jean Chevalier et Alain Gheerbrant, *Dictionnaires des symboles* (Paris: Seghers, 1973), Vol. I, p. 344—47.

[14] "What is the meaning/ Of this blind and deaf world, this dark structure,/ This cloistered, sinister creation/ Without window, without roof, without door, without entrance, without exit, o Terror."

[15] What is destiny? What is Nature?/ But only the same text translated into two languages?/ Is it not only a double branch with the same fruit?

[16] Yves Bonnefoy *Dictionnaire des mythologies* (Paris: Flammarion, 1981), pp. 500—4.

[17] Here C. Renouvier has a harsh criticism, denying the poet Hugo the right to poetic license: "Le critique est obligée de relever, dans cette partie du poème, un contresens, une confusion injustifiable entre la doctrine monothéiste et le monisme brahamanique, entre la création et l'émanation." p. 332. This is simply another example of the erroneous conclusions drawn by critics.

[18] This theme is especially clear in the work entitled *Promontorium Sommni*.

[19] "Qu'est-ce que le progrès? un lumineux désastre,/ Tombant comme la bombe et restant comme l'astre./ L'avenir vient avec le souffle d'un grand vent;/ Il chasse rudement les peuples en avant;/ il fait sous les gibets des tremblements de terre;/ Il creuse brusquement, sous l'erreur qu'il fait taire,/ Sous tout ce qui fut lâche, atroce, vil, petit,/ Des ouvertures d'ombre où le mal s'engloutit./ Va, lutte, Esprit de l'homme! (Verse 2167—75).

[20] "La lecture rétroactive apparaît comme la méthode indispensable au décodage des signes doubles; premièrement, parce que le signe renvoie à un paradigme et qu'un paradigme ne peut être reconnu que s'il a été assez développé dans un espace donné pour que des constantes puissent être perçues." In *Sémiotique de la poésie* (Paris: Editions du Seuil, 1978), p. 119.

[21] L'oeuvre fait partie de ce qui n'existe pas; elle est nivelée par l'ombre avec le néant. Un glacial défi de lumière pèse sur elle. La vaste iniquité des ténèbres la submerge . . . Soudain brusquement, un jet de lumière éclate, il frappe une cime, puis la clarté augmente, le jouor se fait." *Promontorium Somnii*, p. 456

BIBLIOGRAPHY

Bonnefoy, Y. *Dictionnaire des mythologies* (Paris: Flammarion, 1981).

Chevalier, J. and A. Gheerbrant. *Dictionnaire des symboles* (Paris: Seghers, 1973—1974).

Glauser, A. *La Poétique de Victor Hugo* (Paris: Nizet, 1978).

Greenberg, W. Nicholas. *The Power of Rhetoric: Hugo's Metaphor and Poetics* (New York: Peter Lang, 1985).

Huguet, E. *La Couleur, la lumière, et l'ombre dans les métaphores de Victor Hugo* (Paris: Hachette, 1905).

Journet, R. and G. Robert, *Dieu* (Paris: Nizet, 1960).

Nash, S. *Les Contemplations of Victor Hugo. An Allegory of the Creative Process* (Princeton: University Press, 1976).

Renouvier, C. *Victor Hugo, Le Philosophe* (Paris: Armand Colin, 1900).

Riffaterre, M. "La poésie métaphysique de Victor Hugo." *Romanic Review* (Decembre 1960): 268—76.

CHRISTOPHER LALONDE

ILLUMINATING *LIGHT IN AUGUST*

While at the University of Virginia in 1957, William Faulkner was asked if "the title of *Light in August* came from a colloquialism for the completion of pregnancy?" Faulkner said no, and then added, "in my country in August there's a peculiar quality to light and that's what that title means. It has in a sense nothing to do with the book at all, the story at all" (*Faulkner in the University* 74). Faulkner's answer to the student's question seems to be characteristically perfunctory, but upon examination it also appears to be characteristically evasive. To say that the meaning behind the title has in a sense nothing to do with *Light in August* is to at the same time suggest that in some other sense the title is both meaningful and integral to our understanding of the novel which, when begun, had the working title of *Dark House*. Faulkner initially saw his manuscript focusing on the figure of Gail Hightower, the dispossessed and ineffectual minister bound by his vision of an heroic past, but as he worked the story became more that of Lena Grove and, especially, Joe Christmas. Faulkner moves from darkness to light, then, and in so doing suggests that there is something to be illuminated, to be revealed in *Light in August*.

John T. Matthews characterizes *The Sound and the Fury* as a "novel that comes to yearn for an ending," and the same can be said for *Light in August*. Thematically, Joe Christmas yearns to be free of the pattern of his life, while at the same time realizing that he has "never got outside that circle . . . never broken out of the ring of what . . . [he has] already done and cannot ever undo" (*LIA* 373—374). Lena Grove longs to find Lucas Burch, marry, and in so doing end her journey. Byron Bunch wishes to be free of Lena and Lucas, while at the same time longing for marital union with Lena. Gail Hightower simply wishes once more for peaceful days where he can wait until nightfall for his vision to "sweep into sight, borne now upon a cloud of phantom dust" (*LIA* 544). Faulkner, however, plays with the end: we are left uncertain of Hightower's fate; we are unsure of what will become of Byron in his pursuit to be either free of Lena or married to her. What is more, *Light*

149

A-T. Tymieniecka (ed.), Analecta Husserliana, Vol. XXXVIII, 149—161.
© 1992 *Kluwer Academic Publishers. Printed in the Netherlands.*

in August refuses to fix or ultimately figure the two protagonists and their individual strands of the novel.

What then is illuminated in *Light in August*, and how is it illuminated? Among the fundamental properties of light is the characteristic of conveying or transporting information. The information concerns the source of the light itself and any objects that have either partially absorbed, reflected, or refracted the beam of light on the journey from its source to the eye of an observer. In *Light in August* Faulkner introduces three characters late in the novel which transport vital information. Warwick Wadlington points out that Faulkner "disregards a convention of the 'well-made' novel by having three new characters [Gavin Stevens, Percy Grimm, and a travelling furniture salesman] materialize abruptly in the last section of the novel to act as significant narrators and actors" (146—147). Elsewhere I have argued that Faulkner turns the narrative over to the traveling salesman in order to disclose the salesman's understanding of language as power and his need to master Lena Grove in language. Here I wish to suggest that the light in *Light in August* conveys information which illuminates both the fictionalizing process, in order that we might better understand how it is to be human, and the ideologies governing a culture, in order that we might better understand how a culture operates; the light is particularly telling in the nineteenth chapter of the novel, for it is there that Gavin Stevens and Percy Grimm appear and we see how Joe Christmas is ultimately figured.

Joe Christmas has been characterized as "perhaps the most divided and doomed of all Faulkner's major characters" (Minter 130). Unsure of his ancestry, yet convinced that his father was at least part black, Christmas spends his life repeating a pattern that ensures that he will remain on the margin of society. At the same time, Christmas is presented in such a way that the members of various communities are forced to read him before deciding how to deal with him. Consider, for instance, his initial appearance in the novel:

Byron Bunch knows this: It was one Friday morning three years ago. And the group of men at work in the planer shed looked up, and saw the stranger standing there, watching them. They did not know how long he had been there. He looked like a tramp, yet not like a tramp either. His shoes were dusty and his trousers were soiled too. But they were of a decent serge, sharply creased, and his shirt was soiled but it was a white shirt, and he wore a tie and a stiffbrim straw hat that was quite new, cocked at an angle arrogant and baleful above his still face. He did not look like a professional hobo in his professional rags, but there was something definitely rootless about him, as though no town or city was his, no street, no walls, no square of earth his home. And that he carried this knowledge with him always as though it were a banner, with a quality ruthless, lonely and almost proud. (*LIA* 33)

We see that the narrative refuses to fix Christmas, refuses to give the reader anything without in the next instant taking it away. Christmas looks like a tramp; Christmas does not look like a tramp. Christmas does not look like a hobo; Christmas does have a rootless quality. It remains for the men to read Christmas, both in look and in name, in order to figure out the figure posed silently before them.

The men are especially compelled to deal with Christmas' name. The discussion they have centering on Christmas' nationality and color — "Is he a foreigner?" and "Did you ever hear of a white man named Christmas?" are the central questions asked — leads Byron Bunch to think that "a man's name, which is supposed to be just the sound of who he is, can be somehow an augur of what he will do, if other men can only read the meaning in time" (*LIA* 35).

The men, the community of Jefferson, and the reader must read Christmas, his name, and the oxymoronic "white nigger" (*LIA* 379) which becomes his label and drives *Light in August*. That reading, that act of interpretation in light of the information conveyed by the narrative of *Light in August*, must necessarily come to terms with Christmas' final flight and subsequent murder. Christmas' last acts, presented so curiously by Faulkner in the nineteenth chapter of the novel, are peculiarly illuminated by a light which Faulkner makes certain we read.

The narrator is the actualization of the authorial shaping voice of any work. Throughout the first eighteen chapters of *Light in August* the narrator exhibits ample control of both the narrative and the story. Consider two examples: "From that face squinted and still behind the curling smoke from the cigarette which was not touched once with hand until it burned down and was spat out and ground beneath a heel, Joe was to acquire one of his own mannerisms. But not yet" (*LIA* 196); and, "This is not what Byron knows now" (*LIA* 38). In both instances what is suggested is that the narrator knows the story, knows what is yet to come, and that on occasions such as the two pointed out the narrator takes pains to show us what he knows — what, that is, is already there but which he chooses to not yet reveal. Both examples suggest that the narrator possesses the story and is in control of its disclosure as narrative. The narrator is in a powerful position, and his stance suggests an understanding of writing as currency to be alternately hoarded and spent with the aegis of discourse's power.

Given the narrator's control of both the story and its disclosure as narrative we must ask ourselves why Gavin Stevens is allowed to take control of the story of Christmas' final flight from bondage. Stevens, the district attorney who left the South to be educated at Harvard, offers his theory of why Christmas either fled to or finally arrived at Hightower's house. That theory is presented to us as Stevens' recapitulation of the story Stevens tells to his visiting friend from out of town (*LIA* 491). To the extent that Stevens' narrative is a recapitulation of a story of the event, we need to see Stevens as both reader of the story and critic of the story as he extracts from it the materials which comprise his interpretation. Stevens' act of fictionalizing can be read in light of Husserlian phenomenology. For Edmund Husserl, the "element which makes up the life of phenomenology as of all eidetical science is fiction" (*Ideas* 184). To understand the nature of fictions is to gain access to the formal shaping powers of the mind because the act of fictionalizing creates a non-referential construct, noesis without noema, directing us to the representational qualities of the mind. *Light in August* reveals that Stevens' story is a fiction, and therefore as we read "we glance . . . towards the 'image' [Stevens' story] (not towards that of which it is the copy)" [the actual event] and, rather than apprehending something real, apprehend "an image, a fiction" (*Ideas* 291). Fictions ideally illuminate pure consciousness, by virtue of the governing neutrality-modification, but at the same time Anna-Teresa Tymieniecka reminds us that "the spectator [or in this case the narrator] plays an instrumental role in the unfolding of the spectacle as such" (6). Gavin Stevens plays an instrumental role in the spectacle of Christmas' final hour. Although he was not present to see any of the action, Stevens' acts of selection and combination by which he creates his fiction inscribe precisely his and Jefferson's ideological position regarding race. The representational qualities of the mind in this case, disclosed by the fiction, in turn illuminate the shaping or doxic quality of Stevens' discourse.

He begins " 'I think I know why it was, why he ran into Hightower's house for refuge at the last' " (*LIA* 491). In so doing, Stevens linguistically defines himself and asserts his subjectivity. According to Emile Benveniste, " 'I' refers to the act of individual discourse in which it is pronounced, and by this it designates the speaker" (226). The instance of discourse, its orality, is what enables the "speaker to proclaim himself as the 'subject,' " and the formalization of I enables the "speaker to appropriate to himself an entire language" (226). For Benveniste, "language puts forth 'empty' forms which each speaker in the exercise of discourse appropriates to himself and relates to his 'person' " (227) and the "language" he has appropriated. Stevens does nothing less than fill the empty forms of language and the figure of Christmas, and his account defines a self that is governed by and grounded in community. Given the nature of language this is understandable: the speaking subject's attempt at autonomous rule of the narrative is mitigated by language's inherent arbitrariness. The necessary inequivalancy between signifier and signified demands that speaker and audience, "I" and "you," share a sign system in order that communication be achieved. That shared sign system, however, is always culturally determined. Consequently, "every utterance must be conceived as having various levels of signification, and issuing from multiple voices. It is spoken not only by the palpable voice of a concrete speaker, writer, or cluster of mechanical apparatuses, but the anonymous voices of cultural codes which invade it in the form of connotation" (Silverman 50). Reading Gavin Stevens' discourse, then, will enable us to read the other voice(s) present, to see the light in which Faulkner casts Jefferson and, by extension, a culture.

The voice of ideology permeates Steven's reading. The French philosopher Louis Althusser argues that ideology is "simply the 'familiar,' 'well-known,' transparent myths by which a society can recognize itself (but not know itself)" and then adds, "What is the ideology of a society or a period if it is not that society's or period's consciousness of itself, that is, an immediate material which spontaneously implies, looks for and naturally finds its forms in the image of a consciousness of self living the totality of its world in the transparency of its own myths" (144). Ideology, then, is a "system of representations which promotes on the part of the subject an 'imaginary' relation to the 'real' condition of its existence" (Silverman 215). Ideology is, we see, a fiction. We can think of the ideology of modern industrial capitalism, which creates the imaginary corresponding relation between currency, or the wage, and labor in order to cover or mask the laborer's alienation from the product produced in the name of surplus value. Ideologies, "systems of representation," govern societies, just as they govern the social structuring mechanism of rituals and rites of passage, and Althusser argues that we are "always already subjects," and hence can never be free of the restrictive figuring power of the ideologies of a culture.

The ideology comes to us from "cultural agents:" i.e. "a person or a textual construct which relays ideological information" (Silverman 48). In Chapter Nineteen of *Light in August*, Gavin Stevens fills the function of cultural agent, asserts his subjectivity and, in so doing, discloses the ideological information, the transparent myths, governing his reading of Joe Christmas.

Stevens' interpretation rests upon what Eric Sundquist acutely terms the "fantasy" of Christmas' black blood. Sundquist argues that Stevens' reading of Christmas' actions is rooted "in service of an unbearable anxiety that, because it constantly threatens to dissolve into anarchy both a social and a psychic structure, can only be contained by the simplest of theories — one that is necessarily rendered farcical by renouncing the dangerous complexities generated in the surrounding actions of the novel" (70). That anxiety, which is nothing short of the anxiety of figuration (Is Christmas black? is Christmas white? how can we tell?), moves Stevens to articulate a theory of Christmas' warring or disharmonious blood. Stevens feels that, despite the potential promise offered by his grandmother and Hightower, "there was too much running with" (*LIA* 495) Christmas, and that "his blood would not be quiet, let him save it. It would not be either one or the other and let his body save itself" (*LIA* 495).

Stevens, however, discloses his overdetermined attempt at figuration when, before he offers his theory of Christmas' disharmonious and disquieting blood, he tells his friend that "of course I don't know what she [Mrs. Hines] told him [Christmas]. I don't believe any man could reconstruct that scene" (*LIA* 494). This disclosure necessitates that we turn our attention to Stevens as narrator even as we confront his theory. Then we see that Stevens positions himself as reader, writer, and critic. He is reading and interpreting his narrative, his construction. His overdetermination is not directed so much at fixing the figure of Christmas for its own sake, however, as it is at incidentally fixing the figure of Christmas in such a fashion that Jefferson will not be indicted for its actions. Stevens' reading makes Christmas solely responsible for his death: "It was the black blood which swept him by his own desire beyond the aid of any man," where, crouching behind an overturned table, he "defied the black blood for the last time" and "let them shoot him to death" (*LIA* 496). The actions of the townspeople begin with the townspeople's hushed speculation upon the black man the sheriff questions immediately after Joanna's body is found. They want the black man to be the murderer, and they "hoped that she had been ravished too: at least once before her throat was cut and at least once afterward" (*LIA* 315—316) in order that their deepest fears and anxieties might be realized. The actions culminate with the frenzied chase of Christmas and his castration at the hands of Percy Grimm. Stevens' attempt at figuration for the sake of social and cultural salvation, then, only serves as an act of self-figuration and indictment as we see the ideology dictating both his discourse and the community.

The careful post-structuralist reader, such as Sundquist, can see and hear the other voices, the voice of the repressed, in Stevens' figuring interpretation of Christmas. What is most telling is the critique of community and culture which the narrative of *Light in August* advances, as well as how that critique is constructed. In order to understand exactly how *Light in August* critiques community, discloses ideology's voice, we must read the novel's supplement to Stevens' reading: the narrator's own disclosure of Christmas' final flight. Faulkner shows us the subjectivity Stevens is conferring upon the "you" of his discourse, the visiting college professor, by using the enjambing supplement or "interlocking shot" by which the text forces us to re-read and re-interpret Stevens' reading and interpretation. The supplement suggests the deficiency inherent in Stevens' reading and interpretation, a deficiency disclosed by Stevens' admission of overdetermination. That supplement, or re-rendering, calls Stevens' reading into question at least in so far as the later narrative locates the racial and misogynist anxieties in the figure of Percy Grimm rather than in the narrator. More is available however, as the narrative shows how Christmas is both individually unfigured and socially figured. In order to see how this is so we must realize that the final reading of Christmas is also a reading of Percy Grimm.

As driven as Joe Christmas, Percy Grimm is perhaps Faulkner's most reprehensible character because of the object of his desire. Of Grimm we learn that,

He could now see his life opening before him, uncomplex and inescapable as a barren corridor, completely freed now of ever again having to think or decide, the burden which he now assumed and carried as bright and weightless and martial as his insignatory brass: a sublime and implicit faith in physical courage and blind obedience, and a belief that the white race is superior to any and all other races and that the

American is superior to any and all other white races and that the American uniform is superior to all men, and that all that would ever be required of him in payment for this belief, this privilege, would be his own life. (*LIA* 498)

We might recall that in *The Sound and the Fury*, Deacon dresses for parades and imagines a better place for himself in the near future; the result is comic and touching at the same time. Percy Grimm dresses in his captain's uniform and parades down town on "each national holiday that had any martial flavor whatever" with an "air half belligerent and half the selfconscious pride of a boy" (*LIA* 498); the result is a caricature at once ludicrous and painful to behold.

That caricature is presented to us with language as profoundly humorless as earlier passages in *Light in August* are profoundly humorous. Consider just this exchange between Grimm, his name an augur for his actions, and Sheriff Kennedy:

"Come here, boy," the sheriff said. Grimm halted. He did not approach; the sheriff went to him. He patted Grimm's hip with a fat hand. "I told you to leave that [pistol] at home," he said. Grimm said nothing. He watched the sheriff levelly. The sheriff sighed. "Well, if you wont, I reckon I'll have to make you a special deputy. But you aint to even show that gun unless I tell you to. You hear me?"
"Certainly not," Grimm said. "You certainly wouldn't want me to draw it if I didn't see any need to."
"I mean, not till I tell you to."
"Certainly," Grimm said, without heat, patiently, immediately. "That's what we both said. Dont you worry. I'll be there." (*LIA* 502—503)

Faulkner's language is as resolutely playful as ever, as we read the pivotal "certainly not", but it is a cold, tense, calculating play. The breakdown or failure in communication is chilling rather than funny as Grimm uses language to assert his subjectivity and therefore his immunity from the sheriff's power. Grimm's subjectivity is governed by the pistol, by the phallic symbol of authority with which Grimm will inscribe white phallocentric authority.

Grimm's immunity and subsequent domination is grounded in his belief that "We got to preserve order," that "We must let the law take its course. The law, the nation. It is the right of no civilian to sentence a man to death" (*LIA* 498). Grimm conjoins law and nation, making the one synonomous with the other, and in so doing creates a connection of greater gravity than that made in *Sanctuary* between law and community. Law is now equal with nation, with something that at once encompasses and goes beyond Southern community and culture. Grimm will take the law into his own hands, and in his own mind he justifies his actions because he does not see himself as a civilian.

And Joe Christmas' manacled hands flash, glint, glare, and glitter as Percy Grimm takes the law into his own hands and runs Christmas down. We cannot avoid those manacled hands, which cause Grimm to reason "he can't run very fast" (*LIA* 507), and which he sees "glint once like the flash of a heliograph as the sun struck the handcuffs" (*LIA* 509). Those manacled hands do nothing less than signal to Grimm, reflect the light of the sun and flash it for and into Grimm's eyes. Immediately afterward, those hands are "glinting as if on fire" (*LIA* 509), and in Hightower's house they are "full of glare and glitter like lightning bolts" (*LIA* 511).

Early in *Light in August*, before Joe Christmas enters the text, Henry Armstid and Winterbottom read the figure of Lena Grove as she walks on toward Jefferson. Then we learn that Armstid was "there to make Winterbottom an offer for a cultivator which Winterbottom wanted to sell." Armstid "looked at the sun and offered the price which he had decided to offer while lying in bed three nights ago." Winterbottom refuses the offer, Armstid looks "again at the sun" (*LIA* 10—11), and then leaves. For our purposes here what is telling is the narrator's disclosure of Armstid's looks at the sun. Armstid's act of reading works in two directions. On the one hand, to look at the sun is to figure and consequently fix the time of day by fixing the sun's position. On the other hand, to look at the sun means running the risk of blindness. The play between fixing and figuring and temporary blindness is critical in *Light in August*; Gavin Stevens, for instance, falls prey to the danger metaphorized by Armstid's look into the sun. What is more, in the novel's supplement to Steven's reading the sun becomes crucial to our understanding of Joe Christmas and of Percy Grimm's blindness.

In Derrida's "White Mythology" a brief discussion of Plato's *Republic* paranthetically centers on the sun:

In the *Republic* (VI—VII), before and after the line which presents ontology according to the analogies of proportionality, the sun appears. In order to disappear. It is there but as an invisible source of light, in a kind of insistent eclipse, more than essential, producing the essence — Being and appearing — of what is. ("WM" 242)

Light in August presents the sun as essential as well, in as much as it produces the essence, the Being and appearing, of Joe Christmas. We do not see the sun, but its light illuminates by *reflection* the bonded figure that is Christmas. It is a figure, moreover, governed by proportion, " 'I think I got some nigger blood in me' " (*LIA* 216), which creates Being, " 'If I'm not [part] black, damned if I haven't wasted a lot of time' " (*LIA* 280), at the expense of appearance, " 'He [Christmas] don't look any more like a nigger than I do' " (*LIA* 385).

Christmas does not appear to be black, and yet Grimm and Jefferson resolutely hunt him down. Why do they see Christmas as they do, read him as they do? The sun, the center, catches and is caught by the handcuffs. Those handcuffs, symbolic of law and its necessary order and place in society, are the trace of the sun. The community, and especially Percy Grimm, see Christmas in the light of the cuffs. I have already noted that the light off of the handcuffs signals, making the cuffs a heliograph which calls attention to the man whom Sundquist argues must be sacrificed, but the narrative tells us even more about those handcuffs. "Heliograph" also suggests a type of photoengraving; that is, a creative process which fixes a figure immutably. This is precisely what the cuffs do; they define Christmas for and by the community. Grimm chases after the glitter and glare. One can say that Grimm is not blinded because he is seeing what he has all along figured was there; but it would be more accurate to see that Grimm is truly blind, for that is what the narrative suggests, and that Grimm's blindness is indicative of Jefferson's blindness as well. We are at least to some extent back inside Plato's cave, as Grimm and Jefferson unknowingly employ the light off of the handcuffs to justify their reading of the figure of Christmas. They do not see Christmas at all; they see the figure cast by the governing ideological light of ugly racism and the concomitant anxieties regarding misogyny. Heliograph suggests both 'here I am' and 'here I am figured'; Faulkner's narrative supplement to Steven's reading is unrelenting in making clear Steven's wronging figuration by showing us the false light in which Jefferson sees, reads, Christmas.

Grimm's pursuit leads him and several others to Hightower's house, "bringing with them into its stale and cloistral dimness something of the savage summer sunlight which they had just left" (*LIA* 511). Consequently, "It [the sunlight] was upon them, of them: its shameless savageness" (*LIA* 511). The men are at once backlit by that savage sun and of it, embody it, in their actions. Hightower almost immediately recognizes the light in the men's eyes: "Gentlemen!" Hightower said. Then he said: "Men! Men!" (*LIA* 511). At first the minister couches his

plea in the language of society and community, but Hightower immediately replaces his initial appellation with more general and more
humane "men." It is as though Hightower understands that his only
hope is to appeal to the men's humanity; to appeal to their social nature
is to tap into the very source of their savage and misguided actions.

Hightower's call echoes Althusser's process of hailing and interpellation by which ideology " 'recruits' subjects among the individuals (it
recruits them all) or 'transforms' the individuals into subjects (it transforms them all)" (174). Earlier, I pointed out that Stevens hailed his
friend and the reader and that Sheriff Kennedy attempted, and failed, to
hail Percy Grimm; here Hightower attempts the same sort of hailing
action, but the men refuse to recognize Hightower, blinded as they are
by their own ideological light, and therefore refuse to see his subjectivity with its more humane ideology. Interpellation is denied; Hightower's discourse is cut off by Grimm.

Hightower fails, as he must, and Christmas dies. Although he
attempts to hide behind an overturned table, he cannot hide "the bright
and glittering hands . . . resting upon the upper edge" (*LIA* 512).
Faulkner keeps both the hands and the "savage" light before us. But
how is Christmas finally figured? In order to answer that question we
must look closely at the final scene of Christmas' life:

But the Player was not done yet. When the others reached the kitchen they saw the
table flung aside now and Grimm stooping over the body. When they approached to
see what he was about, they saw that the man was not dead yet, and when they saw
what Grimm was doing one of the men gave a choked cry and stumbled back into the
wall and began to vomit. Then Grimm too sprang back, flinging behind him the bloody
butcher knife.

"Now you'll let white women alone, even in hell," he said. But the man on the floor
had not moved. He just lay there, with his eyes open and empty of everything save
consciousness, and with something, a shadow, about his mouth. For a long moment he
looked up at them with peaceful and unfathomable and unbearable eyes. Then his face,
body, all, seemed to collapse, to fall in upon itself, and from out the slashed garments
about his hips and loins the pent black blood seemed to rush like a released breath. It
seemed to rush out of his pale body like the rush of sparks from a rising rocket, upon
that black blast the man seemed to rise soaring into their memories forever and ever.
They are not to lose it, in whatever peaceful valleys, beside whatever placid and
reassuring streams of old age, in the mirroring faces of whatever children they will
contemplate old disasters and newer hopes. It will be there, musing, quiet, steadfast,
not fading and not particularly threatful, but of itself alone serene, of itself alone
triumphant.

(*LIA* 512–513)

What is figured in that scene, what is fixed, is Percy Grimm. Christmas leaves the text, becoming the indefinite pronoun "he" and the indefinitive possessive "his". The preponderence of indefinite pronouns suggests a lack of immutability concerning Christmas. We would do well to remember that linguistically the third person "he" is "not a 'person'" (Benveniste 197); it has no subjectivity. The narrative discloses its refusal to fix Christmas, and the disclosure suggesting a lack of closure works at least two ways. On the other hand, Christmas is never figured in his own mind, and the text indicates this by ultimately denying him the fixing proper noun. Christmas' internal ideology, with which he reinvented and rediscovered himself "in the same ideological representations" (Silverman 217) by which he first knows himself, literally forces him to be a nobody, a nothing. At the same time, the text fixes Grimm and the community in the telling light of an ideology that enables neither Grimm nor Jefferson to need to identify Christmas any more specifically than "nigger murderer." At the end of chapter nineteen, then, only Grimm remains to complete the task sanctioned and required by the community. What is more, there is nothing to suggest that it is Christmas that rises "soaring into their memories forever and ever." It makes more sense that the figure of the apotheosis by Percy Grimm. After all, it is Grimm who is described as "prophetlike" (*LIA* 500), and the image of Grimm standing above the man he has just castrated is undoubtedly memorable. Moreover, it is Grimm who is serene and triumphant, Grimm who is "not particularly threatful" because he is nothing more than the active agent of the community. Whatever the case, it seems clear that while Grimm is quite clearly delineated, Christmas remains fundamentally unfigured in either spoken or written discourse. In fixing Percy Grimm, however, *Light in August* unremittingly figures what is vulgar, what is both common and reprehensible, about the man *and* the community. Christmas' rite of passage ends, then, with both the closure of death and the narrative's disclosure of his continued enclosure in the community's race-governed voice of ideology.

Wesleyan College, North Carolina

REFERENCES

Althusser, Louis, *Lenin and Philosophy*, trans. Ben Brewster (London: Monthly Review Press, 1971).

ILLUMINATING *LIGHT IN AUGUST* 161

Benveniste, Emile, *Problems in General Linguistics*, trans. Mary Elizabeth Meeks (Coral Gables, Fla.: University of Miami Press, 1971).

Derrida, Jacques, "White Mythology: Metaphor in the Text of Philosophy", *Margins of Philosophy*, trans. Alan Bass (Chicago: The University of Chicago Press, 1982), pp. 207—272.

Faulkner, William, *Faulkner in the University*, eds. Fredrick Gwynn & Josephy Blotner (Charlottesville: University of Virginia Press, 1959).

Faulkner, William, *Light in August*: The Corrected Text (New York: Vintage Books, 1987).

Husserl, Edmund, *Ideas* (New York: Colliers, 1962).

Matthews, John T., *The Play of Faulkner's Language* (Ithaca, N.Y.: Cornell University Press, 1982).

Minter, David, *William Faulkner: His Life and Work* (Baltimore: The Johns Hopkins University Press, 1980).

Silverman, Kaja, *The Subject of Semiotics* (New York: Oxford University Press, 1983).

Sundquist, Eric, *Faulkner: The House Divided* (Baltimore: The Johns Hopkins University Press, 1983).

Tymieniecka, Anna-Teresa, "The Aesthetics of Nature in the Human Condition", *Poetics of the Elements in the Human Condition: The Sea* (Dordrecht: D. Reidel, 1985).

Wadlington, Warwick, *Reading Faulknerian Tragedy* (Ithaca, N.Y.: Cornell University Press, 1987).

L. M. FINDLAY

IMAGINING EPISTEMOLOGY: PLATO AND ROMANTIC LUMINARIES

The tradition of visual epistemology is venerable, complex, and remarkable for the ways in which it employs notions of light in the name of enlightenment. In this essay I will examine perhaps the most famous contribution to this tradition made by Plato in the seventh book of the *Republic*, and I will do so in an effort to redefine the poetic and philosophical components of that reflexive gesture by means of which the human subject analyses and/or imagines the conditions of consciousness of the self and its situatedness. I will then examine variously imaginative appropriations of this Platonic legacy by figures of the romantic period with a "view" to redefining the *particular* appeal of Plato to a generation of artists and thinkers haunted by the pretensions and deficiencies of instrumental reason. What will emerge from this account will, I hope, be a sharper and richer sense of the role of the "elemental" in poetic and philosophical *making*, and a fuller understanding of why some versions of knowing have had more authority and influence than others.

First, then, let me turn to the passage in the *Republic* where Plato has recourse to a memorably sustained analogy to bring out aspects of the scene of knowing that will supplement the account given via the figure of the four-part line in Book Six:

"Next," said I, "compare our nature in respect of education and its lack to such an experience as this. Picture men dwelling in a sort of subterranean cavern with a long entrance open to the light on its entire width. Conceive them as having their legs and necks fettered from childhood, so that they remain in the same spot, able to look forward only, and prevented by the fetters from turning their heads. Picture further the light from a fire burning higher up and at a distance behind them, and between the fire and the prisoners and above them a road along which a low wall has been built, as the exhibitors of puppet-shows have partitions before the men themselves, above which they show the puppets." "All that I see," he said. "See also, then, men carrying past the wall implements of all kinds that rise above the wall, and human images and shapes of animals as well, wrought in stone and wood and every material, some of these bearers presumably speaking and others silent." "A strange image you speak of," he said, "and strange prisoners." "Like to us," I said; "for, to begin with, tell me do you think that these men would have seen anything of themselves or of one another except the

163

A-T. Tymieniecka (ed.), Analecta Husserliana, Vol. XXXVIII, 163—182.
© 1992 *Kluwer Academic Publishers. Printed in the Netherlands.*

shadows cast from the fire on the wall of the cave that fronted them?" "How could they," he said, "if they were compelled to hold their heads unmoved through life?" "And again, would not the same be true of the objects carried past them?" "Surely." "If then they were able to talk to one another, do you not think that they would suppose that in naming the things that they saw they were naming the passing objects?" "Necessarily." "And if their prison had an echo from the wall opposite them, when one of the passers-by uttered a sound, do you think that they would suppose anything else than the passing shadow to be the speaker?" "By Zeus, I do not," said he. "Then in every way such prisoners would deem reality to be nothing else than the shadows of the artificial objects." "Quite inevitably," he said.[1]

The appeal of the myth of the cave derives in part from the careful balancing of the familiar and the strange.[2] Individual elements in this scenario are readily called to mind in response to Socrates' urging that we picture (*ide . . . horo*) this or that, but these elements contribute to an overall effect which seems more novel, imaginative, and unsettling than themselves; in other words, to a whole that seems other (if not more) than the sum of its parts. But how could this be? And what does it signify about signification?

We may begin to seek answers to such questions by considering the spatial and temporal co-ordinates of the scene the reader helps create in more or less strict compliance with Socrates' instructions as given by Plato. Figure and ground are, in the case of this mental picture, figures fixed in a particular position underground. And the process of composition of place is further aided by the specification of light, its sources and its consequences. Nature and culture converge in the doubling of a cave as a prison, and in the doubling of light as sunshine and as manmade fire. There occurs next a shift towards emphasising what man has made of this particular environment: his building of a road and wall, and the exhibition above these structures of examples of his technological and mimetic capacities, tools and images of his own and other animal species. We are prepared for the distinction between substance and shadow by the analogy with a puppet theatre and the allusion to a human procession carrying images seen only in outline by the prisoners. Socrates' recourse to an analogy within an analogy helps set up the chain of connections which will link the world of sense experience to the realm of Ideas; it also points to the anxiety of exposition, the desire of the didact to ensure that his audience is following his discourse; and it helps clarify the connections between artifacts specifically designed to create an illusion — puppets, models, replicas — and those that can be adapted to that purpose under special circumstances — implements of all kinds. However, despite these efforts on Socrates' part, the effect on his "immediate" audience is one of estrangement: "A strange image you speak of . . . and strange prisoners." Indeed, the word used twice by Glaucon to register his bemusement is *atopos*, literally denoting that which cannot be easily placed. The composition of place has led to the experience of displacement or homelessness. The call to visualize has precipitated a crisis of imagination. Socrates has presented an allegory, an articulation of otherness which further supports the notion of levels of connected but distinct meanings, but this allegory now calls for interpretation, for the enforcement of the master-analogy's basic claim: *homoious emin*; "like us" these prisoners are.

However, before considering how the allegory is glossed, let me note some of its connections with temporality. The passage begins with a reminder that it is part of an ongoing dialogue aimed at enhancing understanding. It then refers to a past other than its own, namely that of the prisoners who have been fettered here since childhood (*ek paidon*). The present is for them what it apparently has been for many years, a play of shadows on the wall of the cave which they must continuously face. They exist in what seems in essence to be a permanent, unvarying present of sensory control and physical dependence. And the prohibition to them of certain sensory possibilities offers an externally imposed and privative *epoche*, a negative pendant to the Socratic bracketting of historical, biographical, and political considerations for the purpose of clarifying and augmenting our understanding of the essential features of epistemology.

Socrates proceeds to break down his interlocutor's resistance to the strangeness of the allegory in a series of questions. The prisoners, it is agreed, could know nothing of their own physical appearance, that of their fellow prisoners, or of the objects that pass near them, apart from the shadows cast by the fire onto the cave wall. Visual illusion is then connected to two forms of acoustic illusion: that is, the mis-application to the shadow of the name more properly belonging to the substance, and the mistaking of the echo for the original utterance. These prisoners have language as well as sight, but both are seriously compromised by life-long incarceration. There is a crisis of identity and reference which cannot be resolved by one sense calling on the aid of another to confirm or correct its impressions; and, such is the importance of sight and hearing to knowledge, to compromise these two senses is to compromise possible modes of cognition altogether (*panaptasin*).

Visual epistemology thus finds a double or echo in the oral. But replicating a shape, like repeating a sound, creates the conditions not only for connecting apparently discrete particulars but also for misunderstanding such connections and the anterior reality situated behind the current field of vision. Plato has established the regressive momentum which will take him from the world of sensation back to the realm of ideas. The order of release from prison is imminent, its consequences already fairly clear. But what have we learned about the ways in which the allegory authorises itself and fulfills the intentions of its creator? What kinds of seeing (and speaking) are going on, and what kinds of enlightenment ensue?

The allegory of the cave is born of a didactic impulse and purveyed in a dialogic situation in which the allegorist clearly has the upper hand. Socrates already knows what he wants to re-present, and this fore-knowledge is yet another tribute to that which is already known to some but not yet evident to others. The allegory displays the processes and priorities it will be at pains to endorse: the capacity and willingness to imagine; the need to reflect or speculate on the nature of knowledge; the movement from confusion to understanding, from resistance to agreement; and the superiority of the ideal to the empirical. The allegorist manages his materials in a way that may at first seem arbitrary but gradually recommends itself as a form of fiction active in the service of truth. Questions of human freedom and constraint are clarified by an act of temporary, and to a degree involuntary, subordination to the imperatives of an imagination which seems as much poetic as philosophical. However, in resorting to the figurative in this way, Socrates enacts for his audience a dependence on mimesis and mythopoesis that seriously complicates the view of poetry presented in the fifth book of the *Republic* and in the account of the rhapsode in the *Ion*. There is an ambivalence towards verbal imagining that requires a certain amount of discretion on Socrates' part, a certain amount of complicity on the part of his audience, if his account of the scene of knowing is not to be undone, if *mise en scène* is not to dissolve into *mise en abîme*. Somehow Socrates has to control the implications of his analogies so that they do not subvert his argument. He has to exercise mastery over his materials in order to naturalize his preferences and justify his evasions; and he must make the right sort of appeal to the most appropriate authorities in order to convince his audience that, if no example is ever innocent, at least the ones he employs are not implausibly prejudicial. This is perhaps the principal secret of the success of his account of blindness and insight.

But how might the allegory appeal to poets and literati? What does it tell them, for example, about analogy in general, analogy with the mimetic arts in particular, and the nature of language? The displacement of analytical by imaginative discourse at this point in the *Republic* clearly appeals to those who have a stake in the idea of poetic knowing, though it will require them to align themselves with dialectic as a privileged but not entirely reliable mode of access to the realm of Ideas. If they find this alignment problematic, then they may be further concerned about the versions of imitation and wonder conveyed in the analogy with the puppet theatre: *hosper tois thaumatopoios proton anthropon prokeitai to paraphragmata, huper on to thaumata deiknuasin*.[3] An analogy within an analogy has perhaps been embedded in a textualized version of subterranean imprisonment in order to encourage its unflattering association with the prisoners in the cave.

And then there is the problem of language as naming. What is the connection of this activity in the cave with, say, the assessment of the accuracy (*orthotes*) of names in the *Cratylus*?[4] Socrates reconstitutes dialogue as naming, *dialegesthai* as *nomizein* and *onomazein*, that is, as activities once again embedded, this time within the more complex and inclusive repertories of discourse and dialectic on which Socratic dialogue draws. We are not dealing with origins here but with reduced capacities. Just as the visible is not necessarily the accurately intelligible, so the audible can be the symptom or source of error; and this seriously reduced and reductive version of linguistic communication confines the social and epistemological possibilities of language to rudimentary onomastics, the naming of a visible object or speaker. However, this confinement of the oral does not have as obvious a physical cause as does the restriction of the prisoners' vision. The analogy between visual and oral confinement as equally predictable and necessary holds only if we assume that the prisoners have been conditioned to respond exclusively to external stimuli while remaining incapable of impromptu exchange on matters other than the attribution of identity. Such initiative as they show in talking to one another is hence neither playful nor exploratory nor fully interactive; in a literalist, unimaginative way they suppose — here Socrates uses forms of the verb *hegeomai* which denotes taking the lead or taking charge as well as going beyond the self-evident or the verifiable — and their conversation names those suppositions of their ears which simply repeat or confirm the errors of their eyes. To suppose (*hegeomai*) is to pretend to hegemony (*hegemonia*), an activity intended by Socrates to seem necessary and understandable but still illusory. However, his own pretensions to hegemony are only slightly less vulnerable than those of the prisoners whose situation he describes, and any reader of the *Republic* has the option of making much or little of this fact, of recontextualising the allegory of the cave according to a rationalist or otherwise obdurate hermeneutics of suspicion, or of reappropriating it in ways that pay more or less generous tribute to its wisdom and vividness. The apparently controlled semantic play of allegory supports multiple interpretation of its procedures and products, a situation which suggests the reconstitution, at least in this instance, of the definitive as the endlessly suggestive. The quest for stable reference and unequivocal identity, for an incontrovertible account of the nature of knowledge, is an inscription of persistent desire which affords opportunities as well as entailing obligations, and these manifestations of freedom and constraint are realized in ways dependant on general cultural priorities and the specific needs and values of individual interpreters.

Let us next register a few more of the possible emphases and inflections occasioned by the allegory of the cave, beginning with the example of mediation as formal translation in the version of Plato by Thomas Taylor on which many of the English romantics relied:

After these things now, said I, assimilate, with reference to erudition, and the want of erudition, our nature to such a condition as follows. Consider men as in a subterraneous habitation, resembling a cave, with its entrance expanding to the light, and answering to the whole extent of the cave. Suppose them to have been in this cave from their childhood, with chains both on their legs and necks, so as to remain there, and only be able to look before them, but by the chain incapable to turn their heads round. Suppose them likewise to have the light of a fire, burning far above and behind them; and that between the fire and the fettered men there is a road above. Along this road, observe a low wall built, like that which hedges in the stage of mountebanks on which they exhibit their wonderful tricks. I observe it, said he. Behold now, along this wall, men bearing all sorts of utensils, raised above the wall, and human statues, and other animals, in wood and stone, and furniture of every kind. And, as is likely, some of those who are carrying these are speaking, and others silent. You mention, said he, a wonderful comparison, and wonderful fettered men. But such, however, as resemble us, said I; for, in the first place, do you think that such as these see any thing of themselves, or of one another, but the shadows formed by the fire, falling on the opposite part of the cave? How can they, said he, if through the whole of life they be under a necessity, at least, of having their heads unmoved? But what do they see of what is carrying along? Is it not the very same? Why not? If then they were able to converse with one another, do not you think they would deem it proper to give names to those very things which they saw before them? Of necessity they must. And what if the opposite part of this prison had an echo, when any of those who passed along spake, do you imagine they would reckon that what spake was any thing else than the passing shadow? Not I, by Jupiter! said he. Such as these then, said I, will entirely judge that there is nothing true but the shadows of utensils. By an abundant necessity, replied he.[5]

In this excerpt from the Taylor translation I will consider only a few of the ways in which it differs from the Loeb translation quoted at the outset. First, Taylor renders *paideia* as erudition rather than education, thus suggesting that knowledge of the sort about to be discussed is more recondite and exclusive than generally available to all, though it is still detectable in terms of its social consequences, transforming the rude into the learned. We are reminded, if we need reminding, that the universality implied by an appeal to "our nature" (*ten hemeteran phusin*) is based on exclusion and deferred distribution of the fruits of knowledge. Second, Plato begins the appeal to Glaucon with a specifically visual term, *apeikason*, which reveals the iconic, imagistic affiliation of his epistemology. The propriety of this nexus is lost in Taylor's version, but the term he does favour, namely "assimilate," plays interestingly with the earlier transitive sense of this verb, which means making something like something else, as well as its more recent sense of the absorbing of one thing by another. The semantic history of this term attests to the complex relations between self and other wherein connection cannot for long be kept separate from co-option and consumption, where bringing together so often means the bringing to heel of one party or another. Third, the rendering of *thaumatapoios* as "mountebanks" rather than "the exhibitors of puppet-shows" moves mimesis away from aesthetic seriousness in the direction of quackery. It is an intelligent attempt to insist on the fact that the source of the shadow figures appear as it were *mounted* on top of the wall and that they represent an unacceptable approximation to (or distortion of) knowledge of the Good. Taylor maybe thinking here of an other work famous for its dependance on Platonic epistemology, Sidney's *Apology for Poetry*, with its rueful admission that poets "are almost in as good reputation as the mountebanks at Venice."[6] But this echo, whether deliberate or not, is not entirely convenient for Taylor's purpose as faithful translator, reminding us as it does of Plato's ambivalence towards analogy and Sidney's attempt to reclaim Plato for the poets despite himself. Finally, Taylor's selective bias against illusion is evident also in his attribution of the single epithet "wonderful" to the mountebanks' effects (*thaumata*) and to Glaucon's response to the allegory so far (*atopos*). Taylor's respect for Plato causes him inadvertently to conflate two quite distinct kinds of puzzlement, one occasioned by a popular show and the other by a profound allegory aimed at the erudite. Hence, in softening allegory's alienation-effect to a form of *wonder*, Taylor also closes the gap between mere entertainment and philosophical instruction. And this unintended mixture of effects points to the fact that this translator is no more able than Plato himself to eliminate inconsistency and arbitrariness from the staging of the scene of epistemology.

Like any other author, Taylor had only limited control over how his text would be read, as we can see by looking at the excerpt from a work by his friend, William Blake:

If the doors of perception were cleansed everything would appear to Man as it is: infinite.

For Man has closed himself up, till he sees all things through the narrow chinks of his cavern ....

I was in a printing-house in Hell and saw the method in which knowledge is transmitted from generation to generation.

In the first chamber was a dragon-man, clearing away the rubbish from a cave's mouth; within, a number of dragons were hollowing the cave.

In the second chamber was a viper folding round the rock and the cave, and others adorning it with gold, silver and precious stones.

In the third chamber was an eagle with wings and feathers of air; he caused the inside of the cave to be infinite. Around were numbers of eagle-like men, who built palaces in the immense cliffs.

In the fourth chamber were lions of flaming fire, raging around and melting the metals into living fluids.

In the fifth chamber were unnamed forms, which cast the metals into the expanse.

They were received by men who occupied the sixth chamber, and took the forms of books and were arranged in libraries.

The giants who formed this world into its sensual existence, and now seem to live in it in chains, are in truth the causes of its life and the sources of all activity; but the chains are the cunning of weak and tame minds, which have power to resist energy, according to the proverb: "The weak in courage is strong in cunning."[7]

Here, visionary activity of a kind that reworks Dante and Milton and Swedenborg as well as Plato is presented in highly distinctive fashion. For Blake, of course, man's imprisonment in illusion is self-induced, and imagination, not reason, offers the only hope of escape. Despite his disapproval of Plato's paganism, Blake the poet and visual artist finds inspiration in platonic (and neo-platonic) epistemology, although in *The Marriage of Heaven and Hell* that inspiration takes the form of rewriting the allegory of the cave in a defiantly obscure and personal way, moving from the personal cavern of man's own making to the more commodious but still confining location of the five senses in a "Hell" where the poet witnesses the "method" by which "knowledge" is disseminated from "generation to generation." The theme of knowledge provides an occasion for challenge and intrigue by means of an application more radical than Plato's of the principle that "what is not too Explicit [is] fittest for Instruction because it rouzes the faculties to act" (letter to Trusler, 23 August, 1799; *Blake* pp. 6—7). Like Plato, Blake subordinates physical seeing to spiritual vision in the interests of freedom, though not in a dialogue subsequently written down by a philosophical disciple. Blake prefers a text that will revolutionize even as it describes textual production in the infernal printing house. The orthodox culture of the book and traditional scriptism are problematized in an Illuminated Book designed to reveal the true nature of illumination — a book with enigmatic plates and ornaments and unusual coloured inks, a book whose mode of production realizes the emancipatory potential of the processes allegorically intimated in this particular Memorable Fancy. Just as Plato discriminates between Socratic dialogue and the impoverished and mistaken exchanges of the prisoners, so Blake distinguishes between the living and the dead text, the vitally disruptive and the inertly codified. Both Plato and Blake use language with a strongly visual appeal, but Blake supplements and complicates his appeal with a series of pictorial and typographical effects that are far from being simple illustrations of the meaning of the printed text or the systematic subordination of the image to the word. The problematic of textuality is linked by Blake to the question of human identity so as to precipitate once again a crisis in naming: thus the naming of Hell in this poem marks its radical redefinition, while the participants in the dissemination of knowledge are named first as non-human or only partly human, and then as "unnamed forms." The very moment before knowledge is made accessible to "Men," the challenges of allegory give way to the enigma of that which, if it is not Beckett's unnameable, is as yet "unnamed" and therefore the linguistic sign of a lack in language. The term "form" is familiar to printers and to platonists alike, and mediates between titanic energies and the storehouse of the library in a brilliant example of giving and withholding. Variants of this term "form" are used three times by Blake in rapid succession, the first two times as a noun linking the forces shaping molten metal into type and the product of that process, and then as a verb denoting the creative activities of the giant prisoners now fettered by cunning. We know what form books take, but we can only imagine the unnamed forms in the fifth chamber and the processes whereby our world was created. Blake's brand of liberation theology brings together the cave, the printing house, and the library in a scenario whose ironies corrode only that which deserves to be purged, and whose affirmations fully recognize the threat to creativity posed by power-knowledge.

Blake's enthusiasm for Plato was less certain, his suspicion of libraries much greater than that of other English romantic poets, including Coleridge. As arbitrator between two classes of men, Platonists and Aristotelians,[8] and as a poetic redactor of the notion of *anamnesis*, Coleridge did much to rescue Plato from the hostility of the Enlightenment. And the following passage from a letter to Thelwall offers an interesting insight into the reconstitution of relations between philosophic knowing and poetic making that we know as Romanticism:

I am, & ever have been, a great reader — & have read almost everything — a library-cormorant — I am *deep* in all out of the way books . . . I have read & digested most of the Historical Writers —; but I do not *like* history. Metaphysics, & Poetry, & "Facts of Mind" — (i.e. Accounts of all the strange phantasms that ever possessed your philosophy-dreamers from Tauth [Thoth], the Egyptian to Taylor, the English Pagan,) are my darling Studies.[9]

Coleridge qualifies his insatiable appetite for books, indicating his enthusiasm for "Metaphysics, & Poetry, & 'Facts of Mind,'" a configuration that brackets history the better to accommodate continuity and unmediated access to the ancient sources (in Plato's *Phaedrus* and elsewhere) of "philosophy-dreamers." Thomas Taylor comes to mind not simply as the most prominent contemporary translator of Plato but as someone transformed into an "English Pagan" by sustained exposure to platonic and neo-platonic writings. Dreaming is no longer a trivial or escapist but a philosophical activity that connects the dive of the cormorant to the flight of imagination heavenwards.

Coleridge's enthusiasm was shared by Wordsworth, and given expression in a celebrated tribute to platonic *anamnesis* in the Immortality Ode.

Our birth is but a sleep and a forgetting:
  The Soul that rises with us, our life's Star,
  Hath had elsewhere its setting,
    And cometh from afar:
  Not in entire forgetfulness,
  And not in utter nakedness,
But trailing clouds of glory do we come
  From God, who is our home:
Heaven lies about us in our infancy!
Shades of the prison-house begin to close
  Upon the growing Boy
    But he
Beholds the light, and whence it flows,
  He sees it in his joy;
The Youth, who daily farther from the east
  Must travel, still is Nature's Priest,
  And by the vision splendid
  Is on his way attended;
At length the Man perceives it die away,
And fade into the light of common day. . . .

  But for those obstinate questionings
  Of sense and outward things,
  Fallings from us, vanishings;
    Blank misgivings of a Creature
Moving about in worlds not realized,
High instincts before which our mortal Nature
Did tremble like a guilty Thing surprized;
  But for those affections,
  Those shadowy recollections,
  Which, be they what they may,
Are yet the fountain light of all our day,
Are yet a master light of all our seeing;
  Uphold us, cherish, and have power to make
Our noisy years seem moments in the being
Of the eternal Silence: truths that wake,
  To perish never;
Which neither listlessness, nor mad endeavor,
  Nor Man nor Boy,

Nor all that is at enmity with joy,
Can utterly abolish or destroy!
   Hence in a season of calm weather
   Though inland far we be,
Our Souls have sight of that immortal sea
   Which brought us hither,
   Can in a moment travel thither,
And see the children sport upon the shore,
And hear the mighty waters rolling evermore![10]

The first of the two excerpts given here provides a poetic account of the prison-house of physical existence *ek paidon*. Plato's visual epistemology is given a fresh emplotment on the basis of a contrast not between substance and shadow but between two kinds of light, the one originary and far more brilliant than the other. The prisoner of existence has his course determined by the inexorable passing of human time and the unavoidable experience of exile and loss. However, recompense is possible, as the second excerpt from the Ode affirms, with consolation taking the form of contesting (more or less involuntarily) the natural attitude.[11] Once again there is a crisis of naming, as Wordsworth resorts to the word "Blank" to mark a general unease which he proceeds to characterize as ignorance and guilt, the echo of *Hamlet*'s "guilty thing/ Upon a fearful summons" (I.i. 148—9) providing an intertextual enactment of the kind of remembering at issue. This unreadable blankness is then reformulated as an unfathomable mystery which somehow doubles as a source of clarity: "Those shadowy recollections, /Which, be they what they may, /Are yet the fountain light of all our day, /Are yet a master light of all our seeing." Our understanding of such capacities is limited and mediated, but the prison houses of language and perception have inmates who are not entirely fallen from grace, not entirely removed from the sources of their being. Incompleteness hence takes on a more positive aspect in a poem depicting an experience Wordsworth considers to be private, intimate, fitful, yet universal. He empowers himself to speak for all of us who have survived a childhood to which we can imaginatively return, and in so doing he practises economies of argument authorized by an appeal to Plato. The latter's claim that the prisoners in the cave are *like* ourselves is reformulated more metaphorically to implicate us more thoroughly in scene of epistemological loss and gain. Wordsworth elaborates on Plato's symbolic topography in order to revitalise a neglected truth, to rehabilitate sight and hearing in a version of transcending the here and now, a poetic intimation only too aware of the obstacles to such intimacy but determined none the less to rely on the power of poetic mediation.

The success of Wordsworth's Ode gave encouragement to other romantic poets to disclose their own distinctive brands of platonism. Of course, not all Wordsworth's contemporaries were admirers of Plato and platonic mediation, as the famous attack in the opening canto of Byron's Don Juan may remind us:

> Oh Plato! Plato! you have paved the way,
>   With your confounded fantasies, to more
> Immoral conduct by the fancied sway
>   Your system feigns o'er the controlless core
>   Of human hearts, than all the long array
> Of poets and romancers: — You're a bore,
>   A charlatan, a coxcomb — and have been,
>   At best, no better than a go-between.

There was no denying that Plato was increasingly influential at this time, but his influence could be regretted as the pretext for hypocrisy and self-delusion. However, where Byron perceived the bugbear of an ethical system whose author was himself a *ciarlatano* or mountebank, Shelley saw a poet-philosopher of the first order whose work he would translate and imaginatively appropriate in a number of ways.[12]

There is a passage in "Adonais" which is perhaps the best known example of Shelley's platonizing, and adds the element of chromaticism to an account that has been markedly free from any consideration of colour so far:

> The One remains, the many change and pass;
> Heaven's light forever shines, Earth's shadows fly;
> Life, like a dome of many-coloured glass,
> Stains the white radiance of Eternity,
> Until Death tramples it to fragments. — Die,
> If thou wouldst be with that which thou dost seek!
> Follow where all is fled! — Rome's azure sky,
> Flowers, ruins, statues, music, words, are weak
> The glory they transfuse with fitting truth to speak.[13]

This excerpt begins with a pair of antitheses between the immutable and the ephemeral, before introducing the famous analogy between life and the dome. The allegory of the cave gives rise to a new version of confinement in which the opening contrasts between one and many, light and shadow, converge in the plot of plurality and fragmentation, beauty and blemish, in the colours of a world which "Stain . . . the white radiance of Eternity." Shelley's complicated allegiance to human time and eternity causes him at first to upgrade our existential prison into a brighter and more becoming edifice closely associated with divinity. The play on stained glass strengthens the impression that this dome is *domus dei*, though our knowledge of Shelley's hostility to what he called "religion's tottering dome" (*The Revolt of Islam* [1818], II.xliii) may cause us to wonder what kind of religious affiliation, if any, the dome of life can have. Despite the pejorative associations of the term "Stains" (with its echoes of "the contagion of the world's slow stain" a dozen stanzas earlier) there still seems to be a predominantly aesthetic arrangement here, with as it were the stained glass of the middle ages reaching up to and beyond the white light of Brunelleschi's renaissance interiors. Or, more scientifically, one might follow some commentators on this passage who see the laws of optics being invoked by Shelley to account for the contrast between white light and the colours of the spectrum. However, this latter possibility raises difficulties regarding the refractive properties of a dome as distinct from a prism, and there is the further awkwardness of the staining coming *down* from the source of light in the heavens only to be described as a staining *upwards* from an earthly source.

Is Shelley being sloppy here, or does the passage deserve to be admired? He esteemed Plato above all for his imagery[14] and offers a typically imaginative translation of it here that may appeal to a pattern of emission, refraction, and return that recalls Wordsworth's platonizing in the Immortality Ode and the consoling dialectic of the Abramsian "greater romantic lyric." For Shelley too there are compensations on earth which make Death seem as much of a vandal as the verb "tramples" and the disruptive caesura before "Die" suggest. Death can divide us from each other, which leads Shelley to issue an uncompromising challenge to those who feel disabled by an intense sense of loss. The imperative mood is followed by a catalogue of fugitive beauties, the sky offering itself as nature's occasionally monochrome dome, followed by details evocative of Rome and the campagna. The union of the desiring subject with her or his goal can only occur posthumously. In this world the dome contrives our doom, which is a permanent crisis of adequation. Vocal nature, the visual arts, music, language itself are alike deficient because they cannot express "with fitting truth" the glory which they attempt to mediate. Whether complete statues or incomplete ruins, finished compositions or sporadic words, none is a spiritual plenum; all are haunted by a sense of the discrepancy between what they might be and what they are, all encumbered in a way effectively conveyed by Shelley's style at this point, moving as it does from the imperturbable prosody of the One, to the laboured syntax and deferred agency of the stanza's final lines. Weakness is all that can with confidence be affirmed, and the final infinitive form ("to speak") is plainly exposed as a problematic if necessary analogue to the unmodified expressiveness of Eternity.

Such weakness as this may remind us of transfusion as a response to sickness as well the decanting of less vital liquids, but Shelley is not intent on imagining epistemology simply as a debilitating fall from grace, a symptom of hopelessness and imminent suicide. He makes a similar point about transfusion in his *Defence of Poetry*:

Sounds as well as thoughts have relation both between each other and towards that which they represent, and a perception of the order of those relations has always been found connected with a perception of the order of the relations of thought. Hence the language of poets has ever affected a certain uniform and harmonious recurrence of sound, without which it were not poetry, and which is scarcely less indispensable to the communication of its influence, than the words themselves, without reference to that peculiar order. Hence the vanity of translation; it were as wise to cast a violet into a crucible that you might discover the formal principle of its colour and odour, as to seek to transfuse from one language into another the creations of a poet. The plant must spring again from its seed, or it will bear no flower — and this is the burthen of the curse of Babel.[15]

The irreversible flow of existence can be made to work in our favour, if only our capacities for seeing, shaping, and linguistic expression are employed as the main business of our being in the world. Phonetic recurrence is not the restoration of identity but rather one of its most satisfying and instructive surrogates, bringing together as it does *in* language and *as* language "burthen" as the freight of meaning carried by discourse and "burthen" as the patterning of poetic repetition. Shelley's recourse to a highly visual analogy as the focus for experiment and scientific observation is a further reminder that there is much more to semiosis than verbal semantics or the narrowly referential. There are different ways of knowing, different kinds of crucible and fire, different configurations of the elemental which rely on different conventions for a fair hearing, viewing, or alternative apprehension. Shelleyan transfusion may occur under the chromatic dome of life and in the inverted dome of the crucible, reconstituting deficiency as opportunity for appropriate response: meeting imaginative appeal with imaginative reconstruction or refraction in the one case, spurning the hubristic pseudo-science in the other. The visual and the verbal, the shadows in Plato's cave and the linguistic diaspora after Babel, are alike reworked by Shelley to enable and enhance human life.

Where Shelley permits colour into the scene of knowing, Plato was more intent on exploiting the contrast between light and shadow. In so doing he created an opportunity that is intriguingly described by Goethe in his treatise on colour:

The separation of light and dark from all appearance of colour is possible and necessary. The artist will solve the mystery of imitation sooner by first considering light and dark independently of colour, and making himself acquainted with it in its whole extent.[16]

Has Plato then solved the mystery of imitation (*das Rätsel der Darstellung*) by setting his epistemological scene in a quasi-primordial space where fundamental distinctions are made, distinctions which can subsequently be copied or complicated by his successors but never superceded? Is this another reason, perhaps even the main reason, for the influence of the allegory of the Cave? It is time to return to the analogy with the puppets in the cave and their relation to the mystery of mimesis. But first a short detour by way of Kleist.

Kleist's prose dialogue, "Über den Marionettentheater," exploits the conventions of Socratic exchange in a way that has intrigued scholars for a wide variety of reasons.[17] The dialogue is memorable and provocative in its exploration of mimesis, and striking for its apparent conflation of lofty questions with a form of popular entertainment. Like Glaucon in the *Republic*, the narrator is at first bemused and then won over by the surprising contention (*eine so sonderbare Behauptung*) of an acknowledged expert, in this instance the recently recruited and very successful chief dancer at the local opera. As in Socratic dialogue, there will be clarification through verbal exchange, though not the kind of resolution that one participant in the conversation may expect. This verbal exchange takes place in the local marketplace, an enclosed rather than a subterranean space, a context dominated usually by economic exchange but accommodating also on occasion exchange of a more festive kind. The dancer represents the performing arts as they figure in high culture, but he has to give up dance for dialogue in order to initiate the narrator into the mysteries of marionettes, going about this task in a way that problematizes early nineteenth-century notions of representation and may cause us to think again about the activities directed by *thaumatapoios* in the allegory of the cave. Mr. C., as the dancer is called, explains that the control of puppets is much simpler than people may think, primarily involving control of the *Schwerpunkt* or centre of gravity. From such simplicity choreographic diversity results. The narrator is unconvinced and wonders whether the puppeteer must himself be a dancer or at least have "a knowledge of the Beautiful in the dance." The platonic possibility of *ein Begriff vom Schönem* is, however, softened by the dancer to a degree of sensitivity (*Empfindung*) and an exploitation of the dimensions of the human body. After this demystifying response, however, the dancer re-appropriates such mimesis in the name of mystery (*etwas sehr Geheimnisvolles*), indeed nothing less than *der weg der Seeles des Tänzers* that involves the puppeteer becoming himself a dancer. As in so many Romantic interrogations of epistemology, the passage turns on a reflexive term, in this case *sich versetzen*. This in turn leads to a further somersault in the dialogical dance: *Seele* is reduced to *dieser letzte Bruch von Geist* and then to the reconstitution of the marionette as purely mechanical, its dance as "*gänzlich ins Reich mechanischer Kräfte hinübergespielt.*" The dance of the mechanical and the inspired is joined by the human and artificial in the shape of English amputees wearing artificial limbs, before Mr. C. makes another gesture towards "*was sich nicht auch schon hier fände.*" The soul makes another appearance, this time as *vis motrix*, which, when located at the dancer's centre of gravity, makes all current performers seem affected and deficient. We then hear two versions of the loss of youthful innocence drawn from the personal experience of the narrator and C., before the story of the incredible Livonian bear is told, and accepted with an eagerness rich in irony. Kleist has prepared us well for his superbly balanced finale, where matter and spirit, mathematics and optics, are incorporated in a text

whose concluding gesture is directed towards the master-text that is still
being written, the replication that will restore us all to innocence:

Now then, my good friend, you are in possession of all you require to understand my
point. We see how, in the organic world, as reflection grows darker and weaker, grace
emerges ever more radiant and supreme. — But just as two intersecting lines, converg-
ing on one side of a point, reappear on the other after their passage through infinity,
and just as our image, as we approach a concave mirror, vanishes to infinity only to
reappear before our very eyes, so will grace, having likewise traversed the infinite,
return to us once more, and so appear most purely in that bodily form that has either
no consciousness at all or an infinite one, which is to say, either in the puppet or a god.
"That means," said I, somewhat amused, "that we would have to eat of the tree of
knowledge a second time to fall back into a state of innocence." "Of course," he
answered, "and that is the final chapter in the history of the world."

Kleist's play with the unpretentious *Spielart* of puppetry astutely
problematizes the natural attitude towards venerable aesthetic hierarchy, and aggravates the difficulties between grace and consciousness,
Anmut and *Bewusstsein*. Kleist may hence have helped us to perceive
the puppets in Plato's cave as the ineradicable installation of the
aesthetic in the scene of knowing, and to register the ways in which
philosophical as well as poetic enlightenment are *managed* via special
visual and linguistic effects and the refiguration of social as aesthetic
space, the walls that define the city and the stage. As Paul de Man has
shown with Kleist, and Luce Irigaray with Plato,[18] such scenarios work
in part by strategic domination and exclusion and can therefore be re-
read as ideological critique; however, as the romantic luminaries attest,
Plato, and those who imaginatively appropriate his legacy, ought not
simply to be reduced to instruments of domination and exclusion. The
promise of the primordial is always tempting but dangerous; the
economies of philosophy and poetry consistently duplicate loss as gain,
gift as depradation. But such realizations should not be allowed to
disable us, to so encumber human agency that it seems scarcely worthy
of the name or worth the effort. It was not, after all, political naivete or
historical ignorance that led Schiller to affirm in the twenty- fifth of his
Letters on the Aesthetic Education of Mankind that we ought always to
be seeing double:

So long as Man in his first physical condition accepts the world
of sense merely passively, merely perceives, he is still
completely identified with it, and just because he himself is

simply world, there is no world yet for him. Not until he sets it outside himself or *contemplates* it, in his aesthetic status, does his personality become distinct from it, and a world appears to him because he has ceased to identify himself with it.[19]

University of Saskatchewan

NOTES

[1] Plato, *The Republic*, trans. Paul Shorey, Loeb Classical Library, 2 vols. (Cambridge, Massachussets: Harvard University Press, 1930), 514a—c.

[2] See, e.g., John Henry Wright, "The Origin of Plato's Cave," *Harvard Studies in Classical Philology* **12** (1906), 131—42.

[3] For the textual difficulties associated with this passage, see H. Rackham, "Note on Plato, *Republic*, VII. 514B," *The Classical Review* **29** (1915), 77—78. For puppets in ancient Greece, see Max von Boehn, *Puppets and Automata*, trans. Josephine Nicoll with a note on puppets by George Bernard Shaw (New York: Dover, 1972), pp. 6—9. 48ff.

[4] Cf. Richard Robinson, "Theory of Names in Plato's *Cratylus*," in his *Essays in Greek Philosophy* (Oxford: Clarendon Press, 1969), pp. 100—117.

[5] *The Works of Plato*, trans. Floyer Sydenham and Thomas Taylor, 5 vols. (London: R. Wilks, 1804), I.357—8.

[6] *Miscellaneous Prose of Sir Philip Sidney*, ed. Katherine Duncan-Jones and Jan Van Dorsten (Oxford: Clarendon Press, 1973), p. 110.

[7] From *The Marriage of Heaven and Hell* in *William Blake*, ed. Michael Mason (Oxford: Oxford University Press, 1988), pp. 14—15.

[8] This famous distinction occurs in his *Table Talk and Omniana*, ed. T. Ashe (London: G. Bell, 1923), p. 99.

[9] A letter of 19 November 1796, *Collected Letters of Samuel Taylor Coleridge*, ed. E. L. Griggs, 4 vols. (Oxford: Clarendon Press, 1956—59), I.260—61. This passage is followed in the same letter with the sonnet on anamnesis, "Oft of some *Unknown Past* such fancies roll."

[10] *The Poetic Works of Wordsworth*, ed. Thomas Hutchinson, rev. Ernest De Selincourt (London: Oxford University Press, 1965), pp. 460—62.

[11] Wordsworth is also intent on systematically rebutting contentions dear to the Enlightenment. See Marjorie Levinson, "Wordsworth's Intimations Ode: A Timely Utterance," in *Historical Studies and Literary Criticism*, ed. Jerome J. McGann (Madison: University of Wisconsin Press, 1985), pp. 48—74.

[12] *Cf.*, e.g., M. H. Abrams, "Shelley and Romantic Platonism," in *The Mirror and the Lamp: Romantic Theory and The Critical Tradition* (New York: Oxford University Press, 1953), pp. 126—31; C. E. Pulos, "Scepticism and Platonism," in *Modern Critical Views: Percy Bysshe Shelley*, ed. Harold Bloom (New York: Chelsea House, 1985), pp. 31—45; Timothy Webb, *The Violet in the Crucible: Shelley and Translation* (Oxford: Clarendon Press: 1976), p. 31ff.

[13] "Adonais," st.52; *Shelley's Poetry and Prose*, ed. Donald H. Reiman and Sharon B. Powers (New York: W. W. Norton, 1977), p. 405.

[14] See, e.g., Webb, *The Violet in the Crucible*, p. 24.

[15] *Shelley's Poetry and Prose*, p. 484.

[16] *Goethe's Theory of Colours*, trans. from the German with Notes by Charles Lock Eastlake (London: John Murray, 1840), p. 331. I have supplied versions of the original German from the Artemis-Verlag *Gedenkausgabe*.

[17] This work was first published in 1810. I follow the version given in *Heinrich von Kleists Werke*, ed. Erich Schmidt, rev. Georg Minde-Pouet 7 vols. (Leipzig: Bibliographisches Institut AG, n.d.), VII.39—47. I quote from the translation given in *An Abyss Deep Enough: Letters of Heinrich von Kleist with a Selection of Essays and Anecdotes*, ed. and trans. Philip B. Miller (New York: E. P. Dutton, 1982), pp. 211—16. For a range of responses to this story, cf., e.g., Ilse Graham, *Heinrich von Kleist Word into Flesh: A Poet's Quest for the Symbol* (Berlin: de Gruyter, 1975), pp. 11—26; *Heinrich von Kleist Studies*, Hofstra University Cultural & Intercultural Studies 3 (New York: AMS Press, 1981); and Paul de Man, "Aesthetic Formalization: Kleist's *Über das Marionnetentheater*," in *The Rhetoric of Romanticism* (New York: Columbia University Press, 1984), pp. 263—90.

[18] See Luce Irigaray, *Speculum Of The Other Woman*, trans. Gillian C. Gill (Ithaca: Cornell University Press, 1985), especially p. 243ff.

[19] Friedrich Schiller, *On the Aesthetic Education of Man: In A Series of Letters*, trans. Reginald Snell (New York: Frederick Ungar, 1965), p. 119.

CHRISTOPH EYKMAN

THE SYMBOLIC MEANING OF LIGHT
IN EICHENDORFF'S *DAS MARMORBILD*

Joseph Freiherr von Eichendorff (1788—1857), author of poetry, novels, stories, epics, and a history of German literature, ranks as one of the most popular writers of late-German Romanticism. Both in his verse and in his prose, he probes the emotional depths of the Romantic mind while portraying primarily his own social class, the aristocracy. His is a world full of adventurous experiences, of miraculous turns of events, and yet, in spite of the etherial and carefree atmosphere of Eichendorff's "world" which is very much akin to that of the fairy tale, the Christian, more precisely: the Roman Catholic perspective of his Weltanschauung alerts him to the fact that human passions and emotions are linked to man's instinctual nature which can pose a threat to his mental balance. Thus the darker side of man stands in need — just like nature itself — of purification and redemption.

This is the theme of Eichendorff's story *Das Marmorbild* (The Marble Statue), published in 1820, a work which contains all the typical ingredients of Eichendorff's fictional universe. Eichendorff's craft is not that of a realist. His landscapes, his presentation of space in general but also his portrayal of human beings in a certain socio-political and historical setting are mostly only marginally based on close observation and mimesis of the real world around him. In his poems and works of fiction, visible and audible phenomena function as a material embodiment of inner spiritual and emotional qualities and of certain themes connected with these. This is why Eichendorff's world is full of ciphers and symbols. It exhibits an almost stereotypic pattern of recurring constellations of images which are invariably assigned certain symbolic meanings by being placed next to or near certain thematic or emotional key words. A network of interrelated semantic entities is thus created which maintains its validity throughout the text and allows for a "symbiosis" of meaning between contextual elements.

This is particularly obvious with regard to the phenomenon of light in Eichendorff's story. The symbolic connotations of natural light — and in connection with it: of day and night — take on a special signifi-

183

A-T. Tymieniecka (ed.), Analecta Husserliana, Vol. XXXVIII, 183—191.
© 1992 *Kluwer Academic Publishers. Printed in the Netherlands.*

cance in *Das Marmorbild*. Before analyzing them in detail, however, I would like to offer a brief summary of the story.

The young nobleman Florio sets out to travel on horseback across Italy. Near the city of Lucca, he makes the acquaintance of Fortunato, another nobleman, and a young lady, Bianca, who soon falls in love with Florio. He also meets Donati, a wild, restless man who seems to be driven by an evil demon.

During his first night in Lucca, Florio wanders around outside the city walls and finally finds himself at a pond. Its waters surround a marble statue of Venus. For a fleeting moment, the goddess seems to come alive in the magic rays of the moon. Her eyes meet Florio's. Yet only a few moments later she is transformed back into a lifeless artifact. This uncanny experience has a deep emotional impact on young Florio. The next day, he accidentally strays into a beautiful palace garden where he observes a young lady singing a song. Florio shudders when he discovers that her face strangely resembles that of the marble statue.

That same evening Fortunato invites Florio to a masked ball at a friend's villa where he encounters two ladies wearing almost identical costumes of a Greek maiden. One of them appears to be Bianca. The other invites Florio to her castle where Donati takes him a few days later. Totally enthralled by the enchanted atmosphere of the castle which resembles a Greek temple, Florio follows the lady until they both reach one of her chambers inside the castle. Just when Florio is about to succumb to her erotic charms, Fortunato's voice is heard outside. He sings an old Christian song which breaks the spell and prompts Florio to say a short prayer. A sudden stroke of lightning makes Venus and her entourage disappear. Florio, still not quite free of the spell and emotionally perturbed, decides to leave Lucca and joins some other travellers, among whom are Bianca and Fortunato. The latter tells his companions the story of a haunted place where once a temple of Venus stood. Every spring the spirit of Venus rises from the depths of the earth. Her resurrection brings emotional bewilderment to the minds of innocent youths. Only the strength of the Christian faith and the intercession of the Virgin Mary will break the spell and help the victims regain their inner freedom. Florio, who with God's and his friend's help has cleansed his mind of its sinful desires, is now happily reunited with Bianca. Together, they resume their travel.

Eichendorff uses the myth of Venus in order to make palpable the threatening forces of Eros whose elemental and instinctual lure is apt to impair the emotional balance of a young person.[1] He thereby creates a variation of the old romantic theme of nature being in need of gaining salvation through the spirit. As a Roman Catholic, Eichendorff inscribes Christian features into his version of the theme. The imagery of daylight and morning versus moonlight and night in *Das Marmorbild* becomes a function of the struggle between the irrational, pagan, and sometimes even diabolic powers of Eros versus the Ego and the process of sublimation reinforced by Christian values. Light phenomena are thus assigned to one of the opposing realms, i.e. they appear in a carefully assembled context of life — and death symbols, of axiologically charged expressions, of words referring to emotional reaction and of other related images.

The first scene in Eichendorff's story in which images of light become charged with a special meaning derived from the thematic structure of the text can be found in the long Lied (song) sung by Fortunato to entertain a gathering of merrymakers from the upper echelances of the society of Lucca. The song both anticipates and summarizes the events of the story by pitting the pagan against the Christian. It evoques the Greek god Bacchus whose presence is associated with the verb-noun "Glühen" (glowing) and whose eyes are likened to "flames" (530).[2] Venus, compared to a "magic ring" appears steeped "in the glow of dawn" (531). But then the mood of the song changes abruptly and so does the light imagery. The enchanted and seemingly carefree bucolic scene is transformed into a world where the Christian dualism of the "here" versus the "beyond" reigns: "The sounds fade away, /The green leaves pale" (531). In a remarkable fusion of Greek mythology and Christian iconography the figure of Christ is pictured in Fortunato's song holding a flaming torch which points downward (532), an ancient symbol of death. He shows the way to the beyond for the souls imbued with romantic "Todessehnsucht" (longing for death).

Shortly after Fortunato has finished his song, Donati, one of the wild, demonic, doomed characters which wander aimlessly through Eichendorff's stories and novels, makes his first appearance. The narrator describes the expression of his eyes as "shooting mad flames from the depths of the eye sockets" (533). Donati's eyes emit a "sparkling stroke of furious lightning" (534). Yet he is also a "dark figure" (533).

Fortunato compares him to a "pale misshapen moth of the night" (534) and calls him a "moonshine hunter" (535). Indeed, after his brief appearance, Donati exits into the darkness of the night.[3]

The all-important first encounter with the marble statue takes place at night in the moonlight. Here, as elsewhere in the story, moonlight and magic ("Zauber", "zauberisch") are semantically interrelated, and the adjective "still" which occurs five times in this scene becomes an element of the world of Venus. Furthermore, the image of the magic circle reappears: "A few swans were quietly and monotonously circling the statue." (537) In a narcissistic gesture, the statue appears to look at its own reflection in the water. Images of spring and vegetative life round off the description of this enchanted scene. But soon the magic of the statue fades away as quickly as it appeared. The waning of the spell is coupled with a sharp change of mood as well as lighting: "When he looked up again, everything seemed all of a sudden transformed. The moon peeked out strangely between clouds, a sudden gust disturbed the smooth surface of the pond. In the all-pervading silence, the statue of Venus, terribly white and motionless, looked at him in an almost frightful way with eyes of stone." (537) The implicit reference to death in this description prompts a shift in Florio's mood from "Wehmut" (melancholy) and "Entzücken" (delight) to "Schrecken" (fright) and "Grausen" (horror).

Even though, the next morning, Florio tries to shake the spell of his encounter with the mysterious statue of Venus, he is unable to do so because in his heart "the stars were still tracing their magic circles, and in their midst was the beautiful marble statue looking at him with renewed irresistible power." (539) Wandering around aimlessly, he enters the "Lustgarten" of a palace where he spies on a beautiful lady whose uncanny resemblance with the marble statue makes him shudder. Even though "a bright flash of sunlight" (540) for a brief moment illuminates her, her realm is not that of sober daylight but takes on the dreamlike features of a shadowy world like the bottom of a river. The quasi-submerged setting of this scene brings to mind Florio's dream of the sinking ship. While the description of the garden of Venus abounds with references to vegetative life linked with the motifs of stillness and magic, the emotional resonance of the scene in Florio's mind ranges once more from fright to melancholy. When he finally flees from the garden, he finds, still within its confines, Donati in a state of death-like slumber "like a corpse" (542) — yet another example of the fusion of the Venus — and the death themes.

The same night, Florio believes he recognizes the Venus figure once more, thus time behind the window of a house inside the city walls of Lucca.[4] The apparition is placed in a setting of "the glow of dusk", starlight, moonlight, and vegetative images (leaves, blossoms, and flowers).

During the masked ball where Florio encounters the mysterious Doppelgänger in Greek costume, the diffuse lighting arrangements of the event ("only a few lights were still flickering and lit the place dimly" (550)) enhance the ghostly aura of that scene. The song of the beautiful lady whom Florio follows towards the end of the ball and who seems to be yet another embodiment of Venus, contains a reference to moonlight: "I quietly submerge pleasure and sorrow into the gentle waves of the moonlit night." (548) The elements of moonlight, Eros, magic, and dangerous entrapment all find symbolic expression in the image of the "golden net of love" (548) woven by the rays of the moon. When Florio finally seizes the opportunity to talk to the Greek lady and ask for her name she refuses to identify herself and issues him a warning couched in the imagery of flowers and vegetation which evoques both the forces of life and death: ". . . accept the flowers offered by life as the moment gives them to you and don't search for the roots deep down — because down there reigns stillness; it is a reign devoid of pleasure." (549) Significantly, the reader is reminded at this point that this scene is steeped in moonlight: "Rays of moonlight intermittently penetrated the leaves and branches of the trees and fell on her figure." (549). Once back at his abode in Lucca, Florio's confused state of mind finds expression in the peculiar semantic "cluster" of components with which the reader has by now become familiar: the lure of Eros, magic, moonlight, stillness, and fright: "The landscape outside was unrecognizable and still like a miraculously entwined hieroglyphic shape under the magic moonlight. Almost frightened, he closed the window and fell on his bed where he drifted into strange dreams like those of a sick person delirious from fever." (552)

Florio's last and most crucial encounter with Venus takes place in her palace which looks like a Greek temple. Once more, images of the vegetative sphere (flowers, blossoms) abound. When Venus leads him to her chamber it is night and everything is dimly lit by "magic" (*zauberisch*) moonlight. As so often in the story, Florio feels as though long forgotten childhood memories are rising to the surface of his consciousness. Indeed, the process of anamnesis — in psychoanalytic language one might talk in terms of a contact between the spheres of the preconscious and the conscious — is an integral part of Florio's trial and affliction. He has yet to conquer and sublimate the dangerous forces of Eros/nature. At the climactic moment of greatest danger lightning strikes and it seems "as if the lady were standing in front of him, rigid, her eyes closed, her face and arms white." (557) She appears to be transformed back into stone before she completely vanishes like a spook. The sudden change of lighting and mood, quite similar to the one during the scene of Florio's first encounter with the marble statue, is prompted by Fortunato's singing and Florio's short prayer to (the Christian) God. The concomitant theme of narcissism (Venus regards her reflection in a mirror, the pictures of knights on the tapestry all of a sudden resemble Florio and threaten him) connotes death just as the lightning initiates the "death" and disappearance of Venus (". . . that she became ever more pale . . ." (557)). The lurid "Dämmerung" (twilight) of Venus' chamber, however, is finally replaced by the peaceful, disenchanted moonlit city of Lucca.

The morning after the crisis, Florio overhears a gardener greeting the morning with a song: "Gone has the dark night. /So have the magic delusions of evil. /The bright light of the day awakens us to work. /Let's get up and praise the Lord." (558) One day later — again it is morning — Florio is leaving Lucca together with Fortunato and Bianca. They see in the distance, in the "twilight" of the morning, the debris of an old Greek temple. The morning sun shines on a partly destroyed marble statue. This sight prompts Fortunato to sing a long song in which he summarizes Florio's adventures and contrasts the figure of Venus who has arisen from her "Göttergrab" with the appearance of the Virgin Mary on a rain-bow. The latter holds the child Jesus in her arms. If we consider that Venus-Aphrodite is — according to the Greek myth — rising from the ocean and that in Eichendorff's text she is repeatedly associated with the element of water (Florio's first dream of the sirens, the pond with the statue, Venus' reference to "the gentle waves of the moonlit night", her garden which is compared to the bottom of a river) it would not be unduly speculative to see in the Old Testament symbol of the rainbow the product of (and reconciliation between) water, i.e. the pagan world and daylight, i.e. the Christian world, a reconciliation in which, however, Christianity (the Virgin Mary) becomes the dominating feature. Florio's soul is freed from "evil dreams" and the magic spell. The "devilish deception" (562) succumbs to daylight and morning which liberate and cleanse the heart of the afflicted.

Nature and Eros, in Eichendorff's text almost invariably associated with night and moonlight, are restrained and purified by the Christian spirit in conjunction with the healing powers of the poet. As Fortunato puts it: "Believe me, an honest poet can risk a lot, since art which is without pride and sin, calms and soothes the wild earth spirits which rise up from the depths and try to ensnare us." (562)[5] Yet nature itself, as symbolized in the light of the morning, has the power to hold in check the forces which plunge man into the irrational, the instinctual realm, into sin and evil, a sphere which in Eichendorff's fictional universe is so closely allied with death and the emotions of melancholy, shudder, fright, and horror.[6]

The symbolic image of "Untergang" (going under, sinking) which is already prefigured in Florio's first dream and recurs several times thereafter, is finally countered by the upward surge of the rainbow and the flight of larks in the light of early morning. Throughout Eichendorff's novella, morning, sun, and daylight stand primarily for the liberated soul which has shaken off the spell cast by Venus. This semantic/thematic "rule" appears to broken only twice in the novella: in Fortunato's first song at the beginning of the text, Venus and her realm are steeped "in the glow of dawn" (531), and it is but a single ray of sunlight that hits Venus in her otherwise dim and shadowy garden. And only after the spell of Venus has been broken and Florio and his company are able to view the site of the dilapidated temple with the "partially demolished" marble statue from a distance, the morning sun is finally allowed to illuminate this seemingly innocent and peaceful scene which does not betray any trace of past frightful experiences. In the end, the morning sunlight celebrates its victory over the pagan magic of night and moonlight. The light of the morning sun means spiritual freedom (with the religious overtone characteristic of Eichendorff), moral tranquillity, and emotional joy: "Here I am, Lord, I salute the light." (562)[7]

There remains, though, an unresolved contradiction in Eichendorff's story with regard to the theme of death. Whereas, at the beginning, Christ holding the flaming torch invites the weary soul to come "home" to God, throughout the remainder of the novella Christian piety calls the erring soul back to life and light, away from the death-bound pagan forces which, paradoxically, always express themselves through vegetative imagery of life. Life and death are fused in nature, as Eichendorff perceives it. Yet the question remains: which is the worthier stance: the somewhat over-exalted Christian-romantic longing for death as reunification with God or the unredeemed death of the immanence of nature as part of the life cycle?

If one compares Eichendorff's symbolism of light with that of other authors of the Romantic period in Germany, he definitely stands in the Romantic tradition, yet his position also significantly deviates from the Romantic context and thus stands out in a unique way among those of his fellow Romanticists. Novalis, for example, in his "Hymns to Night", describes night as a motherly realm of love beyond time and space. While night and death lift the soul upwards towards God, light, in general means to Novalis: limitation, individuation, unrest, isolated and separate things as appearances. This seems far removed from Eichendorff's world. However, there is also a different philosophy of light in German Romanticism which is much closer to Eichendorff's positive view of morning, daylight, sunlight — and that is the religious interpretation of light found already in the Old and New Testament and in the writings of the mystics where God is light and enters the soul to become the "Seelenfünklein" (Bernhard von Clairvaux). The romantic philosopher Friedrich Schelling interprets light as the divine, immaterial essence of nature, as "Weltseele", and both Friedrich Schlegel and Otto Friedrich Runge equate light with the transcendent realm of the divine.[8] Eichendorff's phrase "Morgenrot der Ewigkeit" (the dawn of eternity)[9] points in the same direction.

The theme of Eros with its pagan-Christian dualism contrasting temptation and seduction with liberation and regained self-control leads Eichendorff to a dualistic use of the symbolism of light in which night and moonlight become components of a negatively charged semantic field of images, concepts, and expressions of emotions. The daylight of the morning, in contrast, symbolizes the redemption of Eros and the dark side of nature through an act of ethical recovery in which God's grace supplants evil magic and where the chaste spirituality of Christian piety defeats the demons of Eros.

Boston College

NOTES

[1] Compare the cautious but convincing interpretation along psycho-analytical lines by Lothar Pikulik, "Die Mythisierung des Geschlechtstriebes in Eichendorff's *Marmorbild*" in *Mythos und Mythologie in der Literatur des 19 Jahrhunderts*, ed. Helmut Koopmann (Frankfurt/M.: Klostermann, 1979), pp. 159—172.

[2] The page numbers given in parenthesis in the text refer to: Joseph von Eichendorff: *Werke*, ed. Jost Perfahl; Vol. 2 Romane, Erzählungen (München: Winkler, 1970). Translations from the German are all mine.

[3] Later in the story, Donati claims that Venus is "an acquaintance" of his (542).

[4] As the appearances of Venus at the masked ball and in the house demonstrate, her temporary reign includes both the area outside the social world of the city and that inside.

[5] Manfred Beller, "Narziß und Venus: Klassische Mythologie und romantische Allegorie in Eichendorff's Novelle *Das Marmorbild, Euphorion* 62 (1968), 117—142, interprets Venus as the Muse of the poet (she carries a lute and sings) neglecting the theme of Eros.

[6] Peter Paul Schwarz, *Aurora: Zur romantischen Zeitstruktur bei Eichendorff* (Bad Homburg v. d. Höhe/Berlin/Zürich: Gehlen) describes that realm somewhat vaguely as "dionysisch-erotischen Totalbezug des Lebens" (190) or as "Auflösung des Individuellen an [sic] das Lebensganze" (191). On the two aspects of nature (nature in need of redemption and nature as a liberating force) compare also: René Wehrli, *Eichendorffs Erlebnis und Gestaltung der Sinnenwelt* (Frauenfeld: Huber, 1938).

[7] As Schwarz (*loc. cit.* p. 81) points out, the morning in Eichendorff's works has two dimensions: a cosmogonic and an eschatological one.

[8] Compare the detailed study by August Langen, "Zur Lichtsymbolik der deutschen Romantik," in *Märchen, Mythos, Dichtung. Festschrift Friedrich von der Leyen*, ed. Hugo Kuhn and Kurt Schier (München: Beck, 1963), 557—485. See also Schwarz (*loc. cit.*) which contains a valuable chapter on light symbolism in German Romanticism.

[9] Joseph von Eichendorff, *Werke*, Vol. I (Gedichte, Versepen, Dramen, Autobiographisches), ed. Jost Perfahl (München: Winkler, 1970), p. 293 ("Im Alter").

BEVERLY SCHLACK RANDLES

VIRGINIA WOOLF'S POETIC IMAGINATION: PATTERNS OF LIGHT AND DARKNESS IN *TO THE LIGHTHOUSE*

To the Lighthouse, an exquisitely formed, musical novel composed of triads, is Woolf's only novel with a Table of Contents, and named (rather than numbered) sections. Part I, "The Window," although it takes up more than half the novel, covers half of one day in the lives of Mr. and Mrs. Ramsay; Part II, "Time Passes," is a brief but extraordinary lyric interlude which occurs after the death of Mrs. Ramsay; Part III, "The Lighthouse," alternates the simultaneous events of an expedition to the lighthouse with the completion of a painting.

Woolf's novels are usually organized to present patterns of meaning in which both characters and events are endowed with symbolic resonance, but *To the Lighthouse* is exceptional even within Woolf's idiosyncratic methodology. Excluding only her other master-work, *The Waves*, *To the Lighthouse* is based entirely upon a coordinated set of primary symbolic values. In discussing this rich and exhaustive network of relations, I shall pay particular attention to the emphasis she has placed upon the agonistic play of light and darkness,[1] which enriches the depth structure of the novel and intensifies its expressivity.

The pervasive metaphor named in the title and the final section functions here as do Melville's white whale, Hawthorne's scarlet letter, and Henry James' golden bowl: they are a "central emblematic image,"[2] pointing to the interrelation between inner and outer worlds. The lighthouse becomes a symbolic equivalent of the idea of androgyny after it has been experienced as representing the Ramsay marriage, itself a symbolic rendering of archetypal attributes of male and female.

Woolf was interested in gender prototypes as both a feminist and a symbolist. Conflicts of masculine intellect and feminine intuition pervade her works, both fictional and non-fictional. Here, although Mr. and Mrs. Ramsay are fully developed, convincingly created human beings, they also sign the mixture of *yin* and *yang* inherent in any marriage. Mr. Ramsay, father and assertive male principle, is *logos* to his wife's *eros* and maternal sensibility; vigilant where she is acquiescent;

193

A-T. Tymieniecka (ed.), Analecta Husserliana, Vol. XXXVIII, 193—205.
© 1992 *Kluwer Academic Publishers. Printed in the Netherlands.*

tough-minded, even brutally insistent upon facts, where she is tender and evasive.

Like Woolf's idea of the androgynous mind (which she developed in *A Room of One's Own*), the lighthouse combines opposing principles of phallus and eye, tower and beam. In her deployment of light and dark symbols, Woolf avoids the implicit masculinization of the symbolic analogues of light and enlightenment to intellect, wisdom or epiphany. This novel postulates darkness as male, and identifies a female, Mrs. Ramsay, with the lighthouse beam.[3] Mrs. Ramsay is instinctive and intuitive, but not in a way which enforces or replicates a sexist symbolism: her beam is linked to its equivalent in the natural world, *moon* light, which is conventional female signing. Mrs. Ramsay's is not the primary sun light of intellection, a power strongly questioned throughout this novel; it is the more diffuse radiation of a unifying spirit of love, pulsating light into the darkness.

In Part III, Mrs. Ramsay sits behind the window beyond which Mr. Ramsay paces and declaims poetry. She radiates a power predicated as contrary to the disruptive force of her husband. The lighthouse and the window suggest a dual function, complexly expressed: the former is a solid structure, external to the window's interiority, but its beam is perceived through the glass. The dialectical ambivalences of the marriage partners are echoed in the descriptions of their respective abilities to see: Mrs. Ramsay is "short-sighted" (21),[4] but her beauty is a dazzling light, a "torch" (64). That Mr. Ramsay takes the long-sighted view is encoded in his profession: he is a philosopher who has written upon "subject and object and the nature of reality" (38). Interested as he is in the relation of perception to things, he sees the light-house as a physical truth entirely defined by its independent factual presence, while Mrs. Ramsay often refuses to see, or at least to acknowledge, the lighthouse's separateness from her own emotional needs and imaginative projections.

In the celebrated argument about the weather which opens the novel, maternal solicitude for young James leads Mrs. Ramsay to predict that the weather will be fine and the expedition to the lighthouse will indeed take place as planned. Against the insistence on bad weather (by both Mr. Ramsay and his toadying accolite, Charles Tansley), Mrs. Ramsay solaces James: " 'Perhaps you will wake up and find the sun shining and the birds singing, . . . Perhaps it will be fine tomorrow' " (26). To Mr. Ramsay's " 'But, . . . it won't be fine' " (10), she counters with " 'But it

may be fine — I expect it will be fine'" (11). Tansley bolsters his
mentor's position: "'There'll be no landing at the lighthouse tomorrow'"
(15). A bit later, an irascible Mr. Ramsay declares there is not "'the
slightest possible chance that they could go'" (50). He declares himself
"enraged" by "the folly of women's minds;" specifically, with how his
wife "flew in the face of facts, made his children hope what was utterly
out of the question, in effect, told lies" (50). He stamps his foot and
says "'Damn you'" to his wife. Leaving aside the issues of his petty
emotional "female" outburst, and his utter failure to take others' feelings
into account (since there is a passage in the novel which addresses this
issue), what dazzles the reader is Ramsay's questionable performance as
a metaphysician, a performance replicated by his robotic follower
Tansley. He has projected his pessimism onto nature as objectivity;
characterized a predictive guess about a future event as a *fact*; made a
weather report — one of the most notorious error-filled vagaries of life
— the basis of his absolute, unqualified assertions; he has labeled a
person positing an opposite meterological opinion a *liar*. While making
a mockery of any standards of objectivity, he and Tansley demean
women, accusing them of lacking precisely this vaunted ability. Mrs.
Ramsay's language has been filled with the shaded contingencies of *if*,
expect, may and *perhaps*; even in a role which very nearly forces upon
her the need to soften her son's disappointment with some truth-
stretching, she hews to proper speculation. That the weather does turn
out bad, and that husband and wife effect a reconciliation in which he
sheepishly capitulates, do not alter Mr. Ramsay's unsavory deployment
of *mind* — a particular grudge Woolf held against male intellection —
as a hurtful instrument of power and dominance.

Woolf slyly casts further doubt upon masculine reason when she lets
us know that Ramsay's sole philosophic contribution has been "one
little book" (39), published when he was twenty-five; "what came after
was more or less amplification, repetition" (39). Through her wisdom-
as-alphabet metaphor, Woolf reveals the sterile reductive dimensions of
academic categorizing. Discrete letters, dispensed in a linear straight-
jacket (and, of course, conventional symbols of philosophic logic) here
signify a plodding, ultimately unsuccessful intent to understand. Woolf's
presentation of Mr. Ramsay's struggle with the alphabet of knowledge
is riddled with awareness of the incapacity of intellect alone to grasp
reality. Ramsay is "bogged down like David Hume in the mud of his
own logic."[5] Within his rigid categorical framework, Ramsay repeats

"every letter of the alphabet from *A* to *Z* accurately in order. Meanwhile, he stuck at *Q*. On, then, to *R*" (55). Symbolism of light and dark informs Woolf's description of Ramsay's task: his philosophic quest is an attempt "to pierce the darkness" (55) and his fears of failing to achieve fame and immortality are fears "his own little light" will be subsumed. He despairs when "the intensity of his gaze" flickers lower and some "eyelid" closes out further light; in such darkness, "*R* was beyond him. He would never reach *R*" (54).

Ramsay, a rich and melancholy paradox, practices a discipline which means *love of wisdom*, according to which the highest virtue may be self knowledge, yet he cannot see as far as *R*, his own symbol. He who lectures on "Locke, Hume, [Bishop] Berkeley" (70) does not understand himself. He is, moreover, insensible to the things of this world: he merely pretends to admire the flowers his wife admires and takes no pleasure in the star light. Mrs. Ramsay complains "he never looked at things" (108) — something of an impediment for a metaphysician!

Very different, however, is Mrs. Ramsay's eagerness to perceive. After she finishes reading a fairy tale to James, they look across the bay and observe the lighthouse becoming operational with two brief strokes of light, followed by a long, steady stroke. With this last beam, Mrs. Ramsay identifies: "it seemed to her like her own eyes meeting her own eyes" (97). She experiences the stroke as "purifying" because it is "without vanity . . . stern, . . . searching, . . . beautiful" (97).

Mrs. Ramsay relishes those moments of solitude when she feels the active bustle of her life shrinking to "a wedge-shaped core of darkness" (95) beyond all attachments and distractions: "Beneath it is all dark, it is all spreading, it is unfathomably deep" (96), yet the busy, social *persona* she presents to others never exposes this "core of darkness" which is her private self. That secret inner self (to which Mr. Ramsay is not privy, either in her or himself) is synthetic — it contains both light and darkness, illumination and shadow.

The self Mrs. Ramsay presents to the outer world is magnificently conveyed in the dinner party scene. Fifteen people assemble for Boeuf en Daube; one of the guests, seeing the house windows ablaze for the event, is so impressed he can only chant "lights, lights, lights" (119). This is dinner as ritual communion, triumph over life's disparate moments, a meta-dinner, more fulfilling than filling.

Presiding at the head of the table, Mrs. Ramsay dispenses soup and falls prey to pessimism after intuiting the spiritual strife embedded within her guests, antagonisms which will prevent them from merging into a genuine community. Discord reigns: there is Mrs. Ramsay's own sexism ("she pitied men always, as if they lacked something — women never" (129)) and Tansley's corrosive misogyny ("silly, superficial, flimsey" women), accompanied by his gleeful assertion "'No going to the lighthouse tomorrow, Mrs. Ramsay'" (129). Lily Briscoe stews in resentment of Tansley's taunting "women can't write, women can't paint" (130). Mr. Bankes muses upon the human race's unattractiveness as a species (134), while Mr. Ramsay frowns and scowls, not troubling to hide how bored he is.

Mrs. Ramsay orders eight candles to be brought to the table; they change everything. They illumine a dish of fruit in a surreal way, so that it seems "possessed of great size and depth" (146); they illumine the faces around the table so that they are "brought nearer . . . and composed, as they had not been in the twilight, into a party" (146). The light empowers human solidarity within the house. Night is "shut off" (147) by windows which keep chaos and darkness at bay. Inside light prevails; the guests feel an atavistic comfort in their communal resistance to the ominous black fluidity "out there" (147). The candlelight has annihilated isolation; Mrs. Ramsay feels her uneasiness depart and Lily feels "sudden exhilaration" (147).[6]

When Mrs. Ramsay glances out of the uncurtained window "with its ripple of reflected lights" (158), the distortion does not give her pause. In the grip of a certainty of coherence and stability, she does not recognize any possibility of inaccurate perception. As with Mr. Ramsay's intellectuality, Woolf undercuts Mrs. Ramsay's solipsistic wishful thinking. The clear window of daytime is now black with night; it does not reveal, it reflects, like a mirror. It nows blocks the "out there" world behind it, and replicates a fabricated ontology whose origin is within Mrs. Ramsay's own wishes and needs. Candles have been marshalled against the natural force of night, but the light they give out is a man-made contingency.

Soon enough Mrs. Ramsay is assailed by the melancholy truth of evanescence. The dinner party ends, as it must, with her awareness that it has become "already the past" (168); she goes "upstairs in the lamplight alone" (169).

Lily Briscoe also feels the disintegration set in, and within this rendering of a failure to compose something of lasting value dwells Woolf's critique of social life and the traditional woman's role. Mrs.

Ramsay, attempting to find solid reality in the midst of the accepted roles of perfect wife, mother and hostess, will be no more (if not less) successful than Lily Briscoe, the solitary artist who does not participate in the approved roles for women. Mrs. Ramsay, whose quest for a unifying truth causes her to identify with the searching lighthouse beam, is nevertheless required to dissemble — as mother, for example, when she covers over with her shawl the fact of death which the skull in her children's bedroom represents, or when she assures them with fairy tales. Her need to participate in illusion as well as reality is perhaps behind her ambivalent observation about the lighthouse beam: it is the "steady light, the pitiless, the remorseless [beam] which was so much her, yet so little her" (99).

Mr. and Mrs. Ramsay sit reading in their room after the party and he is "relieved" — presumably of his relentless overground march through the alphabet of thought, that forced competitive march which has controlled and shaped his life. He comes to feel "it didn't matter a damn who reached Z" (179). Bathed in the enlarging empathy that literature enduces, Ramsay revels in "the astonishing delight and feeling of vigour that it gave him" (180). Might this not be Woolf's hint that insight into the significance of the life experience comes best not from philosophy but literature?

In a state of emotional readiness induced by literature (Mrs. Ramsay has been reading a Shakespeare sonnet), they look to each other for solace and assurance. Both are ready to receive; he is not capable of giving. He reverts to his abrupt, reproving austerity, informing her that she was no more likely to finish her knitting this evening than he and the children are to sail to the lighthouse tomorrow. She concedes both points; he smiles at her capitulation. Yet, it is she who makes the last move in the marital chess game of power politics. She feels "she had triumphed again. She had not said it" (186). By withholding that expression of love which her husband wanted to hear, she has answered his dominating force with manipulative passivity.

"Time Passes," the brief middle portion of the novel, is a "sustained impersonal meditation on man and nature, on consciousness and its non-conscious environment."[7] The night which concluded Part I, the darkness behind the window, has become the global nightmare of world war. Night, like war, is a male force; the narrator calls it *he*, as nature is called *she*.[8]

Assorted Ramsay children, Mr. Bankes, Lily Briscoe and Mr.

Carmichael the poet arrive at the house on a moonless evening of heavy rain and "immense darkness" (189). This male darkness possesses both psychoanalytic and ontological dimensions; it has an animate life; it "creeps in at keyholes and crevices, . . . [steals] round window blinds," invades rooms and settles upon the objects therein; the very furniture is "confounded" (190). Pitted against this all-pervasive dark, human consciousness is nearly over-whelmed. How is the human world to establish itself in the face of an indifferent or annihilating natural universe?

For Woolf, the answer to what sort of struggle for identity and consciousness can be made against that enduring physical force was nearly always the same. To the awful omniscience of universal darkness — broken only occasionally by "some random light" (191) from moon, stars or the lighthouse — Woolf juxtaposes a poet, reading. Creative consciousness is her answer to mindless chaos: Carmichael is reading Virgil and keeps the "candle burning rather longer than the rest" (189).

The choice of a poet of antiquity reinforces *continuity* of human endeavor: in reading, reader and writer keep each other alive, or as W. H. Auden would have it, the death of a poet is kept from his poems.[9] Out in the "chaos and tumult of the night," the narrator finds only "idiot games" of "brute confusion" (203). Into the context of a long, dark winter comes the news that Mrs. Ramsay has "died rather suddenly" (194), leaving Mr. Ramsay's out-stretched arms empty.

With the nurturing female presence gone, the darker forces of nature "met nothing . . . that wholly resisted them" (194). Feminist metaphysics (a struggle between male destructiveness and a female generative principle) pervades the entire section. The sea wind attacks the empty house, loosening the shawl Mrs. Ramsay had thrown over the skull's head. Her endeavor to combat and conceal death appears about to be overcome by unadorned existential facts (facticity being male). Destruction lingers everywhere. Rust, dust, mildew and warp prevail. Wallpaper fades and flaps against the dilapidated walls. When it would appear that nature can and will destroy human handwork utterly, there arrives upon the desperately disintegrating scene a female savior.

Scrub bucket and dust rag in hand, Mrs. McNab opens all the windows, real and symbolic. This "witless" and "toothless" (196) cleaning lady is transformed by the narrative genius of the passage into a cosmic fixer-upper, housekeeper to the universe, a female domestic as God. The narrator calls her "care-taking woman" (196), commending her persistence and humor. She battles moldy books, moth-eaten clothes, plaster falling from walls, leaky windows, sodden carpets, rabbit-infested flower beds, rats in the attic. Seventy years old and weary, McNab hobbles about, dusting and wiping, singing as she lurches from room to room. She embodies "some incorrigible hope" (197), and that she can smile and sing at all suggests "some cleavage in the dark . . . some channel in the depths of obscurity through which light enough issued" (197).

Human consciousness and nature are absolutely separate orders — the narrator renders information about human life within brackets, Woolf's version of phenomenological reduction. Within brackets Mrs. Ramsay dies, even as the human brackets of Mr. Ramsay's arms reach out for her. Within brackets Prue Ramsay marries, accompanied by the coming of spring. Within brackets she dies in childbirth, granted no greater significance than the rain, flies and weeds described by the godlike narrator. Within brackets Andrew Ramsay dies in combat in France. The resurrection of the physical world, great stirrings of plant growth and bees humming, does not preclude mortality; cosmic bracketing ruthlessly humbles human activity.

Consciousness and nature are simultaneous occurrences in a large, vital experience that is value-free. Thus, Prue Ramsay dies trying to give birth in a season of birth; Mr. Carmichael fares better within the prisoning brackets and gives birth, as it were, to his own form of child, a volume of poetry.

Once McNab departs, the house is again at peril. Toads join the mice, plaster continues to fall, Mrs. Ramsay's death-covering shawl sways precariously, weeds proliferate, swallows nest in the drawing room. Woolf's ontological feminism is neither simple nor reductive, however. She grants that in addition to their function of cleaning up after the universe, women also embody a mindless generative force. Obscenely fertile nature replicates itself crazily: "let the poppy seed itself," the narrator complains, let "the carnation mate with the cabbage" (209). As rampant fertility and the caretaking and preserving impulse reach a crisis point — at which the house will either be saved or fall to ruin — ontology's cleaning lady returns with additional troops.

Equally old and weary Mrs. Bast combines with Mrs. McNab to banish destruction: they "stayed the corruption and the rot; rescued [the house] from the pool of Time" (209). The ladies do call in some marginal masculine help (Mrs. Bast's son catches the rats and weeds the garden; builders perform repairs), but it is to the female principle that the narrator returns in Homeric praise, citing their rescue of rotting books, including the very Scott novel that once briefly reduced Mr. Ramsay to tears.

The rhythmic glare of the lighthouse is now both perceiver and perceived; it interacts with consciousness and the physical world. Its fixed, regular beam penetrates the windows, revealing reality even when no human beings are there to perceive it doing so. It sends "its sudden stare over bed and wall" and looks "with equanimity at the thistle and the swallow, the rat and the straw" (208). It participates in changes through time and seasons, having a severe "authority" (199) in winter, but a softer presence in the house in spring, when it mixes with moonlight (200). When its long, third stroke strikes across the bed beneath the shawl-covered skull, it reasserts the presence of a female unifying force: Mrs. Ramsay's spirit survives in the house.

Late one fall evening, Lily Briscoe arrives, the first to return a living female consciousness to the house, and to record "the voice of the beauty of the world" (213). The house then fills with others and things reconstitute themselves. Mr. Carmichael reads by candlelight once again, and as dawn breaks, Lily Briscoe stirs from sleep. Human consciousness and the natural world are reconnected. The last sentence of the section is in fact one (crucial) word: "Awake" (214).

In the final section, "The Lighthouse," ten years after the events of Part I, the beam of Mrs. Ramsay's vision is providing direction to the traveler. The passive viewing of the world from the window has become an active journey to the lighthouse. Mr. Ramsay now sees the trip as a memorial to his wife; the dialectic dimensions of the Ramsay marriage, with its contrasts of light and dark, of intellect and intuition, are to be healed. The instrument of the reconciliation is the lighthouse, which embodies transcendence of personal limitations in androgynous comprehensiveness.

Three persons in particular achieve a unifying solution through the lighthouse: Mr. Ramsay will accomplish his wife's wish; James will successfully overcome his Oedipal hatred of his father; Lily Briscoe will resolve her relationship to both Ramsays and encode her understanding aesthetically, within her painting.

The children are sullen and resistant to the journey; they feel their father has forced this trip in his usual tyrannical manner. Yet when Mr. Ramsay reads in the becalmed boat, new feelings for him emerge. The man who has failed to reach Z, even R, persists in his quest with unflinching resolution, obstinately, in the face of his limitations and scant temporal fame. This begins to look much like courage. The relentless pessimism with which he plagued those near him has another face: a noble one of honesty, candor and intellectual integrity. His journey to the lighthouse is yet another quest for truth, another odyssey in which the traveler becomes a hero.

To this focused, stern totem of probing consciousness and human effort James must relate, by confronting his hatred and fear of his father's dominating presence. James likens his Oedipal emotions to a forest where there is both bright sunlight and dark shadow. In maternal terms, he recalls the lighthouse of his past: "a yellow eye that opened suddenly, and softly in the evening" (276). Looking at it in the present, seeking psychological reconciliation with his father, he sees the phallic dimensions: "the tower, stark and straight; . . . barred with black and white" (276—77). In a moment of androgynous illumination, he concludes both are true, "for nothing was simply one thing" (277).

Reaching the lighthouse, Mr. Ramsay makes contact with a truth outside himself, surrendering the uniqueness of his ego to a more impersonal reality. It is, moreover, an oblique admission that Mrs. Ramsay's optimism works, that a journey not completed yesterday may still take place tomorrow.

Alternating with the sailing to the lighthouse is the on-shore activity of Lily Briscoe. Like James, she too has reconciliations to make with Mr. and Mrs. Ramsay, and the lighthouse will help her transcend disunity. For Lily, the drama is one of aesthetic struggle. As she watches the boat approach the lighthouse, Lily ponders her lack of attachment, her felt loss of *relation* (218): "What does it mean then, what can it all mean?" (217).

The novel's lighthouse and window symbolism differentiates between commitment to impersonal values and involvement with interpersonal human relationships. Lily now has to discover both aesthetic and personal meanings in the idea of *relationship*. Thus, as the lighthouse image shrinks in importance, the painting increases in pluri-significance; Lily supplants Mrs. Ramsay, art becomes the ultimate expression of integration.

Lily's non-representational canvas, which balances shapes and shadows, has been called "a philosophical painting."[10] Her wish in the first section of the novel was to paint a relatively conventional Madonna and

Child portrait of Mrs. Ramsay and James; now she feels a need to represent human values as purely aesthetic, relational truths of mass, light and darkness. She realizes that if a corner of the canvas is bright, another has "need of darkness" (81), that "a light here required a shadow there" (82).[11]

Lily finds a curious correspondence between her shapes and the lighthouse developing as she paints, making a "first quick decisive stroke" (235), then a second and a third — an exact analog of the rhythms of the lighthouse beam. As Lily realizes that the strokes and pauses are related (236), the reader sees that the aesthetic pattern of this novel also relates and integrates its disparate elements. Her meditations upon formal design lead to a philosophical illumination: the effort to shape chaos is the effort "to make of the moment something permanent" (241). Even the question of the meaning of life must be approached in terms of contingencies, not absolutes. She finds not "great revelation," but "little daily miracles, illuminations, matches struck unexpectedly in the dark" (240).

The best of these "matches," whether canvas, philosophical treatise, or (Carmichael's) book of poetry, turns out to be creative activity. What remains is creative achievement: "all changes, but not words, not paint" (267), Lily decides. She has not yet achieved the desired equipoise in her canvas. It lacks the "necessary razor edge of balance between two forces" (287). Looking at the house and one of its windows (which recalls Mrs. Ramsay sitting there), Lily sees it whiten as someone sits in the chair behind the pane of glass. An "odd-shaped triangular shadow" (299) is cast upon the stairs and Lily's painterly eye finds the slightly changed configuration of light and shadow instructive.

As the wave of whiteness moves over the window pane, Lily feels the ghostly presence of Mrs. Ramsay, yet she is in search of that razor-edged balance she had envisioned as essential. She turns from a potential entrapment within Mrs. Ramsay's power (the mystique of womanly-woman, mother-and-child) toward the sea, toward the lighthouse and Mr. Ramsay. Confronting relational truths of both Mr. and Mrs. Ramsay, she achieves her own self-definition.[12] Reconciliation of dialectic poles is attained in art and in life simultaneously.

Observing the boat in the bay, Lily informs Mr. Carmichael, "'He had landed. It is finished'" (309). Turning back to her canvas, she finds she is able to integrate the Ramsays' separate meanings, "she with her impulses and quickness; he with his shudders and glooms" (296). She draws a line down the center of the canvas, supplying a central spine, the long stroke to which the other shapes in her painting are related. The Ramsays are balanced: she has combined his epistemology of mundane experience with his wife's intuitive illuminations — connecting their emotional worlds of light and shadow.

"It is finished" applies equally to her picture (for the line in her picture is the lighthouse Mr. Ramsay has reached) and to the novel which contains her own last thoughts: "it was finished . . . I have had my vision" (310).

These final sentences of the novel, its last word, *vision*, approximate the final thoughts of any thinker or artist. Woolf sees the reconciliation of antagonistic or disruptive forces as the function of art, which triumphs over darkness, dissolution, and chaos. Lily Briscoe's painting has brought all the parts together, as has Woolf's novel.

From the defective limitations of male and female roles, an androgynous incorporative truth has emerged. From the dialectic of human consciousness and the physical world, Woolf extracts inspiration to create the illusions — or are they truths? — which help us live wisely and well. She too has had a vision, which is offered to readers both as resignation and affirmation, steady and complete, like the lighthouse which houses tower and eye.

No less satisfactorily than Woolf's characters and Virginia Woolf herself do we know the healing integration of arriving at the lighthouse.

Adirondack Community College,
Glens Falls, New York

NOTES

[1] The dialectic of light and dark permeates Woolf's other novels; e.g., *The Waves, The Years*, and *Between the Acts. Night and Day* is the title of an early novel, her second.

[2] Northrop Frye, *Anatomy of Criticism: Four Essays* (New York: Atheneum, 1979), p. 92.

[3] Yet in her essay, "Lives of the Obscure," Woolf speaks of great men as falling "upon the race of life like beams from a lighthouse. They flash, they shock, they reveal, they vanish" (*Collected Essays* (New York: Harcourt, Brace and World, 1967), Vol. IV, p. 131).

[4] Virginia Woolf, *To the Lighthouse* (New York: A Harvest Book, 1955). Hereinafter, pagination will be given in the text.

[5] Eugene F. Kaelin, *Art and Existence: A Phenomenological Aesthetics* (Lewisburg: Bucknell University Press, 1970), p. 112. Kaelin notes that Ramsay's knowledge, being

"conceptual" and "general" (112), is "separated from its objects by the signs he must use to think with" (112—13), thus "removed from the reality he would like to describe" (113).

[6] Yet another radiance pervades the party: the engaged couple, Minta and Paul, exude the glow of their passion, as if they could "throw any light upon the question of love" (155).

[7] S. P. Rosenbaum, "The Philosophical Realism of Virginia Woolf," in *English Literature and British Philosophy: A Collection of Essays*, ed. S. P. Rosenbaum (Chicago: University of Chicago Press, 1971), p. 342.

[8] For example: "Did Nature supplement what man advanced? Did she complete what he began?" (201—2), and "Night fell, his head crowned; his sceptre jewelled" (213).

[9] W. H. Auden, "In Memory of W. B. Yeats," line 11: "The death of the poet was kept from his poems."

[10] S. P. Rosenbaum, *op.cit.*, p. 343.

[11] Compare Merleau-Ponty's observations on the ontology of painting, especially his description of painting as "a *logos* of lines, of lighting, of colors, of reliefs, of masses — a conceptless presentation of universal Being" (Maurice Merleau-Ponty, *The Primacy of Perception and Other Essays*, trans. J. M. Edie (Evanston, Illinois: Northwestern University Press, 1964), p. 188.

[12] Compare Merleau-Ponty on painters as "artisans of Being" (*op. cit.*, p. 180) and of their vision as encountering "as at a crossroads, all the aspects of Being" (p. 188).

JORGE GARCÍA-GÓMEZ

THE SWAN AND EROTIC LOVE: LIGHT, COLOR, AND MYTH IN RUBÉN DARÍO'S POETICS

As the title suggests, I would like to examine Rubén Darío's poetry by placing it in a most specific setting, namely, the one which is constituted by looking at it from the standpoint of the swan and yet this formulation of the approach I am adopting here may prove misleading, unless I introduce some preliminary qualifications.

No doubt the role of the swan as symbol is of some significance in this poet's work, but it would be both an injustice and a travesty to leave it at that. For Darío, the swan is certainly a symbol, but only if we understand this term in a very precise sense, namely, as the standard-bearer of *otherness*, to be sure, but of an otherness which gives itself on the *face* or *surface* of the symbol, and neither as a purely enigmatic presence behind the symbol nor as some thing or event disclosable by means of the symbol, but only by the expedient of some convention, rule, or conceit. No, the swan is first and foremost a definite object, to wit: the goal that Darío proposes for himself as that which is to be brought into being by him in his creative activity by means of the instrumentality of the symbol bearing its name.

But even this approximation would not measure up to Darío's accomplishment, were I not to add that the swan is so constituted by him and for him by letting it be conformed to two different norms, namely, those of Greek mythology and erotic love. It is in this manner, then, that the swan arises *and* acquires definition, but not as if we were alternately playing the same motif in two scales. In fact, in his way with the swan, he can only succeed by means of the synthesis of erotic love and mythology or, more precisely, in terms of erotic love mediated by Greek mythology. Let us try to see this with some care.

In the remarkable book[1] he devoted to his Nicaraguan *confrère*, the great Spanish poet Pedro Salinas does not present us with a simple figure, who would consistently display a selfsame visage and register, as would someone who primarily lets his erotic memories and yearnings pour into his poems. In fact, Darío's career as a poet could be understood as the struggle for self- and world-knowledge carried out by the

207

A-T. Tymieniecka (ed.), Analecta Husserliana, Vol. XXXVIII, 207—235.
© 1992 *Kluwer Academic Publishers. Printed in the Netherlands.*

instrumentality of the poem. In other words, he spent a major portion of his life in the effort of knowing himself poetically in relation to the world, in so far as it opens itself up to him in that special manner which can be characterized as *proportionate* to his glance and as *co-constitutive* of it. And such a struggle and effort is no other than his love of woman. As Salinas has demonstrated, Darío's life, conceived in this fashion, cannot possibly turn out to be a one-sided and repetitive affair; it is rather a matter of increasing depth and of illusion, melancholy, and *Weltschmerz*, by which he anticipates death and purifies his life in its ever-renewed, multi-levelled challenges to disclosure. One could venture the notion that Darío's existence as a poet is the attempt to win over his life by way of his love of the Other, in so far as the fleeting and perishable in life may be overcome. But this involves a paradox, and yet one which does not consist in pursuing the conquest of becoming by means of some recourse to eternity, as a sort of intemporal domain alien to this world; rather, he seeks to vanquish the passing moment by way of the passing moment, an adventure which — if we creatively reflect on it, as any great poet can do in his unique way — would lead to the sense and realization of the immensity of time and space and of the possible nullity of individual human life. Hence the paradox and the melancholy and *Weltschmerz* which, as correlates and results, suffuse Darío's existence as the growing flavor of his creative life.[2]

Undoubtedly, Darío is both a sensuous and a sensual poet. As depth psychology has clearly shown, however, of these two dimensions of human sensibility, *eros* is not only the more profound, but as well the one which gives orientation and motivation to sensuousness itself. In so far as he is a man, Darío is no exception to this rule. And yet we have to pose the question, the answer to which would determine whether or not anyone in this predicament is a genuine poet. It could be formulated thus: *Is eros sufficient for him?* If it were, Darío's work could only be abusively characterized as poetry, for it would amount only to being a sort of diary or memoir, i.e., the autobiographical acknowledgment of yearning and desire. In fact, if any man were to lead a far-reaching but genuine erotic existence, he could not limit or devote his life to it; he would rather have to sublimate and purify *eros* and learn how to practice and regard it in depth. In other words, he would have to make it his own; he would need to *spiritualize* it. Now, this is precisely what obtains in Darío's creative work. Salinas formulates this point with precision, when he asserts that ". . . when erotic yearning seeks to go beyond . . . [the world of immediacy] in search of a more encompassing space, one is forced to enter into various other mediate worlds . . ."[3] A poet *qua* poet is in need of a *mundus imaginabilis*, and yet this experience of his is no *viaticum* by which he would seek to evade the *mundus sensibilis* or at least to make it acquire the status of provisionality or even of substitutiveness. On the contrary, the poet's *mundus imaginabilis* is the device he creates precisely in order to live the *mundus sensibilis* even more profoundly than ordinary mortals may in terms of their encounters with the lifeworld and one another in everydayness. And this is precisely what I mean by such a need for spiritualization.

It is to be noted that Salinas speaks, in this context, of a *plurality* of possible imaginary worlds which could be put to the use that the poet intends. The fact that only one is chosen indicates, however, that the various imaginary worlds are not given to the poet himself *in statu indifferentiae*. One could argue that for every poet there is one or at least a few such worlds which would really matter for the task at hand. Now, this restricted set is determined by the special sort of openness to reality which characterizes the given poet (or to be more precise, for "determines" bespeaks necessity, it is the set of those imaginary worlds that are compatible with the essential world-openness which defines the poet in question.)[4] But this certainly implies that, unless the poet examines the attitude he adopts, he would be unable to achieve self-knowledge and thereby the creation of genuine poetry. And yet this is a matter of intolerable ignorance and nothing akin to instinct, spiritual or otherwise. In my view, this position is warranted only if we understand self- and world-knowledge as correlative and co-constitutive facets of experience. There is no Book of Life where we may find already inscribed what anyone is. Accordingly, we have to see in the poem, to begin with, the suitable pedagogical method of self-scrutiny and self-knowledge available in the existence of a poet. Having said this, one must nevertheless be careful to understand this contention aright, for the poet's life is no attempt to know himself as such. Self-knowledge is always the way of access to world-knowledge, and vice versa, in perfect mutuality. Although generally true, this thesis acquires a special form in the creative life of the poet, since what he says or does is not externally or accidentally dressed up in "poetic" garb, as Plato would have us believe.[5] We must learn to appreciate that the poet's manner of self- and world-knowledge is constituted for what it is in and by his forming or creative work. All in one, the poem is a *sui generis* power of self- and world-knowledge that renders subjective and objective dimensions available which would be inaccessible otherwise; in fact, it is the fruit and synthesis of the special correlation of world- and self-knowledge in which poetic creation consists and abides in and for a given poet.

Salinas attempts to formulate this very point so far as Rubén Darío is concerned, and yet he manages to do so only in a somewhat enigmatic manner. This is what he says:

Greece is no object of knowledge, but only the lodestar [gathering] his various separate desires [which he immediately lives as] in search of direction. This was the significance of our Greek heritage for Rubén — it allowed him to secure a measure of stability for the urging restlessness of his desires.[6]

In my opinion, it is important to remark on several points made or suggested in this passage. First of all, we are told which sort of world is this *mundus imaginabilis* by means of which Darío wants to come better to know his own sensibility, i.e., his own self as absorbed in the task of sensuously coming to terms with the world. Such an instrumentality is no other than Greek mythology. Any yet Darío's relationship to this tradition is not presented as one that is abstract or external or, for that matter, as one resulting from inquiry or even mere scholarship. No, the Greece of *mythos* is for him intimate and familiar, for it is his lodestar, a guideline for his life. In other words, upon choosing Greek mythology as his means, Darío is not leaping into the void; he is not behaving arbitrarily; he is not kindling a sheer sense of curiosity. Rather he finds in himself, if I am allowed to use Goethe's expression, an elective affinity for the Greek *mythos*, and this means that he discovers in it the suitable way of coming to know himself, for only if there is a self-identification of this sort, however partial and provisional it may be, will it be possible to know and create in the genuine sense of these words. Secondly, the Greek *mythos* functions as a lodestar for Darío, and this means that it serves him well to, fix the bed of his desires; in other words, it allows him to know them in so far as they are given shape in the poem. But Salinas does not rest his case there, for further on he adds: "the sense Darío has that his being is rooted in the Greek heritage can hardly be said to arise from any bookishness; it is much more a matter of human faith".[7] And this is the third aspect to keep in mind, to wit: that Darío's desirous nature is identified and set for him on the basis of an act of faith. Now, this implies that he is running a risk, namely, that of mistaking himself for someone else, of taking as his own reality and as that of his world something that is truly alien to him, in which case his poems would only be *simulacra* and not those contexts destined for the eventuation of truth. In this manner, we can appreciate how Darío — in a non-theoretical and yet most meaningful way — realizes that he has bet his entire life on one card, a commitment which discloses that his poetic activity is irreducible to mere aesthetic playfulness.

In Darío's mythologically inspired poetry, we encounter a great variety of beings, such as centaurs, sirens, nymphs, and tritons,[8] and the gods themselves appear at the head of the pack. The interesting question is the one we may pose concerning their role or function therein. Rubén does not care about their picturesque natures, much less about their individuality; rather he focusses on them and incorporates them in his poetry just as means, symbols, or avenues of access. As Salinas explains, ". . . Apollo, Eros, Endymion, so many names and as many legendary accounts, did constitute an entire imaginary system . . ."[9] And yet we may wonder about the purpose of such a system. As a first step, we could say that it will be "the new flesh in which Rubén's erotic yearnings take shape".[10] However instructive Salinas's formula just quoted may be, I find it ultimately unacceptable, and this not only or even fundamentally because Salinas is there sinning on the side of superficiality, but also and above all because such a formula is riddled with ambiguity. I am referring here to the ambiguity inherent in poetry, i.e., the basic possible occasion of entrapment which genuine poetry always is. I have already pointed at a dimension of the problem when I spoke of the temptation to reduce poetry to the autobiographical level, especially if it is of feeling or passion, and yet the gravity and peril I have in mind is much greater, for poetry can be understood as our path towards the more perfect Other or, equivalently stated in the language of desire, as our way to the possible (but perhaps unattainable) meridian or zenith of our love. If we choose to give expression to this projection and striving in terms of Venus (a most important creature in this mythological system, for she is the goddess of love), we have to join Salinas when he argues further that, above and beyond the failings and manners of decadence to which the earthly beauty of woman is subject,

. . . we find Venus, who withers not, and stands firm on the heights in which she dwells and where she remains untouched by earthly inconstancy, thus reassuring all women that, as the titular representative of human beauty, even if their personal beauty came to an end, human beauty *qua* myth could never perish. Venus is the Olympian manner of the desire for eternal beauty which is the usual companion of feminine nature.[11]

But to this I would add that such a view is also true of the lover of woman, for who is he but the one whose desire seeks to possess eternal beauty?[12] And yet here lies a source of deception, for myth has two possible functions to perform, namely, the clarification of the nature of desire by the disclosure of its intended goal, and the obfuscation of desire by bringing it to rest in the implicit belief that desire is ultimately capable of fulfillment, thus giving rise to an ideal or unceasing striving after beauty. Rubén has not been entirely exempt from this temptation or free from self-deception in this regard, and yet he has managed to overcome being finally ensnared by it all, as this masterful verse of his may perhaps indicate:

From the abyss, Venus would cast her eyes on me, sadly.[13]

The heights have now become the unfathomable abyss. Venus is not just the beauty who withers not, but as well and above all the unattainable one. Thus, the one who endows desire with sense places herself beyond desire. Accordingly, sadness, even melancholy come to form an essential dimension of the wisdom being established by the poet in his creative life. In this light, we can appreciate the meaning of that formula of Salinas which seeks to give expression to the complex web of relationships between poetry and mythology in Rubén's work. He says: "Mythology is the best possible symbolics of desire".[14] Now we can see quite clearly what Salinas has discovered in Darío: mythology allows him not only to identify and fix desire by way of the embodiment of an act of faith in the object of desire, but also permits him to realize that desire is solely a means, an instrumentality. Desire urges the poet, moving him to self-transcendence time and again, permanent satisfaction being foreclosed in principle. In this manner, the human being (i.e., either poet or reader) comes to know himself precisely in and by means of the object of his desire and search, for it is there (and by opposition to perfection lovable and lovely in itself) that he constitutes himself for what he is, namely, a finite striving, an imperfectible desire. The beings of mythology, and the world of facts and events in space and time to which they are conformed, therefore become symbols or representatives of desire or, more exactly, of the truth of desire, that is to say, of unquenchable thirst. Herein lies the ultimate root of Rubén's melancholy and thereby of his poetry.

THE RELEVANT MYTHICAL TRADITION

One is confronted, first of all, with the task of presenting the pertinent mythological matter, even if only most succinctly, before one has any right to examine the various poems in which Darío shapes it in various ways. Among the Greek-mythological entities Rubén resorts to, however, I would only like to pay special attention to Zeus, Leda, and the Swan, primarily in terms of their relations, since, for our purposes, they are both revealing and full of wonderment.

Zeus engages in the pursuit of Nemesis, who is not to be identified with the notion or experience of divine vengeance. Rather, she is the Nymph-goddess bearing the same name, but who is better known as Leda.[15] We encounter, although not surprisingly, two versions of the likely story in question:

1. In the pre-Hellenic account, it is the goddess who engages in the pursuit of Zeus. The manner of this pursuit is most striking: the divine king undergoes various transformations that are in keeping with the seasons of the year, and he does so precisely to escape Leda, but she changes accordingly, until she finally captures and devours him at the summer solstice.[16]

2. The Hellenic presentation paints precisely the opposite picture, since therein we find Zeus involved in pursuing Leda: she flees and changes shape, while Zeus keeps up his pursuit until she is overtaken and violated by him.[17]

Nemesis or Leda was "the Moon-goddess as Nymph".[18] In the pre-Hellenic account of the myth, we can find a correlation between Leda's changes and the seasonal transformations of the divine king: hare, fish, bee, and mouse (or, as a variation of it would have it, bird instead of bee and grain of wheat in place of mouse).[19] During Hellenic times, however, the story undergoes a remarkable alteration: "With the victory of the patriarchal system, the chase was reversed . . ."[20]

For the goddess, the swans were sacred animals.[21] Probably this was due to their white plumage and to the fact that they fly in V-formation, a female symbol.[22]

The usual version of the myth is that of Hellenic or patriarchal times.

It is precisely in this form that we encounter it in Darío and also in William Butler Yeats (to whom I shall return at the end.) In such an account, the reason for the pursuit is the simplest: Zeus has fallen in love with Nemesis. Leda attempts to escape from Zeus by plunging into the waters and adopting the shape of a fish, but Zeus wades through the river by taking up the form of a beaver (= *castor*). Leda wins the other bank and continues her flight, successively changing her appearance to that of various beasts, the natures of which follow an increasingly pugnacious and swift sequential order. At last, Leda attempts to fly away as a wild goose, and Zeus, having changed himself into a swan, possesses her at Rhamnus in Attica. Nemesis or Leda then "shook her feathers resignedly, and came to Sparta . . ."[23] There she "found a hyacinth-colored egg . . . [from which] Helen of Troy was hatched".[24]

As we can see, the commerce between god and beast has yielded its fruit, namely, Helen, the most beautiful woman of the Ancient World and sister to Castor and Polydeuces (or Pollux, if we go by his Latin name).[25] Castor and Clytaemnestra were the mortal children born to Leda as the result of her union with Tyndareus, king of Sparta. The children she begat by Zeus were Helen and Polydeuces.[26]

According to Hyginus,[27] the outcome is the same (i.e., the birth of Helen), but the manner of the violation is different: Zeus succeeded in deceiving Leda "pretending to be a swan pursued by an eagle"; Leda's resulting distraction allowed him to take "refuge in . . . [her] bosom, where he ravished her"; in due course, Leda "laid an egg, which Hermes threw between Leda's thighs, as she sat on a stool with her legs apart".[28]

The best known, indeed the usual version of the violation of Leda runs like this: Zeus, adopting the form of a swan, possessed her "beside the river Eurotas", and this event resulted in her laying "an egg from which were hatched Helen, Castor, and Polydeuces".[29] Consequently, she was "deified as the goddess Nemesis".[30] But since "Leda's husband Tyndareus had also lain with her the same night",[31] we discover again that the paternal attribution is a confused affair.[32]

This is, in brief, the mythological matter elaborated by Darío in the poems that concern us. Let me now proceed to examine them.

THE SWAN POEMS

Various and most interesting are the poems in which Rubén Darío sings of the swan or of Leda. If I am not mistaken, all the important ones are to be found either in *Prosas Profanas* or in *Cantos de vida y esperanza*. I would like now to consider these poems severally and with some care, so as to be able to appreciate how the myths concerning Leda and the swan serve Rubén well in his task of self- and world-knowledge.

As Salinas points out, the swan is "hardly endowed with a fixed sense in Darío's lyrical work".[33] In fact, as he goes on to indicate, it is precisely the many-sidedness of the swan, especially in its capacity to give expression to contradiction, that most attracted Darío and inclined him to employ it as a symbol. And yet, for all its value, this contention is ultimately misleading, for there is no necessary incompatibility between multiplicity and wealth of meaning, on the one hand, and unity of signification, on the other. Granted, this unity may remain concealed and function primordially in the grounding depths of creative activity, but then multiplicity and even contradiction in the sphere of creative meaning would work themselves out on the basis of such a foundation. Unity is matrix, and the many arises from, is supported by, and returns to the matrix, which thereby is not in isolation from or independently of its offspring, but rather exists and exists only in the elaboration it undergoes in terms of its offspring. Let me try to show this.

First of all, as Salinas himself acknowledges, the swan appears as a "genuine jewel"[34] in the poem entitled "Noble Ancestry".[35] In order to signify and express this, the poet has chosen, for the most part, metaphors that are visual in nature. Some examples of this practice are the following: "Olympian snowswan", "agate-rose beak", "lyre limb", "Greek-amphora haft". The snow-white quality of the swan is as "sister to flax" and kin to "the bud of white rosetrees" and to "the whiteness pure of adamantine golden fleece/on tender Paschal lambs". The poet has masterfully combined the data presentations which are strictly visual (that is to say, of graspings in terms of color) with those of perceptions of shape and form, which properly belong to the sphere of touch. Accordingly, we do find, as Salinas had indicated, a many-sidedness pertaining to the swan, and yet the situation is much more complex than Salinas imagined, for in fact the complication is twofold. On the one hand, we find the visual and tactile experience of the poet; on the other, we are presented with the swan multiplying itself into color (white and rose) and form (beak, limb, haft, bud, lamb). In my opinion, here lies the key to our difficulty. It is to be noted that neither colors nor forms and shapes are given abstractly; rather, what we are given is the whiteness of flax, of the bud of rosetrees, and of tender

Paschal lambs, and the agate rose of the beak; and we are also presented with a lyre limb or an amphora haft — in fact, the swan's wing "opens up in the sun as a chaste fan".

Now, what is the meaning of all this? I could say that it is something striking in its simplicity and which is, to boot, in perfect accord with the fullness of Darío's sensuality. There is no occasion here for the dissolution of the sense-perceptible into sheaves of qualities, which would thus be subject to abstractness and dis-realization (leading, say, to the natures "whiteness" and "arc of a circle"), but neither do we encounter human sensibility broken into so many unrelated or independent capacities or faculties, such as vision or touch. Rather, we are faced here with the phenomena of coenesthesia and their expression: what the poem renders manifest and available is precisely the depth unity characteristic of the sense-perceptible and of sensibility.[36] One sees as one touches, one touches as one sees. Formulations like these, however, can be misleading, if one surreptitiously takes them merely as expressions of simultaneity. But this is not the case at all. Reality not only unfolds, thus begetting multiplicity; it does so and thus increases its own treasure, but by way of the constitution of *concrete* wholes, which come to speech in expressions of some complexity, such as "wing/chaste fan", "agate rose/ beak", "neck/lyre limb/Greek-amphora haft", or "white bud/flax/lamb". Reality unfolds and is thereby unified. The newly arising concrete unities unfold again in unsuspected ways and become unified once more, again to repeat the process in unsuspected ways and recurrently until the final synthesis is achieved. I mean of course the concreteness from which the poet departed in the first place, although then it was only a question, a marvelous task to discharge, but presently is a problem resolved. The original "Olympian snowswan" is now an enriched treasure, for it has turned into "gods . . . of an endearing landscape, /they consist of perfume, ermine, /light, dawn, of silk and dreams".

And yet there is more. The transformation undergone by the swan in terms of intensification, diversification, and unification does not thereby come to an end. The sense-perceptible plane *stricto sensu* is now overcome, for the swan is the "Composer of rimes gathering in ideal assembly". This dimension of *ideality* was already suggested in the presentation of the swan as Olympian in the very first verse, but now such a characterization grows and becomes this: "consisting of ermine are its lyrical robes". The appearing of the swan in snow-white becomes intensified not only in further concretions and ever-growing sensuous unities; it is also magnified so far as the swan's dignity is concerned: whiteness becomes ermine, fitting for "winged nobility". In sum, Darío's poem has succeeded in reaching greater and greater depths in the sensuous and ideal wealth of the swan, a reality which, up to the moment the poet attempts his transformations, *remained inaccessible in the recesses of silence.* The *lógos* — and here specifically its poetic manner — is not repetitious but insightful and creative. It is precisely the poem which becomes the instrument to constitute, put together, and render the swan manifest. It is in this *sui generis* fashion that the poet fulfills his defining mission, to wit: that of completing the cosmic work of God. In my opinion, Salinas has a glimpse of this when, referring to the last verse of the poem but failing to mention it, he says: "And if all of this were not enough, [the swan now turns out] to be made of still another substance, an insubstantial substance, for it is made of dreams".[37]

Taken as a visual synthesis of qualities,[38] the swan reappears in the first poem of the collection entitled "The Swans".[39] Here the swan's function undergoes further purification, for its ideal dimensions continue to develop. Darío himself remarks on it in that splendid beginning where he says: "What signal are you drafting, oh Swan, with your bending neck/as the sad, wandering dreamers pass you by?" The very capitalization of the word "swan" seems to suggest that ours is no ordinary swan; in fact, it is its potentiation when it is taken precisely as signal. If this impression is correct, then we are entitled to ask about the direction along which the swan would be leading us. To this one may reply that the swan both symbolizes *and* fulfills our search for consolation. As Darío puts it: "[Oh,] swans, let the fans of your refreshing wings/most purely caress our pale foreheads, /let your white expressive shapes steal dark thoughts away from our minds". It is to be noted that these verses give expression to a *desire*, in so far as it becomes incarnate in possible qualities and actions of the swan, for it is the swan that refreshes, relieves, and brings us consolation. That this is at all possible rests with our discovery of a secret quality of the swan towards the end of the poem, indeed of a power where we meet the fidelity characteristic of swans given final shape, even and especially as the poet becomes disillusioned, for hope is rendered manifest in "the immortal . . . dawn".

Now, as suggested, a remarkable thing takes place at this point in the poem. We had gained entry into it in the company of the swan, in so far as it was the living compossibility of the concrete qualities of silence, beauty, whiteness, lordship over the waters, and impassiveness to flowers. In fact, the silence of the swan was given as grounded in those other sense-perceptible and mental qualities. And yet at the end of the poem the swan is transfigured and exalted, for it is now that the swan speaks to the poet and discloses reality to him. It is by the *lógos*, *mirabile dictu*, that the swan effects the salvation of the poet, for it is in the word that it is capable of uncovering for him the notion that hope is possible at all, that a new dawn will always be reborn. But this revelation is a source of wonder on two counts, for the changing swan not only continues to undergo a transformation, but the transformation itself gives rise to a further unsuspected unity. *In one and the same swan* we come to find the *lógos* and qualities non-verbal, and yet only in so far as they are the foundation of each other.

However thought-provoking or illuminating this interpretation may be, it does not yet exhaust the matter under scrutiny. There is further occasion for wonder, inasmuch as the swan's transformation into *verbum spei* is in fact occurring at deeper and deeper levels. In a poem we examined before (i.e., "Noble Ancestry"), the voice appeared as a regal feature of the swan, since it was a dimension not to be visited or exercised, except under unique circumstances of privilege, for it is only "in death that its soul composes the rimes of song". To appreciate this well, we must come to realize that the transformation in question was already under way, as we can verify in the following stanza of the poem, "The Swan":

> It was a divine moment for humankind.
> The swan would sing only on its way to die.
> But we came to hear the tones of
> Wagner's swan at dawn, a time to be reborn.[40]

Let me insist on this point and its significance. The swan's transformation into voice implies a parallel transformation of man. Rubén insightfully tells us that it "was a divine moment for humankind". This is the *locus lucis*, the time of being born. It is no wonder that Darío here refers to the myth of Leda and to her birth. If on that event the swan became the means for attaining to physical beauty and for its entry into the world, now it is the occasion for the birth and cultivation of the poetic word. The swan is idealized, purified, and enriched once more, as it turns into the source of poetic creation. Composing a song to the swan — and this is tantamount to purifying, enriching, and bringing it to unity — is already poetry. And man thereby arises as poet, an outcome which is a new advent in world and soul at once:

> under the shadow of your white wings
> does young Poetry in glory of light and harmony conceive
> eternal, pure Helen, flesh to the ideal.[41]

The voice or song of the Swan, an unceasing song indeed, is now heard and succeeds in mastering "the tempests raging in the human ocean", namely, the hammer and the sword, as the first poem of "The Swans", of which I have already spoken, also indicates.

This notwithstanding, I would like to argue that the highest degree of intensification or potentiation of the being of the swan is yet to be reached. It lies precisely in the portentous event of Leda's transformation or, more exactly, in the realization that Leda herself is the secret being of the swan. But what could this possibly mean? Let me attempt to present its signification step by step.

The very beginning of the fourth poem of "The Swans"[42] will serve to confirm the truth of the fundamental sense of the interpretation that I am proposing. Again we witness an enrichment in the *selfsame* being of the swan, since, as Darío puts it on addressing the woman, "Above all, glory be to you, oh, Leda!" Let us take here the word "glory" in the noble sense of *doxa*, which is the only meaning that seems to fit the context. Accordingly, Darío appears to be proposing that we approach Leda in the splendor and exaltation of her being as woman. As the swan is exalted, so is Leda. The swan, potentiated in itself, is Leda. Salinas offers the following commentary on this event:

The fourth poem [of "The Swans"] proceeds from describing to the level of exalting in song the union undergone by woman and beast. . . . This action is presented as heavenly and supreme, [for] it portends a novel phase in the life of the world, to the extent that . . . the animal and divine dimensions are in search of each other and interpenetrate and harmonize.[43]

Let us keep in mind that here Zeus is the divine principle, and that he is and has become Nemesis-Leda. Furthermore, the animal principle involved is constituted in the synthesis of beaver/swan and fish/goose. Let us now listen to Darío's presentation of this truly consequential event:

With silk the God covered the sweetness of your womb.
Honey and gold pouring on the gentle wind!
Alternation in sound:
Pipes and crystals, Pan and fountain.
Earth becoming song, Heaven a smile![44]

Now then, this union of beast, woman, and the divine is an eclosion taking place in the world itself. Again, we become privileged witnesses to a new transformation and enrichment, since it is not a matter just of the preservation of the unity achieved, but of its growth in scope and depth as well. The violation of Leda is the *gaudium* of the universe, since it is the port of access for the universe to accomplish the *telos* already embedded in its name, i.e., the complete and dynamic unification of the All, the discovery and *proclamation* of the universe *qua* unity of concretion, as signified in the pairs "Earth/song" and "Heaven/ smile". This is what it means for Leda to become the swan who is possessing her: we are not facing here the annihilation of Leda or the vanishing of Zeus, just as before they did not disappear into the manifold transformations undergone either by the pursuer or the pursued in the mythical storyline of their love affair. Rather, the case is this: on possessing Leda, Zeus the Swan gains access to being Leda, and upon being possessed and impregnated, Leda becomes divine and attains to being Nemesis. It is precisely in the events pertinent to union and reciprocal transformation that the universe is poetically constituted for what it is, inasmuch as the animal, human, and divine principles are established therein as a unity in difference. Darío brings this to words (and does so magnificently) as he says: "In the presence of the act heavenly and supreme, /gods and beasts consummated their alliance". Leda's exaltation, which was accomplished by the mediation of the swan's deed, now can be grasped in its genuine significance, for it truly is a cosmic, totalizing event, and not merely a parochial occurrence, perhaps affecting one or another quarter of the universe.

As a consequence, the inhabitants of earth are fittingly influenced and transmuted. The larks are given "the light of day", "the owls their wisdom", the nightingale its melody, the lions their victory, the eagles their glory, and love is granted to the dove. And yet it is the swans that underwent and deserved a transformation by far the greater, an exaltation most sublime, for they turned into "divine princes" ennobled above their own world and became "wanderers like vessels/unblemished as linen cloth, /wonders like birds". In their true color, their beaks are seen as "pure coral"; their deeds become eternal "in infinity" and turn into "exact rhythm, daydream voices, mythical lights". The swan is thus totally transformed in consonance with the exaltation to which is brought the entire universe of which it is and remains a part. Or as Darío chooses to put it:

> Oh, white vessels of harmony!
> You are the sum of Olympian pride.
> Jewels of ivory moved by a divine spirit's
> heavenly melancholy.

In this state of exaltation, the summation or synthesis achieved by the universe is rendered manifest, for the harmonious nature of these jewels of ivory no longer lies in concealment within the containing walls of the vessel the swan is and has been. Containment and exaltation, concealment and glory — these are the mutualities of the *alétheia*[45] of the swan. And all of it takes place in an instant, violent and sublime, in which the swan, the swan's kiss, "traversed silken fields, /and climbed up the rose peak/of Leda's sweet hills".[46] The swan's inner life, of which the beast is never dispossessed, is at this crucial point lying both exalted and exposed, for it is moved by the melancholy spirit giving it breath. But whence would this situation arise, if not from "having loved, /near the fountain in the grove, the shining neck stretching out/between the white thighs of Leda's"? Darío's poetic vision here is, in my judgment, correctly interpreted by Salinas, when he says that this manner of "melancholy consists of solitude, the feeling of having to miss forever the brief instant of the embrace, in which a happiness never imagined by the beast happens to befall it, to be gone all at once".[47]

Let me now underscore the fact that it is in this context that a bridge towards being a poet begins to be constructed. At the onset of our discussion, I asserted, as an anticipation, that Darío's poetry consists in the effort of achieving a special sort of reciprocity of world- and self-knowledge. At this point, I believe we can appreciate most concretely the truth of my contention. In fact, the many-sided lesson he has learnt about the real by placing himself and abiding at the heart or center of the solitary swan will at this juncture prove useful in the poet's striving after self-knowledge, but this will be the case, of course, only if he senses and continues to feel the being of the swan in all its unfolding phases, up to the glorification by which — and correspondingly — the unity of the cosmos is poetically achieved. In my opinion, the last stanza of Poem IV, a piece I quoted in its entirety and then proceeded point by point to interpret, becomes the suitable means to understand Poem III, despite the fact that it obviously succeeds it in the order of poetical presentation.[48] Let me explain what I mean.

It is precisely the swan's melancholy that allows the poet to come to know himself as a desiderative and thereby unfulfillable animal, provided that we see this feeling arising from its permanent motive, namely, the memory of that sublime, unique moment in the swan's life. The poet too comes to live his life in melancholy, a subjective exaltation that is the correlate of the world's. But isn't this exactly what Darío gives expression to in the two decisive stanzas of Poem III? Here they are:

> For a moment, oh Swan, I will join my yearnings
> with your yearnings, those of your two wings
>   (which held Leda in an embrace, . . .
> Swan, your white wings for an instant will be mine,
> and the rose heart in your sweet breast
> will throb in mine in its abiding blood.[49]

For an instant, just for a moment "Love will abide in happiness". Salinas's commentary on these verses is to the point: "The poet's yearnings (and we know it is his erotic ones that matter here) seek out those [already] stirring in the swan's wings".[50] And he proceeds to add that the

... beauty and her beauty, Leda and her loveliness, shall be reached and possessed by virtue of the poet's bodily identification with the swan. The meaning of the swan is that of being the most beautiful symbol for the fulfillment of the erotic yearnings for possession which the poet has ever found. In terms of this mythical story, [we realize that] the swan is the form of [erotic] possession.[51]

Accordingly, one can say that the swan is, all at once, symbol and reality. It is that which signifies the world, in so far as it is capable of being expressed as the unity of a manifold, and it is reality too, to the extent that, in the act of possessing Leda, such unity is fulfilled and rendered manifest. The possession of beauty is — in one — the actualization and the proclamation of the unity of the universe. And this twofoldness is constituted precisely in the poet's song, in his poem. It would then be no surprise to discover that the poet does not just sing; in his song, he becomes aware of what he does and is thereby transformed. In other words, he does not merely sing of the possession of

Leda; he himself becomes the possession of Leda, the union of the animal, human, and divine dimensions in a harmonious synthesis, if only ever so briefly. The poet is now the swan itself as a means to the exaltation and unification of reality as a whole, of which he is, paradoxically, a part — an integral component of the universe who nevertheless is beside it, in the manner of a witness. In my opinion, this is Salinas's meaning when he argues as follows: "And, upon asking the swan to lend him its wings, what is the poet doing but exactly what Jupiter did? He is playing the role of god".[52] Hence, the poet's condition and destiny are no better than the swan's: "Oh, poor prince! . . . In his adventure he is just the mediator carrying out the task the god has chosen for him, as it should be".[53]

Finally, I would like to examine "Leda",[54] a poem that I believe is an accomplished synthesis of the two dimensions I have identified as being at work here, namely, the poet's self-knowledge and his proclamation of the world for what it is. And yet this is neither an abstract nor a contingent harmonization of the two. On the contrary, it is at once a most concrete and irreplaceable coming together of the dimensions in question, specifically in the coupling of Leda and the Swan. Let me attempt to show it.

First of all, I must underscore the visual nature of the poem, for it perfectly matches the fixity of the poet's glance. In fact, it is almost a photographic still, indeed the expression of an Apollonian attitude. No wonder then that the appearance of the swan's manner of being in the world becomes thereby determined as such. All at once we are confronted with a static take, wherein "The swan in the shadows seems cast in snow/its beak is in amber, against the light of the dawn". And this occurs in such a way that the interplay of light and shadow accentuates the formal outline of the swan, an effect which lies in between to those produced by Dürer and Rembrandt.[55] A little further and the swan's surroundings are established by means of color and light:

> And then, on the sky-blue waves of the lake,
> after the red tint of the dawn had faded away,
> having folded its wings and bending its neck,
> the swan is of silver, bathed in sunlight.

Time has been suspended, and this comes to words in the past "had faded away". The poet's search is for the right expression to convey the wonderment provoked by the synthesis of reality and ideality he meets in the Swan. And his intuition seems to guide him aright, for he now puts together the manners of smith and painter. He finds himself incapable of resolving the swan into pure color, for then it would vanish into the domain of ideality, but he cannot just choose any metal for his work as a smith, since the swan could then gain excessive bulk, too much reality. Silver is however the suitable material to give the swan its proper shape and weight. As a result, the swan comes to cut a figure in the world and is granted its proper bodiliness, just as a real, concrete entity of light resting in selfsameness, for silver acquires form only against the light. Accordingly, Darío succeeds in endowing the swan with the night measure of materiality and ideality — as he says: "the swan is of silver, bathed in sunlight".

This notwithstanding, time has already begun making its sallies, gnawing away at selfsameness. In the first stanza, it had barely shown its head, so as to produce, however paradoxical this may sound, an Apollonian illumination-effect. That time is a stranger in the swan's world is suggested by the employment of the present tense, especially since it is done against the background of the "mellow sunset", a self-extinguishing witness to time itself: "the mellow sunset fleetingly passes, /a blush rose on the snow-white of the wings". Here we are privileged to see time almost undone by the coming into being of this wonder-ful creature of light. And yet, by the third stanza, time makes its final onslaught. We are now living Leda's own time. The stillness of the swan becomes pure action at this point. The Nymph-goddess draws the swan out of itself, beyond its dwelling of light, and vision gives way to touch and hearing, for here we encounter "feathers of silk", "lips in blossom", "sounding water-springs". It is then that the "Olympian bird, wounded by love" *violates* Leda, "its beak seeking after her lips in blossom". Now the secret is completely disclosed: light becomes desire; the stillness and selfsameness of the silver swan are torn by love, for the Olympian's wound maddens it to the point of violation and search.

As the swan is transformed, as the divine and Olympian sphere becomes the realm of desire and needfulness, so does the world undergo a corresponding change. It is no doubt true that Leda has found in her flesh the impression of divine desire, and yet what is occurring here goes much further than that, affecting the universe itself. Or as Darío allows it into song when he says:

The beauty, naked and vanquished, utters a sigh,

and as her plaints into the air escape,
out of the greenish depths of the thicket
sparkle Pan's disquieted eyes.

The sounds of satiated divine desire reach the air and the surrounding thicket, leaving a trace and effecting a mutation in what lies beyond Leda and the swan. We are now face to face with the cosmic exaltation already sung by Darío in Poem IV of "The Swans", but here it acquires a special significance. The scene is endowed with an exceptional sense, for it is also the correlate of the experience of a privileged witness. Pan lies concealed in the greenish depths of the thicket, wherefrom "sparkle . . . [his] disquieted eyes". The divine and bestial creature has become disturbed by virtue of the desire provoked in his loins as he looks upon the unusual coupling of the beauty and the beast — of humanity, animality, and divinity coming to unity. But who could Pan really be? Who shall redeem Pan's ugliness, the measure of ugliness which Plato saw as inherent in desire?[56] Could it possibly be that Darío has learnt here a way of access to his innermost and secret self? Is it perchance true that Pan is the poet himself, in so far as he, too, is called to become one with Leda, to transmute himself into the swan as it possesses Leda, thus at once redeeming the ugliness of his desire and participating in her beauty in the most *active* of fashions? Darío does not reply: his silence leaves us all alone before the enigmatic last verse of the poem. But perhaps here lies the way to touch the intimate bond between self and world, indeed the unity of ground at the root of the universe, that which evermore beckons our faculty of desire.

A COMPARATIVE EXCURSUS: CONCERNING THE SWAN IN GUILLÉN AND YEATS

In his poem, "The Swan",[57] Jorge Guillén engages in a poetic inquiry into the essence of the swan. His purpose is the same as Daríos, at least *in genere*. He seeks to gather and disclose the secret of the swan. In order to understand him aright, I must reassert that the swan's being is not something already given or even pre-given in some pre-reflective fashion; otherwise, the inquiry, whatever its manner, would be idle or redundant. This does not however mean that we have no notion about the swan as we begin, or that we are bereft of any clues to follow in our effort at determination. The fact of the matter is that the swan's essence is given as a task, and it therefore does not arise apart from the instrument of the inquiry and its employment, which in this context is the poem itself.

Surprisingly, the outcome of Guillén's poetic search is just the opposite of Darío's. Let us see how this comes to pass. Guillén begins as follows:

> [Gathered] in purity between air and wave,
> the swan, the nature of whiteness,
> plunges its exacting beak and fathoms
> the uncertain harmony.

To all appearances, we find ourselves in the same sphere as that we entered into at the end of the first stanza of Poem I of Darío's "The Swans", for there we encountered the swan in the bosom of its whiteness and exercising its lordship over the waters. Darío even anticipated Guillén's own conclusion, namely, "Silent are the white ones!", when he said: "Why are you so silent by dint of whiteness and beauty, /by lording it over the waters and being impassive to flowers?" And yet this apparent coincidence of minds does not really take place. The very interrogative form of Darío's utterance already suggests that he suspects that, above and beyond the stillness in his heart, there is a deeper secret which is the swan's (and thereby his own). But in Guillén's poem the truth of the swan consists in being itself, in withdrawing into its pure selfsameness. Instead of culminating in motion and search, as Darío does, Guillén, by contrast, makes his poetic beginning on the basis of motion and search. This accounts for Guillén's words, "plunges its exacting beak and fathoms/the uncertain harmony", an expression which leads him merely to one discovery: "Idle talk of the waters!" In the space between song and conversation, it is not possible ultimately to fathom anything: "Useless search, musical in emphasis!" But if this adventure toward sound is inconclusive, for only "Beaks bereft of prey are gathered by the breeze/pursuing the briefest things", the definitive entry into the new sphere would eventually bring us back to the sheer being of the swan. This is strongly impressed on us by the contraction of time and substance into the area of the briefest. Just begun, the swan's attempt to become a voice ends in failure: "Afterwards would the Slender one want to outstretch its curve". It is surprising to find that Guillén's profound poetic intuition, which brings him to the threshold of the potentiation and unification of the sense-perceptible (i.e., to connect form, sound, and the purely visual in the unity of the swan), does not somehow allow him to cross over it. One does not observe here what one did in Darío, who, as you may remember, multiplied the being of the swan and synthesized its manifold appearances into a concrete essence, encompassing visual, tactile, and sound dimensions in unity. In Darío, one witnesses the swan actually becoming its voice and, in so doing, allowing the poet to overcome his condition, as he progresses from the state of disillusion to that of hope for the imperishable dawn. The swan's nature is there being perfected as voice, whereby the poet achieves his own completion.

But it is by means of the two perfecting processes that the totality of the universe becomes perfect or one as such. Accordingly, one must assert that the universe is the harmony constituted in the poem, that it is, to employ Guillén's own expression, the *chord* or agreement of sound, color, and form. And yet the meanings assignable to "chord" turn out to be not just different, but even opposite in Darío and Guillén. In Darío's case, the chord is the one established between the poet and the swan, i.e., the agreement constituted for the entire universe at the precise juncture of that encounter, that which comes to pass by means of the transformation of the swan into song. The poet's creation is just the *lógos* of the swan's voice. In Guillén's work, on the contrary, the chord is brought into being as the swan withdraws into its visual purity in the midst of silence, when "Its entire plumage traces its fateful system of silence". In fact, the swan is disclosed as identical with its withdrawal into selfsameness. The harmony that the searching beak had been unable to fathom, and which afterwards the swan had unsuccessfully attempted to capture in the voice, it now finds within itself. As Emilia de Zuleta expresses it so well, despite such failings, ". . . its chord becomes intensified and its plumage outlines a system",[58] the system of its own intimate being. And yet the chord in question is no "transcendent harmony, but . . . one graspable here and now".[59] This is a point well taken, since for Darío the possibility of finding the system inherent in each thing or the harmony proper to every thing depends entirely on the poet's search after the chord or agreement between things. In brief: Darío takes the poem as the fruit of transcending sensuous immediacy by means of the potentiation, multiplication, and unification of what is sensuously given to the poet, culminating as he

does in the harmony of all-encompassing concreteness of the cosmos.
To all appearances, however, Guillén's stance is just the opposite. Let
us hear him as he sings:

> And the swan, faithfully enduring
> through its tranquility's transparency,
> is beholding its own soul, silent and remote:
> a divinity of the flow.

One must needs gain access into the interiority of the thing itself, thus
avoiding a flight into the transcendent by means of the voice, whether it
be into the subjective spirit of man or into God's consciousness and
might. One may thus search after tranquility in pure immanence, i.e.,
the soul or inner world of the thing in question. Only in this manner is
it possible for the swan to achieve its own being, to become a "divinity
of the flow".

Now, to say the least, this position is a paradox, and it is one on two
counts:

First of all, if applied to each and every thing in the world and to
the poet himself (as is seemingly intended by Guillén),[60] the process of
internalization involved would *de jure* comprehend even the outermost
stretches of the universe. Accordingly, the interconnection and unification of the many would be fulfilled in terms of the intensification and
purification of immanence, the immanence or soul of every thing. As
Zuleta herself points out, "chord or agreement lies in continuity . . .
only in continuity can one find perfection . . ."[61] But this continuity is
empty; in fact, it is established precisely in the breach. Hence, the
universe vanishes altogether, and even this conclusion and the path
leading to it become impossible and incomprehensible, for are they
not mediated by the song of the poet, now imprisoned in his own
Innerlichkeit?

Secondly, at least in the case of the swan, the process of internalization is established in terms of tranquility and silence. Over against
Darío, Guillén holds that it is not by way of song (and the transcendence and openness constituted thereby) that the genuine nature of the
swan comes to be disclosed (and consequently the true being of world
and poet as well). The royal road to this end is, according to Guillén,
precisely the opposite of the song; we find it by traversing the silence
characteristic of the swan's being *a se* and *ex se*. And yet this is a
finding made by Guillén, by the poet who is composing the swan's song.

And here lies the other paradoxical dimension of Guillén's poetic stance. His objectivism seems to go hand in hand with some form of subjective idealism, a combination which, in my opinion, succeeds in dissolving both the object and the realm of the song.

Is it possible somehow to overcome the contradiction inherent in Guillén's position? I mean the one which results from the fact that it is the poet's song that is to achieve the disclosure of the being and continuity of the world, precisely on the occasion of the swan's failed attempt to sing and its consequent annihilation. In my opinion, the difficulty is much graver than it may at first appear, for it is not limited to the case of the swan or to some quarter of the universe. What is at stake is the very possibility of the poetic *lógos* itself. I believe that Guillén cannot succeed in his attempt at reconciliation, at least if I judge in terms of his poem "Swan", for this is seemingly a most radical expression of his attitude towards poetry and reality. At least, the awareness of the difficulty would impose upon us the task of harmonizing the stance intrinsic in this poem with the observable success and existence of Guillén's poetry. And this would require that we work out his poetics, both as a theory and a practice, but this venture we cannot go into in the present context. Suffice it to say that this poem does not contain the key to the contradiction between the constituted song of the swan and the silent "divinity of the flow". Moreover, I think it is fair to say that Guillén does not even suspect the paradoxical nature of his song. And yet, is it not in the bosom and context of paradoxes that discoveries are born? Heraclitus once recognized as much when he said: *Pólemos pánton men patér esti, pánton de basileús . . ."*[62] The evidence that *a posteriori* establishes this point one may find precisely in the fact that in both poets the result is essentially identical, for the universe is disclosed, if one regards it as the correlate of their poetic activity, as a totality characterized by unity, continuity, multiplicity, and perfection. To be sure, the emphasis chosen by each poet is different, just as their respective poetic sensibilities are not the same. Furthermore, as we have seen, the procedures followed by the two poets are not identical; in fact, they are opposite in kind. And yet both poets move from multiplicity to unity; even the transcendent realm created by Darío is by no means a device to evade or replace the world of concreteness and everydayness; rather, it is the means to find the unity of one thing in another in a voyage towards the universal.

Darío's method (especially in the context of mythology, where he applies it) is exposed nevertheless to an inherent peril. In fact, it is one which Darío successfully avoids (as I think I have already shown), but this does not make it any the less real and pressing. Possibly it is his special sensibility that allows him not to fall prey to it; but, be that as it may, let me insist on an important point. As we have seen, Darío's procedure consists in symbolically transforming reality into myth, in order to discover its intrinsic interconnectedness and, on that basis, sensuously and ideally to potentiate it and bring it to unity. In this context, one can say that the danger in question lies in the possibility of replacing a thing by another, or in dissolving it into a symbolic network, or even in forcing it to occupy a place foreign to it by inserting it in an alien mythological system. Apparently, this is what occurred in William Butler Yeats's case, according to Ezra Pound, T. S. Eliot, I. A. Richards, and Robert Lowell. They all contended, in one way or another, that Yeats's creative stance did not permit him to recognize the independent status and existence of things. A swan, for instance, would only be a swan in appearance; accordingly, Yeats did not hesitate to subject it to his will and to substitute for it anything which, in his view, it would symbolize.[63] To be sure, on referring to this problem, I do not mean to engage in the endeavor of removing such a peril, or even in that of bringing its nature sufficiently to light; much less do I harbor the intention of examining the quality and problems of Yeats's work as a whole. What I propose to do is at once simpler and preliminary, namely, to consider Yeats's poem "Leda and the Swan", [64] in order — by contrast — better to recover Darío's own poetic method.

First of all, I must underscore the fact that Yeats's poem is reduced to regarding one moment and one moment alone, namely, the instant in which Leda's violation takes place. Indeed, it is this focussing on the special event in question that endows the poem with a very high degree of intensity. As a consequence, Yeats manages to bring time to a halt, as if the flow were to cease and time became identified with that instant, a *contradictio in adjecto* if there is one. The reader experiences a violent impression, as if he were encountering an unidentified force kept in check, but about to make the poem explode into smithereens. In my opinion, what allows for this impression is, paradoxically, the fact already noted, namely, that time has become the instant. And I say "paradoxically", because motion is not however banished from the scope and sense of the poem. On the contrary, it points forward, as the first stanza clearly shows:

> A sudden blow: the great wings beating still
> Above the staggering girl, her thighs caressed
> By the dark webs, her nape caught in his bill,
> He holds her helpless breast upon his breast.

The mood is one of *pure expectation*; the stanza portends surprise and destiny. Now, this certainly contradicts Darío's own vision of the event, as can be immediately gathered by his refusal to focus on the privileged instant or to underscore its inevitability. His concern is rather with the moments before and after. For Darío, time is not so much imminence, as it is preparation and fruit. This is negated by Yeats's own accomplishment, which we can appreciate by regarding — with his own eyes — the moment just preceding the fateful event. There he ponders the impossibility of avoiding Leda's destiny:

> How can those terrified vague fingers push
> The feathered glory from her loosening thighs?
> And how can body, laid in that white rush,
> But feel the strange heart beating where it lives?

It is as if, before the fact, we were witnesses to the clash between two irresistible partners in opposition — his "strange heart" and her "loosening thighs". We are thus confronted with fate, violent fate. Nothing but Leda's violation by the swan could ever take place:

> A shudder in the loins engenders there
> The broken wall, the burning roof and tower
> And Agamemnon dead.

A perfect picture, indeed: motion and event are reduced to stillness, the stillness of the instant of inevitable consummation achieved in just three plain brushstrokes. Agamemnon is dead,[65] and yet do we know what has really taken place? Do we find perchance, as we did with Darío, a union and a synthesis, the coming together of the divine, human, and animal principles, or the event of poet and swan becoming one? In the encounter between Leda and the swan in Yeats's poem, do we gain access to a universal communion of all that is? Is there here anything like the alliance which "gods and beasts" had brought to fulfillment "in the presence of the act heavenly and supreme"? We must not lose sight of the fact that these are Darío's clues to coming to terms with and establishing the most noble sense of the opening words of Poem IV of his "The Swans", where he hailed the woman as follows: "Above all, glory be to you, oh, Leda!" In my opinion, Yeats's poetic way does not allow for Leda's exaltation, and that certainly implies that the swan's exaltation, and the poet's own and thereby that of the universe, are necessarily foreclosed. The reason, I think, is simple and — at this point — evident: the time which reduces itself to the instant and to imminence both annihilates itself and alienates itself from eternity. This may be confirmed by Yeats's own last stanza, where he says:

> Being so caught up,
> So mastered by the brute blood of the air
> Did she put on his knowledge with his power
> Before the indifferent beak could let her drop?

No transitional events are presented here, so as to establish at least the possibility of Leda's eventual coming to the state of exaltation. Instead, what we find again is a sense of imminence, which in this case is the foretaste of abandonment. There is no love in this poem, no genuine union which, in its very fleetingness, would remain in the melancholy feeling of our memory, precisely as Rubén experience and sings of it. In its indifference, the beak could let her drop at any moment; in fact, we expect this to happen at the slightest tremor or bit of change, so great is the sense of detachment. And Leda? One can no doubt wonder whether any lasting effect has left its imprint or trace in her, whether having been possessed by the swan had in any way transformed her, even before the fated moment of abandonment. As Yeats himself asks: "Did she put on his knowledge with his power . . .?" To all appearances, she did not; but, if this is so, how could anyone entertain the hope that the world would undergo any significant transformation as a result of the fated event? If Leda remains Leda, if she cannot become Nemesis, how can one even imagine that Helen's beauty would originate precisely out of this encounter? How could anyone place his trust in an indifferent swan and in a Leda who does not give of herself, and then expect to witness a resulting exaltation and unification of the world? These are vain hopes and obfuscated desires, which could only achieve fulfillment in Darío's swan and his Leda, or in a poetic manner consistent with them.

Long Island University
Southampton, New York

NOTES

[1] Cf. Pedro Salinas, *La poesía de Rubén Darío* (Barcelona: Seix Barral, 1975).

[2] Cf. Francisco Sánchez-Castañer, *Estudios sobre Rubén Darío* (Madrid: Cátedra "Rubén Darío", Universidad Complutense, 1976), pp. 162—64 and 170—74.

[3] P. Salinas, *op. cit.*, p. 75.

[4] Cf. P. Salinas, *La realidad y el poeta* (Barcelona: Ariel, 1976), pp. 39 ff. To use Salinas's terms, we must distinguish between two correlative aspects in poetic creation, namely, the phase or dimension of reality disclosed and constituted in the poem, and the attitude by means of which the poet opens up to reality in order to create or form it. It is the latter that I have in mind at this point.

[5] Cf. *Republic* X, 601b.

[6] P. Salinas, *La poesía de Rubén Darío*, p. 77.

[7] *Ibid.*, p. 79.

[8] *Ibid.*, p. 84.

[9] *Ibid.*

[10] *Ibid.*, p. 86.

[11] *Ibid.*, p. 87.

[12] Cf. Plato, *Symposium*, 199d—201c, 204d, 206d, 210b—212a.

[13] Rubén Darío, "Venus" in "Sonetos áureos", *Azul* in *Poesías Completas*, ed. Alfonso Méndez Plancarte, 11th. ed. (Madrid: Aguilar, 1975), p. 536. All translations of Darío's poetry into English are mine.

[14] P. Salinas, *La poesía de Rubén Darío*, p. 89.

[15] Cf. Robert Graves, *The Greek Myths* (New York: George Braziller, 1957), 32.2; C. Kerényi, *The Heroes of the Greeks* (New York: Grove Press, 1960), p. 107.

[16] R. Graves, *op. cit.*

[17] *Ibid.*

[18] *Ibid.*, 62.1.

[19] *Ibid.*

[20] *Ibid.*

[21] Cf. Euripides, *Iphigenia in Tauris*, vv. 1095 ff. Latona is Leda. Cf. R. Graves, *op. cit.*, 62.2.

[22] R. Graves, *op. cit.*, 32.2.

[23] *Ibid.*, 62.

[24] *Ibid.* Cf. Homer, *Cypria*, p. 334b; Sappho, *Fragment* 105; Eratosthenes, *Catasterismoi* 25.

[25] Cf. Edith Hamilton, *Mythology* (New York: The New American Library, 1942), p. 179. She was *also sister* to Clytaemnestra. (Cf. C. Kerényi, *op. cit.*, p. 238). This may have relevance to W. B. Yeat's verse, "And Agamemnon dead" in his "Leda and the Swan", since Clytaemnestra is Agamemnon's adulterous and murdering wife. This is possibly an allusion to the killing of her husband by her own hand. How this event is connected with Leda's violation by Zeus (= the Swan) is unclear. Cf. *infra*, p. 231.

[26] Cf. E. Hamilton, *op. cit.*, p. 41. This matter is most obscure, as anyone may appreciate from the fact that Leda's mortal son is called Castor, which is precisely the name of one of the animals whose shape is adopted by Zeus in his pursuit of Leda. (Cf. R. Graves, *op. cit.*, 62.1.) Furthermore, even greater confusion results from the usual

practice of grouping Castor and Polydeuces together and calling them *Dioskuroi* (i.e., the sons of Zeus) in certain contexts and *Tyndaridae* (i.e., the sons of Tyndareus) in others. Cf. E. Hamilton, *op. cit.*

27 Cf. *Poetic Astronomy*, ii, 8.

28 R. Graves, *op. cit.*, 62.

29 *Ibid.*, 62c.

30 *Ibid.* Cf. Lactantius, [*Divinae Institutiones?*], i, 21; Hyginus, *Fabula*, 77.

31 R. Graves, *op. cit.*, 62c.

32 Cf. *supra*, n. 26.

33 P. Salinas, *La poesía de Rubén Darío*, p. 95.

34 *Ibid.*

35 "Blasón", *Poesías Profanas* in *Poesías Completas*, pp. 557—58.

36 Cf. James Ward, *Psychological Principles* (Cambridge at the University Press, 1920), pp. 41, 110 f., 116, 135, 249; G. F. Stout, *Analytic Psychology* (London: Swanson-nenschen and Co. 1896), II, p. 134; Wilhelm Wundt, *Grundzüge der physiologischen Psychologie*, 4th. ed., I, p. 434. By "coenesthesia" I do not mean so much the general, undifferentiated sense of our bodily self as the subjective-objective complexes corresponding to it. Accordingly, I do not contend, as Wundt for one does, that it involves sensations that are "exclusively subjective". At best, such sensations would result from an abstractive procedure to which coenesthesia would be subjected.

37 P. Salinas, *La poesía de Rubén Darío*, p. 95.

38 Rubén honors the swan in his song, in so far as it is "white" and "beautiful", as it "lords it over the waters and remains unmoved by the flowers". It is to be noted that Darío proceeds to bring the visual qualities to unity with other features belonging in the mental order. The swan thus acquires feeling: it is an unmoved tyrant.

39 "Los cisnes", I, *Cantos de vida y esperanza* in *Poesías Completas*, pp. 648—49.

40 "El cisne", *Prosas Profanas* in *Poesías Completas*, pp. 587—88.

41 *Ibid.*, p. 588. To all appearances, the interpretation I am proposing here meets with an unsurmountable difficulty, for it seems it is a matter of contradiction. It is as if Rubén did away, quite arbitrarily, with the silent nature of the swan. And yet I think this is not at all the case. Perhaps a solution to the riddle is to say that the swan gives itself as silent *only from without*, since the possibility of song abides in its *Innerlichkeit*, in so far as the latter consists primordially in witnessing. (Cf. "Los cisnes", II, first stanza, *Cantos de vida y esperanza* in *Poesías Completas*, p. 649.) Concerning the verses quoted in the text and corresponding to this note, I would like to add that the scope of the interpretation of the stanza should not be limited to a definite historical setting. Such a restriction would see in it only a manifesto for the literary movement known as Modernism in Spanish and Spanish-American letters. Even if Darío kept this reference in view (as I believe it is most probable), a fact of this nature would be no stumbling block to an *objective* extension of the scope of the interpretation, for the poem actually and potentially says much more, the poem itself being always the ultimate rule and measure of the task of interpretation.

42 *Cantos de vida y esperanza* in *Poesías Completas*, pp. 650—51.

43 P. Salinas, *La poesía de Rubén Darío*, pp. 97—98.

44 *Cantos de vida y esperanza* in *Poesías Completas*, pp. 650—51.

45 Cf. José Ortega y Gasset, *Meditaciones del Quijote* and Julian Marías, "Commentario" (Madrid: Ediciones de la Universidad de Puerto Rico, Revista de Occidente,

1957), pp. 80 ff. and 296 ff. ("Comentario"); Martin Heidegger, *The Origin of the Work of Art* in *Basic Writings*, ed. D. F. Krell (New York: Harper and Row, 1977), pp. 167 ff.

[46] "Blasón", *Poesías Profanas* in *Poesías Completas*, p. 558.

[47] P. Salinas, *La poesía de Rubén Darío*, p. 99.

[48] "Los cisnes", *Cantos de vida y esperanza* in *Poesías Completas*, p. 650.

[49] *Ibid.*

[50] P. Salinas, *La poesía de Rubén Darío*, p. 99.

[51] *Ibid.*, p. 100.

[52] *Ibid.*, p. 101.

[53] *Ibid.*

[54] *Cantos de vida y esperanza* in *Poesías Completas*, p. 664.

[55] Cf. José Ortega y Gasset, "Sobre el punto de vista en las artes", *Obras Completas*, Centenary Edition (Madrid: Alianza Editorial/Revista de Occidente, 1983), IV, xi—xii, pp. 450—52 and xv, pp. 456—57; Heinrich Wölfflin, *Principles of Art History. The Problem of the Development of Style in Later Art*, trans. M. D. Hottinger (New York: Dover, 1950).

[56] Cf. *Symposium*, 202c—d.

[57] Jorge Guillén, *Cántico 2* in *Aire Nuestro* (Milan: All'Insegna del Pesce d'Oro, 1968), p. 157. All translations of Guillén's poetry are mine.

[58] Emilia de Zuleta, *Cinco poetas españoles* (Madrid: Gredos, 1971), p. 128.

[59] *Ibid.*, p. 129.

[60] *Ibid.*, p. 131.

[61] *Ibid.*

[62] Fragment 53.

[63] Cf. Dennis Donoghue, "The Hard Case of Yeats", *The New York Review of Books*, No. 9 (May 26, 1977), p. 4.

[64] W. B. Yeats, "Leda and the Swan", *The Collected Poems* (New York: Macmillan, 1966), pp. 211—12.

[65] Cf. *supra*, n. 25.

WILLIAM S. HANEY II

METAPHOR AND THE EXPERIENCE OF LIGHT

The experienca of elemental or light, though a common occurrence in the course of human history, has increasingly come under attack by critical theorists who, without any direct experience of this light themselves, have had to resort to its metaphorical representation in literature. Because the experience of light, or what Mircea Eliade calls the world of Spirit,[1] is ultimately a personal discovery, its metaphorical representation can lead to confusion about the nature of light if language and consciousness are understood solely on their most superficial dimension. Metaphors operate through a comparison between a word and not a single reference but several references that seem to have something in common. While the proper use of a word may suggest one reference, its metaphorical use in an improper context will result in that context suggesting another reference, or as some critics will argue, any number of references. Thus, as Donald Davidson asserts, "there is no limit to what a metaphor calls to our attention. . . . When we try to say what a metaphor 'means,' we soon realize there is no end to what we want to mention."[2] Moreover, through their deconstructive enterprise, Jacques Derrida and Paul de Man collapse the distinction between literary and philosophical language because metaphors cannot be eliminated from philosophical discourse. Derrida claims that while all language is polysemous, literary metaphor is especially so because it is autotelic, a complete departure from the world of reference. Karsten Harries, on the other hand, argues for a definition of metaphor between the purely aesthetic and the inevitability of referring to a world beyond the text.[3] This paper will argue two major points: that the metaphor of light, the heliotropic model of all metaphors, is both purely aesthetic and referential; and that inner light can be experienced through metaphor as a presence which corresponds to an outward reality but is not dependent on the sun as a sensory object.

The question of whether or not metaphor and especially the metaphor of light constitutes proper knowledge has been answered from many perspectives. Although each answer may be considered equally valid, they are not all equally complete. Harris observes that because a

237

A-T. Tymieniecka (ed.), Analecta Husserliana, Vol. XXXVIII, 237–245.
© 1992 *Kluwer Academic Publishers. Printed in the Netherlands.*

literary work is defined as a unified whole, its metaphors must also be unified and therefore self-sufficient.[4] This purely aesthetic value of metaphor seems to preclude the possibility of referring to a meaning beyond the text. In its resistance to the mimetic function of art, metaphor aspires to the status of an immediate presence. According to Susan Sontag, "transparence is the highest, most liberating value in art," where "transparence means experiencing the luminousness of the thing itself, of things being what they are."[5] The transparence of art as a self-sufficient presence, though, has traditionally come with the sacrifice of truth, defined as a referential knowledge of the world at large. Most art that aspires to an aesthetic presence ends up being contaminated by reference anyway, but even in falling short of its intended purity, art is still not considered a reliable source of knowledge.

For one thing, each metaphor will turn out to have its own history of former meanings, and its ancestory will often extend to another language. For example, the modern French word for moon, "lune," derives from the Latin word for light, "lux." The English metaphor in the word moon derives from the Latin word for month, "mensis." These metaphorical stratifications of language tend to be overlooked by modern speakers. On the whole, it seems that metaphors would have difficulty becoming an immediate presence given both the polysemous character of language and the intertextual nature of literature.

How, then, can the metaphor of light express a meaning with any truth value, either aesthetic or referential? Derrida claims that "the sun is never properly present in discourse."[6] On the one hand he asserts that the sun is the ideal sensory object because "[i]t is a paradigm of the sensory *and* of metaphor: it regularly turns (itself) and hides (itself)."[7] Like any aesthetic object, the sun can either hide itself or present itself. On the other hand, Derrida asserts that because the sensory sun can never be known properly, it is improperly named and therefore supplies an improper metaphor. Since, as Aristotle states, we can not be sure of the sun's properties or even of its sensory characteristics, Derrida argues that any time there is metaphor the sun is involved, but "it is no longer completely natural." He says "it is always, already a luster, a chandelier . . . an *artificial* construction."[8] According to this logic, whatever is left of nature has the ability like the sun to emerge from itself, to transform itself into its other, or as Derrida says its " 'artificial' light."[9] The sun, like nature in general for Derrida, is never completely natural but always metaphorical, an abyss that infinitely stratifies itself, "simultaneously widening and consolidating itself,"[10] that is, simultaneously expanding and contracting, like the pulsating universe itself.

By defining metaphor as a function of freeplay or the movement of *différance*, Derrida attempts to deconstruct the unified presence of both aesthetic and natural objects, thereby blurring the distinction between art and reality. One implication of such a strategy is that the distinction between the aesthetic and referential function of literature is also blurred, since there is no longer a natural world beyond the text to which a metaphor can properly or even improperly refer. Any deconstruction of the self-presence of either the purely aesthetic or the phenomenal world thus depends on the notion of freeplay or the movement of *différance*. The principle of *différance* or diversity, however, belongs to the field of relativity and, as I will argue below, has little impact on the direct experience of elemental light. Moreover, the notion of *différance* can be shown to characterize the very essence of presence when understood from the level of transcendental consciousness, a state of three-in-one collectedness in which the awareness knows itself to be the knower, known, and process of knowing, a state with its own corresponding physiological condition that differs radically from that of ordinary waking consciousness.

Paradoxically, then, the movement of the signifier, which separates the metaphor from any decidable reference and the sensory sun from any sure knowledge of its properties, has the effect of negating the difference between the referential and the purely aesthetic. Both art and reality become bad metaphors yielding improper knowledge. This leveling or unifying function of *différance* has an important implication for the experience of elemental light.

Karsten Harries notes that pure poetry results less from observation than from the desire for satisfaction and plenitude.[11] This desire to transcend the boundaries of the human condition involves a sense of pride. As Sartre writes, "the best way to conceive of the fundamental project of human reality is to say that man is the being whose project is to be God.[12] Sartre and Kant both believed the project to be in vain, since reality always seems to escape our grasp. The modern poet therefore seeks to create his own reality not dependent on established language or the things of the world. But even if the poet can never escape temporal reality, even if, as Yeats shows in "Sailing to Byzantium" the monuments of man's unaging intellect depend on nature for their art, the gesture towards eternity is never completely in vain. If we accept the biblical assertion that in the beginning was the word, and the word was with God, and the word was God, then the medium of language must provide a means toward the experience of eternity. According to the ancient Vedic Science of India, as summarized by the physician Deepak Chopra,

> At its primordial level, the whole relative world . . . is made of sound . . . these sounds are the subjective experience of the infinitely diverse frequencies that physics identifies as the basis of all matter and energy. Before these sounds manifest themselves in our awareness as thoughts, emotions, or desires, there is a deeper level at which they are all unmanifest sound — we can think of this as the seed of sound where a structure exists without any material form, yet is starting to sprout something material. These unmanifest sounds are the actual fabric from which the network of sutras that is the finest structure of the universe is made.[13]

The poet's search for aesthetic purity, then, does not depend only on innovative language but also on how language is experienced.

Saussurean semiology describes language as consisting of an arbitrary system of differences in which the sign is divided from its object. In post-structuralism, the sign is divided not only from its object but also within itself, with the movement of the signifier resulting in the transcendental signified being infinitely deferred. This spatial and temporal gap between sound and meaning, however, seems to apply only to the expressed dimension of language experienced when sounds manifest themselves in our awareness as thoughts and feelings. Vedic language theory, in contrast to Saussurean semiotics, describes four levels of language that correspond to different levels of consciousness. The levels of *vaikhari*, or outward speech, and *madhyama*, or inward speech, correspond to ordinary waking consciousness, while the levels of *pashyanti* and *para*, the unmanifest seed of sound, correspond to transcendental consciousness or *samadhi*.[14] Whereas madhyama, or inward speech, is experienced temporally as having a gap between sound and meaning, pashyanti is experienced at the junction point between waking and transcendental consciousness where sound and meaning are completely unified. For post-structuralists the problem with the traditional notion of a pre-verbal transcendental signified or absolute meaning is the apparent contradiction in the possibility of a transcendental signified being experienced independently of language in a state of intuitive self-presence. Even if meaning can be experienced in a purely subjective realm, post-structuralists question how it can have a lasting existence without being expressed in writing. The notion of a transcendental signified seems to exclude the sound or form necessary for the experience and communication of meaning.

The critique of the transcendental signified, however, results from treating it as a notion of the intellect rather than an object of direct experience. Although the vaikhari and madhyama levels of language consist of a temporal division between the signifier and signified, this division disappears in the pashyanti and para levels, which according to Vedic poetics is beyond space and time. In pashyanti and para, the transcendental signified is not pre-linguistic or a subjective illusion but the very essence of sound. It is a unified whole in which the signifier, while beyond ordinary sense perception, is still available to direct experience. When the awareness of the poet or reader expands toward unbounded consciousness, then he or she can experience the transcendental signified not only as a finite concept but as a unified, polysensory whole. That is, when fully developed, the awareness can function on the level known as *ritam bhara pragya*, "that level which knows only truth," or *Jotish mati pragya*, "that all-knowing awareness." Experience from this level of awareness in pashyanti, the transcendental signified acquires polysensory characteristics through which it is simultaneously heard, visualized, felt, tasted, and smelled.

Although this level of reality inherent in language is always accessible to the subject, it is made available primarily through aesthetic experience. According to Vedic language theory, the metaphor is not a gesture toward an ideal beyond itself — or a metaphor of presence. Rather, it acquires the status of the fully present insofar that its literal and figurative terms each constitute a unified whole containing a transcendental signified open to direct experience. Reality, therefore, is not an ideal accessible only to God. It spans both the subjective and objective realms, both the knower and the known between which the metaphor functions as a process of knowing. In the aesthetic experience, the knower, known, and process of knowing move toward complete unification.

The aesthetic approach seen from a Vedic perspective does not require that the world established by poetic metaphor escape from the already establish world of daily experience. As Harries put it, the poet "cannot be seen as a godlike creator."[15] The poet discovers new relations between the world established by metaphor and the world in which we live, but these relations often convey a knowledge more subtle than that available through ordinary sense experience; they convey ultimately the experience of bliss. Moreover, this experience occurs by means of, rather than in spite of metaphor. From a Vedic perspective, it would be incorrect to say with Harries that "There are moments when the inadequacy of our language seizes us, when language seems to fall apart and falling apart opens us to what transcends it."[16] Language falls apart only in the sense that metaphor allows us to transcend from the vaikhari and madhyama levels of language toward the pashyanti, an experience of a transcendental unity of sound and meaning within language. This transcendence induces an experience of what can be described as elemental light. As suggested by quantum physics, inner light is subjective as well as objective.

As we have seen, Derrida attempts to deconstruct the presence not only of the transcendental signified but also of the sun as a natural object of experience. The experience of inner light, I would suggest, is linked to the experience of the transcendental signified. Both occur at the junction point between ordinary waking consciousness and transcendental pure consciousness. This junction point is analogous to what quantum physicists describe as the junction point between the so-called true vacuum, or the unified field of intelligence in nature, and the false vacuum, or the first impulse toward manifestation. In the words of Victor Weisskopf, a well-known physicist, "the history of our universe started with a fluctuation of the empty true vacuum into a small region of false vacuum, which exploded, almost immediately, into a very much larger region of false vacuum. That was the primal Bang."[17] What is interesting for us about this junction point in the microsecond after the Big Bang is that, as Weisskopf says, "the universe was filled with hot, dense gasses of quarks and antiquarks, electrons and positrons, and a very intense, high frequency thermal light radiation." He says that the "plasma was bathed in shining light, visible light," that the "energy of the false vacuum created all light, all particles and antiparticles, which developed into what exists about a microsecond after the explosion." Current scientific thought thus confirms the old testament account of the world as beginning on the first day with the creation of light, and explains that the fact of our sun having been created no sooner than the fourth day is not a contradiction, for the universe was filled with different kinds of light long before the sun appeared. As Anna-Teresa Tymieniecka points out in "Light and the Word," the advent of elemental light provides the basis not only for the metaphor of light but also for the metaphors of time, space, and causality.[18]

That this objective boundary between the true and false vacuum is analogous, if not identical, to the subjective boundary between ordinary waking and pure consciousness has also been proposed by the physicist John Hagelin in his groundbreaking article, "Is Consciousness the Unified Field? A Field Theorist's Perspective." But scientists can only theorize about his juncture, while poetic metaphor can lead to its direct experience. As described by Vedic aesthetics, metaphor has the effect of swinging the awareness of the reader by means of suggestion from the concrete to the abstract, from the finite to the infinite. The power of suggestion (or *dhvani*) produces a sense of identity between the literal and figurative terms of the metaphor that transcends the ordinary path of logic.[19] In the highest type of poetry, the expressed form of metaphor is subordinated to what the critic Charkrabarti calls its "charming suggested content."[20] Both the expressive sound and the expressed sense are subordinated to a suggested content produced by their unification — as represented by pashyanti. In this experience of metaphor, the awareness moves from the concrete individual perspective toward an all-inclusive perspective that characterizes the unity of transcendental consciousness. Harries describes this experience as a transcendence to a "vision of the world that would be truly objective and transparent, free from perspectival distortion."[21] But Harries associates this experience with white mythology, with a forgetting of the limiting original scene of metaphor demanded by the need for a sense of control over objective reality. Vedic aesthetics, however, locates the irreducible reality of things subjectively on the ground of consciousness. Metaphor thus becomes less important for its expressed sense than for its suggestive function of expanding the reader's awareness toward the point between waking and pure consciousness, that basis of phenomenal reality where the reader can experience the quantum light of revelation inherent in language.

The subjective experience of illumination associated with metaphor thus corresponds to the objective radiation of light that characterizes the most fundamental time/distance scale of the universe. At the juncture to the unified field of natural law, the division between subject and object, sound and meaning begins to disappear. In terms of Vedic language theory, as we have seen, this level of reality is embodied by pashyanti and para. The integration of sound and meaning here constitutes a meaning-whole or eternal word, known as *sphota*, which is latent in the consciousness of every person. Nevertheless, the content conveyed through sphota can be manifested to different degrees. In vaikhari and madhyama the sphota is conveyed through temporal sequence, while in pashyanti it flashes forth as a noumenal whole instantaneously through the power of suggestion.[22] Derrida's play of *différance* represents only one version of the temporal experience of language. In pashyanti this play is subsumed by the three-in-one collectedness between knower, known, and process of knowing, and by the unity of the signifier and signified, a unity-amidst-diversity.

Through metaphor, as implied by modern physics and Vedic aesthetics, the reader ultimately experiences the fluctuations of pure consciousness, which parallels the fluctuations of the true vacuum and the first manifestation of light. The unified wholeness of meaning glimpsed as the awareness moves toward pashyanti through the power of suggestion, therefore, is not a metaphor of presence in the sense that language depends on something beyond itself. Instead of being a transparence, metaphor collapses the distinction between inside and outside, subject and object. But unlike Derrida, Vedic aesthetics extends the domain of language in such a way that the text beyond which nothing exists is defined in terms of its most unbounded dimension, a transcendental unity of the signifier and signified, and not merely in terms of the signifier. In Vedic aesthetics, moreover, "the purpose of speech is to promote bliss in the listener."[23]

Maharishi International University

NOTES

[1] Micrea Eliade, *The Two and the One*, trans. J. M. Cohen (Chicago: The University of Chicago Press, 1962), p. 21.
[2] Donald Davidson, "What Metaphor Means," *On Metaphor*, ed. Sheldon Sacks (Chicago: The University of Chicago Press, 1979), p. 44.
[3] Karsten Harries, "Metaphor and Transcendence," *On Metaphor*, ed. Sheldon Sacks (Chicago: The University of Chicago Press, 1979), pp. 71—88.
[4] *Ibid.*, p. 74.
[5] Susan Sontag, *Against Interpretation* (New York, 1967), p. 13.
[6] Jacques Derrida, "White Mythology," *Margins of Philosophy*, trans. Alan Bass (Chicago: The University of Chicago Press, 1982), p. 251.
[7] *Ibid.*, p. 250.
[8] *Ibid.*, p. 251.
[9] *Ibid.*, p. 251.
[10] *Ibid.*, p. 253.

[11] Harries, p. 80.

[12] Jean-Paul Sartre, *Being and Nothingness*, trans. Hazel E. Barnes (New York: 1956), p. 566.

[13] Deepak Chopra, "Bliss and the Quantum Mechanical Body," *Modern Science and Vedic Science* 2 (1988): 68.

[14] Harold G. Coward, *The Sphota Theory of Language* (Columbia, Missouri: South Asia Books, 1980). pp. 126—137. The four level of language in relation to consciousness is also explained by Maharishi Mahesh Yogi in *Phonology of Creation* (Part 2) [Videotaped lecture, 26 December 1972, La Antilla, Spain.] This explanation is incorporated by Rhoda Orme-Johnson, "A Unified Field Theory of Literature," *Modern Science and Vedic Science* 1, 323—373.

[15] Harries, p. 87.

[16] *Ibid.*, p. 87.

[17] Victor Weisskopf, "The Origin of the Universe," *The New York Review of Books* xxxiv, No. 2 (2/16/1989): 10—14.

[18] Anna-Teresa Tymieniecka, "Light and the Word," presented at The Fourteenth Annual Convention of The International Society of Phenomenology and Literature: "Poetics of the Elements in the Human Condition," Boston, April, 1989.

[19] T. P. Ramachandran, *The Indian Philosophy of Beauty, Part Two* (Madras, India: University of Madras Press, 1980), pp. 60—80. Also see Maharishi's Vedic Science on the swings of awareness as summarized in Rhoda Orme-Johnson, "A Unified Field Theory of Literature," *Modern Science and Vedic Science* 1: 355.

[20] Tarapada Chakrabarti, *Indian Aesthetics and Science of Language* (Calcutta: Sanskrit Pustak Bhandar, 1971), pp. 174—177.

[21] Harries, p. 85.

[22] K. A. Subramania Iyer, *Bhartrhari* (Poona, India: Deccan College, 1969), pp. 147—180.

[23] Maharishi Mahesh Yogi, "Videotaped Lecture" (New Delhi, 1989).

PART FOUR

SHERLYN ABDOO

JAKE BARNES' INSOMNIA AND FIESTA
NIGHTMARE IN *THE SUN ALSO RISES*

Ernest Hemingway's obsession with death was probably his major preoccupation in life. In *The Sun Also Rises* the symbolical event that is never absorbed or superceded as experience is World War I, because Jake Barnes carries the remnants of the conflict with him as a permanent badge of honor. Jake's wound did not earn him rewards of glory, or medals symbolizing glory; rather, permanent disfigurement and shame of his lost manhood are his prizes.

With castration as the central symbol of his first novel of 1926, Hemingway immediately located the anxiety away from the symbolical and forced an exploration of something more profound: the nature of the spiritual crises suffered by the major players in the text.

Jake's wound becomes an emblem for a much deeper psychic trauma — the desertion of someone close to him — and allows Hemingway to unravel the ways Jake's anger about his impotence has resulted in the stoical vulnerability he feels, but tries to hide. The facade of strength that attracts people to him disappears when he is alone in his room and forced to confront the bitter truth that his incapacity is the source of his loneliness and isolation and that nothing can be done to alter his situation.

Jake Barnes, the novel's passive hero, tells a story about the events a circle of American and British expatriots experience when they spent a week together in Pamplona celebrating the annual Fiesta of San Fermin. Using male rivalry as the focal point and agent that binds his characters together, Hemingway draws the reader tightly into the center of his investigation of death: first by exploring the death of Romantic Love as an ideal and the resulting disintegration of family values; secondly, by revealing that chivalry and the heroic ideal are no longer valid codes of behavior in the modern world; and, lastly, that death is the drama of human life itself, struggling against what Freud calls "'internal' reasons" to "become inorganic once again" (*Beyond the Pleasure Principle* 32). In contrast to the idea that the "'aim of all life is death'" is Freud's other dictum that "sexual instincts . . . are the true life instincts" (32, 34). Jake, whose sexual life is dead, is trapped in the unbearable

249

A-T. Tymieniecka (ed.), Analecta Husserliana, Vol. XXXVIII, 249–267.
© 1992 *Kluwer Academic Publishers. Printed in the Netherlands.*

situation of being compelled to continually re-live his wounding incident, to "'repeat' the repressed material as a contemporary experience
instead of . . . 'remembering' it as something belonging to the past" (12).
It is only through his compulsion to repeat the "unpleasurable" that
Jake can "take an 'active' part"(9) in searching to master his situation.
But, of course, the cycle is unredemptive. Jake is forced to witness and
accept the sexual promiscuity of Brett Ashley, the woman he loves, and,
in one instance, even arranges her assignation with the young bullfighter,
Romero. As the consummate faithful friend, Jake's role is that of
observer, confessor and story-teller. As observer of the sexual antics of
his friends, he becomes an unwilling voyeur; as confessor, he is forced
to listen to the varying "decent version[s]" of his friends' love affairs
(TSAR 48);[1] as storyteller, he is assuming an active role which enables
him to not only bear witness to events as they happened, but is yet
another instance in which he is compelled to repeat the events by
writing about them. Jake, after all, is a journalist and seeking out the
facts is as deeply ingrained in him as is his investigation into the
meaning of his life which he, at one point, ruminates upon:

Perhaps as you went along you did learn something. I did not care what it was all about.
All I wanted to know was how to live in it. Maybe if you found out how to live in it you
learned from that what it was all about. (148)

I

"'You, a foreigner . . . have given more than your life'" (31).

Among the first things we learn about Jake Barnes is that he is an
insomniac. His inability to shut out "the old grievance" (30), as he
refers to his situation, haunts him perpetually. "Perhaps I would be able
to sleep" (30) he tells himself shortly after he and Brett Ashley have
verbally reaffirmed their love for one another, and Jake's self-examination in the mirror of his room as he puts on his pajamas, is a grim
reminder of the impossibility of their affair. Having tried to reassure
himself that the whole thing is a joke, albeit an ironic one: "Of all the
ways to be wounded. I suppose it was funny" (30), Jake succumbs to
tears:

I lay awake thinking and my mind jumping around. Then I couldn't keep away from it,
and I started to think about Brett and all the rest of it went away. I was thinking about

Brett and my mind stopped jumping around and started to go in sort of smooth waves. Then all of a sudden I started to cry. (31)

Trying to come to terms with his dilemma, Jake misleads himself into believing that "I never would have had any trouble if I hadn't run into Brett when they shipped me to England" (31). But Brett's presence, which makes him happy as well as sad, excoriates his already too sensitized feelings, and is more complicated than that of a woman who "only wanted what she couldn't have" (31). After Jake finally gets to sleep, Brett arrives, excusing her bad manners of waking him with, "'Just wanted to see you'" (36). The real reason for her visit is to keep his feelings for her engaged, which she does by announcing her rejection of Count Mippipopolous' offer of "'ten thousand dollars to go to Biarritz with him'" (33). It is as if she was compelled to tell Jake that her faithful rejection of so huge an amount of money was because their love for one another compensated her enough for the fact that they can't be lovers:

Told him I was in love with you. True, too. Don't look like that. He was damn nice about it. (33)

Nevertheless, after Brett makes her announcement, she leaves him for a "'breakfast in the Bois'" (33) with the very man she has told Jake she rejected, leaving him to once again deal with his insomnia: "It is awfully easy to be hard-boiled about everything in the daytime, but at night it is another thing" (34).

The second time Brett visits Jake in his apartment with Count Mippipopolous, she changes her role from unrequited lover to comforter. Having stepped fresh from the shower, Jake greets his guests in his bathrobe, and reminds Brett that she had stood up their lunch date earlier in the day. He then seeks private assurances of her love and, in the process, reveals the extent of his own vulnerability: "'Oh, Brett, I love you so much'" (54). Once his admission is out, she responds, not as a lover, but as a mother. She kisses him "coolly on the forehead" (54), then "sat on the bed . . . and stroked [his] head" (55), just as if she had been soothing away a small boy's nightmares. Each time Brett visits Jake he is dressed in bedroom attire which puts him at a distinct disadvantage in the domestic scene charged with unspent emotion. As the obvious paternal figure in this ménage à trois, the Count cools his heels in the next room while Jake and Brett play out their game of charades in which Brett has rejected both men as lovers, but singled Jake out as the preferred son. Brett rejects Jake's plea to "'just live together'" (55), saying "'I'd just "tromper" you with everybody'" (55). Knowing that she would either deceive, cheat or disappoint him, clearly indicates that even though Brett makes many protestations of love, her feelings are condescendingly distant. As she keeps Jake at arm's length, Brett vascillates between the two poles of acting the unrequited lover and the caring mother-figure, and in the process keeps Jake's feelings high so that he is never allowed to escape the memory of the incident that caused his loss of sexual function, nor the subtle torture that loving, but not having, Brett entails. When Brett rejects Jake's propositions, her excuse is "'I couldn't live quietly in the country. Not with my own true love'" (55); but she has already made plans to go to San Sebastian with Robert Cohn. Jake's anxiety is roused by a premonition that something unpleasant is about to happen:

I had the feeling as in a nightmare of it all being something repeated, something I had been through and that now I must go through again. (64)

It is not just that Jake senses a painful repetition, but Brett's compulsion to engage in illicit love affairs is also repetition of something in her raging out of control. Jake and Brett are locked in a deadly Oedipal cycle that wounds him as deeply and as symbolically as castration. Even as Brett rejects Jake as a lover, she expects him to condone her numerous affairs with other men, and to rescue her when she is in trouble. And Jake, who is either unwilling or unable to resist her bidding, is effectively prohibited from finding another woman who can accept him the way he is.

Three nights before the fiesta begins Jake has a second episode of insomnia. At first he is "quite drunk" and tries to rationalize it away: "I did not want to shut my eyes because the room would go round and round" (147). As he tries to regain his equilibrium by reading Turgenieff's "A Sportsman's Sketches" (147), Jake hears Brett and her fiancé, Mike, retire into the next room, talking and laughing together. When he "turned off the light and tried to sleep" he was unable to stop his mind from working and again wonders why his life seems so unbearable in the darkness:

I could not sleep. There is no reason why because it is dark you should look at things differently from when it is light. The hell there isn't!. . . . To hell with women, anyway. To hell with you, Brett Ashley. (148)

The reasons for Jake's insomnia are explained as his thoughts roam from association to association. First he realizes that "for six months I never slept with the electric light off" (148). Then he is ashamed of himself for enjoying the torment Mike Campbell has caused Robert Cohn over Cohn's brief affair with Brett:

> I liked to see him hurt Cohn. I wished he would not do it, though, because afterward it made me disgusted at myself. (148—49)

Seeing Cohn get hurt, like watching himself suffer over Brett, is an exercise in masochism. Jake enjoys it vicariously, but has conflicted feelings about enjoying something that seems to be morally reprehensible. And finally, Jake ruminates about the emotional cost of his love for Brett:

> Women made such swell friends. Awfully swell. In the first place, you had to be in love with a woman to have a basis of friendship. I had been having Brett for a friend. I had not been thinking about her side of it. I had been getting something for nothing. That only delayed the presentation of the bill. The bill always came. That was one of the swell things you could count on. (148)

Because of the "oversensitized state of [his] mind after too much brandy" (149), Jake stays awake all night, reading, in an effort to displace his painful thoughts about Brett sleeping in the next room with Mike. For, as Jake informed us early in the novel: "I have a rotten habit of picturing the bedroom scenes of my friends" (13). But Jake's effort to lose himself in his book is a futile exercise in sublimating his real problem and it isn't until "Along toward daylight" (149) that he catches just enough sleep to keep him going.

A couple of nights later, before the running of the bulls, Jake is again deprived of all but two hours of sleep:

> I remember resolving that I would stay up all night to watch the bulls go through the streets at six o' clock in the morning (159)

but he gets so "sleepy that [he] went to bed around four o'clock" (159), and is awakened by "the sound of the rocket exploding that announced the release of the bulls from the corrals" (160).

Avoidance of sleep seems to be an important part of the ritual of festival:

> 'We go too long without sleep in these fiestas. . . . Damn bad thing not to get sleep. Makes you frightfully nervy.' (204)

While Jake's insomnia fits the requirement of the festivities, the huge amounts of alcohol he consumes to keep his raw nerves dull is deadly when its effects wear off, and requires continual refueling.

The first night of the fiesta Jake is knocked out in a fist-fight by Robert Cohn who accuses him of being a "pimp" (190) for having arranged Brett's assignation with Romero. When he regains consciousness he is in the midst of an hallucination that projects him backward into the nostalgic dreamscape of his youth when he had "been kicked in the head" during a football game. It is another instance in which Jake is unable to stop himself from re-living the past. Jake compares how he felt then to what he feels now: "I felt as I felt once coming home from an out-of-town football game" (192). So clearly does Jake re-experience the past, that in his hallucination, he imagines he is "carrying a suitcase with [his] football things in it" (190). In fact, his "phantom suitcase" is so real that, at one point, he emulates the gesture of setting it down (192). Juxtaposing the longed-for past onto the present situation, Jake perceives that "It all seemed like some bad play" (192) and he longs for forgetfulness in "A deep, hot bath, to lie back in," "a hot bath in deep water" (193—94). It is the forgetfulness of returning to the warm safety of the womb that Jake longs for. His desire to return 'home' — not only to the home of America, but to the home of the body of the nurturing female, both as the child of the womb and in the fulfillment of his sexual longing, is what is so poignantly expressed here. The suitcase is not just the suitcase carrying the clothing associated with his youthful combat in football games, but also represents the intolerable weight of his failures carried throughout the long intervening years since youth. What Jake hopes for but knows he will not achieve until death is blissful rest, because as he advised Cohn in the early pages of the novel:

"You can't get away from yourself by moving from one place to another. There's nothing to that." (11)

In his stupor Jake seeks and finds a suspiciously sarcophagus-like "deep stone tub" (195), but when the water will not run, he retreats to his room and spends another mostly sleepless night:

It must have been half past three o'clock when I had gone to bed and the bands . . . waked me at six. (199)

After the last bullfight on the last night of the fiesta, Jake is again very drunk and again he cannot sleep. But he "pretended to be asleep" when Bill and Mike look for him, and after an interval follows them "downstairs to the dining-room" (224) for something to eat. Rather than confess his fears, Jake blames hunger as the reason for his wakefulness: "'I got hungry and woke up'" (224). He is ashamed of his insomnia because admitting it would be too much like confessing to be the sissy little boy who cannot sleep unless a night light is on.

As the three of them sat, Jake thinks "it seemed as though about six people were missing" (224) and remembers another supper he and his friends had shared three nights before the fiesta began, which he described as being:

like certain dinners I remember from the war. There was much wine, an ignored tension, and a feeling of things coming that you could not prevent happening. (146)

Jake clearly associates the last meal of the fiesta with the two friends who survived the ordeal with him, to the last shared meal of the war before he suffered the fatal incident that wounded him. As the memory of one meal becomes conflated into the memory of another, Jake's "world" seemed "inclined to blur at the edge," erasing the boundaries of time and place. Even his perception of himself becomes distorted as Jake, looking in a mirror, thinks: "I looked strange to myself" (224).

Jake's insomnia, while triggered by the immediate events of his disastrous love affair with Brett Ashley, is really the residue of the war trauma which caused his incurable wound. His pathological fear of the dark results in sleepless nights, nights when he sleeps with the lights on, or nights when he sleeps only after sunrise. The only time in the entire novel Jake mentions a good sleep is on the first night of his fishing trip to Burguete when he and Bill share a room. Even then he wakes in the night to satisfy himself that nothing has happened:

Once in the night I woke and heard the wind blowing. It felt good to be warm and in bed. (111)

What Jake fears is, of course, death, and in order to keep his fear under control, his vigilance is directly nightly toward staving off the long dark nightmare of sleep for as long as he can.

II

"I suppose it is some association of ideas that makes those dead places in a journey" (41).

The central passage in the novel which explains Jake's affair with Brett comes from a book Jake is reading:

The book was something by A. E. W. Mason, and I was reading a wonderful story about a man who had been frozen in the Alps and then fallen into a glacier and disappeared, and his bride was going to wait twenty-four years exactly for his body to come out of the moraine, while her true love waited too. (120)

That Jake thinks the story is 'wonderful' is certainly a telling factor, for what he is reading about is his double — a mirror-image of himself — a man frozen in place and at a time before he is able to consummate his love affair. Like Mason's frozen bridegroom, Jake is still waiting. For, just as the groom is mourned by his disappointed bride who waits for her 'true love' to return, so too does Brett tell Jake that she "'couldn't live quietly in the country . . . with my own *true love*'" (italics mine, 55).

One source of the A. E. W. Mason story is E. T. A. Hoffman's "The Mines at Falun." In that fuller version of the tale, Elis Fröbom, Hoffman's protagonist, forsakes his bride early on the morning of their wedding and descends into the mysterious depths of the mines he loves, which offer him "splendours of the . . . immeasurably rich treasure which lay hidden there" (Hoffman 334) and where he dreamt he had heard his mother's voice beckoning to him in the guise of a "beautiful young woman who stretched her hand down to him through the vaulting and called his name" (318—19). During the intervening years since Fröbom's disappearance in the mines, his bride takes widow's weeds, and waits faithfully for him to reappear, until one day, exactly fifty years later, he is found:

in a pool of vitriolic water . . . The body appeared to be petrified when they brought it to the surface. The lines of the face were so well preserved, the clothes and even a flower attached to the jacket were so completely free of decomposition, that the youth might have been merely sleeping. (336—37)

When Fröbom's bride, by then "an ancient woman . . . on crutches" (337), is reunited with her lost lover, she clasps him tightly against her body and dies as his petrified corpse dissolves slowly into dust — literally the "dust to dust, ashes to ashes" of a mock funeral service.

In Hoffman's story, the hero clearly prefers the mysterious darkness and symbolical death in the mines to the convention of married life. In the story's prophetic opening lines, Fröbom was a "solitary sailor, a slim handsome youth hardly twenty years old" (312) lamenting his mother's demise:

'Oh, if only I were at the bottom of the sea — for in life there is no one with whom I can be happy!'(133)

Fröbom's desire for the dark depths is fulfilled when he willfully consigns himself to the mines' bowels, symbolically as both a tomb and a womb.

While the fantasy of the faithful bride who waits until death for her bridegroom to reappear, is a main component in both stories, perhaps more important is the image of the, likewise, chaste and faithful bridegroom who dies before the wedding ceremony takes place, and is thereby relieved from his wedding night duty. In death, Mason's frozen groom and Hoffman's petrified groom have become unnaturally rigid, as if to emphasize the unremitting grotesqueness of their rigormortis.

Because of his war wound, Jake is a third embodiment of the unwilling bridegroom syndrome. Unwilling because, unconsciously, each story reflects the situations of three characters who would rather die than sacrifice their youthful vigor for the sake of a woman. Jake's life situation is a type of frozen death in which growing up has been postponed; a state of willed limbo is achieved as the moment of death is suspended and the appearance of eternal youth is preserved. The frozen and petrified men are preserved in their youthful bloom while their grieving brides grow old and feeble from grief. What is clear is that the fear of growing up and accepting life for what it offers, goes hand-in-hand with the fear of accepting adult responsibilities, and the inevitably of death.

In Mason and Hoffman the disappearance of the physical bodies of their protagonists serves to keep their memory alive in the minds of their waiting "widows" who, too, are unable to transcend the grieving experience, and to heighten the impact of the youthful death image when it is revealed.

Jake's story is as grotesque or perhaps even more so, than the two versions that precede him, because though Jake has, after a fashion, survived the physical trauma of his castration, he is destined, psychologically, to be haunted by the spectre of himself endlessly re-living the nightmare of his wounding, only to realize nothing has changed to solve his problem.

III

> "the point of the book for him [Hemingway], . . . was 'that
> the earth abideth forever' " (Baker 81).

The one explicit statement in the novel which identifies impotence as Jake's problem takes place during the fishing trip Jake and Bill take, when Bill, probing Jake to confess the truth about his affair with Brett, accurately describes his situation:

> 'You're an expatriate. You've lost touch with the soil. You get precious. Fake European standards have ruined you. You drink yourself to death. You become obsessed by sex. You spend all your time talking, not working. You are an expatriate, see?'
> . . .
>   'You don't work. One group claims women support you. Another group claims you're impotent.' (TSAR 155)

Jake's immediate response is to defensively side-step the issue: " 'No, . . . I just had an accident' " (115). We know Jake is responding only to the charge of impotence because he is afraid that the revelation would damage their friendship: "I was afraid he thought he had hurt me with that crack about being impotent" (115).

As an emblem of death, Jake's presence becomes all the more eloquently human when he is in the midst of nature's ripeness:

> We . . . watched the country out of the window. The grain was just beginning to ripen and the fields were full of poppies. The pastureland was green, and there were fine trees, and sometimes big rivers and chateaux off in the trees. (87)

Or, when he is walking through "thick woods" full of fattening cattle and sees "wild strawberries growing on the sunny side of the ridge," "great fields of yellow gorse," and a "field of buckwheat on the hills" (117—18). The fast-flowing rivers are so full of fish that even before he can bait his hook "a trout shot up out of the white water into the falls," then "another trout jumped . . . making the same lovely arc and disappearing into the water that was thundering down" (119).

During the pastoral idyll Jake shares with Bill Gorton, the imagery of nature's bounty makes death's presence all the more ominous. At the inn in Burguete where they eat their evening meals, three "dark and smoky-looking" paintings hang on the wall, disturbing testaments to the dark side of sportsmanship:

There was one panel of rabbits, dead, one of pheasants, dead, and one panel of dead ducks. (110)

The repetition of the word 'dead' itself is a type of verbal punctuation that reinforces the reader's perception that what is important about the rabbits, pheasants and ducks as art objects, is that they are beautiful because they are dead.

Later, the ritual of fishing requires "fighting" a fish that "bend[s] the rod almost double, out of the boiling water" and then "bang[ing] its head against the timer so that he quivered out straight" (119) before it is gutted and packed in layers of ferns. What is apparent in the close tactile description is that there is an aesthetics of death that is repeatedly invoked and celebrated here.

Even Bill's and Jake's lunch conversation gravitates to death, first revolving around the joke about whether the chicken or the egg came first, then moves casually to the recent death of a mutual friend named Bryan:

'First the egg,' said Bill. 'Then the chicken. Even Bryan could see that.'
'He's dead. I read it in the newspaper yesterday.'
'No. Not really?'
'Yes. Bryan's dead.' (121)

In tribute to their dead friend, Bill adds a prayer: "'Our stay on earth is not for long. Let us rejoice and believe and give thanks'" (121).

In fact, the novel's death imagery spares no one. The only person who claims to be safe is Romero who declares with childish innocence: "'I'm never going to die'" (186).[2] When Mike realizes his fiancé has gone off with Romero, leaving him a humiliated and broken man, Jake notices Mike begins looking "like a death mask of himself" (210). In Paris, Count Mippipopolous credits his happy state of being to having discovered that the true meaning of life is in knowing the value of things. In the Count's simplistic view of the world: "'You haven't any values. You're dead, that's all'" (61). Sleep, traditionally associated with a state of limbo somewhere between life and death, is a state Jake often has trouble achieving. But when Robert Cohn quietly falls asleep during the fiesta, Bill unhesitatingly diagnoses his situation: "'I think he's dead'" (158), and when Cohn wakes up tells him, "'You were only dead'" (159). Whether 'dead' is meant to be a shorthand version of "dead to the world" or "dead tired," the impact of hearing one's companions express so openly a veiled death wish, even if it was expressed in the form of a tasteless joke, is a shocking foreboding.

During the fiesta the procedure of coralling bulls is costly because of the number of horses that are brutally sacrificed when the bulls, protesting the lockup, gore them, often disemboweling them in the process. Jake warns Brett in advance:

'Don't look at the horses, after the bull hits them, . . . Watch the charge . . . but then don't look again until the horse is dead.' (162)

Likewise, the sacrifice of human life during a fiesta is expected. Vincent Girones, the "man who was killed" (189) during the running of the bulls, died, as a waiter tells Jake, of " 'A big horn wound' " (197). When he died, it was

'All for sport. All for pleasure. . . . All for fun. Just for fun.' (197)

Unable to stop himself from repeating the litany, the waiter exclaims again and again, marvelling at the sheer madness of it all:

'You hear? Muerto. Dead. Dead. He's dead. With a horn through him. All for the morning fun.' (198)

Hemingway's use of the word 'dead', always in triplets, is almost seductive in its insidious invitation. Bill marvels at the uncontrollable madness that grips the fiesta crowds and drives young men prematurely to their graves:

'The damn police kept arresting chaps that wanted to go and commit suicide with the bulls' (200)

as if to say, why stop them. If a man wants to commit suicide, let him.

The compulsion to die by the bulls includes Brett's metaphorical description of herself as a 'goner,' dying for love of Romero, the matador;

'I'm a goner,' Brett said.
'How?'
'I'm a goner. I'm mad about the Romero boy. I'm in love with him, I think.' (183)

IV

" 'Nobody ever lives their life all the
way up except bullfighters' " (10).

A post-World War I novel, *The Sun Also Rises* is unavoidably and to a great extent about the war. The novel is subtly shaded with combat imagery and many of its characters express regretful nostalgia that the war years are over.

One obvious way of expressing their nostalgia is through the sporting events that occur during the course of the action. In the first sentence of the novel, Robert Cohn is introduced as "once" having been "middleweight boxing champion of Princeton" (3). As a passive-aggressive character, Cohn, in the end, proves his ability to fight when he beats not only his best friend, Jake, but Mike and Romero — his rivals for the woman he has fallen hopelessly in love with — in a series of fist-fights. Boxing, like tennis and football, is a sport Jake and his circle approve of, and their enthusiasm is an essential part of the invisible bond that keeps them together. Whether in war or engaged in competitive sport, it is all the same: they belong together as members of a special fraternity that requires the invitation of experience and sympathy to join.

In addition to Cohn's mastery of the sport, boxing is mentioned three more times in the novel: first, when Bill describes a boxing match he witnessed in Vienna in which another American expatriate, a Black boxer, knocked out this Viennese opponent rather than ignominiously throw the fight as he was expected to. Bill was so impressed with the boxer's heroics that he helped him escape an angry mob and loaned him enough money to get home. Shortly afterward, Jake and Bill take in the "Ledoux-Kid Francis fight" (81), and during the festival, Jake admires one of the bulls primarily because he moves like a boxer:

'Look how he knows to use his horns . . . He's got a left and a right just like a boxer.' (139)

With the exception of Bill and Robert Cohn, all the main characters were directly involved with the war: Jake, as we know, was wounded; Harris, the English fishing buddy Jake and Mike hook up with in Burguete, has had a difficult time since the war and measures his pleasure in fishing by a post-war time frame: " 'I've not had much fun since the war,' " he tells them, grateful for their companionship: " 'I say. Really you don't know how much it means' " (129).

Mike Campbell's war experience was one of absence rather than presence. Though he had been in the army, Mike never saw combat; his greatest danger was of falling off his horse when it " 'bolted down Piccadilly' " (134). Never permitted the opportunity of proving his courage (probably because of the influence of his privileged family),

Mike is something of an impostor, and suspects that he is unworthy of his inheritance, which is controlled by his mother and doled out to him in the form of a monthly allowance. Mike is always waiting for his money to come (82) and Brett, his fiancé, is just another possession when he refers to her as "'lovely piece,'" "'this thing'" (79) or a "'lovely healthy wench'" (166). Nevertheless, he, too, is nostalgic about the war years:

What times we had. How I wish those dear days were back' (134)

and tells a long joke about some "war medals" he borrowed from his tailor so he could attend "'a wopping big dinner'" in the presence of "'the Prince of Wales'" and for which the invitation stipulated "'medals will be worn'" (135). As Mike tells it, he didn't get to wear his borrowed medals because "'it was the night they'd shot Henry Wilson, so the Prince didn't come and the King didn't come'" (135). In a frivolous gesture Mike gives his medals away to some girls as a "'Form of souvenir'" (136).

The subtext of Mike's story, which is meant to be understood as an elaborate joke, is a profound commentary on Mike's situation. His blatant disregard for both the owner of the medals and the tailor who lent them to him, is indicative of his raging desire to destroy the symbolical value of heroism, especially someone else's heroism, in order to erase or sublimate the importance his lack of heroic symbols means to him. On another level, his destructive action is also a veiled act of revenge against the privileged class which has sheltered him from proving his manhood. Without medals Mike has not proven himself in the world of fighting men. And, appropriately, Hemingway gives Mike the character of an irresponsible loser, careless of everyone and everything that gets in his way. Mike is a discharged bankrupt and a drunk; he is humiliated twice in front of his friends when both Cohn and Romero cuckold him; and he never participates in sport which adds to the soft, defeated, whining image he projects. Pursued throughout the festival by people he owes money to, he borrows from everyone, including Montoya, the hotel proprietor, in order to pay his bills, then discharges his debt to Montoya by borrowing from Brett, even as she is leaving him to go to Madrid with Romero.

Brett Ashley was a V.A.D. volunteer during the war, first nursing Jake who was wounded, then Mike, who, though never wounded, perceived that he had a need for it. She married her second husband Ashley, a "'Ninth baronet'" (203) after her first died in the war of "'dysentery'" (39). Having lost two husbands to the war, Brett's present situation is best understood in connection with Ashley, a sailor so traumatized by combat that he slept "'on the floor . . . with a loaded service revolver.'" But protection from the enemy that continued to haunt him was, at best, ephemeral, and when he had "'bad spells'" he would tell Brett "'he'd kill her'" (203). Brett's friendship with Jake, then, is explained partly as a repetition of her situation with Ashley. She is attracted to Jake because he is safely wounded and poses no sexual threat; though she loves him, his war wound gives her an excuse to distance herself from him emotionally, while allowing her to indulge in romantic fantasies, complaining about what they can't have, which serves to keep Jake feeling guilty and bound to her at the same time. Jake plays the pseudo-husband or father in that he will always be available to rescue Brett from her indiscretions, and she is dependant upon his loyalty.

Even so peripheral a figure as Count Mippipopolous has "'been in seven wars and four revolutions'" (60). He unhesitatingly displays the "'arrow wounds'" he claims to have received "'on a business trip'" "'In Abyssinia'" when he was "'twenty-one years old'" (60). His business, it seems, was like a war and as dangerous.

Jake's nostalgia for the war years centers on the fellowship of pre-combat dinners and the ease that alcohol provides. Now that the war is over, all that is left of the war-games are the sporting events and the alcoholic haze they collectively reach back into, searching for the aura of the glory days.

Behind the war talk stands the legendary heroism of Roland, Charlemagne's nephew and commander, during the battle of Roncevalles in 778 when Charlemagne's rear guard army was betrayed and slaughtered, killing Roland and Oliver, his comrade. In *The Sun Also Rises* Jake and Bill quickly locate "the monastery of Roncevalles" "on the shoulder of the first dark mountain" (108) as they enter the village of Burguete the first night of their fishing trip. With Harris they visit the monastery. Though Bill and Harris both disavow the importance of the place to them, neither wanted to miss having seen it:

'It's a remarkable place, though,' Harris said. 'I wouldn't not have seen it. I'd been intending coming up each day.' (128)

In the face of his friends' lack of sympathy for the heroic idealism the place symbolizes, Jake's silence can only be understood as reverence.

For Jake and his friends, the war experience looms large in their imaginations and the only thing that compensates is watching single combatants pitted against each other, first in boxing, and then in bullfighting. So closely are war and sport intertwined with one another that Jake describes the heightened sense of feeling derived from spectatorship as a "disturbed emotional feeling ... the feeling of elation" (164), until after the last fight when elation becomes a let-down: "we both took a bullfight very hard" (221).

In addition, to the emotional investment in the fights, the fiesta, itself, sounds like a war zone. The fiesta did not begin; it "exploded" with a "rocket" (153). Then, a "ball of smoke hung in the sky like a shrapnel burst, ... trickling smoke in the bright sunlight" (153). Even the music is martial:

we heard the pipes and the fifes and the drums coming ... the pipes shrill and the drums pounding. (153)

Later, a "military band" plays while a "fireworks specialist" tries to "send up fire balloons" (178—79) and the whole town takes on the aspect of "'a wonderful nightmare'" (212):

Everything became quite unreal finally and it seemed as though nothing could have any consequences. (154)

For Jake who says he would "'believe anything. Including nightmares'" (212), the high points of the fiesta are the bullfights. Jake, because he is an "aficionado ... one who is passionate about the bullfights" (131), is among a select group of men who test each other in

a sort of oral spiritual examination with the questions always a little on the defensive and never apparent, there was this same embarrassed putting the hand on the shoulder, or a 'Buen hombre.' But nearly always there was the actual touching. It seemed as though they wanted to touch you to make it certain. (132)

His relationship with Montoya is, likewise, special, determined by their shared feeling for the bulls:

He always smiled as though bull-fighting were a very special secret between the two of us; a rather shocking but really very deep secret that we knew about. He always smiled as though there were something lewd about the secret to outsiders, but that it was something that we understood. It would not do to expose it to people who would not understand. (131)

Jake's bond with Montoya, as brother 'aficionados', has been enhanced by his yearly patronage of Montoya's hotel, and gives Montoya reason to solicit Jake's help in protecting the newest young bull-fighter from being exploited by unethical, greedy managers, or women — in particular, from the "'one American woman down here'" who "'collects bull-fighters'" (172):

'He's such a fine boy,' said Montoya. 'He ought to stay with his own people. He shouldn't mix in that stuff.' (172)

After Jake agrees with the plan, Brett implores him to help her because she has fallen in love with Romero. Against his better judgement, Jake arranges an assignation, betraying, in the process, Montoya, Romero, and ultimately, himself:

Just then Montoya came into the room. He started to smile at me, then he saw Pedro Romero with a big glass of cognac in his hand, sitting laughing between me and a woman with bare shoulders, at a table full of drunks. He did not even nod.' (177)

Heightening and complicating the drama of the situation is Jake's own propensity to identify with Romero. First there is a bond of chastity — Jake's by virture of his impotence, and Romero's self-imposed abstinence from both drink and women, a common practice among boxers and bull-fighters in training before they enter the ring. While it is Brett who falls in love with Romero, a man almost young enough to be her son (he is nineteen years old and she thirty-four), Jake also notices Romero's physical beauty: "He was the best-looking boy I have ever seen" (163). The second reason Jake identifies with Romero is because Romero's ritualized killing is a highly eroticized one, and Jake vicariously enjoys the death-combat in which the matador is always the victor.

Because "He loved bull-fighting, and . . . he loved the bulls" (216), Romero's technique conveys "real emotion" and "absolute purity of line" (168). In fact, what Romero's exhibition projects is a seductive death dance in which the bull is first seduced, then betrayed to its death. When "Romero smiled" (218) after he "offered" the bull "the cape" (217), it was because

The bull wanted it again, . . . Each time he let the bull pass so close that the man and the bull and the cape . . . were all one sharply etched mass. . . . It was as though he were rocking the bull to sleep. (217)

Before Romero can complete the kill, however, he has "to make the bull consent with his body" (217); then, at the moment of the killing thrust,

as the sword went in, and for just an instant, he and the bull were one. (218)

The language of love used here obviously describes a ritual copulation and its punishment, death. Like a lover revealing and perhaps apologizing for the true nature of his betrayal, Romero "spoke to the bull" (219) before it succumbed "slowly, then all over, suddenly, four feet in the air" (219).

The dance of death that Romero enacts three times a day each day of the festival takes place in a circular arena, which is a visual image of the sun: "the sand of the ring was smooth-rolled and yellow" (211). In boxes stacked one on top of another spectators watch the bull's death become a blot on the artificial sun's surface, wedding the life force in its timeless struggle with death's urge. The power of the ritual re-enactment confirms what Freud, in *Civilization and Its Discontents* (1930), came to conclude was "the meaning of the evolution of civilization." It was the "struggle between Eros and Death, between the instinct of life and the instinct of destruction . . . work[ing] itself out in the human species" (69).

At the beginning of *The Sun Also Rises*, Jake tells Brett Ashley that his wound is not very important because

'what happened to me is supposed to be funny. I never think about it.' (27)

But, as we've seen, Jake never stops thinking about it. His wound is the overriding concern of his life, and in one way or another, occupies not only his waking hours, but what few sleeping hours he has as well.

New York University

NOTES

[1] For economy's sake, I have adopted the abbreviation "TSAR" for *The Sun Also Rises*; citations are noted intertextually by page number.
[2] Romero's belief that he will 'never die' is a repetition of Nick Adams thinking, at the end of "Indian Camp," that "he felt quite sure that he would never die" (19).

WORKS CITED

Baker, C. *Hemingway: The Writer as Artist* (Princeton: Princeton University Press, 1973).

Freud, S. *Beyond the Pleasure Principle*, Trans. and Ed. by James Strachey (New York: Norton, 1961).

Freud, S. *Civilization and Its Discontents*, Trans. and Ed. by James Strachey (New York: Norton, 1961).

Hemingway, E. "Indian Camp" *In Our Time* (New York: Scribner's, 1970), 15—19.

Hemingway, E. *The Sun Also Rises* (New York: Scribner's, 1970).

Hoffman, E. T. A. "The Mines at Falun" *Tales of Hoffman*, Trans. with an Introd. by R. J. Hollingdale (Middlesex: Penguin, 1982), 311—38.

SELECT BIBLIOGRAPHY

Backman, Melvin. "Hemingway: The Matador and the Crucified" *Modern Fiction Studies* **I**: 3 (1955): 2—11.

Cochran, Robert W. "Circularity in *The Sun Also Rises*" *Modern Fiction Studied* **XIV**: 3 (1968): 297—305.

Drinnon, Richard. "In the American Heartland: Hemingway and Death" *The Psychoanalytic Review* **LII**: 2 (1965): 149—175.

Grenberg, Bruce L. "The Design of Heroism in *The Sun Also Rises*" *Fitzgerald/Hemingway Annual* (1971): 274—89.

Moore, Geoffrey. "*The Sun Also Rises*: Notes Toward an Extreme Fiction" *A Review of English Literature* **IV**: 4 (1963): 31—46.

Mosher, Harold F. Jr. "The Two Styles of Hemingway's *The Sun Also Rises*" *Fitzgerald/Hemingway Annual* (1971): 262—73.

Murphy, George D. "Hemingway's *The Sun Also Rises*" *The Explicator* **XXVIII**: 3 (1969): 23.

Ross, Morton L. "Bill Gorton, The Preacher in *The Sun Also Rises*" *Modern Fiction Studies* **XVIII**: 4 (1973): 517—27.

Rouch, John S. "Jake Barnes as Narrator" *Modern Fiction Studies* **XI**: 4 (1966): 361—70.

Schneiderman, Leo. "Hemingway: A Psychological Study" *The Connecticut Review* **VI**: 2 (1973): 34—49.

Scott, Arthur L. "In Defense of Robert Cohn" *College English* **XVIII**: 6 (1957): 309—14.

Spilka, Mark. "The Death of Love in *The Sun Also Rises*" *Hemingway and His Critics*, Ed. with an Introd. by Carlos Baker (New York: Hill and Wang, 1961), pp. 80—92.

Wertheim, Stanley. "The Conclusion of Hemingway's *The Sun Also Rises*" *Literature and Psychology* **XVII**: 1 (1967): 55—56.

Yevish, Irving A. "The Sun Also Exposes: Hemingway and Jake Barnes" *The Midwest Quarterly* **X**: 1 (1968): 89—97.

DAVID BROTTMAN

LIGHT-VALUES AS EXISTENTIAL INDICES
IN THOMAS PYNCHON'S EXTRAVAGANT
COMIC REVERY

*"Idiopathic Archetypes" of the Ego, Its Shadow,
Its Preconscious Being, and the Self in the Spectrum
that is* Gravity's Rainbow

Henri Bergson's insights regarding the encrustation of spontaneous being by reifying mechanisms that promote obliviousness[1] and Mikhail Bakhtin's recognition of the recuperative transvaluations topographically bodied-forth in the carnival celebration of phenomena associated with the lower-bodily stratum[2] together clearly indicate the definitive diagnostic and therapeutic predilections of comic extravagance as a mode of literary revery. Recognizing with Gaston Bachelard that the images of revery are manifestations of Being,[3] there is, then, compelling warrant for considering specific instances of extravagant comic revery from the orientation of phenomenological psychiatry and *Daseinsanalysis* in which dominant and recurring imagery is appreciated as the indexical manifestation of an existential a priori or dominant mode of intentionality and attunement delivering to an existence a lived-world characterized by particular attributes and not others and ultimately reflecting the dominant mode of relation to Being as such by which *Dasein's* structural potentialities for relatedness have been constricted.[4] Phenomenological recuperation of the dominant attunements of comic extravagance provides access to its thematic preoccupations, as well, insofar as those preoccupations conceptually extrapolate a predisposition to value or to devalue specific attributes and qualities in accordance with the mode's definitive redistribution of imaginal energy in the evocation of phenomena. This redistribution of engaged attention provides an index to a fundamental transvaluation of values originating in the comic's radical reorientation toward Being.

In the case of Thomas Pynchon's *Gravity's Rainbow*[5] not only do the dominant constituent attributes of its images provide indices to the existential reorientation and redistribution of imaginal energy constituting comic transvaluation, but the redistribution of energy is itself the

269

A-T. Tymieniecka (ed.), Analecta Husserliana, Vol. XXXVIII, 269–295.
© 1992 *Kluwer Academic Publishers. Printed in the Netherlands.*

imaginal paradigm determining its sprawling, seemingly chaotic yet overdetermined, forming and deforming pattern. Phenomenological attention to the constituent attributes of the most vividly realized images of *Gravity's Rainbow* discloses a common denominator so insistent that it must be acknowledged the intuitive basis of the text's pattern of conceptual articulations. The concentrated point and its diminished surround, and more specifically, the concentrated point of light and its penumbra of dissolution, provide in their dialectical relation the principle indexical manifestation of the existential value distributed throughout the stratum of Pynchon's images. Foregoing this paradigmatic dialectical relation not only discloses the fundamental redistribution of energy and value proceeding by means of the descriptive evocations of characters, situations, and incidents, it also discloses what is existentially at-stake in recognizing them as imaginal manifestations of what might be designated, borrowing Pynchon's own provocative but unelucidated term, certain *Idiopathic Archetypes*. In accord with Pynchon's abundantly evident diagnostic predisposition, imaginal manifestations of light, dark, and the spectrum foreground certain attributes as symptomatic indices to a morbid state or condition without precedent in any other — a state or condition of morbidity tending to be concentrated in a particular part, profile-type, or group due to *the particular susceptibilities of its intrinsic structure*. Specifically, then, what is at-stake in many of Pynchon's most extravagant images is an implicit archetypal idiopathology of the ego's morbidity as a concentrated and concentrating point of light (socially embodied as a transcendentalizing gnostic elect), and that morbidity's dialectical generation of its Shadow, as well as its intimations of its preconscious maternal ground and its Self — all best understood not merely as endopsychic agencies or complexes but as expressions of dominant perspectival modes of being within the pantheonic spectrum of potential modes that *Dasein's* existential structure fundamentally affords. Though it is by no means limited to it, this idiopathology is most immediately disclosed by the mode of being-in-relation of Pynchon's paradoxically central yet marginal character, Tyrone Slothrop and his experiences in the deconstructed Zone "between."

If Slothrop begins as a nebulous focus and proceeds to blur to indistinction, it is because he is in Pynchon's comically distantiated vision like all his other characters, but a temporary, loosely bonded, molecular or sub-atomic moment. However, given the undeniable diagnostic and therapeutic predilections of comic extravagance, the question arises, what is to be gained in losing Slothrop in the shifting mass of Pynchon's spectrum of attention? The answer resides I think in the recognition that Slothrop's indistinctness and lack of distinction constitute his saving grace and that there is something comparably salutary for the reader in having his or her conventionally concentrated focus of attention diffracted to a vastly expanded spectrum of consideration. While Pynchon emphasizes the disintegration of Slothrop in terms that seem to degrade him as a hero in order to prevent habitual sentimental identification with him, in his personified passage from a point of concentration to mindless dispersion beyond its shadowy margins and across the spectrum of the Zone, Slothrop provides direct access to his creator's valorizations. His slapstick paperchase for salvation through definition, epitomizes the continuous displacement of being by becoming and of the phenomenal by the conceptual that characterizes the so-called search for identity. Once the phenomenon of Slothrop's loss of integral identity is approached as it would be in Daseinsanalysis, with a phenomenological description of what disintegration seems to entail for Pynchon's imagination and a consideration of to what it gains Slothrop (and the reader) access, his ostensible failure becomes more clearly a matter of conceptual designations that have "long worded over all ability to know victory or defeat."

But before judging the values implicated in the constituent attributes of disintegrative processes, one must first determine what valorizations are attached to phenomena associated with concentration, centralization, and integration. The valorizations intrinsic to these spatializing principles can be most immediately engaged in the lived-world of Slothrop's nemesis, the oppressively punctilious behaviorist, Pointsman, whose mode of relation nominates him the indexical opposite of the sloppy Slothrop's dispersive tendencies. Pointsman's world-design is the very articulation of the conceptual vocabulary of concentration. He himself is the very incarnation of the narrow constriction implicit in focalizing and of all its centralization can effect in the marginal expanse beyond its parenthesis, the "noose" that is "the gold-lit borders of consciousness" (76). More than this he is, as his poetic meditation on the act of focusing indicates, the vampiric spirit of reductivism personified, appropriating phenomena from the environs much as he abducts his canine specimens and narrowly directing their expropriated vital energy as tributary and tribute to his own project of abstract and projective attribution. His description of the "inhibitory dissolve" of the surround is best read as Pynchon's own phenomenological meditation on the peril implicit in the narrow focus of extreme concentration and its potential for effecting distributive imbalance whenever an expression of the existential tendencies for which Pointsman is named:

> Around the bloom, the stimulus, the need
> That brighter burns, as brightness, quickly sucked
> From objects all around, now concentrates
> (Yet less than blinding), focuses to flame.
> [The presence of other things] canceled, for this moment, by the flame:
> [displaced] perhaps to roll
> Beyond the blank frontiers of memory . . .
> Yet this, be clear, is no 'senile distraction,'
> But concentrating, such as younger men
> Can easily and laughing dodge, their world
> Presenting too much more than one mean loss [. . .] (226—227).

The point is that Pointsman's narrowed world cannot afford such losses, and so the hermetic must be established as a means of control, as it is through the laboratory. But what is perhaps most worthy of remark is how much this description, in rendering a single-minded intentionality, evokes the obsessive fetishism that generally characterizes the exclusionary yet appropriative mode of paranoia. In this mode some attribute or quality of Being is abstracted under the stimulus of its felt-absence and in projection made the nucleic image around which an unnaturally cathected world is engendered, while the rest of the potentially available is cast into oblivion.

The relevance of Pointsman's description to Bergsonian comic preoccupations can be made more apparent when the terms of the Pavlovian formulation from which Pointsman's poem springs are contextually framed by the general concerns of phenomenological psychoanalysis. Speaking of a narrowed, monocular focus that impairs any relating to the environment Pavlov writes, "Concentrating on one stimulus [that is, a phenomenal attribute or quality] we exclude by negative induction other collateral and simultaneous stimuli [the spectrum of potentially available attributes or qualities] because they often do not suit the circumstances [the pattern of valorized designations], are not complementary reactions in the given setting [the world-as-designed]." Pointsman's reaction to Slothrop as a "sudden angel, thermodynamic surprise" (143) is thus an index to any abrupt appari-tion of imbalance within the field of entropic equivalence that is Pointsman's habitual indifference (obliviousness) to anything outside the focus of his projects. The otherwise marginal Slothrop becomes for him a phenomenon that demands to be appropriated; indeed Slothrop becomes for Pointsman nothing more than a configuration of his appro-priative design, an opportunity for his theories. Stripped to is essence, one has in Pointsman's meditation a description of his own habitual existential a priori, a privileging narrowness that aggrandizes itself by bringing into virtual being some phenomenon that has singled out to receive the fixating projection of its own narcissistic image. This self-perpetuating, appropriative yet exclusionary, narrowness constitutes the existential mode of the ego. The ambivalence of the penultimate image of Pointsman's poem — an ambivalence measured in the difficulty of distinguishing the repressive from the masturbatory as reciprocal self- and world-obliterating acts — is an index to the ambiguous motivational origin and world-affect of this mode:

> Excitatory processes eased to cinders
> By Inhibition's tweaking, callused fingers,
> [. . .]
> Each light, winking out [as in a city's blackout] (226—7).

Because points of disclosure must always be a kind of closure for Pointsman, a closing out of most of existence from the oblivious parenthesis of focus, his image provides access to the transvaluative implications of Slothrop's compensatory "dwindling white point of himself" (383). Pointsman is in this regard just one of a constellation of such indications of implicit valorization. Phenomenological scrutiny of the attributes constituting other of Pynchon's most vividly realized images will disclose intrinsic value-associations that suggest Slothrop's "diminish[ing] like the light" in the manner of the psychic medium Eventyr (a Tyrone evenly dispersed) is indicative of a loosening and undoing of the ego-complex and its unnatural bondings prerequisite to a return to the pre-conscious state of psychic distribution. Slothrop's dissolution as a character, or concentrated value-complex, can be said to body-forth a redistribution of energy comparable to the dispersion of the miser's hoard that is one of the comic's greatest archetypes insofar as the imbalance of value in anyone's world originates with the establishment of the ego and is perpetuated by its design. This principle is in accordance with the ontological status and condition of the ego as it is conceived by Pynchon, who asks his reader to

Think of the ego ... that suffers a personal history bound to time, as the grid. The deeper and true Self is the flow between cathode and plate. The constant, pure flow. Signals — sense-data, feelings, memories relocating — are put onto the grid, and modulate the flow. We live lives that are waveforms constantly changing with time, now positive, now negative. Only at moments of great serenity is it possible to find the pure, the informationless state of signal zero. (404)

A temporalizing center of inertness, the ego engenders its world through a system of distribution, a world-design that grids (categorizes and allocates) phenomena in such a manner as to modulate (valorize) these manifestations of the always-already in correlation with its own lived-relation to Being/Non-being. Implicit throughout the pattern of Pynchon's images is a vision of paranoia as representing a mere exaggeration of the valorizing procedures by which ego perpetuates its own ontological imbalance by perpetrating an imbalance in its world such that some phenomena are valued excessively (as signs of information, say) at the expense of others that are not valued, or lived, at all.

The claim made by and for the One creates the not-one, the preterite many or multitude of zeros that are marginalized in being passed-over, decentered by the centering acts of some supposed center of election. Here again Pointsman is the exemplar of this mode of exclusion, as another character indicates when he tells Pointsman that because he has become "so used to talking, and to light" that he cannot see nor hear the blacks "in their darkness ... their silence" (172). Pointsman's design, what he is capable of imagining, what his punctiliously discrete categories make available to him before the rest is relegated to oblivion as unworthy of attention, reflects an either/or mode of relation to Being:

in the domain of zero to one, not-something to something, Pointsman can only possess the zero and the one. He cannot [. . .] survive anyplace in between. Like his master I. P. Pavlov before him, he imagines the cortex of the brain as a mosaic of tiny on/off elements. Some are always in bright excitation, others darkly inhibited. The contours, bright and dark, keep changing. But each point is allowed only the two states: waking or sleep. One or zero. [He] assumes the presence of these bi-stable points. (55)

But the assumptions intrinsic to the binary vocabulary of a conceptual design may function to bar the gates of Eden, preventing the existence from ever getting "Into It far enough to start talking about God" (752–8). Thus Pointsman is said to have been "led down the garden path by symmetry" in "assuming that a mechanism must imply its mirror image" in accordance with Pavlov's formulations concerning "[i]deas of the opposite," which purported to demonstrate "how mirror-images Inside could be confused." Indeed, designated symmetries ramifying on and on into further sub-categories of oppositions that subject the flow of Being to their "coordinate systems" are themselves an index to some "sickness" — "[s]igns and symptoms" or a "pathology" culminating, Pynchon avers, in rocketry manifesting the obliteration latent in categorical antagonisms (144).

Although Pointsman's dominant mode is pathological, his exemplary meditation on dialectic manifests both an imaginal tendency pervading Pynchon's comic revery and an existential principle that is paradigmatic for his thematic preoccupations. Formulated by the transcendence-obsessed, self-dooming Weissmann-Blicero, this principle is recalled by his lover Gottfried as the latter contemplates those who wish upon first stars, while himself ascending toward them in a rocket: "The true moment of shadow is the moment in which you see the point of light in the sky." "The single point" engenders "the Shadow that [gathers] you in its sweep" (760). This is the same principle expressed in Pavlov's diagnosis of paranoia, as summarized by Pointsman, his disciple:

Pavlov believed that obsessions and paranoid delusions were a result of certain — call them cells, neurons, on the mosaic of the brain, being excited to the level where, through reciprocal induction, all the area around becomes inhibited. One bright, burning point, surrounded by darkness. Darkness it has, in a way, called up. Cut off, this bright point, perhaps to the end of the patient's life, from all other ideas, sensations, self-criticism that might temper its flame, restore it to normalcy. He called it a 'point of pathological inertia.' (90)

When conjoined on the basis of their constituent imaginal attributes these two passages separated by almost seven-hundred pages indicate how the elect's impulse to transcend comes to be implicated as a manifestation of the operative structure within the self-fetishizing design-tendencies of the ego's concentrated point of light, and the pall of morbidity that it effects everywhere else. Together these passages suggest the parallel reciprocal relation of the ego to, on the one hand, its projected ideal Other — which as its transcendentalized Absolute is shrunk by distantiation to a void-surrounded point of desire — and on the other, to the pathologically inert character of the fixating complex of valorized attributes that, as the nucleus of the paranoid ego's narrowed transcendental category and world-narrowing design, determine the nature of its lived-world. In doing so they go far to indicate how Pynchon comes to imagine the concentrated point of light as deleterious to the spontaneous flow of things, as in his description of a spotlight in whose beam migrate birds are "held till they dropped exhausted out of the sky" (134).

Significantly, the many elements of Pynchon's thinking about the bright focal point and its world come to a point in a passage about fetishism. In the typical degradatory manner of the carnivalesque, Pynchon seeks to provoke an "unwholesome giggle" at the transcendence-presumptions of Western values and the phenomena they valorize by tainting them with the innuendo of ubiquitous sado-eroticism and its secret suicide-lust:

How the penises of Western men have leapt, for a century, to the sight of this singular point at the top of a lady's stocking, this transition from silk to bare skin and suspender! It's easy for non-fetishists to sneer about Pavlovian conditioning and let it go at that, but [. . .] there is much more here — there is a cosmology: of nodes and cusps and points of osculation, mathematical kisses . . . *singularities!* Consider cathedral spires, holy minarets . . . mountain peaks rising sharply to heaven, such as those to be noted at scenic Berchtesgaden . . . the edges of steel razors, always holding potent mystery . . . rose thorns that prick us by surprise . . . even, according to the Russian mathematician Friedmann, the infinitely dense point from which the present Universe expanded . . . In each case, the change from point to no-point carries a luminosity and enigma at which something in us must leap and sing, or withdraw in fright . . . Do all these points imply, like the Rocket's, an annihilation? What is that, detonating in the sky above the cathedral? beneath the edge of the razor, under the rose? (396)

The problem is of course that out of such detonating singularities expand lived-universes by coordination of the points of cathexis into a logos and the consignment of all silent no-points to the annihilating shadows of the inconsequential.[6]

The constituting logic of the bright galvanizing nodes is that as they become fetishized they must be projected into that place of lived-absence, those undifferentiated "black frontiers" of Pointsman's meditation that they have rendered indistinct and unremarkable by the logic of the either/or (having no point the undifferentiated cannot be meaningful). A diagnostic reconnaissance map of the paranoid's lived-experience would reveal a binary topography of either detonated object-moments delivering their psychic payloads of information or their negatives of torpid vacancy of meaning. However, "staring at a recco map" can cause "bomb craters [to] flip inside out" (713). This image may be said to formulate a diagnostic principle regarding the potential ironic consequence of any either/or design insofar as the reversion of background to foreground and vice-versa is said to be the dialectical result of a fixating mode of relation. Following Pavlov, Pointsman designates this inversion of values attributed to phenomenal qualities the "ultraparadoxical phase," describing it as a "seek[ing] in the silence, for the stimulus that is not there" (90).

It is Slothrop who best epitomizes those who would fix their attention upon some meaning-cathected star surrounded by an information-less state of silence that can only be experienced as the void's "black frontiers." And it is also Slothrop who provides the best, though not the only, model for how in the ultraparadoxical phase of the ego's paranoid mode the Shadow comes to emerge from the field of coordinated nodes of fetishizing concentration. In this phase the ego engenders (i.e., makes manifest) its own darkness through an obsessive focus on its putative enlightenment — much as when the hyper-rational Franz Pokler goes "to switch on a light — but in the act of throwing the switch" realizes that "the room had really been lit to begin with, and he had just turned everything out, *everything*" (400). In this parable of "the confusion of ideas of the opposite," Franz' ego-intentionally would foreground light, would effect enlightenment in its character as pointsman or switching-path of distribution; but by asserting its point of light as mechanically as a reflex ego-intentionality obliterates the already-given, which in its obtuse inattentiveness it could not appreciate until too late.

Just as at one point he is said to awaken to "light-values still to be put together" (437), Slothrop seeks strenuously for the enlightenment that will put and keep himself together, even though by the time of his disappearance there are "few who can still see [him] as any sort of integral creature any more," most having long given up "trying to hold him together, even as a concept" (740). But phenomena such as the play of light can in certain moments of graceful interdiction be discovered to have their own value in and of themselves before their being appropriated as data into a pre-established interpretive design that habitually designates, combines, and schematically places them in terms of their teleological worthiness as clues. By contrast, when purposively conceived as an object to be arrived at, put together, and possessed, rather than as an ongoing activity of reciprocal encounter, ego-identity must always effect a narrowing of focus in terms of similar categories of priority. As a case in point, Slothrop's paranoia is motivated by a desire for an integrating center identified with the assemblage of the 000001 Rocket. Slothrop's delusion demands that he concentrate on the One, causing him to narrow the spectrum of phenomena available to him such that he either ignores or abandons whatever cannot be appropriated in its name.

Considering the obsessive degree to which Slothrop establishes the *Aggregat* rocket as the center of what he conceives to be his identity and purpose it must be designated Pynchon's premier example of a world-engendering nucleic fetishized point of concentration ("Whether you believe or not . . . you had a feeling — a suspicion, a latent wish, some hidden tithe out of your soul, *something* — for the Rocket," [673]). As an object of fetish, the Rocket "must answer to a number of different shapes in the dreams of those who touch it" (727); but it is the desire for a "Destiny with a shape" that provides the general teleology for its aggregation. The rumor that the Rocket's assembly is somehow Slothrop's assembly as well[7] merely literalizes Pynchon's figurative characterization of the formation of the ego-identity as the gnostic expression of a self-aggrandizing ontological anxiety; thus the "assembly of the 000001" is described kabbalistically as "a Diaspora running backwards, seeds of exile flying inward in a modest preview of gravitational collapse, of the Messiah gathering in the fallen sparks" (737). As the embodied principle of aggregation and concentration to a point in anxious response to the dispersed, the Rocket provides the most diagnostically salient of many indices to the transcendentalizing tendency of the ego — its desire to solipsistically project itself as absolute in its autonomy and freedom from contingency. Configured as a prosthetic extension of the ego's "psychic prostate," the Rocket is exposed as the recipient of the existential equivalent of Maxwell's Demon, which "concentrates[s] energy into one favored room of the Creation at the expense of everything else." "The dynamic space of the living Rocket" (301) lends itself, then, to identification with the cosmos of the phallic "I" because in their self-aggrandizing proclivity both constitute themselves by engorging upon the energies that they attract from the margins that their centrality engenders, imperially making all phenomena pay tribute to them as if they were its colonies and their essential attributes exploitable raw materials.[8]

However, as the "male embodiment of a technologique that embraced power [. . .] for just those chances of surrender, personal and dark surrender, to the Void," the Rocket is also implicated in "the confusion of ideas of the opposite," just as are all attempts of the ego-mode to sustain the pretence of autonomous existence. Tacitly defining itself in terms of specific attributes (concentration, fixity, centrality), the ego-mode reveals its suicidal inclination toward Non-being whenever those attributes are foregrounded as absolute metaphysical values which deflect appreciative attention from the undifferentiated onto-logical ground that sustains them. Given the associative pattern of the predisposition that Pynchon diagnoses as the paranoia of the ego, to foreground is to cause to raise *above*, thereby preventing the possibility of a lateral field or spectrum of equally valued phenomena or their attributes. Thus election (i.e., being plucked out of a penumbral field of oblivion) is imagined as the foregrounding intentionality of a transcen-dentalized "I" whose index is that bright focal point of light we have seen before: "Sunday light, elevating and washing the faces above the pulpits defining grace, swearing *this is how it does happen — yes the great bright hand reaching out of the cloud*" (29). What must be appreciated, however, is Pynchon's comic predisposition to subvert the conventionally foregrounded so as to recuperate the manifold that has been passed-over by demeaning the desire for the Absolute implicit in the elect's claims to having direct access to or recipience of its attributes.

A proleptic volition drives Slothrop's paranoid quest for teleological validation of his election, just as Weissman-Blicero is obsessed with "the radiance of what we would become" (723—4). But the temporal deformation of the existential capacity for presence by an exclusively anticipative mode of intentionality is evocatively suggested by Sloth-rop's own revery on life in the futuristic Raketen-Stadt, in which instructions are delivered for a mission to:

go and find the Radiant Hour . . . Your objective is not the King — there is no King — but momentary targets such as the Radiant Hour . . . which has been abstracted from the day's 24 by colleagues of the Father, for sinister reasons of their own. (674)

What makes this injunction an aspect of "father's daily little death-plots" against a son who "[d]idn't know it was lost," is its implicit nega-tion of the quotidian, an attitude which by means of value-designations that distil the aggregate of phenomena and their attributes into a fetish of concentrated illumination would tacitly redistribute the potential fulness of Being available within any and every given moment so as to exclude most as inconsequential and necessarily to be taken for granted. The narrow, targetting, will-driven mode of attunement that characterizes metaphysical quest can manifest bad faith insofar as the necessarily paranoid seeker must always look elsewhere, to the absent, to what is not given — to the transcendent — for his or her self-justifying vivification. Slothrop's parabolic traversal of the Zone suggests that focus directed toward metaphysical irradiance engenders ontological shadow: projects designed to "rescue" or retrieve some attribute, aspect, or moment of Being thought to be privileged express the "[p]ernicious" character of the "Paternal Peril" that is the transcendentalized ego. "[H]unting [. . .] to be shown," Slothrop had become "a Saint George after the fact, going out to poke bout for droppings of the Beast" (490) — "catching up to" the always-already being the very nature of gnostic paranoia's self-imposed "work-therapy." Presence becomes the hidden-in-plain-view whenever a projective seeking deflects attention away from the full range of the multivarious phenomenal attributes randomly constituting any moment:

> Big globular raindrops [. . .] begin to splat into giant asterisks on the pavement, inviting him to look down at the bottom of the text of the day, where footnotes will explain all. He isn't about to look. Nobody ever said a day has to be juggled into any kind of sense at day's end. He just runs. (204)

Slothrop's eventual wayward drifting in the Zone causes him to be "weeded out" in the "Holy-Center Approaching" competition, but it is this intuitive obliviousness to the Absolute even as he consciously seeks it that constitutes his saving grace.

As an absolute center of organizing value establishing a field of either/or distinctions in relation to it, such a "plexus" or bright focal point might provide "a good enough vision of what's shadowless noon and what isn't." Because of its attributes the star we designate the Sun has throughout history lent itself as an index to those attributes to which the human aspires, while at the same time seeming to locate the distant realm of value to which the human must transcend in order to acquire or reacquire those attributes; thus the gnostic paranoid fantasies of Enzian, Weissmann-Blicero's African lover and convert to Western-style fetishism, invoke a transcendental vocabulary of values: "the high, rising . . . the blazing, the great one." But Pynchon's revery on the sun, greatest of concentrated points of light, bright eye, solar gaze of the detached Father, the transcendentalized ego that sees and judges all things according to His lights, goes beyond its traditional identification with the ego's image of itself, the self-valorization of consciousness. It goes on extravagantly to foreground the oppressive transparency of the ego-mode:

For millions of years, the sun has been roaring, a giant, furnace, 93 millionmile roar, so perfectly steady that generations of men have been born into it and passed out of it again, without ever hearing it. Unless it changed, how would anyone know?

The unremittant imagined as a virtual atmosphere of the unattended — surely this is a parabolic paradox. While the repressed produces its oppression as the felt-presence of an absence (ego-anxiety registering a present existential void projected into the future and returning as the ego's certainty of its diminishment), in this case the constancy of an implicit given has obscured its own presence such that it guarantees, indeed necessitates, that it be taken for granted. Lived as a transparency, it is actually an implicit medium through which experience must pass, although because it is unacknowledged there is no possibility for any awareness of how experience has been altered or phenomena preterized thereby. By providing an ambivalent index to the hidden-in-plain-view, and to what the hidden in plain view may hide (the "silence you never get to hear"), this imaginal evocation of the steadily un-remarked exposes the obscurantizing tendency of whatever is habitual and ubiquitous. The tyranny of a too-much-with establishes no other continuum but that of the insufficiently-there. By virtue of its comparable affect the light's roar of concentration is disclosed as the ontological origin or existential a priori of an egological metaphysic and world-design, "the great Vacuum in the sky they have taught you." But moments of presence-to are possible and, not surprisingly, they are associated with the enshadowed preterized portion of that which is:

Except that at night now and then, in some part of the dark hemisphere . . . sound-energy from Outside is shut off. The roaring of the sun *stops*. For its brief life, the point of sound-shadow may [descend upon someone for whom it is] audible only by virtue of accidental bits of sound-debris that may happen to be caught in the eddying.

This may well be the only image within Pynchon's vast pattern that explicitly associates shadow rather than light with the centering point of attention; and it does so as a transvaluative redistribution that recuperates lower-bodily attributes (accident, debris). For when the transcendental is eclipsed by its Shadow it is immanent Being that is materially foregrounded: "the Titan's drum of his heart."

Some of the most powerful images of *Gravity's Rainbow* indicate Pynchon's recognition that the manner in which an existence experiences the quotidian reflects the manner in which the ego has or has not come to terms with Being, whose presence to it is greater than its presence to itself, or would be did not the designations of its world-design serve to reduce the vast spectrum of Being's emanations and manifestations to a concentrated point of erstwhile light. Nowhere is the existential difference better indicated between being present-to a phenomenon as a manifestation of Being and attempting to appropriate that phenomenon to a design-tendency unequal to its being than in Pynchon's evocations of the Titans. As presences, as manifestations of *the implicit* — of the ongoing givenness in the full energy of its presence — the Titans are consistently valorized as the sublimity potentially recognizable within the quotidian as provocations to fulness of being whenever their essential extravagance is not habitually repressed. Discountenanced and marginalized while retaining the uncanny "familiarity" of the repressed, they remain in Slothrop's endlessly deferring search for significations, a "vain and blinding tugging at his sleeves *it's important . . . please . . . look at us*" until they recede once again to "only wind, only *g*-loads" (312) as his life continues to be a sequence of inadequate responses to a spectrum of phenomena that might have become *presences* had they not been appropriated by the reductive vocabulary of the ontologically narrow Apollonian ego — its "grim rationalizing of the World" (588) and its "rather strictly defined, clinical version of truth" that "seek[s] no wider agency" (272).

Though marginalized into preterition by the demarcations of reason, the Titans may yet make themselves available to those whose metaphysical designs have been eclipsed, those who have "now and then re-eras[ed] brain to keep it clean for the Visit." Geli the witch is granted a vision confirming the Titans as a sublime implicit or material being that "stir[s] far below." As "all the presences we are not supposed to be seeing . . . that we train ourselves away from," the Titans are pre-ego-intentionalized phenomena, the unacknowledged and the taken for granted that may be recuperated whenever the fundamental stratum of human existence, elemental bodyhood, discloses itself to revery. Thus Geli is said to see "the World just before men," which is to say, of the moment out of which "human consciousness, that poor cripple, that deformed and doomed thing, is about to be born" and an epochal redistribution effected. Gazing down into the lower-bodily stratum of Being where the phenomenal originates for consciousness, where the two open on to each other reciprocally as the realm of *Dasein*, she sees "canyons [. . .] opening up [. . .] fumaroles steaming the tropical life there like greens in a pot." She witnesses Being prior to its subjection to the stasis and control that characterizes and is valorized by the ego's grid:

> [t]oo violently pitched alive in constant flow ever to be seen by men directly. They are meant only to look at it dead, in still strata, transputrefied to oil or coal. Alive, it was a threat: it was Titans, was an overpeaking of life so clangorous and mad, such a green corona about Earth's body that some spoiler *had* to be brought in before it blew the Creation apart.

The Apollonian reduction of the sublime to the proportions of the ego, its "routinization of charisma," combine with the attributes complected in the images of concentrated light to clarify the implication of Pynchon's energy monopoly, Phoebus. Though one of many possible complexes,[9] the ego would exist as a monopolization of psychic energy and its only available channel. And, "One way or another," this monopoly is "in the business of providing the appearance of power, power against the night, without the reality" (647). It is this pretence against which Byron the inextinguishable lightbulb struggles once he has realized that "Bulb must move beyond its role as conveyor of light-energy alone" because enlightenment does not ensure against impotency.[10] Byron recognizes that "Phoebus has restricted Bulb to this one identity," although "there are other frequencies, above and below the visible band." These frequencies — the spectrum of modes potentially available to being — are clearly to be associated with what to the Absolute (the transcendentalized ideal of the monopolistic gnostic ego) could only appear as the criminally subversive deities of Earth's body, the Titans; for not only can Bulb "give heat" to redress the Grid's "freezing back [of] the tumultuous cycles of the day to preserve [its] cube of changlessness" (678), it "can provide energy for plants to grow, illegal plants, inside closets, for example" (652) — which is to say, it can foment the "green uprising."

If the transcendentalized and transcendentalizing "I" originates as an epochal reactionary imbalance "holding down the green uprising," the Titans' capacity for vividly manifesting the energy of the lower-bodily stratum, qualifies them as an underground. The "defection rate" at which a few egos go over everyday to their titanic Selves gauges "their striving subcreation" as a subversive redistribution directing the imagination to extravagant lower-bodily transvaluations, "out, and through, and down down," "under the net," the "information network" — the totality of rationalized explanation and totalitarian paranoid conviction that effects the deferral of *presence to Being* and prevents the renewed disclosure of things to renewable human being. The Titans embody the threat that the sublime represents for a mode of being that cannot, will not, acknowledge the presence of a correspondent quality in itself ready to reemerge upon the stimulus of any phenomenon witnessed in its essential extravagance: "Suddenly, Pan — leaping — its face too beautiful to bear, beautiful Serpent, its coils in rainbow lashing" emerging from "the constantly parted cloak of our nightwalk" (720—1).

In much the same manner, the sun as a bright galvanizing point and center of absolute value elsewhere reaches its climactery and transvaluative turn in images of the nova as an instance of the greatest sublimity, of Being so titanically present to being that the existent must necessarily be unequal to its manifestation. Thus Enzian's paranoid revelation finally "*breaks* [upon him] as that light you're afraid will break some night at too deep an hour to explain away" (520). Brightness of focal concentration makes for darkness of mind, the overbearing glare of such "revelations" being epitomized by the colossal and mystic Kirghiz Light, which casts all other experiences of a life into the shadow of its one moment; indeed, the "charismatic flash" of the Absolute "flaring up to the same annihilating white" may efface the elect just as the "sheep huddled so vulnerable on their bare hillside [were] bleached by the Star's awful radiance" (58). In the classic comic manner, Pynchon redistributes the value of dubious election by degrading the clumsily inadequate "abreaction" of his human seekers to an equivalence with "the bewildered roach sitting paralyzed and squashable out on the bare boards, rushing, reliving the terror of some sudden blast of current out of nowhere and high overhead the lambent, all-seeing Bulb" (648).

The significance of the nova-image is its evocation of the centrifugal disintegration of a too-condensed nucleic point, the diasporic irradiation of a formerly over-concentrated One. Thus Pointsman, under the increasing pressure of self-absorption's excessive gravity, begins to register intimations of the "labyrinth collapsing in rings outward [. . .]

inside the light of himself, the mad exploding of himself" (143). The point is that the nova-phenomenon represents an event that is always-already happening though the ego's resistance temporizes so that the waves of intensity reach it, reach Pointsman, as if from star-years distance in dim intermittent pulsations of anxiety rather than as "a violence, a nova of heart that will turn us all, change us forever to the very forgotten roots of who we are" (134).[11] For the nova indexically registers what Bachelard designates *innovation*, the image's renewal of the intensity of being that the child experiences in the disclosures of phenomena first encountered.[12] In this sense all images of the sublime are novas and all sublimities disintegrations of the sun as ego-complex. The nova is an index, then, to the ego's returning to sublimity in the emanational dispersion of itself into the multiplicity of fragments prerequisite to its creative accommodation of the liberated spectrum of multiple Others.

The revery that is gravity's rainbow reflects, then, a creative redistribution: a breaking-down under the pressure of an extremely centripetal focus — the ego's mode of concentrating-at-the-center so as to constitute itself as a permanent, autonomous entity at once hermetic and appropriative. The subsequent breaking-up of this focal point manifests itself in images that, in archetypal terms, express its dispersive scattering into a spectrum of elemental particles and titanic elementals liberated below by the prismatic disintegration of the glaring Sun-Father above. It is not insignificant in this regard that the first syllable of Slothrop's name garbles "sol," the coil-like rune for sun which is said by Pynchon to have devolved from the solar-circle during "a time of discontinuities, tribal fragmenting perhaps alienation, whatever's analogous, in a social sense, to the development of an independent ego by the very young child" (206). For the eventual disintegration of Slothrop as an integral identity provides many indications of his submission to the submontane attractions of "Frau Holda," a pun on gravity as an ensconced, subterranean female force functioning as the equivalent of what Neumann terms the Uroboric Great Mother, the endopsychic expression of the as-yet undifferentiated ego and the operative mode governing the *participation mystique*.[13] Slothrop's established mode of relation exemplifies how the root of solipsism is to be located at the center of the Absolute — how the discontinuities that he experiences and which his paranoid design is intended to bridge are promoted by ego-intentionality. Yet his orphic descent down a Harlem toilet and into the sewers underground in pursuit of his blues "harp" initiates the prerequisite redistributive contact with the lower-bodily stratum that characterizes the disintegrative *nigredo* phase of the "alchemistic transformation of the human personality" (Neumann, pp. 60—1).[14] This phase of immersion in the elemental preterition of the enshadowed, amorphous stratum of the fecal and the carbonic,[15] may be said to culminate in his emersion from a muddy river under the eye of the Mother in her terrible aspect, Greta Erdmann, whose crazed imagination transfigures him to some resurrected titan:

[o]ne of those children [that she had murdered] — preserved, nourished by the mud, and radium, growing taller and stronger while slowly, viscous and slow, the currents bore him along underground, year by year, until at last, grown to manhood, he came to the river, came up out of the black radiance of herself to find her again, Shekhinah, bride, queen, daughter. And mother. Motherly as sheltering mud and glowing pitchblende — (479)

In order to incandesce, the "*Seele*," or *carbon* filament of German lightbulbs, (654) must be screwed into its *Mutter*, its grounding socket — this is the wisdom of comic materialization, of the descent of the noumenal into the earth.

Whether rocket arc or rainbow, the parabola is the parable insofar as gravitation locates the dialectic between the upward thrust of a detached identity further detaching itself (the election of the ego, its election to transcend, transcendence as a validation and guarantor of that election) and the downward pull into the continuum of the lower-bodily stratum. Pynchon's diagnosis therefore takes the shape of a degradatory materialization of the Icarian archetype in which the attempt to defy the field of gravitational presence-to constitutes the ego's manner of delivering itself to its own death wish. Those who have too closely approximated some Absolute fetishized center of too radiant value are like *Gott*fried, dubiously freed and most certainly fried by such as Weissman-Blicero, the bleacher at bliss-zero. But Slothrop falls out of the validating eye/I, the withering gaze of the transcendental ego, the solar Father within whose field he has for too long desired to orbit — "The Man [who] has a branch office in each of our brains, [whose] corporate emblem is a white albatross" and whose "local rep has a cover known as the Ego" (712—13). He meanders the Zone "plucking the albatross of self now and then, idly, half-conscious as picking his nose" (623—4). By abandoning the integrality of a determinant self and its centeredness — the foregrounding of identity and the isolation consequent to it — Slothrop may be seen (more accurately, not seen) to have merged with the marginal:

> They keep passing him and he remains alone, blotted to evening [. . .] — if they do see him his image is shunted immediately out to the boondocks of the brain where it remains in exile with other critters of the night. (379)

The last we do not see of Slothrop he has abandoned his "Rocketman" persona and been completely "dissolve[d]" into the Humility, having reportedly become part of a communal identity, the rock band, the Fool, although "[t]here is no way to tell which of the faces [on their album cover] is Slothrop's" (742). However, in being "plucked [. . .] *stripped*" of accustomed identity and habitual modes and "scattered all over the Zone" (712), Slothrop would seem to have approached the titanic condition, since "[p]ast Slothrops, say averaging one a day, ten thousand of them, some more powerful than others, had been going over every sundown to the furious host" (the hoarded turns to hoarde with the encroaching Shadow) (624). He also achieves something of the bodily redistribution often associated with the totemic titans, for "[s]ome believe that fragments of Slothrop have grown into consistent personae of their own. If so, there's no telling which of the Zone's present-day population are offshoots of his original scattering" (742). In this reference the earlier intuition of a "reknotting seed-flow" of light has through extravagant revery been imaginally transformed to a (re)generative sowing that turns the dismembered to renewed pan-theonic being.

In *Gravity's Rainbow* Pynchon dreams the "dual body" of the extravagant comic image somewhat in the manner of von Goll, his megalomaniacal artist, whose work makes manifest "the Double Light [that] was always there." Once illuminated from below, the lower-bodily stratum simultaneously casts its shadow across the conventionally illumined stratum of the head in such a way that the reciprocal relation of the ego and its Shadow is literally bodied-forth in ambivalent images. The point of light that in those comic moments of cosmic field-reversal reveals the black anti-self "hidden always in the blinding sun" illuminates the Shadow as the index of two denials, as the index at once of the Other as intimated Self and the Other as ego's repudiated mirror-image. The Shadow bodies-forth all that the ego could not begin to imagine, has tacitly claimed it is not, has devalued, neglected, or sought to rid itself of. It is, then, an indexical manifestation of the continuum of Being from which the ego-complex has sought to detach itself as a world-narrowing mode of intentionality, a complex of motivations intended to establish itself as the coextensive personification of that by which all that is has come to be. The Shadow is, ultimately, the Absence that the ego pretends does not exist but by which it is always-already in affected response. It is this existential absence that manifests itself whenever there "breaks" a light whose glare discloses its own "nuclear blackness" (390) — discloses the preterition within its putative election, discloses the nihilism at the heart of the hoard appropriated through systematic either/or designations that ramify the conviction of a meta-physical center of absolute value (for "as the vortex grows more sure, [so] preferential paths are set up" [253] — a quasi-Cartesian description that serves to clarify the essence of the ego-complex as a consolidation around an Absence).

As a lurking presence on the periphery of attention, the unshrunken, unnarrowed amorphousness of the Shadow tacitly pressures the ego to be present to Being. The Shadow is that for whom the ego constructed its labyrinthine design; but like the titanic, mucose Adenoid that emerges from the nose of Lord Osmos to swallow him, it is capable of extravagantly going-beyond conceptual borders and barricades in sub-lime manifestations that correspond to the ego's diminishment and further its dissolution and re-absorption. However, as a monster too expansive to be penned in the designations of language, the Shadow of the paranoid ego can produce the affect of unacknowledged desire as well as anxiety because its expansivity can be retained by the ego in the course of its own transformation: "terribly tense with the waiting, unable to name whatever it is approaching, knowing — too awful to say — it is herself, her Central Asian giantess self, that is the Nameless Thing she fears" (341). But to name is to admit, in both senses of the word. Recognizing upon meeting him that Enzian is "ego-mad", Katje nevertheless is forced against her will to experience him as a bodying forth of both what she will not acknowledge in herself and the unreal-ized, unactualized, potentiality, that lies beyond that acknowledgement. While trying unsuccessfully "to keep from having to move into his blackness" she begins to

[u]nderstand it isn't *his* blackness, but her own — an inadmissible darkness she is making believe for the moment is Enzian's, something beyond even the center of Pan's grove . . . a set of ways in which the natural forces are turned aside, stepped down,

rectified or bled to ground and come out very like the malignant dead: the Qlippoth that Weissman [in his madness] has 'transcended,' [. . .] a city-darkness that is her own, a textured darkness in which flows go in all directions, and nothing begins, and nothing ends [. . .] It is shaking itself into her consciousness. (661).

Here, face to face with the uroboric shadow, adumbrative yet undifferentiated, in a tone of dread and fascination, is recognizable the core experience of an existential phenomenology of the various cognate procedures of marginalization, colonization, vampirization, sanitization, and desensitization that Pynchon demonstrates are aspects of the preterization of the phenomenal.

The Shadow may foreshadow the curse of ambivalence — "working under a shadow, forever" — as it seems to to one double-agent. But, as the aptly-named Merciful Evans gracefully rejoins, "think of the freedom . . . I can't even trust myself? can I. How much freer than that can a man be?" (543). The comic celebrates perversity as a means of grace capable of eluding the constraints of will and of allowing opportunities to substantiate the Shadow by acknowledging it as the presence of attributes and their correspondent mode of attunement ready to emerge. Insofar as the Titans provide an index to the uncanny Other that is the returning human legacy of the "wider agency," the pantheonic Self — Being's sublime multiplicity existentially already given in *Dasein*'s spectrum of potentialities; and insofar as this pantheonic Self threatens the ego and its transcendentalized ideal One and Absolute with intimations of a more powerful presence;[16] it is particularly appropriate that Pynchon should refer to the Brocken spectre-phenomenon as "God shadows." For in one of his few moments of inspiration, Slothrop projects himself into identification with a Titan, his physical gesture revealing an inclination for embodying the Shadow of the repressed spectrum:

Slothrop raises an arm. The arm-shadow trails rainbows behind as it moves reaching eastward for a grab at Göttingen. Not ordinary shadows, either — *three dimensional* ones, cast out on the German dawn, yes and Titans *had* to live in these mountains, or under them.

Typical of the ambivalence of the comic image, while the fullness of Being is evoked as expansivity and amplitude of achieved dimensionality or presence in the world, a pun parodies the Absolute's paranoia — the pretended Promethean overreaching that would appropriate *Gott* (a projection of the overweening encroachment characteristic of the ego itself).

The moment of opening-on to Being closes as Slothrop, having become self-conscious of his extravagance, lapses into the melancholy of the comparative mode, dismissing the Titans as "[i]mpossibly out of scale."[17] The Titans seem lost to Slothrop, no longer available to him as indices of the Self because the quotidian given can only return to an existence whatever was the predisposition of the existential a priori: "only their deep images [. . .] left, haloed shells lying prone above the fogs men move in." Yet grace again ensues as Geli recalls the lower-body to sex and dancing and "[t]he spectra wash red to indigo, tidal, immense, at all their edges." Even though "the shadow phenomenon is confined to dawn's slender interface, and soon the shadows [. . .] come shrinking back to their owners" (330—31), and even though the sublimity dwindles with shame and repression in accord with the sun's ascendance,[18] in the eternity of its revery the bodily periphery — index of all that has been marginalized by the focal — is baptismally bathed in and receives the rainbow flux, the widest available bandwidth indicative of the fullness that grants well-being.[19]

The eponymous Spectro, colleague and opposite number of the equally eponymous Pointsman, does not "differentiate as much as he between Outside and Inside," opting for the / that signifies the zone *between* the either/or. Witnessing "the cortex as an interface organ, mediating between the two, but *part of them both*," Spectro is led to ask "how can we, any of us, be separate?" Although Pointsman, too, begins to wonder whether "Outside and Inside [could] be part of the same field? If only in fairness," only at one point does he seem to verge on the intuition that there is a collaborative mode of the Self, an actualized spectrum of the modes potentially available within the structures of *Dasein*. Characteristically, this intuition is the paradoxical result of narrowing and diminishment. Just as he becomes aware of the focus of his consciousness as the periphery fades to dark, so too he begins to truly experience his Being only in the presence of the Other's darkening — in this case the sequential deaths of the corporate owners of the sacred Pavlovian text:

and with each one, he thinks he feels patterns on his cortex going dark, settling to sleep forever, parts of whoever he's been now losing all definition. . . . Soon, by the dialectic of the Book, Pointsman will be alone, in a black field lapsing to isotropy, to the zero, waiting to be last to go [of] the human field of seven he once was. (141—2)

Much in the manner of Pointsman's deprivation experiments, Nothing-ness stimulates the experience of the opposite: an awareness of pleni-tudinal Being and a flickering recognition that *Dasein* is a composite, a pantheon, a lateral continuum of equivalence, a spectrum of relation-ships.

With his hermetic interpretive design and its "the closed white version of reality" (264), Pointsman can only contemplate the dark mystery of the spectrum potentially available to the human through its structures of existence. As he leaves behind the stratum of the earthly, Gottfried's awareness can only gradually dwindle in abrupt oscillation between nostalgia and anticipation, between the remembered "skin of an apple, bursting with nebulae" and the revelation of death as

a carrying of whiteness to ultrawhite [. . .] bleaches, detergents, oxidizers, abrasives [. . .] extending, rarefying the Caucasian pallor to an abolition of pigment, of melanin, of spectrum of separateness from shade to shade, it is so white that CATCH the dog was a red setter, the last dog's head, the kind dog come to see him off can't remember what red meant [. . . .] (758—59)

But it is Slothrop who has the innate capacity to celebrate unknowingly the fact that color is "primary". In colors of "the available spectrum" Slothrop's map bodies-forth "the ad hoc adventure" of his living. At once cortexical and endopsychic, this map comprised of "constella-tions" of irradiative "girl-stars" and circumscribed "rocketstrike circles" registers a "multicolored, here and there peeling firmament" of "den-sity" interspersed with areas of "nebular streaming" (19). As an indexical manifestation of Pynchon's predilection for dreaming the process of distribution and redistribution it is second only to the imaginal valorization evoked by the medium, Roland, as he arrives on the "Other Side": "Lights he had studied so well as one of you, position and movement, now gathered there at the opposite end, all in dance . . . irrelevant dance."

While the imaginal vocabulary of scattering and thinning, the process of becoming imageless, undoes the value-designations associated with the unduly concentrated, the too bright point and the pall it effects around it, Pynchon's image of a flask of liquid, light "reknotting through the seedflow inside the glass" (55), indicates as well that there is for him always the potential within the flux of the undifferentiated for a spermatic clustering along some intrinsic line of force, some renewing principle of associative formation that may again manifest, at one level, an individual and unique instance of Being, and at another, an image of that being, an ego — some centering nucleus of identity and its world.

NOTES

[1] Henri Bergson, "Laughter," in *Comedy*, ed. Wylie Sypher (Garden City, New York: Doubleday and Co., 1956).

[2] Mikhail Bakhtin, *Rabelais and His World*, trans. Helene Iswolsky (Cambridge, Massachusetts: M.I.T. Press, 1968). This stratum of the elemental locates the cosmos of bodily organs and orifices, their acts and their intentionalized objects, through which the human comes to experience the virtual.

[3] Gaston Bachelard, *The Poetics of Reverie: Childhood, Language, and the Cosmos*, trans. Daniel Russell (Boston: Beacon Press, 1969).

[4] For the principles that provide the foundations of phenomenological psychiatry and Daseinsanalysis see Ludwig Binswanger, *Being-in-the-World: Selected Papers*, trans. and "Critical Introduction" Jacob Needleman (New York: Harper and Row, 1963) and Medard Boss, *Existential Foundations of Medicine and Psychology*, trans. Stephen Conway and Anne Cleaves (New York: Jason Aronson, 1979). For examples of its diagnostic and therapeutic practices and the kind of insights such an orientation and method afford, also see the case histories of Binswanger and Eugene Minkowski in *Existence: A New Dimension in Psychiatry and Psychology*, ed. Rollo May, Ernest Angel, Henri F. Ellenberger (New York: Basic Books, Inc., 1958).

[5] Thomas Pynchon, *Gravity's Rainbow* (New York: Viking Press, 1973). Because of Pynchon's frequent use of ellipses, my own elisions of his text will be indicated by brackets.

[6] The consequential programmatic distraction dialectically implicit in that which galvanizes attention can be registered as the fatality it is in another image from the same passage, regarding "the crunch of trainwheels over the points as you watch peeling away the track you didn't take." Tacitly repressed, design-proscripted phenomena are relentlessly passed over by the ineluctable one-track thinking of all monomania.

In a separate but parallel passage Mister Information scolds Skippy for going "off on another of [his] senseless and retrograde journeys" of logic away from "the points," to which he must be made to "come back." While obliquely addressing the way a logic can compel misleading tangents of thought ("you rattled over the points onto the wrong track"), Mister Information redirects the attention of the elliptical "little fool" to a principle of bifurcating symmetry (or, distributive design) implicit in the reflexive mechanism of man, which he personifies as "the pointsman" who "throws the lever that changes the points" sending us either to "Happyville" or to "Pain City" (644—5). Perhaps the most salient feature of this generally featureless pointsman is that he is located at the point "where the paths divided," a retrospective phrasing that contextualizes this distinction-making tendency within the epoch of some ramifying dispersion, whether cosmological, psychological, or existential. Certainly it is clear that the pointsman is indicative of a principle that is both bifurcated (constituted) and bifurcating (constituting). The suggestion is, I think, that the binary either/or principle functioning with the neural and cortexical mechanism has an analogue in that which determines the existence of the design-system and regulates the predictable tracks of its delusive associative logic: "Even you could push it, Skippy. If you knew where it was [. . . .] He could have sent you on the right trip back there, Skippy. You can have *your* fantasy if you want, you probably don't deserve anything better [. . . .]"

It might also be added that the few descriptive elements to which the attention is directed (for Mister Information is, pointsman-like, throwing some switches of his own) are meant to disturb for all the assurance of his benevolence: at once executioner and member of an esoteric elect, the pointsman's face and smile are effaced by a shadow cast by his white hood. The quintessentially fecal element of the lower bodily stratum — a dominant motif in Pynchon's revery — will by implication suggest the indexical aspect of the pointsman's *brown* shoes, the only other attribute ascribed to him. Let it here suffice to say that the relation of the constituent attributes to this image the placement of the colors, provides indexical access to the ambivalence which Pynchon thematizes throughout.

7 Slothrop is rumored to have been "sent into the Zone to be present at his own assembly — perhaps, heavily paranoid voices have whispered, *his time's assembly*." Certainly what is said of Enzian the Schwarzkommando, also applies equally to Slothrop's fanciful delusion, that "As the Rocket grows toward its working shape and fullness, so does he evolve, himself, into a new configuration" (318).

8 In accordance with the same imaginal logic governing the complex of values that associates the assemblage of the rocket with the aggrandizement of the "I" and the erection of the rocket with the I's (im)posture of transcendence, the description of Slothrop's erect penis as "the metropolitan organ [. . .] all other colonial tissue forgotten and left to fend for itself" provides another indexical manifestation of the insistent image of the fixating center of concentration whose marginal "black frontiers" escape oblivion only by becoming tributary to its vampiric insistence. An imperial entity drawing tribute blood from its surround, the "I" stands, engorged capital, as an index to the ego's vertical "Raketen-Stadt," a.k.a. "the City Paranoiac", which for "its very survival" needs the "resources" of "our submission so that it may remain in power [and] our lusts after dominance so that it can co-opt us into its own power game" (737). Within the same complex of values, when Pynchon avers, "a hardon, that's either there or it isn't. Binary, elegant" (84), he may put his finger on the origins of those narrowed design-systems of abstractive antagonisms which he exclusively associates with certain masculine modes of relation that he says culminate in rocketry. In the classic manner of comic degradation, this literalizing embodiment provides an imaginal vivification of the conception of anxiety as a lived-Nothingness — the felt-absence of a foregrounded concentration being here the paradoxical root of all either/or categorization.

9 The supplantation of the zodiacal pantheon of archetypes in the constellation of the ego-complex, the one and only shape, is sardonically imagined as a constellation of the Brennschluss points of all the Rocket's various firing sites into a thirteenth sign of the Zodiac. "[T]he specific shape whose center of gravity is the Brennschluss Point" indexically manifests the suspension fantasy of not being "bound . . . to time"; this gnostic desire that "It was never launched [and] It will never fall" (301) is valorized by Pynchon in such a way as to emphasize that "[t]he Eternal Center can easily be seen as the Final Zero," for "[n]ames and methods vary, but the movement toward stillness is the same" (319). The stillness of the concentrated center registers values hopelessly

tainted by a suicidal nostalgia for the Absolute, values originating in the ego as the prototype, the hidden center, of "inertias unknown" — a phrase distinctly reminiscent of the Bergsonian diagnosis. Pynchon concludes his description of the constellated Brennschluss points with a remark that suggests the condition of the ego as the prototype of the hidden-in-plain-view: "but they lie so close to Earth that from many places they can't be seen at all." However, by entering into the multi-perspectival and undesigned condition located spatially by the Zone "they can be seen" and indeed seen "to fall into completely different patterns" (302).

[10] Because the "I" exists to itself as a serial continuity of habituations, a manner of retention in some ways analogous to the eye's illusory persistence of vision, it is appropriate that Pynchon should remark about the lightbulb's concentrated point of light: "It's only that the wire inside the bulb unbrightens slow enough before the next peak shows up that fools us into seeing a steady light," rather than "a train of [usually] imperceptible light and dark" (642).

[11] Though he has come to glimpse elliptical stretches of the routes of power distribution through the Grid, Byron the inextinguishable comes to recognize that his knowledge leaves him virtually indistinguishable from his mortal brethren, and that "information" is "glow modulated, harmless, nothing close to the explosions in the faces of the powerful" (650).

[12] "Reveries Toward Childhood," in *The Poetics of Reverie*. Pynchon's glaring example is the Kirghiz Light, whose power "must change us to children" and reduce our conceptual vocabularies to "the meaningless sounds of a baby" (358).

[13] Erich Neumann, *The Great Mother: An Analysis of the Archetype* (Princeton: Princeton University Press/Bollingen, 1963). In keeping with the themes of value (re)distribution within the imaginal stratum and of modes of attunement delivering existential presence, it might be added that Neumann often resorts to the vocabulary of physics to describe the "magnetic field" of the archetypal image and its capacity as an "energy transformer." As a preconscious orientation and organizational predisposition, an archetype configures the lived-world of an existence in its own image insofar as it dynamizes all aspects and structures of human being by means of symptomatic modalities attuned to certain attributes of phenomena and not others.

[14] This dissolution of the ego and its categorical discretions back into the *massa confusa* — the Zone where "categories have been blurred badly" (303) — corresponds to comic degradation, in which the lower bodily stratum becomes the *vas* that locates the transmutation of lived-substances. Pynchon specifically refers to the second stage in the alchemical transvaluation of lived-matter, "moments of high albedo": "To much *confusion* out here [. . .] [o]nly the older scope hands can still maintain a sense of the appropriate: over the watches of their Durations [. . .] they have come to understand *distribution* . . . they have learned a visual mercy" (489, my italics). The prerequisite capacity of the bodily fundament in the cleansing that transforms attitude and perception could hardly be better expressed than by Brigadier Pudding's ditty: "Wash me in the water/That you wash your dirty daughter,/And I shall be whiter than the whitewash on the wall" (231). The existential goal of the alchemical redemption of matter as liveable-value, the *rubedo* phase, might be said to be briefly glimpsed in the moment that a gaze "into [the] curved reddening space" of an apple that is "at last [. . .] apple-colored" evokes a condition of being in which "[e]verything is where it is, no clearer than usual, but certainly more present" (758).

[15] "[D]ead black, no light," the carbonic represents the "passed over" (166), bearing witness in itself to the preterition of whole species. It is even the means to another's election since coal tar is "Earth's excrement, purged out for the ennoblement of shining steel," the Rocket and the structures of the Rocket City. Wherever it makes its appearance the excre*mental* threatens and must be repressed as the grotesque vivifying power of the fecund imagination and its capacity to recuperate and bestow the potentially-given. If the "unfolding . . . is one meaning of mauve, the first new color on Earth, leaping to Earth's light from its grave" it is because "[a] thousand different molecules waited in the preterite dung" to be delivered. Within the same logic of imaginal attributes, the carbonic is imagined as a "jet black, softly bubbling" primal soup of healing "grace" (475ff).

[16] The tendency of the comic to glorify the multiple perspective gains psychological and existential relevance in the light of James Hillman's argument in "Psychology: Monotheistic or Polytheistic?" (published as an appendix to David L. Miller, *The New Polytheism*, [Dallas, Texas: Spring Publications, 1981]), in which he indicts the mono-theistic ideological bias of the predominant paradigm of psychology for its inability to appreciatively register the differentiated complexes constituting the psyche or to liberate their imaginal manifestation from a single-minded abstraction, integration ("When the One means 'only' [one-sidedness], literalism is inevitable").

[17] This is the existential relevance of the often implicit, occasionally explicit, reference to the Heisenbergian principle that "the very need to measure interfere[s] with the observations" (452); for often the purpose of the comparative mode is to reduce the powerful presence of the singular, "*that singularity, those few seconds of absolute mystery*" whose unmodulated static momentarily breaks up the stasis of the fixed signal of the Absolute.

[18] Compare also, "noon flared the shadows in tightly to their owners" (316). Virtually the same movement of the imagination manifests itself in this description of the concen-trated point of light and its relation to its penumbra: "The sensitive flame dives for shelter, shadows across the table sent a dance, darkening toward the other room [shades of Maxwell's demon!] — then it leaps high, the shadows drawing inward again" (31).

[19] The bandwidth image appears elsewhere as well; compare the radioman and mystic, Kurt Mondaugen's articulation of Pynchon's version of the principle of attunement, a spatialization of existential temporalization: "Personal density . . . is directly propor-tional to temporal bandwidth.

'Temporal bandwidth' is the width of your present, your *now* . . . the thicker your bandwidth, the more solid your persona. But the narrower your sense of Now, the more tenuous you are." (509)

ALAN PRATT

A NOTE ON HEIDEGGER'S DEATH ANALYTIC: THE TOLSTOYIAN CORRELATIVE

Heidegger's analysis of the meaning of death in *Being and Time* has been widely claimed as his most important contribution to philosophy. Critics have suggested that his investigation incorporates traces from the thought of Rainer Maria Rilke and Karl Jaspers.[1] In the death analytic, however, Heidegger himself mentions neither the poet nor the philosopher but references only Leo Tolstoy's *The Death of Ivan Ilyich*,[2] significantly, the only prose fiction work mentioned in *Being and Time*. Clearly Tolstoy's novella made a lasting impression on Heidegger because in it he could find dramatically illustrated most of the characteristic behaviors and evasive attitudes uncovered in his own phenomenology of death. *The Death of Ivan Ilyich*, then, is an illuminating supplement — specific, personal and emotional — to what Heidegger universalized in his philosophy.

* * *

Long before writing *The Death of Ivan Ilyich*, Tolstoy had thought long and hard about the meaning of death. In fact, it became the focus of a chronic, agonizing and psychologically exhausting rumination. He describes his first encounter with the extreme significance of death, stripped of passifying rationalizations, in "Memoirs of a Lunatic." In it, Tolstoy explains that while on a long business trip, for reasons unknown, he was suddenly and violently struck with his own radical finitude. With this epiphany came the cosmologically sabotaging Why?: "Why am I driving? Where am I going?" After this experience, he was filled with an unshakable horror; and although for all appearances he resumed an ordinary life, Tolstoy writes that henceforth he was dominated by the experience.[3]

The Death of Ivan Ilyich, one of Tolstoy's later works, expresses in fictional form the fears and insights developed only after a long preoccupation with the phenomenon of death. It is this habit of rumination coupled with the author's genius for discerning and then describing what is generally overlooked which has made this novella one of the major explorations of death in Western literature. No wonder, then,

A-T. Tymieniecka (ed.), Analecta Husserliana, Vol. XXXVIII, 297—304.
© 1992 *Kluwer Academic Publishers. Printed in the Netherlands.*

that in it Heidegger could find most of the characteristic behaviors and evasive attitudes uncovered in his own phenomenology of death.

Based loosely on an actual event,[4] *The Death of Ivan Ilyich* concerns the experience of a rather nondescript lawyer who at forty-five has acquired moderate success, marriage and a family. While decorating his apartment one day, he falls and bumps a window latch but thinks nothing of it or the mild pain he experiences. The pain persists, however, and grows, at first casually and then ravenously. He begins going from doctor to doctor to find relief, but the treatments do nothing to reduce his pain. It finally dawns on him that he is dying.

Until the moment that Ivan Ilyich realized his illness was terminal, he had never given the inevitability of his own demise so much as a passing thought. With death now looming on the horizon, however, he gains insight which separates him from his family and friends. With his enlightenment — an enlightenment without radiance — the exquisitely organized world of everyday concerns in which he had lost himself erodes, and the once clear concepts, ideas and goals which defined and motivated his existence are obscured. Tolstoy highlights Ivan's new cleared perception by repeatedly contrasting it with the artificial perceptions of wife, children and colleagues. They hide, ignore and otherwise pervert Ivan's most personal experience into a chance unpleasantness, all the while making plans to live on without him. As Heidegger notes, it is not just Ivan's reactions but the reactions of those near the dying man which he found memorable.

According to Heidegger, rather than face the menacing specter of non-Being, we tend to be always fleeing from it, concealing it beneath the surface of our time-consuming and taxing everyday concerns. The means by which we minimize and finally alienate ourselves from the existential implications of our impending demise is with the mode of being Heidegger calls "falling." Falling is characterized by an all-absorbing interest with the demands of the phenomenal world where we are required to learn and adopt an essentially "public" mode of existence.[5] In section 51 Heidegger plots the various ways of "falling" by which "they" avoid an authentic understanding of what it means to be:

... temptation, tranquillization, and alienation are distinguishing marks of the kind of Being called "*falling*." As falling, everyday Being-towards-death is a constant *fleeing in the face of death*. Being-towards-the-end has the mode of *evasion in the face of it* — giving new explanations for it, understanding it inauthentically, and concealing it. (*BT* 298)

When caught up with others and the things of the world, as Ivan, his family and friends are, we understand ourselves by an uncritical acceptance of the public standard, the prefabricated flux of collective sentiment. "They" are who we must match wits with; "their" established standards of material and psychological success are what we constantly measure ourselves against; and in this contest, we unavoidably, yet willfully, sacrifice our authentic self to "them," all this in order to "fall" away from our most sobering possibility.

The attempt by others to treat Ivan's dying in terms of the innocuous manner of "They" does, indeed, constitute much of the novella. Neither family nor friends have time for dying, and, moreover, they are reluctant to give Ivan's imminent death any attention. Instead of facing the fact that he will die and confronting the realities such a realization gives rise to, they minimize the experience by informing Ivan that he is not really seriously ill and that he will soon be better if he only follows the doctor's orders. Ivan, his sensitivity heightened by his experience, sees such consolations and encouragement for what they are — idle talk and passifying deceptions. By having his characters give such advice, Tolstoy concretely and dramatically illustrated what Heidegger would generalize in his analysis:

> This evasive concealment in the face of death dominates everydayness so stubbornly that, in Being with one another, "neighbors" often still keep talking the "dying person" into the belief that he will escape death and soon return to the tranquillized everydayness of the world of his concern. (BT 297)

All the cliches and soothing talk, all the conventional expressions by which we deal with the deaths of strangers, neighbors and friends provide a cover to protect us from our most extreme and absolute possibility. Death is not something that "they" will readily discuss, and actually *thinking* about it is a social taboo, something to be regarded as morbid or pathological. While Tolstoy dramatically illustrated the phenomenon, Heidegger de-personalizes it and analyzes its meaning.

As Ivan's illness leads to its irrevocable conclusion, friends and family eventually grow tired of espousing platitudes and finally become irritated with and callous about his experience. Tolstoy writes that they reacted to the dying man as they would to "a bit of unseemly behavior (they reacted to him as they would to a man who emitted a foul odor on entering a drawing room)."[6] Heidegger recognized the universality of this behavior, noting that in the face of death "they" denigrate dying to a "social inconvenience, if not a downright tactlessness, against which the public has to be guarded" (*BT* 298). Ivan is fully aware how his dying annoys his associates and family and also realizes that there is no one with whom to share his disasterous experience — it is his alone, absolute and non-relational, as Heidegger describes it.[7]

As he drifts inexorably toward his end, the non-relational nature of his experience further severs Ivan from his "public" identity, and what has been his fallen mode of "Being-in-the-world" crumbles and is swept away under the gaze of an authentic death consciousness. Tolstoy accentuates what this illuminating perspective reveals by having the dying man recall a syllogism, "Caius is mortal" (*DI* 93). Previously, such pronouncements had always seemed perfectly correct and normal, Ivan muses, but when taken from the alienating level of abstraction and applied to himself, the syllogism discloses something ominous and intimidating. Ivan's "resolute" perception moves beyond his analysis of this phrase, and soon he is reinterpreting his entire life.

When the neutralizing effects of "falling" cease to dominate our perspective, that is, when the conventions and pretensions with which we organize our existence become apparent, the affairs of life acquire a new significance. For Ivan, who had always done what he was supposed to, the revelation is catastrophic, The careful respectability which he had spent his entire life cultivating is an enormous deception, something appallingly trivial or worse, pointless.

It's as though I had been going steadily downhill while I imagined I was going up. That's exactly what happened. In public opinion I was moving uphill, but to the same extent life was slipping away from me. And now it's gone and all I can do is die! (*DI* 120)

At this moment and thereafter, he begins to discover the essential Self which he had so long forfeited to the "They-Self." In the parlance of Heidegger, in the light of his encounter with non-Being, Ivan has recognized his freedom and now must begin to comport himself toward his own Being as his ownmost possibility. Ironically, with his new attempt to achieve a modicum of existential harmony, Ivan understands that precisely what is real are the scarcely perceptive impulses which he had always suppressed in favor of what "they" thought. This realization plagues him to the moment of his death.

"Ivan Ilyich is dead," one of his former colleagues reads in the newspaper. Finally, the dying man makes the transformation from Dasein to "deceased."[8] For Ivan's friends and family, though, the monumental significance of this change is minimized in the manner of falling. For the most part, they remain firmly grounded in the realm of beings, pondering the effects of Ivan's death not in relation to their own mortality but solely in terms of "what effect it would have on their own transfers and promotions or those of their acquaintances" (*DI* 39). Only reluctantly, motivated by the standards of respectability established by "them," do Ivan's colleagues agree to pay last respects. Heidegger describes this behavior as a clever guise by which " 'they' . . . puts itself in the right and makes itself respectable by tacitly regulating the way in which *one* has to comport oneself towards death" (*BT* 298).

Undoubtedly, the most compelling images of how the "They-self" confronts death by fleeing from it are found in the home of the deceased. Presumably this would be the case because it is there, face to face with the most menacing and inevitable of possibilities, where what it means to *be* for human beings comes close to being fully realized. How the threat of death is defused in this circumstance is exemplified by the actions of Ivan's colleague, Pyotr Ivanovich.

Not surpisingly, Pyotr has made his visit to the family only after complaining of the inconvenience. As he enters to view the body, we learn that what most concerns him is not the death of his friend but the proper etiquette for this situation. Is it proper to bow? What would *they* do? Unable to resolve the problem, he compromises by making a slight movement like a bow and feels he has preserved respectability without compromising his pride (*DI* 38). Although the close proximity of death makes him uncomfortable, he continues his masquerade when he meets Ivan's widow:

Pyotre Ivanovich knew that just as he had to cross himself in there, here he had to press her hand, sigh, and say: "I assure you!" And so he did, and having done so felt he had achieved the desired effect: he was touched and so was she. (*DI* 41)

The unspoken but "understood" deference "they" accord death is also evident in the manner which Ivan's widow responds to the death of her husband. Superfically she performs as one is expected. Her underlying concerns, though, are much different, illuminating the subtleties by which "falling" affects our escape from authenticity. Its attractiveness is directly related both to its ability to conceal our nature as "Being-towards-death" and to its link with essentially pragmatic concerns. Hence, the possibility that a cigarette may singe the carpet compels Ivan's widow to stop weeping just along enough to pass an ashtray.

Moreover, her grief in no way prohibits her from making detailed inquires about a grave site and arriving at a "very sound decision" (*DI* 43).

The same business-like behavior is evident when the widow approaches Pyotre to address the most important issue — Ivan's pension,

but he [Pyotre] saw that she already knew more about this than he did, knew exactly, down to the finest detail, how much could be had from the government, but wanted to know if there was any possibility of extracting a bit more. (*DI* 45)

Although such pragmatic concerns could be considered indiscreet by the conventional standards of respectability demanded by "them," it is still behavior that focuses on the everyday and characteristic of "falling." Proximally and for the most part, it achieves the desired result of concealing unpleasant existential concerns.

After he speaks with Ivan's widow, Pyotre — solely for the sake of propriety — returns to see the deceased, and once again he is overcome with an uneasy feeling which this time is suddenly transformed into raw panic: "Why the same thing could happen to me at any time!" Just as suddenly, "he himself didn't know how," he is rescued from such thoughts when he recalls the "customary reflection" that "all this had happened to Ivan Ilyich, not to him, that it could not and should not happen to him; and if he were to grant such a possibility, he would succumb to depression" (*DI* 44).

With this line of reasoning Ivan's colleague is able to set his mind to rest. What he has done is transform the possibility of death into the *actuality* of others dying, making death the less threatening death of another. Heidegger too describes the rationalization which occurs by such reasoning: "One of these days one will die too, in the end; but right now it has nothing to do with me."[9] "One" remains anonymous and vague, and when "one dies" it is, in fact, no one. Hence, Pytor is able to convert his terrifying awareness into passifying abstractions.

After investigating the meaning of death, Heidegger concludes that we cannot understand the full significance of death through observation alone because the realm of the actual is secondary to that of the possible, which is strictly and uniquely personal. Perhaps this is the case; however, few accounts in literature can match the evocative power of Tolstoy's unsettling observations of one man's death, and it is difficult to read *The Death of Ivan Ilyich* with detachment. As such, it is much different than Heidegger's analysis, but, like Heidegger, Tolstoy realized that to understand life requires standing face to face with death.

To the extent that Heidegger's own phenomenology of death distinctly parallels Tolstoy's fictional account, we know he too was struck by the accuracy of Tolstoy's observations. In this instance, then, art and philosophy are integrally linked: *The Death of Ivan Ilyich* reinforced Heidegger's own observations and dramatically supplements his death analytic.

Embry-Riddle Aeronautical University
Daytona Beach, Florida

NOTES

[1] For a fuller discussion of the origins of Heidegger's thoughts on death see Vincent Vycinas, *Earth and Gods* (The Hague, Netherlands: Martinus Nijhoff, 1961) and Roger Waterhouse, *A Heidegger Critique* (Atlantic Highlands, New Jersey: Humanities Press, 1981).

[2] Heidegger writes that in this work Tolstoy "presented the phenomenon of the disruption and breakdown of having 'someone die' " (*Being and Time* 298 n. xii.). *Being and Time* will throughout this article be abbreviated as *BT*. My quotations are from the translation by John Macquarrie and Edward Robinson using their pagination (New York: Harper and Row, 1962).

[3] Leo Tolstoy, "Memoirs of a Lunatic," *The Existential Imagination* (Greenwich, Conn.: Fawcett Publications, Inc., 1962), pp. 75—87.

[4] According to Roland Blythe, Tolstoy was moved by the death of a provincial judge, Ivan Ilyich Mechnikov, whose death was described to him in some detail by the dead man's brother. (See Blythe's introduction to *The Death of Ivan Ilyich* [New York: Bantam Books, 1981]).

[5] By adopting a "public" mode of being ". . . proximally and for the most part Dasein covers up its ownmost Being-towards-death, fleeing *in the face of it.* Factically Dasein is dying as long as it exists, but proximally and for the most part, it does so by way of *falling*" (*BT* 295).

[6] Leo Tolstoy, *The Death of Ivan Ilyich* (From now on abbreviated as *DI*), trans. Lynn Solotaroff (New York: Bantam Books, 1981), p. 103.

[7] Foremost among the elements constituting the structure of human existence is the fact that our Being is integrally bound to non-Being, a fact which not only determines actions in the present but also colors the interpretation of the past. "Death is something that stands before us, something which is impending" (*BT* 294). Heidegger's rather unassuming pronouncement, typical of *Being and Time* as a whole, summarizes how the phenomenon of death *is* for human beings. Only by "resolutely" facing death as the most absolute and extreme possibility, will one be liberated from one's lostness in those possibilities which may accidentally thrust themselves upon one; and one is liberated in

such a way that for the first time one can authentically understand and choose among the factical possibilities lying ahead of that possibility which is not to be outstripped. (*BT* 308)

[8] Heidegger uses the term "deceased" to distinguish a human corpse from any other kind of lifeless material thing "just-present-at-hand-and-no-more." This distinction is necessary because for those who remain behind, the deceased is an object of concern more significant than merely "the useful" of other "beings-in-the-world" (*BT* 282).

[9] This is necessary, Heidegger notes, because "*the 'they' does not permit us the courage for anxiety in the face of death*" (*BT* 298).

PART FIVE

HANS H. RUDNICK

PER ASPERA AD ASTRA:
ASPECTS OF DARKNESS AND LIGHT
IN WESTERN LITERARY CONSCIOUSNESS

The ancient Egyptians, Babylonians, and Persians as well as the
Christian tradition relate light and fire with the divine. God's nature
manifests itself in light long before the world was actually created. It is
not the sun at this initial stage of creation that functions as the source of
light, it is God and nothing else. The creative act begins with *fiat lux*,
"let there be light!", an imperative of will, determination, and purposeful
energy. A plan of creation, a cosmogony, is in the process of being
implemented. Daylight is there from the first moment of creation,
clearly before the sun came into existence. Light and darkness are
separate and independent entities. The divine plan is that they, darkness
and light, alternately rule over the earth in a constant succession of day
and night. When one of them is predominant, the other withdraws and
awaits its predetermined turn.

Only after beginning with darkness and light did God create the
heavenly bodies, the sun, the moon, and the stars. It was their task to
provide regularity, a dimension of order, to the duration of days,
months, and seasons that determine the agricultural and religious
calendar. The biblical writers insist that the light which we perceive
with our eyes is and remains a mysterious creature, symbolic of God's
terrifying power as we well know, for example, from Job's experience.
In the Old Testament Yahweh is identified with the light (thou coverest
thyself with light as with a garment, Ps. 102: 1—2), "God is the light" (1
Jn. 1:7), and "God is in the light" (ibid.), and in the New Testament
Jesus calls himself twice "the light of the world" (Jn. 8:12; 9:5).

The divine light is so bright that it is blinding. Paul, for instance, is
blind for several days after his conversion. This is not only an indication of the brightness and power of the divine light, but also a powerful
figurative device in the writer's hand to dramatize the radical event not
only by a change of name from Saul to Paul, but also by a new vision
that someone experiences after he has — now proverbially — "seen the
light."

The three magi also saw light, this time the light of an unusually

307

A-T. Tymieniecka (ed.), Analecta Husserliana, Vol. XXXVIII, 307—314.

bright star, that led them through the darkness of the night to Beth-
lehem where, as we now know, a historic event had happened by which
most of us count our days ever since. That star was standing in the east,
certainly, from a literary perspective, not accidentally, since we are
accustomed to light coming to us on this earth from the east, from the
rising sun which Homer constantly refers to as "when dawn spread its
fingertips of rose" or as "in the East dawn confirmed the third day [of
Odysseus' floating in the sea before reaching the Phaiakians]." Churches
usually locate their altar so that the congregation is facing east. Orient
and occident have received metaphorical meanings beyond the literal
which identifies the orient as the place where the light of the sun comes
from, where it rises (mostly from the sea), and the occident as the place
where it sets (also mostly into the sea). The east points to the coming of
light and a new day with its potentialities, the west marks the place
where the light disappears and darkness begins to fall. These are, of
course, the hermeneutics of the Judeo-Christian tradition, whereas, for
example, the modern American interpretation of the west meant riches
and a bright future as in the slogan "go West, young man!" It is no
surprise, therefore, that young American students interpret the fate of
the two British prisoners in Frank O'Connor's short story "Guests of
the Nation" much more optimistically than European students. At the
end of the story O'Connor simply says that the prisoners were taken
over the hill toward the west. For the European student it is clear that
the prisoners were executed, whereas for the American student they
seem to be given their freedom.

Darkness and light have been assigned their places in our respective
value systems. Light comes from above, darkness looms below. The
first one seems to imply elevation and perhaps sublimation to a higher
level of human existence and consciousness, whereas the other threatens
to draw us down into the realm of evil and suffering. Bogs, caves, and
evil monsters threaten the lives of ancient heroes as much as superior
warriors who enjoy the favor of a member of the Greek or Indo-
European pantheon. Blind seers like Theiresias and the omniscient
Pythia of the Delphic oracle seem to see so much clearer about the fate
of the mortals than anyone else living on this earth. Beowulf, the
Niebelungs, and the heroes of the Icelandic Sagas live as much under
the desire to know about their own fate and the course of the civilized
world as Odysseus, Aeneas, and Dante who descend into the darkness
of the underworld to learn about themselves, the world, and the inter-

relation between both. More recently, Goethe's Faust, prototype of the modern quest hero, "the image of the godhead", wants to know very much like a modern scientist "was die Welt im Innersten zusammenhält" (the innermost design of the world) and promises his soul to Mephistopheles who is at one place characterized as "scum . . . , misbegotten filth and fire." Right after the Easter stroll Faust makes his pact with Mephistopheles expecting that this will be the only way to receive the answer to his ultimate question.

While Faust wagers his soul right after Easter for the so much sought-after ultimate knowledge, it is Dante who will emerge from his adventure, that has led him to the brightest light of Paradise, just in time to celebrate at Easter his own new lease on life that the mediaeval cosmogony can grant to this near-Renaissance man. Goethe's Faust shows independence from the powers of the past, he feels Promethian, "he hears the message, but is lacking the faith" and, right before Easter, filled with hopelessness and despair, he is ready to commit suicide. Dante, however, hears the message very well, he understands it, and joins with the rest of mankind to celebrate the resurrection, the new beginning which is still his own and Christ's.

Modern mankind does no longer hear the message, does no longer know its limits, does no longer listen to the conditions of its being, similarly to Yeats' falcon (in the poem "Sailing to Byzantium") who cannot hear the falconer as he is drawing his ever-widening circles around the center that cannot "hold." Kafka, Ionesco, and Beckett further reinforce this impression. Deconstruction is making a sport of received values that function as markers of orientation at least for those students who are trying to understand the basic tenets of the human condition. E. D. Hirsch, on the other hand, tries to prescribe values that are to have validity for all. Has darkness descended and covered this world with nothingness and relativity that will rule supreme? Has the Faustian and Promethian rebelliousness overshot its goal of independence? Do we have to submit to the wanton destruction of cultural values or do we have to quietly accept superimposed values that are assumed by selfish others who determine from their well-meaning but nevertheless misguided perspective what is to be good for the rest of humankind?

The Latin phrase in my title means "from darkness to light" or "through night to the stars." Both versions of my translation carry an optimistic note. Seneca may have expressed this idea first, although this is only an educated guess with scant evidence. There is no doubt that modern man has taken his fate in his own hands. Where is the modern equivalent to the *locus amoenus* which we find in the older tradition of Western literature? Gottfried von Straßburg's *Tristan* abounds with this literary device, as is Cervantes' *Don Quixote*. Here I shall only refer to *Tristan's* Cave of Love that is located in such a place of natural perfection. This grotto held a bed

cut from a slab of crystal . . . . In the upper part of the grotto some small windows had been hewn out to let in the light, and these shone in several places.

Where one went in and out there was a door of bronze. Outside, above the door, there stood three limes of many branches, but beyond them not a single one. Yet everywhere downhill there were innumerable trees which cast the shade of their leafy boughs upon the mountainside. Somewhat apart, there was a level glade through which there flowed a spring — a cool, fresh brook, clear as the sun. Above that, too, there stood three limes, fair and very stately, sheltering the brook from sun and rain. The bright flowers and green grass, with which the glade was illumined, vied with each other most delightfully, each striving to outshine the other. At their due times you could hear the sweet singing of the birds. Their music was so lovely — even lovelier here than elsewhere. Both eye and ear found their pasture and delight there: the eye its pasture, the ear its delight. There were shade and sunshine, air and breezes, both soft and gentle. Away from the mountain and its cave for fully a day's journey there were rocks unrelieved by open heath, and wilderness and wasteland. No paths or tracks had been laid towards it of which one might avail oneself. But the country was not so rough and fraught with hardship as to deter Tristan and his beloved from halting there and making their abode within that mountaincave. (Hatto transl., 261—262).

This classic *locus amoenus*, idealized, but of this world nevertheless, presents the perfect natural setting in which darkness and light, shadow and sunshine, cool water, shade trees, air, breezes, and animals hold a peaceful balance. Similarly in tune with each other are the lovers, enchanted by love's blindness and the blinding beauty of Isolde in her prime. Nature and humans are inseparably united into one grand harmonious whole. Only the Romantics some 600 years later would ever come close to pretending such perfect interaction between nature and the creative artist.

The *locus amoenus* is provided by nature in which Tristan and Isolde live and of which they are integral and inseparable parts at least as long as they are to be shown as being under the spell of love. Later in the history of human consciousness this balance between darkness and light is broken, the individual is thrown out of nature into the civilizing forces of guilt and reason which prescribe propriety. St.

Augustine's conversion that comes after half a life of youthful exuberance culminates in "the sing-song voice of a child" that "again and again ... repeated the refrain '*Take it and read, take it and read.*'" Although a child's voice does the beckoning, the content of the message is an invitation to submit to new rules, it is an invitation to alienation from nature, from the past, and the self. Such a radical reorientation in accordance with new values redefines Augustine's entire past. He castigates his foolish behavior, is grateful for having finally seen the light, and within the coordinates of the new hermeneutics his son's name will be henceforth Adeodatus, the one who was given by God. This was later imitated by Erasmus when he chose Desiderius as his first name although he was very much an undesired child if one were judging by the rules of legitimacy prevailing at his time.

Optics in both senses played a major role in the lives of the enlightened who pushed our civilization forward. The exploration of the skies with the help of lenses, in effect looking for specks of light within the darkness of space, the interpretation of these observations and facing the sometimes life-threatening consequences instigated by the Inquisition, and analysing the spectral composition of light, are all distinctive markers of human curiosity and creative thinking that were indelibly set by Copernicus, Bruno, Kepler, Newton, and Goethe.

Light was also symbolic of the French and American revolutions which liberated the common people from feudal and colonial oppression. Bartholdi's Statue of Liberty at the entrance to New York harbor depicts liberty as a woman holding a torch high into the sky so that its light may shine as far as possible and that it may be seen and enjoyed from a distance by as many people as possible.

The dark dungeons of suppression that affect the human will are deep and treacherous. They may even cause the darkest depression from which many of our contemporaries suffer. This is the "aspera" of my Latin phrase, the uncomfortable darkness of night that surrounds us. But we must not submit; as the Latin phrase continues, the "astra", the light and the stars are waiting for us. We are destined to *strive* like Faust for the ultimate answer, like Einstein for the ultimate formula. The answer will not be ours to know, but nevertheless, "wer immer strebend sich bemüht, den können wir erlösen" (whoever keeps honestly trying, shall be rewarded). This will ultimately be the justification for Faust's rescue from the clutches of Mephistopheles.

What makes Faust's rescue possible has to serve as encouragement for all the generations of creative people to follow his example. Rembrandt made use of light and darkness to highlight the essential traits of character he intended to bring out, particularly in his portraits, but also in other paintings where, for example, rays of light shining down from the sky illuminate three oak trees situated near the line of the horizon.

Most striking are the Romantics and Impressionists with their enthusiastic and revolutionary treatment of light in their paintings. Around 1860, they leave the confines of the atelier behind to do their painting outside in the open air. Their fascination with light and the atmosphere is legendary. Turner's ships in the haze and mist of the Thames and Monet's haystacks, poplars, and façades of the Cathedral of Rouen painted many times just to capture their varying appearance under different lighting conditions are the best-known examples of this celebration of light in modern art. The pointillism of Neo-Impressionists like Seurat pursues the refraction and dissolution of light into tiny dots of color to excess so that later artists will return to the primacy of form and its dissolution into cubistic and mathematical spheres.

The dynamics of creativity, however, remain the driving forces that define and push human civilization forward from the mysterious and frightening dark toward the light of discovery and meaning. We might in this context even speak of Heidegger's *lumen naturale* that resides in the creative human being. This human being is inspired or, in Heidegger's words, "erleuchtet," it is "illuminated" literally, and figuratively "enlightened" through its intuition and hermeneutic faculties so that for itself it creates the "clearing" of meaning, the "self"-evidence that is disclosure and discovery at the same time. This is the "Lichtung", the perceiving of a sense-making light emanating from inspiring and creative forces resident within (cf. *Being and Time*, 133).

Hölderlin's hymn without title beginning with the line "Wie wenn am Feiertage . . ." ("as on a holiday"; Michael Hamburger's translation, 163), well known as a poetic rendition of the poet's creative powers, has been chosen by at least seven different interpreters for explication, among them are Heidegger, Kerényi, Böckmann, W. Rehm, Szondi, and Otto. One editor (Zinkernagel) decided to name this hymn "The Heavenly Fire", another (Hübscher), as unauthentically, called it "To the Poets", which Hamburger retains in his translation. Certainly, this poem addresses the poet's task. But it also refers to the wider, more general task of human creativity and meaningful human existence *per se*. Particularly the third stanza of this unfinished poem speaks to our concern with light and its connection with the human creative faculty. After a night of rain, thunder, and lightning, the divinely beautiful Nature seems to repose at certain times of the year in the sky, among the plants, or among the people. That is the time when the poets are sad, when they feel deserted, when their inspiration has dried up; but it is nevertheless also the time when they still "foreknow" ("ahnen") like Nature herself "foreknows" during her repose. The third stanza marks the awakening of Nature and the shared foreknowing with the poet

> But now it dawns! I waited and saw it come,
> And what I saw, it is holy, let my word convey.
> For she, herself, who is older than the ages
> And higher than the Occident's gods and the Orient's,
> Nature now has awoken with clamor of arms,
> And from the Aether above to the abyss beneath,
> Engendered, as once before, according to rigid law,
> Out of holy Chaos[:]
> Rapture, — the all-creative [—] now feels renewed.

At the light of dawn the all-creative Nature, apparently also the source of inspiration for all subsequent creativity, engenders rapture (*Begeisterung*) in the observing poet

> And as a fire gleams in the eye of that man
> Who has conceived a lofty design: so now
> Once again by the signs, by the deeds of the world
> A fire has been lit in souls of the poets.

We as human beings must feel like this inspired poet, we must learn and be educated to strive for and try to understand like Faust and his modern successors that the sublimation of our human existence lies in recognizing the limits of our own powers. This insight defines our boundaries within the constant strife between the darkness and the light of our own existence. We are seeking light, like a moth seeks light; we still refuse to look beyond the object of our desires, we rely on forgiveness and blindly trust the Lord's words to Mephistopheles; "a good man in his dark and secret longings/ is well aware which path to go" (Salm, 21). Experience teaches us that awareness does not necessarily lead us on the proper path "per aspera ad astra." However, there must always remain hope for the civilizing force of enlightenment.

Southern Illinois University,
Carbonadale, Illinois

BIBLIOGRAPHY

Saint Augustine. *Confessions*, trans. with an introduction by R. S. Pine-Coffin (London: Penguin, 1988).

Goethe J. W. von. *Faust*, Part I, rev. ed., transl. with an introduction and notes by Peter Salm (New York: Bantam, 1985).

Heidegger M. *Being and Time*, trans. by John Macquarrie and Edward Robinson (New York: Harper and Row, 1962).

Hölderlin F. *Hölderlin, His Poems*, trans. by Michael Hamburger with a critical study, 2nd ed. (New York: Pantheon, 1952).

Straßburg G. von. *Tristan*, trans. with an introduction by A. T. Hatto (London: Penguin, 1987).

Szondi P. *Einführung in die literarische Hermeneutik. Studienausgabe der Vorlesungen*, Bd. V (Frankfurt: Suhrkamp, 1975).

William Butler Yeats, *Collected Poems*, definitive ed. with the author's final revisions (New York: Macmillan, 1956).

GEORGE L. SCHEPER

ILLUMINATION AND DARKNESS
IN THE SONG OF SONGS

As a tiny pebble dropped in a pond sends its ripples across the surface
to the furthest shore, so the Song of Songs, one of the shortest books of
the Bible and one in which neither the name of God nor any national or
religious concern is ever explicitly mentioned, remarkably resonates
and reverberates throughout Jewish and Christian culture, as though it
were understood to embody the central truth and mystery of the human
condition. The Song and its imagery resonate backwards and forwards
through the other books of the Old and New Testaments, establishing a
rich intertextuality in which the original blessing of Creation, epitomized
and embodied in the one-flesh union of Adam and Eve (Earth-man and
Life-mother) in the garden, seen as lost or distorted in the present
alienated human condition, presentifies itself as restored and redeemed
in another garden in the graced, non-oppressive love relation of the
lovers of the Song of Songs. And this image, in turn, is viewed in
Christian typological eschatology as foreshadowing the messianic Marriage of the Lamb in the heavenly garden — as in Van Eyck's Ghent
Altarpiece.

A crucial trajectory therefore connects: (1) the opening chapters of
Genesis; (2) the succession of privileged convenantal marriages from
Abram and Sarai, and Hosea and Gomer, to Elizabeth and Zachariah,
and Joseph and Mary; (3) the paradigm of the Song of Songs; and (4)
the leitmotif of nuptial allegory, from the prophetic metaphor of God's
betrothal of Israel, and the presentation in Wisdom literature of
Hochmah/Sophia as the consort of God, to the New Testament images
of the messianic Bridegroom and the eschatological wedding feast. It is
a trajectory that, in the Jewish tradition, creates a privileged intertextual
link between the creation story of Genesis, the Song of Songs, and the
Exodus (which the rabbinical commentators, following the lead of the
prophets, interpret throughout in terms of the divine nuptial allegory),
and which in the Christian tradition creates a privileged link between
the creation story of Genesis, the Song of Songs and the Apocalypse —
links which are demonstrable, respectively, in exegetic history, liturgy,

315

A-T. Tymieniecka (ed.), Analecta Husserliana, Vol. XXXVIII, 315–336.
© 1992 *Kluwer Academic Publishers. Printed in the Netherlands.*

religious art, and mystical theology. Because of this trajectory, special resonances connect certain key images and phrases:

"Let there be light"/ "Lo, the winter is past"/ "Lo . . . flashes of lightning . . . seven torches . . . and as it were a sea of glass, like crystal"

"Be fruitful and multiply"/ "Let him kiss me with the kisses of his mouth"/ "For the marriage of the Lamb has come, and his Bride has made herself ready"

"Your desire shall be for your husband and he shall rule over you"/ "I am my beloved's, and his desire is for me"

"Upon my bed by night I sought him whom my soul loves"/ "And the Spirit and the Bride say, 'Come.'"

But before addressing the imagery of the Song of Songs, specifically the interplay of images of light and darkness with images of vitality and eroticism, a word must be said about the enormously complex exegetic and literary history — the reverberations — emanating from the book. For almost as though it represented some sort of obsession, the Song of Songs over the centuries has provoked an amount and diversity of interpretation and paraphrase far out of proportion to the book's modest scope of 117 verses; as I have noted in an earlier article, "the number of commentaries is astounding. The early catalogues and bibliographies tend to list more commentaries on the Song than on any other biblical book save the Psalms, all of Paul's epistles taken together, and the Gospels."[1] It is only fitting, therefore, that Marvin Pope's compendium commentary on the Song of Songs is one of the thickest volumes in the Anchor Bible series.

The diversity of interpretation was marked from the earliest times. Theodoret, the fourth century bishop of Cyrrhus, commenced his commentary on the Song with a refutation of those holding divergent views about the book, and from then on it became a matter of course for Christian exegetes to begin with a similar caveat. Similarly, in the 10th century, Rabbi Saadia Gaon began his commentary by warning, "Know, my brother, that you will find a great diversity of opinion as regards the interpretation of the Song of Songs; and it must be confessed that there is reason for it, since the Song of Songs is like a lock, the key of which has been lost."[2] In our own century, Robert Pfeiffer says in his *Introduction to the Old Testament*, that "the scope of interpretations has grown until it has surpassed by far differences of opinion about any other part of Scripture."[3]

The array of interpretations is difficult even to encapsulate. The love dialogue in the Song of Songs has been variously regarded: as allegorizing the history of Israel's relationship with God from the Exodus through the messianic fulfillment (the Targum, *Midrash Rabba* and *Zohar*); as allegorizing, in general, God's relationship with the Church (Origen, Augustine, Gregory) and, in particular, with the faithful individual soul (Bernard), the newly baptized Christian (Ambrose), the consecrated virgin (Jerome), the contemplative mystic (Teresa, John of the Cross), or in a special way the Virgin Mary (William of Newburgh); as celebrating the wedding of Spirit and Flesh in the Incarnate Christ (Athanasius), or of the union of the Active Intellect with the material intellect (Moses Ibn Tibbon); as recording, symbolically, the dialogue between Solomon and Wisdom (Leon Herbraeus) or, historically, between Solomon and his Ethiopian bride (Delitzsch), or as dramatizing a love triangle between a seductive King Solomon, a chaste country maid and her shepherd lover (Ewald); or the book has been viewed as a series of folkloric Palestinian weddings songs or *wasfs* (Budde), or a collection of transmogrified fragments of Mesopotamian sacred marriage hymns (Meek), or — as is it is most commonly seen today — as a "secular" anthology of erotic love lyrics, pure and simple (Herder, Gordis, Falk).[4]

Modern humanist commentators have been particularly hostile to the medieval allegorizations of the Song as a neurotic obsession of the monastic milieu. F. W. Farrar, for instance, commented that "There was one book of the Bible which left scope to their imagination to revel in thoughts which seemed to be innocent because they were supposed to be scriptural, and which gratified those yearnings of the human heart which are too strong and too sacred to be permanently crushed. It was the Song of Solomon ... The monkish commentaries upon it were unwholesomely numberless ... grotesque [and] ... melancholy," indulging in a rhetoric "of which it would be charitable to say nothing worse than that it is too poetically sensuous for any commentary on Holy Writ."[5] Similarly, Dean Inge wrote, "As to the Song of Solomon, its influence upon Christian Mysticism has been simply deplorable. A graceful romance in honor of true love was distorted into a precedent and sanction for giving way to hysterical emotions, in which sexual imagery was freely used to symbolize the relation between the soul and its Lord. Such aberrations are as alien to sane Mysticism as they are to sane exegesis."[6] Delitzsch dismisses the allegorical commentaries with contempt: "To inventory the *maculator* of these absurdities is a repulsive undertaking, and, in the main, a useless labour, from which we absolve ourselves."[7] Such commentators betray their own Victorian fascinated fear of sexual imagery, but a contemporary advocate of "erotic spirituality," William Phipps, similarly heaps scorn on the "inverted interpretations" of the "eunuch" Origin and such monks as Jerome and Bernard, "who had contempt for the flesh and females," and who, while they "polemicized against coitus on the physical level . . . [were] engrossed in it on a fantasy level."[8]

Such polarized controversy represents in itself an ensnarement in a dualistic mentality. In fact, the implicit "sacred"/"secular" nomenclature creates a false dichotomy in the first place, as feminist Biblical scholar Phyllis Trible has well pointed out.[9] For one thing, there is no evidence that such an anachronistic distinction would have been at all meaningful in ancient Israel; that the lyrics of the Song of Songs could, at once, have been read as erotic love poems and as a mystical expression of God's love for the people would be natural in the Israel of Hosea or the Israel of Ecclesiasticus — although by the first century, perhaps under the influence of Hellenistic Stoic philosophy, Rabbi Akiba would pronounce anathema on anyone "who gives his voice a flourish in reading the Song of Songs in the banquet-halls and makes it a secular song."[10]

There is no inherent reason why the imagery of the Song of Songs should not resonate simultaneously in literal, parabolic, allegorical or mystical/arcane dimensions, or why its imagery should not be readable and revelatory at once and holistically in terms of erotic psychology, biblical anthropology and mystical spirituality, thereby intersubjectively mobilizing the "innermost virtualities of the human condition."[11] Mesopotamian sacred marriage rite, Jewish and Christian allegory, Palestinian wedding custom, and erotic love poetry are not inherently mutually exclusive trajectories — except to the exclusively discursive, left-brained polarizing mentality that insists on valorizing one resonance or one reverberation over all others. But the persistent poetic power of the Song of Songs to engage the creative imagination in every milieu, even despite this contentious history of interpretation, testifies to the fact that the Song of Songs is itself a prime datum of phenomenological poetics, is itself a result of "the crucial interplay between the vital forces of Nature and the *Imaginatio Creatrix*."[12]

So we must begin with the pregiven world which presences itself, whose word is spoken in the Song of Songs. This pregiven world involves first a dramatic presentifying of the many moods and phases of erotic love, as expressed in the monologues and dialogues of a pair of lovers as played out against and interwoven with the background of the theatre of nature. The lovers are seen in a series of lyric moments and dramatic situations: in longing and in anticipation, in separation and anxiety, and in blissful reunion. The woman, whose point of view predominates in the poems, is seen now in longing and heartsickness and now in ecstatic fulfillment; she is seen now in public disgrace, scorned for her sunburnt complexion by the "daughters of Jerusalem" and reviled and mistreated by the watchmen during her nocturnal search through the city for her beloved (Cant. 1: 6, 5: 7), and now in public triumph, borne through the desert on a resplendent nuptial litter and admired in her bridal sword-dance by those same "daughters of Jerusalem" (6: 10, 13). The rhetoric of invitation, and a yearning, subjunctive mood predominate throughout the poems: "let him kiss me . . . ; let my lover come to his garden . . . ; O that you were my brother, . . . I would kiss you; let me hear your voice . . . ; arise, my beloved . . . ; open to me, my sister . . . ; draw me, bring me . . . ; come, my lover . . . ; be swift, my lover . . . ."

On occassion, the male lover is called or compared to King Solomon, as the maiden is at one point called a prince's daughter, but this most likely represents not a reference to a royal couple, but to the tradition of the Palestinian *wasfs*, wedding songs in which bride and groom were extravagantly praised, including imagery reflecting their symbolic status as king and queen; similarly, while the setting occasionally is urban, and even courtly (as though the lovers were Solomon and his queen), undoubtedly that reflects the same folkloric metaphor of the bridal couple as a royal pair.[13] Otherwise the imagery is essentially pastoral, reflecting a world primarily of fields, pastures, gardens, groves and, especially, vineyards. Time is experienced in relation to that pastoral world, with diurnal and seasonal references to resting flocks "at noon" and pasturing them "until the day breathes and the shadows pass away," and to seasons of pruning, budding, blossoming or harvesting, to the passing of winter rains and the coming of the time for singing. And always the natural setting is infused with the dynamics of eros:

Come, my beloved . . . let us go out early to the vineyards, and see whether the vines have budded, whether the grape blossoms have opened and the pomegranates are in bloom. There I will give you my love (7: 10—12).
    Let my beloved come to his garden, and eat its choicest fruits.

I come to my garden, my sister, my bride, I gather my myrrh with my spice, I eat my honecomb with my honey. I drink my wine with my milk (5: 1)

As such passages suggest, the images of nature in the Song of Songs are really inseparable from their erotic connotations: the vineyard and the garden are not only settings, they are metaphors for the beloved herself, with their clusters of grapes, their budding pomegranates, their mountains of myrrh and hill of incense and windblown fragrances, just as the inventory of delectables — honey, spices, perfumes, oils, fruits, flowers — are so many metaphors for sexual delight. There are some fifteen animals and twenty-one different plants referenced in the Song of Songs, and a veritable catalogue of foods, spices, herbs, perfumes, unguents, jewels and precious metal — mostly introduced in the course of metaphoric blazoning of one another's beauty. As Phyllis Trible says about this garden of love redeemed, every ambivalence about the natural world that might have been passed down from the Genesis story is banished: here all serves Eros.[14]

No other book of the Bible offers such a panoply of natural history as these short 117 verses of the Song of Songs, nor such a constant appeal to the world of the senses: the aromatic scents of the perfumed garden, the scent wafted from the hills of Lebanon, the scent of the lover's garments, the scent of the lover's breath and body; the taste of honey, of apples, of the lover's breast, the lover's lips ("Your lips distill nectar, my bride; honey and milk are under your tongue") and the lover's body ("With great delight I sat in his shadow, and his fruit was sweet to my taste"); the sound of singing and the "voice of the turtledove," the voice of the beloved, calling out to hear the lover's voice ("The voice of my beloved! Behold, he comes, leaping upon the mountains . . . 'O my dove . . . let me hear your voice, for your voice is sweet"); the exquisite sense of touch, her breasts like twin fawns, or like the clusters of a date palm ("I will climb the palm tree and lay hold of its branches"), the lover "held captive" in the tresses of her hair, the embrace of the lovers ("His left hand is under my head, his right embraces me"), her visceral response ("my bowels were stirred"); and, everywhere, the delight of the eyes: "Behold, you are beautiful, my beloved . . . let me see your face . . . your face is comely . . . your cheeks are like halves of a pomegranate behind your veil"; "My beloved is all radiant and lovely . . . his body like ivory work, encrusted with sapphires"; "Who is this that looks forth like the dawn, fair as the moon, bright as the sun?" — and the eyes recursively give back as much delight as they receive: "Turn away your eyes from me, for they disturb me . . . You have ravished my heart with one glance of your eyes . . . ."

The aesthetic of the pregiven world of nature that speaks its word in the Song of Songs is, to use terms suggested by Tymieniecka, panoramic, symphonic and plurivocal, and that word is reverberated in poetry that manifests those same panoramic, symphonic and plurivocal qualities.[15] The hallmark of the imaginative world of the Song of Songs is its *fullness*, a fullness manifest first of all in an unprecedented inventory of places, creatures and substances, including many exotic plants and animals not native to Palestine and whose foreign names are often simply transliterated into Hebrew; these, along with other Persian and Greek loan words, Aramaisms and archaisms, altogether give the microcosmic garden of the Song of Songs the feeling of the inclusive fullness of the garden of Eden, where Adam was charged with naming everything, or of Noah's ark. The name itself, Song of Songs, *Shir ha-shirim*, literally signifying "most excellent of songs," serves in itself as a cognomen coveying the idea of fullness and inclusiveness.

Secondly, the mood of erotic richness and joy — whether taken literally or symbolically — is one of openness, invitation, receptiveness, without hint of reticence or qualification, expressing the fullness of human virtuality. When the canonicity of the Song of Songs was debated by the rabbis at Jamnia at the end of the first century C.E., Rabbi Akiba proclaimed, "God forbid! — no [one] in Israel ever disputed about the Song of Songs (that he should say) that it does not render the hands unclean [i.e., is sacred], for all the ages are not worth the day on which the Song of Songs was given to Israel; for all the writings are holy, but the Song of Songs is the Holy of Holies."[16] Centuries later, the writer of the *Zohar* agrees, declaring the Song of Songs is the holy of holies because "all its words are instinct with love and joy . . . wherein is to be found the summary of the whole Torah, of the whole work of Creation" and of all the rest of sacred history, elaborating that "On the day when this song was revealed the Shekinah descended to earth."[17] The ultimate "mystery" of the Song of Songs, according to the *Zohar*, is that it expresses the union of the Shekinah with the King her Husband, a union which, when fulfilled, will cause to be poured out every sanctification and benediction upon the world.

Rhetorically and stylistically, this quality of plenitude is expressed by images of fullness and overflowing ("You are altogether lovely . . . your navel is a rounded bowl that never lacks mixed wine"), and by a rhetoric of excess and immoderation. And not only the modern appreciators of the poem celebrate this quality. The Cistercian abbot Bernard comments about the opening line of the poem:

See with what impatient abruptness she begins her speech . . . From the abundance of her heart, without shame of shyness, she breaks out with the eager request, "Let Him kiss me with the kiss of His Mouth." . . . "He looketh upon the earth and maketh it tremble," and she dares to ask that He should kiss her! Is she not manifestly intoxicated? No doubt of it . . . And if she seems to you to utter words, believe them to be the belchings of satiety, unadorned and unpremeditated . . . It is not the expression of thought, but the eructation of love . . . Hence it is that the Spouse, burning with an incredible ardour of divine love, in her anxiety to obtain some kind of outlet for the intense heat which consumes her, does not consider what she speaks or how she speaks. Under the constraining influence of charity, she belches forth rather than utters whatever rises to her lips. And is it any wonder that she should eructate who is so full and so inebriated with the wine of holy love?[18]

Having offered these general observations about the poetics of the Song of Songs, I should like to turn our attention to the phenomonology of illumination and darkness as presentified in its lyrics. Attention has always focussed on the garden and natural-history imagery of the Song, but the interplay of illumination and darkness in the poem proves to be a particularly powerful infralinguistic sign system recorded in the language of the text, and informing the supralinguistic rhythms and structural/imagistic patterns experienced in reading or listening to it.

In the pregiven world of the Song, as always in the experience of nature, *fullness* of illumination seems to give not only itself, the flowing sphere of light, but everything else along with it,[19] as though it is light that presences for us every other natural form, every creature, every person, each of which is apprehended by the eye according to its own manner of reflecting that light, whether dull or shiny, bright or obscure: from the natural earth-tones of the cedar rafters of the lovers' bedchamber to the highly reflective glitter of the ornaments of Pharoah's chariots, and from the swarthy, sun-burnt complexion of the Shulamite to the brightness of her eye, which, her lover says, "drives him wild" (6: 5). The brilliance of the desert sun in the Song of Songs we come to know from the maiden's testimony that she is "black and beautiful," admonishing the daughters of Jerusalem, "Do not gaze at me because I am swarthy, because the sun has scorched me" (1: 5—6). We also know that the shepherds rest their flock at "noon," in the heat of the day, and that to sit in the shadow of an apple tree is pleasant — although what the maiden prefers is to sit in her lover's "shadow," where "his fruit" is "sweet to [her] taste" (2: 3).

Conversely, the virtual *absence* of illumination, sheer darkness, seems not only inapprehendible in itself, it is as though that absence deprives us of everything else, and we seem to grope helplessly: "Upon my bed by night I sought him whom my soul loves; I sought him but found him not" (3: 1), and the litter of Solomon, the poet reminds us, is guarded by sixty warriors, "each with his sword at his thigh, against the terrors of night" (3: 7—8). Of course it only *seems*, to the first level of consciousness, that illumination presences everything for us and that darkness absents everything — the lovers, and we, can, after all, still touch and hear and smell in the garden, as could Keats "darkling" listen to the nightingale and sense what "soft incense hangs upon the boughs . . . in embalmed darkness."[20] But that is matter for another level of consciousness . . . . For the first, we have the old primeval fear of darkness and night, and their association with separation, loss, anxiety, and the primeval exhuberance and relief that accompany light and day, and it is these primeval feelings that give such emotional potency to the maiden's nocturnal search in the city, on the one hand, and the lovers' mutual invitations to come forth into the springtime and into the daylit vineyards, on the other.

And in between full illumination and complete darkness, there are, in the world of the Song of Songs, recreated those innumerable intermediate experiences of light, such as the sudden emergence of dawn on a desert horizon, which occasions a figurative description of the lover, resplendent in her wedding regalia, or perhaps just resplendent in the fullness of her love: "Who is this that looks forth like the dawn, fair as the moon, bright as the sun, terrible as an army with banners?" (6: 10). Notice the beautifully orchestrated incremental intensity of the images of rising dawn, fair moon, bright sun, and "terrible" army, effecting a successive heightening of the impact the maiden has on those who behold her. Notice, too, how only in the barbaric colorfulness of an army arrayed for battle could the poet find a way to surpass the impact of the sun's refulgence. In another verse the lover is described in his turn as "radiant and ruddy," which might remind us of the converse metaphor of Psalm 19, describing the emergence of the sun, "which comes forth like a bridegroom leaving his chamber." And when we allow ourselves the freedom of reverie with these too-familiar images, we can recapture the beautifully playful and striking interplay here of eros and nature, of the erotic radiance of the sun and the radiant eros of the lover.

Less intensely dramatic than the description of the rising dawn, fair moon and bright sun of verse 6: 10, is the twice-repeated softly lyrical description, "until the day breathes and the shadows pass away" (2: 17 and 4: 6). It could be a description of the cool breath of evening and the onset of night, erasing the shadows of day (as Marcia Falk reads it[21]), but it could also describe the breath of dawn and the chasing away of the shadow of night itself, as seems more likely from the implied erotic context. In the one passage the lover is said to "pasture his flock among the lilies until the day breathes . . ." and in the other he describes her breasts as being like two fawns that feed among the lilies, following this with the thought that "Until the day breathes and the shadows flee," I will hie me to the mountains of myrrh and the hill of frankincense. The interesting associational web gives the thought that it is lovemaking that should last "until the day breathes . . ." — which means either that they make love all day and part at evening or that they make love all night and part at dawn, the latter being not only the more conventionally realistic image, reflected in the *aubade* tradition, but the more powerfully symbolic one as well.

Other light-related images carry seasonal associations. Especially prominent is the description of the advent of spring, the dawning of the seasonal new year, analogous to the dawning of a new day and to the dawning of erotic feeling, a nexus of associations captured in the well-known lines in which the lover invites his beloved to "Arise . . . and come away," for the flowers have appeared, "the fig tree puts forth its figs, and the vines are in blossom [and] give forth their fragrance" (2: 10—13). The maiden, in her turn, goes "down to the nut orchard, to inspect the blossoms of the valley, to see whether the vines had budded, whether the pomegranates were in bloom" (6: 11), and then invites him to join her: "Come, my beloved . . . let us go out early to the vineyards, and see whether the vines have budded, whether the grape blossoms have opened and the pomegranates are in bloom. There I will give you my love" (7: 11—12). Similarly implying a summery outdoor setting are the description of the Shulammite's dance (6: 13), and the image of "Solomon's" wedding: "Go forth, O daughters of Zion, and behold King Solomon, with the crown with which his mother crowned him on the day of his wedding, on the day of gladness of his heart" (3: 11). It is of great interest that a passage in the *Mishnah* cites this latter text in describing the practice of religious folk dances supposed to have been performed in the days before the destruction of the temple in association with the harvest of summer fruits and autumnal vintage — and the choosing of mates:

There were no happier days for Israel than the 15th of Ab and the Day of Atonement, for on them the daughters of Jerusalem used to go forth in white raiments . . . to dance in the vineyards. And what did they say? Young man, look up and behold the maiden you are going to choose. Set not thine eyes on beauty but on family. Likewise it saith, *Go forth ye daughters of Sion, and behold King Solomon with the crown wherewith his mother hath crowned him in the day of his espousals and in the day of the gladness of his heart* [Cant. 3: 11]: *In the day of his espousals* — this is the giving of the Law; *and in the day of the gladness of his heart* — this is the building of the Temple. May it be built speedily in our days! Amen. (Taanith 4: 8)[22]

Consonant with these images of outdoor, daylight love is the array of natural imagery associated with the fields, vineyards, groves and gardens, imagery marked by qualities of growing, budding, blooming, flowing and glistening — buds, flowers, apples, halved pomegranates, living waters, wine and milk — and the array of artifice imagery associated with the lovers' bright adornments or used figuratively of the lovers' charms — Solomon's silver and gold palenquin, strings of jewels, scarlet thread, a tower hung with bucklers, battlements of silver, limbs like ivory and alabaster set with gems — a panoply of light-reflective imagery.

But, as we noticed above, the scenes of intimacy and consummation of love are set at night, when "the day breathes and the shadows flee away" — scenes set indoors, on the maiden's couch or bed, in the place she calls in one passage the "wine-cellar" and in other passages her "mother's house." It is from the dark intimacy of this bed in the maternal house that one imagines the opening lines spoken by the black and beautiful Shulammite, "Let him kiss me with the kisses of his mouth" — as though a call from a chthonic goddess, a Kali or black

Astarte. And this leads us to a reconsideration of the primal privileging of light and fear of darkness registered in the first consciousness, alluded to above. Such a polarization leads, as is now well known, to a mythopoeic association of light, spirit, culture, God, deliverance and the so-called "male principle" or yang on the one hand, vs. darkness, flesh, nature, chaos, bondedness and the so-called "female principle" or yin on the other — a dualistic schema that became so entrenched and dominant in the mainstream Hellenistic, Roman, medieval and enlightenment cultures that Robert McAffee Brown, following the lead of feminist theologians, has called it the Great Fallacy [Phallacy?] of Western patriarchal culture.[23] Thus mainstream Jewish and Christian spirituality, under the impetus of Orphic and Gnostic cosmologies, has over the centuries committed itself to a theology of Light and a soteriology of Illumination, which in the Christian tradition, in particular, especially since Augustine and Jerome, has evolved as a transcendentalist spirit vs. flesh spirituality whose ideal of perfection centered on virginity, asceticism, self-mastery, mastery of nature, and "contempt for the world."[24]

It is not surprising, then, that the conventional allegorical commentaries on the Song of Songs, Jewish and Christian alike, have interpreted the imagery of the poem according to this theology of Light. In these commentaries the springtime represents the New Dispensation of grace succeeding upon the harsh, dark winter of the Law; high noon would be Paradise itself. The comparison of the bride successively to the dawn, moon and sun represent the Synagogue's, or the Church's, progressive evolution toward what Philo of Alexandria called the Divine Light-Stream.[25] The anonymous Neoplatonic medieval commentary on the Song of Songs called *Deiformis*, for example, interprets every passage in the book in terms of the soul's progressive approximation toward the Divine Luminosity, to the point where it becomes wholly assimilated into Light and therefore divinized.[26] Conversely, in the commentaries, the sun that scorches the Shulammite's complexion is the chastening Sun of Justice, and the blackness of her complexion represents her sinful condition, or else her persecuted condition, while her sleep and nocturnal search for her absent lover represent the period of Israel's captivity, or else the persecution of the Church.[27] In terms of personal spirituality, however, many of the traditional commentators viewed the Shulammite's nocturnal ordeal in the city and her mistreatment at the hands of the watchmen as symbolic of the purgative way, a painful but necessary stage on the soul's journey to salvation (e.g., Ambrose, or Gregory of Nyssa). Similarly, in this vein, her blackened complexion would signify not so much persecution or her sinfulness, but rather the penitential condition of a catachumen (Origen); or, as the *Aurora consurgens*, a 12th century alchemical allegory based on the Song of Songs, has it, her blackness represents the state of *nigredo* or *putrefactio*, the necessary prelude to *sublimatio* and *coniunctio*, the union of opposites and transformation of base metals to gold which symbolizes the perfection of the soul in Christ.[28]

In all this, the Song commentaries follow the conventional patterns of the theology of Light. But, as a collection of love lyrics, the Song of Songs, as we have seen, also embodies a much more ambivalent attitude toward light and darkness. For while the poem is full of effusions of springtime, and of the daylight-flooded world of blooming gardens and budding groves and vineyards as a folkloric setting for seasonal rituals of courtship and love-celebration, and while it also portrays the night as a time of love-longing, separation-anxieties and personal ordeal, it is, not so paradoxically, in that same deep night that ultimate consummation is achieved. In fact, it is precisely in consequence of the maiden's ordeal that she discovers her lover. In chapter five it is the impatient question by the daughters of Jerusalem ("What is your beloved more than another beloved . . .?") that prompts her ecstatic description of his beauty, as though his image has now newly dawned in her consciousness ("This is my beloved, and this is my friend"), followed by her own realization about where her lover has gone: he "has gone down to his garden" (6: 2). In chapter three also, it is after the encounter with the watchmen that she finds "him whom my soul loves. I held him and would not let him go" (3: 4).

It is, after all, at *night* that the lover, the "gazelle," feeds "among the lilies. Until the day breathes and the shadows flee away" — until, that is, the day separates them. This moment in the poem is, as already suggested, an *aubade*, a brief poem of lovers' parting at the first sign of dawn. Is it not, then, out of the deep darkness that we imagine rising the lover's desire ("Let him kiss me with the kisses of his mouth") or the image of their intimate union ("His left hand is under my head, his right hand embraces me")? Or who has ever imagined the vehement flame of love, which waters cannot quench nor floods drown (8: 6—7), as burning by day rather than blazing up in the dark night?

So the rhythms and patterns of the pregiven world of the Song of

Songs, the premised intersubjectivity of living nature and living human eros, resonate with a peculiar and a powerful authenticity in our own responsive imagination. Desire, there and here, rises like dawn, blazes up like the sun or like fire, or it blossoms and buds and sends forth its perfumes, and invites us to go forth to dance in the vineyards — until our mutual love-longing leads us to the wine-cellar, to "our mother's house," and to the ecstasy of consummation which comes like a sudden plunge into darkness, a deep darkness of union and of utter self-forgetting.

That is how it is — there, and here. As we have seen, neither the conventional moralistic allegorizations, nor the conventional humanistic readings can make anything of this. But myth and poetry recognize it well. The Shulammite's night-quest for her lost lover reads just like a mythic *descensus ad inferno*, specifically like those ancient Near Eastern versions of the goddess' search to bring her missing consort back from the underworld, the search of Isis, or Ishtar/Inanna. The Akkadian account of Ishtar's descent to the nether world to recover her consort Tammuz even includes her being subjected to abuse at the hands of the gatekeepers, who strip her of her ornaments and clothes, as the Shulammite is stripped of her veil.[29] In terms of the poetics of love, this mythic descent into darkness, whether in the story of Orpheus and Euridyce, Demeter and Persephone, Ishtar and Dumuzi or the Shulammite and her lover, symbolizes not persecution or sinfulness or penitence, but rather the overwhelming, redemptive power of passion.[30]

It is above all the mystics in whom the erotic imagery of the Song of Songs has most powerfully reverberated. Being themselves wholly absorbed in a passionate love story, the mystics were able to be led by and give themselves up to the erotic poetics of the Song of Songs as neither the traditional moralizers nor the modern humanist critics have been able to do — so that the mystics become our most reliable phenomonologists of the world of the poem. In the experience and the writing of the contemplative mystics, guided and inspired by the Song of Songs, the phenomonology of light and darkness is turned inside out and upside down. For them, the wakeful sleep of the Shulammite ("I sleep but my heart wakes" — 5: 2) is not sloth or ignorance or imperfection but contemplation itself, and the dark night in which the lover is absent to her is not a condition of sin or punishment or persecution but the paradoxically luminous dark night of the soul, the cloud of unknowing.

The first source to which we turn for such a reading is the negative theology, the *via negativa*, associated with the writings of Pseudo-Dionysius, the anonymous fifth-century Syrian author believed in the middle ages to be St. Paul's Athenian convert Dionysius and whose unconventional ideas therefore bore great credibility and exerted a powerful influence through the ninth century translations of John Scotus Erigena. For Pseudo-Dionysius the Divine Nature is incomprehensibly beyond any human categories of knowledge, so that It cannot be named or known: "nor is It darkness, nor is It light, or error, or truth; nor can any affirmation or negation apply to It" — although negation is apter than affirmation. The Divine Nature is in this world a "Ray of Darkness," and the closer a soul approaches It, the more the soul is wrapped in a "dazzling Darkness" (the Biblical paradigm was Moses on Mount Sinai, as explicated by Philo Judaeus).[31] Led at first to an imperfect knowledge of the Divine Nature as reflected in creatures, the contemplative's faculties are progressively stripped and emptied "in order that we may attain a naked knowledge of . . . Unknowing . . . and that we may begin to see that super-essential Darkness which is hidden by all the light that is in existent things."[32]

The mystical *via negativa* is more familiar to students of medieval English literature through the anonymous 14th century treatise *The Cloud of Unknowing* which transforms this theology of "Nothing" and "Nowhere" to a spirituality of love-longing, as in the famous saying that God "may well be loved, but not thought. By love he can be caught and held, but by thinking never."[33] *The Cloud of Unknowing* even more explicitly than Pseudo-Dionysius sets forth a spirituality of emptiness, analogous to Buddhist *sunyatta*, or "emptiness-yoga." The great obstacle to union with God, the author says, is the "stark awareness of your own [separate] existence. . . . Everyone has something to sorrow over, but none more than he who knows and feels that he is." Be willing, therefore, the author says, "to be blind, and give up all longing to know the why and the how, for knowing will be more of a hindrance than a help" (*Cloud*, p. 73). "Reconcile yourself to wait in this darkness as long as is necessary, but still go on longing after him whom you love. For if you are to feel him or to see him in this life, it must always be in this cloud, in this darkness" (p. 62).

The natural affinity of this "dark night" theology with the erotic poetics of the Song of Songs is everywhere evident in the Western mystical tradition, where in example after example we can see how in reaching to describe or articulate this experience of infused contemplation the mystics, Jewish and Christian, have recourse to the imagery of the Song of Songs. One of the earliest and best sources for this connection are the fourth century homilies on Canticles by the Greek theologian Gregory of Nyssa. Already, in his symbolic *Life of Moses*, Gregory had explicated Moses' vision of God in a dark cloud by explaining that "spiritual knowledge first occurs as an illumination in those who experience it ... [and that] Indeed, all that is opposed to piety is conceived of as darkness; to shun the darkness is to share in the light. But that as the soul makes progress, and by a greater and more perfect concentration comes to appreciate what the knowledge of truth is, the more it approaches this vision ... the true vision and the true knowledge ... [that] what we seek consists precisely in not seeing, in an awareness that our goal transcends all knowledge and is everywhere cut off from us by the darkness of incomprehensibility."[34] Thus, in commenting on Canticles 3: 1, Gregory says that here, the soul in contemplation, believing she has attained union with her beloved, is "suddenly introduced into the realm of the invisible, surrounded by the divine darkness," and feeling the absence of her divine Lover — until she realizes that this absence represents his very closeness, for in giving up every finite mode of comprehension, she indeed finds him whom her soul loves (Gregory, pp. 201—202). Similarly, on Canticles 5: 2, Gregory describes the "strange and contradictory fusion" of sleeping and waking as a contemplative state of "pure and naked intuition" (pp. 241—42). Thus, spiritual progress, for Gregory, is a movement that proceeds at first from darkness to light, but in the stage of mystical contemplation it is an entry into the "secret chamber of ... divine knowledge, ... the divine darkness" (p. 247). Thus even the stripping of the Shulammite's veil by the watchmen is understood as a paradoxical good (p. 270), as the stripping away of every illusion and every consolation but this: the incomprehensible unitive experience in which she becomes oned with that invisible "archetypal Beauty" (p. 282).

The greatest and most renowned exponents of this passionate "dark night" theology are, of course, the 16th century Carmelites John of the Cross and Teresa of Avila. The experience of infused contemplation is described, for example, in John of the Cross' *Spiritual Canticle*, using the metaphors of Spiritual Betrothal and Spiritual Marriage in conjunction with imagery drawn from the Song of Songs, and the same is true, as is well known, in Teresa's *Interior Castle* and her lesser known commentary on the Song of Songs, *Conceptions of the Love of God*, while the most vivid description of a personal experience of such passionate annihilation and ensoulment is Teresa's account in her spiritual autobiography of the 'transverberation' of her heart with a golden spear by an angel of flaming light.[35]

But it is John of the Cross, in particular, in his treatise *The Dark Night of the Soul*, a commentary on his own poem of the same title, who offers the most fully elaborated evocation of the experience of the love of God in terms of the erotic love lyrics of the Song of Songs, infused with images of the living flame of love, the wound of love, the inebriation of love and the ultimate self-giving of lovers to each other in the "emptiness" of "thick darkness."[36] The contemplative soul, he says, is "dissolved in nothing and annihilated," knowing nothing (p. 73), and "by means of this dark contemplation . . . [is] brought actually into darkness" (p. 121). "In this way, being empty . . . it may be informed with the Divine" (pp. 122—23). Thus, stripped, and wounded, and blinded, and emptied, the soul in this thick darkness is consumed by the living flame of love and, as he says in stanza five of the poem, is wholly ensouled in the lover:

> O dark of night, my guide!
> O sweeter than anything sunrise can discover!
> O night, drawing side to side
> The loved and lover,
> the loved one wholly ensouling in the lover.[37]

The Spanish Carmelites have left an unprecedented imprint on the western imagination, because nowhere else has the poetics of erotic spirituality achieved so rich an expression, and it continues to reverberate in European and American poetry, sometimes with conscious influence, as with Donne, Crashaw, Novalis, Hopkins and Brother Antoninus — more commonly without it, as other poets independently, but without the resources of the received mystical tradition, apprehend the mystical dark night. Blake struggled to bring about the marriage of heaven and hell, but was perhaps too entrapped in a gnostic theology of Light to assimilate a dark night theology. Wordsworth, too, Romantic though he was, was still essentially a product of the enlightenment and committed to a natural theology of light — although in Book XIV of

The Prelude the unexpected experience of a moon-flooded landscape on the summit of Mount Snowdon becomes symbolic of a state of imagination surpassing anything known by the daylight mind (ll. 11—129), just as Romantic painters, such as Washington Allston, would occasionally try to reach beyond their sun-flooded illuminist visions by painting mysterious nightscapes. The Mount Snowdon experience was for Wordsworth a realization of the Romantic version of the spiritual marriage he alludes to in "Home at Grasmere": "For the discerning intellect of Man, /When wedded to this goodly universe/In love and holy passion, shall find these/A simple produce of the common day" (ll. 52—55).

A more explicit "dark night" spirituality occurs in Theodore Roethke's "In A Dark Time," which offers a contemporary expression of the *via negativa*:

> In a dark time, the eye begins to see. . . .
> What's madness but nobility of soul
> At odds with circumstance? the day's on fire!
> I know the purity of pure despair.

and whose last two stanzas invoke the Dionysian image of dazzling darkness and a culminating unitive experience:

> A steady storm of correspondences!
> A night flowing with birds, a ragged moon,
> And in broad day the midnight come again!
> A man goes far to find out what he is —
> Death of the self in a long tearless night,
> All natural shapes blazing unnatural light.

> Dark, dark my light, and darker my desire
> My soul like some heat-maddened summer fly,
> Keeps buzzing at the sill. Which I is *I*?

> A fallen man, I climb out of my fear.
> The mind enters itself, and God the mind,
> And one is One, free in the tearing wind.[38]

Closer to the Canticles-inspired imagery of the Carmelite mystics and consciously echoing it, is the poem "The Encounter" by Brother Antoninus (William Everson), which begins:

My Lord came to me in the deep of night;
The sullen dark was wounded with His name.
I was as woman made before His eyes;
My nakedness was as a secret shame . . .

My Lord came to me in my depth of dross;
I was as woman made and hung with shame.
His lips sucked up the marrow of my mind,
And all my body burned to bear His name.[39]

Here the mystical experience is mediated not only by the metaphor of
erotic spirituality, but by a particularly graphic gender-transformed
passion imagery conceivable only in the dazzling darkness of the "deep
of night."

These examples from contemplatives, medieval to modern, seem to
relate the insights of "dark night" spirituality entirely to personal inner
experience and sometimes they are interpreted in such a way as to
reinforce a transcendentalist, world-denying mentality. But theologian
Matthew Fox has made a project of teaching us to re-read mystics like
Julian of Norwich, Hildegard of Bingen, Mechthild of Magdeburg and
Meister Eckhart in such a way as to recover what he has called their
authentically erotic and "creation-centered" spirituality, which has been
obscured by the pervasive polarized, dualistic thinking of patriarchal
Christianity and phallogocentric Western culture.[40] Inspired by the
creation-centered mystics, who are erotically in love with the world and
with God as sacramentally (panentheistically) present in the world and
in its creatures, Fox calls upon us to realize the profounder dark night
of ourselves, our society, and our planet, crucified by industrialism, mil-
itarism, nationalism, economic injustice, ecological havoc and nuclear
nightmare, a dark night in which God-in-the-world calls out to be
kissed and held and offers mystical union in a dazzling darkness
invisible to a humanity bathed in the glaring artificial light of reductive
and positivist ideologies.

Essex Community College (Baltimore, MD)

NOTES

[1] George L. Scheper, "Reformation Attitudes toward Allegory and the Song of Songs," *PMLA* **89** (May 1974), 556.

[2] Theodoret, "Commentary on the Song of Songs," in *The Voice of the Church*, 2 vols. (London, 1850), I, 193. Rabbi Saadia Gaon, quoted in Christian Ginsburg, *The Song of Songs* (London: 1857), pp. 36—37.

[3] Robert Pfeiffer, *Introduction to the Old Testament* (New York: 1948), pp. 714.

[4] For surveys of the history of exegesis on the Song of Songs, see Marvin H. Pope, *The Song of Songs/ A New Translation with Introduction and Commentary* (New York: Doubleday, 1977), pp. 89—210; H. H. Rowley, "The Song of Songs: An Examination of Recent Theory," in *The Servant of the Lord and Other Essays* (London: 1954), pp. 189—234; F. Ohly, *Hohelied-Studien: Grundzuge einer Geschichte der Hohenliedausle-gung des Abendlandes bis zum 1200* (Wiesbaden: 1958); A. Robert and R. Tournay, *Le Cantique des Cantiques/Traduction et Commentair* (Pairs: 1963), pp. 43—55; George L. Scheper, "The Spiritual Marriage: the Exegetic History and Literary Impact of the Song of Songs in the Middle Ages," Ph.D. Diss. (Princeton: 1971). Roland E. Murphy, *The Song of Songs/ A Commentary on the Book of Canticles or The Song of Songs* (Minneapolis: Fortress Press, 1990), pp. 11—41.

The modern sources mentioned in the text are: Franz Delitzsch, *Commentary on the Song of Songs and Ecclesiastes*, trans. M. G. Easton (Edinburgh: 1877); H. G. A. Ewald, *Das Hohe Lied Salomos* (1826); Karl Budde, "The Song of Solomon," *The New World*, III (1894), pp. 56—77; T. J. Meek, "The Song of Songs and the Fertility Cult," in *The Song of Songs/ A Symposium*, ed. W. H. Schoff (Philadelphia: 1924), pp. 48—79; Robert Gordis, *The Song of Songs and Lamentations: a Study, Modern Translation and Commentary* (New York: Jewish Theological Seminary, 1974); Marcia Falk, *Love Lyrics from the Bible/ A Translation and Literary Study of the Song of Songs* (Sheffield: Almond Press, 1982).

[5] Frederick W. Farrar, *History of Interpretation* (London: 1885), pp. 256, 32, and 257.

[6] W. R. Inge, *Christian Mysticism* (New York: 1964), pp. 43.

[7] Delitzsch, *op cit.*, pp. 15.

[8] William E. Phipps, "The Plight of the Song of Songs," *JAAR*, *XLII* (March, 1974), 89—90.

[9] Phyllis Trible, "Love's Lyric's Redeemed," in *God and the Rhetoric of Sexuality* (Philadelphia: Fortress Press, 1978), pp. 144—65.

[10] *Tosefta Sanhedrin* 12: 10; cf. Babylonian Talmud, *Sanh.* 101a (ET, *II*, 684).

[11] Anna-Teresa Tymieniecka, "The Aesthetics of Nature in the Human Condition," in *Poetics of the Elements in the Human Condition: the Sea*, ed. A-T. Tymieniecka, *Annalecta Husserliana*, XIX (1985), pp. 4, 15.

[12] *Ibid.*, p. 18.

[13] For the wedding-week/*wasf* interpretation of Canticles, see J. G. Wetzstein, "Remarks on the Song," Appendix in Delitzsch, pp. 162—76; and Budde, *op cit.*; also Falk, chap. 4, pp. 80—87.

[14] Trible, p. 150, pp. 160—61

[15] Tymieniecka, pp. 4—13.

[16] *Mishnah Yadaim* 3: 5 (*The Mishnah*, trans. Herbert Danby [London, 1938], 782); cf. *Tosefta Yad* 2: 13—14.

[17] *Zohar* 145b (*The Zohar*, trans. Harry Sperling and Maurice Simon, 5 vols. [London, 1933], *IV*, 12—13). Also see Paul Vulliaud, *Le Cantique des Cantiques d'apres la tradition juive* (Paris: 1925), pp. 117—18.

[18] *St. Bernard's Sermons on the Canticle of Canticles*, trans. by a priest of Mount Melleray, 2 vols. (Dublin: 1920), I, 50—51; *II*, pp. 281—83.

[19] Anna-Teresa Tymieniecka, "Light and the Word," presentation delivered at 14th Annual Convention of the International Society of Phenomonology and Literature (Cambridge, Mass.), 12 April 1989.

[20] Keats, "Ode to a Nightingale," stanzas 4—6.

[21] Falk, pp. 93—94; cf. Pope, p. 408.

[22] *Tannith* 4:8 (*Mishnah*, pp. 200—201).

[23] Robert McAffee Brown, *Spirituality and Liberation: Overcoming the Great Fallacy* (Louisville: Westminster/John Knox, 1988).

[24] See Peter Brown, *The Body and Society/Men, Women and Sexual Renunciation in Early Christianity* (New York: Columbia, 1988); John Bugge, *Virginitas* (Hague: Martinus Nijhoff, 1975); Elaine Pagels, *Adam, Eve, and the Serpent* (New York: Random House, 1988).

[25] For traditional comments on Cant. 2:11—12 and 6:10, see Pope, pp. 394—98, 571—74; and Richard F. Littledale, *A Commentary on The Song of Songs from Ancient and Medieval Sources* (London: 1869), 93—97, 284—89. For Philo's theology of Light, see Erwin Goodenough, *By Light, Light/The Mystic Philosophy of Helleistic Judaism* (New Haven, 1935), esp. pp. 23, 160—64.

[26] See the analysis of *Deiformis* in Edgar de Bruyne (who attributes the text to Thomas Gallus), *Etudes D'Esthetique Medievale*, 3 vols. (Brugge, 1946), III, pp. 58—71.

[27] For traditional exegesis on Cant. 1:5—6 and 5:7, see Pope, pp. 307—22, 527—29; and Littledale, pp. 21—25, 230—34.

[28] For the "via negativa" reading of Cant. 5: 7, see Gregory of Nyssa, *Commentary on the Song of Songs*, trans. Casimir McCambley (Brookline: Hellenic College Press, 1987), 220 f., and for a similar reading of Cant. 1: 5—6, see Origen, *The Song of Songs/ Commentary and Homilies*, trans. R. P. Lawson, ACW **26** (New York: Newman, 1956), 91—113. For the alchemical allegorization, see *Aurora Consurgens/A Document Attributed to Thomas Aquinas on the Problem of Opposites in Alchemy*, ed. Marie-Louise von Franz, trans. R. F. C. Hull and A. S. B. Glover. Bollingen 72 (New York, 1966).

[29] For the Akkadian account of Ishtar's descent into the netherworld, see *Ancient Near Eastern Texts Relating to the Old Testament*, ed. James B. Pritchard, 2nd ed. (Princeton: Princeton University Press, 1955), pp. 106—109; and see discussion in Pope, p. 527.

[30] For an interdisciplinary consideration of the Orpheus myth, see *Orpheus/The Metamorphosis of a Myth*, ed. John Warden (Toronto: University of Toronto, 1985); on Demeter, Persephone and the Eleusinian Mysteries, see C. Kerenyi, *Eleusis/Archetypal Image of Mother and Daughter*, trans. Ralph Manheim. Bollingen LXV. **4** (New York: Pantheon, 1967).

[31] Dionysius the Areopagite, "The Mystical Theology," in *The Divine Names and the Mystical Theology*, trans. C. E. Rolt (London: SPCK, 1979), pp. 191—201.

[32] *Ibid.*, 196, cf. Meister Eckhart, sermon 17, in *Breakthrough/ Meister Eckhart's Creation Spirituality in New Translation*, Introduction and commentaries by Matthew Fox (New York: Image/Doubleday, 1980), pp. 239—40.

[33] *The Cloud of Unknowing and Other Works*, trans. Clifton Wolters (New York: Penguin, 1978), 68.

[34] *From Glory to Glory/Texts from Gregory of Nyssa's Mystical Writings*, selected by Jean Daniélou, trans. Herbert Musurillo (London: John Murray, 1961), p. 118.

[35] See St. John of the Cross, *Spiritual Canticle* trans. E. Allison Peers (New York: Image/Doubleday, 1961): stanzas xii—xxvii recount spiritual betrothal; stanzas xxviii—xxxix spiritual marriage. St. Teresa of Avila, *Interior Castle*, trans. E. Allison Peers (New York: Image/Doubleday, 1961): the fifth mansion concerns spiritual betrothal; the seventh, spiritual marriage. Also, Teresa, "Conceptions of the Love of God," in *Complete Works of Saint Teresa of Jesus*, trans. E. Allison Peers, 3 vols. (New York, 1950), II, pp. 352—99. On the "transverberation" of Teresa's heart, see *The Life of Teresa of Jesus*, trans. E. Allison Peers (New York: Image/Doubleday, 1960), chap. xxix, pp. 274—75.

[36] St. John of the Cross, *Dark Night of the Soul*, trans. E. Allison Peers (New York: Doubleday/Image, 1959), p. 106.

[37] *The Poems of St. John of the Cross*, trans. John Frederick Nims (New York: Grove, 1959), p. 21.

[38] Theodore Roethke, "In A Dark Time," in *Modern Poems/An Introduction to Poetry*, ed. Richard Ellman & Robert O'Clair (New York: Norton, 1973), p. 295.

[39] William Everson [Brother Antoninus], *The Veritable Years/1949—1966* (Santa Barbara: Black Swallow Press, 1978), p. 86.

[40] Matthew Fox, *Original Blessing/A Primer in Creation Spirituality* (Santa Fe: Bear & Co., 1983) and *The Coming of the Cosmic Christ* (New York: Harper & Row, 1988).

FREEMA GOTTLIEB

LIGHT AND THE AESTHETICS OF HOLINESS IN
THE JEWISH SPIRITUAL TRADITION

Light, according to the biblical creation story, was the first "thing of beauty" ever created by an artist, the first symbol, first image, and first work of art.

There is a general misconception that Judaism, because it is a monotheism, is not a culture that encourages aesthetics. This view can be combated by examination of imagery of light contained in Jewish spiritual sources. In the Jewish spiritual tradition images such as those of light and jewels, ornaments and garments and objects of physical beauty are used, as an outward expression for the deepest and most inward movements of the psyche.

The whole case for Jewish art rests on the minute description of the images and figures in the Temple, and the most severe case against it is contained in the ten commandments housed in the Holy of Holies within that Temple.

In the ten commandments we find:

You shalt not make for yourself a sculptured image, or any likeness of what is in the heavens above, or on the earth below, or in the waters under the earth. (Exod. 20: 4)

With whatever suspicion the illustration of this or that object in creation was regarded, the strictest prohibition concerned any attempt to make a representation of God Himself:

The Lord spoke to you out of the fire, you heard the sound of words, but perceived no shape — nothing but a voice . . . For your own sake, therefore, be most careful — since you saw no shape when the Lord your God spoke to your at Horeb out of the fire — not to act wickedly and make for yourselves a sculptured image in any likeness whatever. . . . (Deut. 4—12, 15—16)

In this case, fashioning the image of an animal or an insect or a fish is not merely wrong because one has made an image of that particular object but for the larger implication of trying to represent God. And that is really at the root of why it is forbidden.

Authoritative interpretations of the prohibition against image-making contained in the second commandment explain that it had to be taken

337

A-T. Tymieniecka (ed.), Analecta Husserliana, Vol. XXXVIII, 337—349.
© 1992 Kluwer Academic Publishers. Printed in the Netherlands.

in juxtaposition with the following verse: "You shall not bow down to them or serve them" (Exod. 20: 5). That is, images of natural objects were forbidden only when used for idol worship. Motifs drawn from the vegetable world were considered entirely innocuous objects for representation. The higher up in the echelons of creation, however, the model to be copied, the more suspect it became presumably because it would be more likely to be set up in rivalry to the Deity. Thus, there was a very strong bias against the representation of animals or humans, especially in three-dimensional forms like sculpture, which would give an additionally lifelike appearance.

Despite the stringency of these prohibitions, the Holy Temple itself boasted not only expensive and glorious "this-worldly" furniture, and the holy vessels were decorated not only with patterns based on geometrical and floral shapes, but figures of animals, birds, and even naked human beings featured largely in addition.

"Visages" or *Parsufin* of nonhuman creatures were allowed, notes the Jerusalem Talmud, and were to be found in the temple itself.[1] But from the Biblical text and from the observations of Philo it seems that even the two cherubim standing guard over the Holy of Holies wore faces that were very human indeed! (1 Kings 6: 23—35). It looks as though the cherubim under whose wings the Holy of Holies nestled, consisted of a boy and girl — naked but for their wings. Equally surprising are the apocalyptic murals envisioned for a restored Temple by the Prophet Ezekiel. These were to be decorated with:

cherubim and palmtrees . . . and every cherub had two faces; so that there was the face of a man toward the palmtree on the one side, and the face of a young lion toward the palmtree on the other side. (Ezek. 4: 18—20)

So much for the proscription of the representation of animal or human forms!

A skilled apologetist such as Josephus found it difficult to explain the discrepancy between temple art and the second commandment. He was so hard put to it that he charges Solomon with senility:

As he (Solomon) advanced in age and his reason became in time too feeble to recollect the customs of his own country . . . he sinned and went astray in the observance of the laws, namely when he made the image of the bronze bulls that supported the molten sea and the image of the lions around his own throne, for it was impious to make them. (*Antiquities*, v—111, 7, 5)

In the Bible text as we have it, however, not only is there no suggestion of "impiety" in the fashioning of such objects, but they were divinely prescribed. And a whole temple artistic tradition influenced the synagogue styles that were to follow.

In the third century, animal and human figurative art on synagogue murals was widely tolerated, and by the fourth century some rabbis withdrew objections that had been voiced in previous generations to mosaic pavements.

In a paraphrase of Leviticus 26, Targum Pseudo Yonatan defines the situation:

A figured stone you shall not put down on the ground to worship it but a colonnade with pictures and likenesses you may have in your synagogue, but not to worship it.

The Palestinian Talmud puts it on record that certain artistic techniques are acceptable in some periods and cultural circumstances and not in others:

In the days of Rabbi Yochanan they began to paint on the walls, and he did not prevent them. In the days of Rabbi Abun they began to make designs on mosaics, and they did not prevent them. (Babylonian Talmud Avodah Zarah, 4a)

The Babylonian Talmud quietly observes:

The practice of man is that he draws a picture on a wall, although he cannot instill it with a spirit and breath and entrails and organs. (BT Berakhot 10a, Shabbat 149a)

To draw the human figure is a natural propensity from childhood on and a complete ban upon such a natural proclivity would be as absurd as to outlaw laughter. The Talmud on this occasion is so accepting of this instinctive tendency only because it is very rational about the natural limits of art. The very limitations of the artist give him a certain license. He can outline the contours of the image, but he "cannot instill it with a spirit and breath and entrails and organs." He can only create the illusion, like a child playing at being grownup, but he cannot create the real thing. Thus awareness of art's limits and weaknesses paved the way for a greater liberalism in artistic expression which extended even to representations of the human form. What is forbidden is to produce a complete three-dimensional picture of a human-being. A sculpture with an imperfection of any kind is permitted. Since man has limited capacities for creation — although he can portray the physical, he cannot instill it with the breath of life — the picture he produces is necessarily incomplete and can be no serious competition with his Creator — therefore there is room for permitting it.

The Midrash (homiletical part of the Talmud) reflects in similar vein upon the ineptitude of human artistry as compared with the divine. One definition of creative genius has been someone who has a whole conception simultaneously, or who can evoke with a few bold strokes a total reality. While the human artist has to use a series of colors from his palette, God works simultaneously:

And who is a rock (tsur) except our God? (Ps. 18: 26). Hannah also said: "Neither is there any rock (tsur) like our God." (1 Sam. 2: 2)

Do not read "Neither is there any rock," but "Neither is there any artist (tsayyar) like our God."

The artist — he cannot draw a figure all at once, only little by little; but the Holy One, blessed be He — He makes a figure, all of it, in one stroke, as is said He is One who forms all (at once). (Jer. 10: 16).

The artist — he cannot paint unless he have many pigments, white, and black, and green, and red, and other hues: but the Holy One, blessed be He (can) . . .

But the most obvious difference between divine creation and human art is that, while God can instill the breath of life in His work-of-art, man cannot!

By pointing out the inefficacy of these dummies, the psalmist is also exposing the weaknesses of those who uphold them as well as highlighting the real likeness that exists between artist and work.

Their gods are of silver and gold, the work of human artistry. They have mouths, but they cannot speak, eyes but they can't see, ears but they can't hear, noses but they cannot smell. They have hands but they cannot feel, feet but they cannot walk; nor can they make a sound with their throat.

May those who make them become like them, whoever trusts in them . . . !" (Ps. 115)

It seems that the various beliefs the ancient world shared about cause and effect need not necessarily follow. First, they believed children and works of art and human beings were created in the likeness of their creators and progenitors and reflected credit or otherwise upon them. Then they believed that a "First Cause" or parent is necessarily superior to children. While the former approximates more to the original, they are merely the copy.

According to the Platonic Theory of Ideas as depicted in the Myth of the Cave, art is an imitation or fiction for some ideal reality dramatised by the interplay of shadows with the objective and transcendent light of the Sun. According to Plato, art is merely an imitation and at a second remove from reality. It is with this tacit assumption of the superiority of the original or First Cause to subsequent imprints, of parent to child, of God's Infinite Light to any of the subsequent spiral of emanations, that the Midrash contrasts human creativity with God's by stressing that while the impression of a king's features on the coinage of the realm appears fainter and fainter with each application, and while each imprint is identical, in divine creation each human being, while bearing a fresh imprint of the "Divine Image" has a personality that is entirely their own.

According to the Jewish spiritual tradition, God Himself is light. All He did in creating the world was to withdraw so as to prepare space into which He could project that light in form of a series of lamps or reflector-images. When God uttered the words: "Let there be light!" He did not create anything new. What He did in fact was what all artists and all fathers and mothers do, He took something inside Himself and projected it into the external world, pouring His light into the container of created space. With God's utterance: "Let there be light!," the Menorah candelabrum that was already there was simply placed on its pedestal for all to see.

God had this Menorah in mind before He even created the sunlight. According to the natural unfolding of events, first there is plant life, then a garden; first there is creation, then the Temple; first there is nature, then civilization. According to both Aristotelian and Jewish thinking, the last thing to be realized is often the first in conception and the whole point of it all. In a sense, therefore, the objective preexists what leads up to it. . . . First we set our sights on the goal and then we take the intermediary steps to attain it. "God looked into the Torah and created the world" (Bereishit Rabba 1: 1). According to this view the Torah is not simply law that came into existence at a certain period of historic development. It is a divine blueprint pointing to the secret formulae and principles underlying nature. And similarly with primordial light. First God dreamt of a Menorah and then He created the light of sun and moon.

This notion of preexisting idea or quintessence which we can imagine through images of light is entirely consonant, as we have seen, with Greek and Platonic theory.

God had this Menorah in mind before He even created the sunlight.

According to the natural unfolding of events, first there is plant life, then a garden; first there is creation, then the Temple; first there is nature, then civilization. According to both Aristotelian and Jewish thinking, the last thing to be realized is often the first in conception and the whole point of it all. In a sense, therefore, the objective preexists what leads up to it. . . . First we set our sights on the goal and then we take the intermediary steps to attain it. "God looked into the Torah and created the world" (Ber. Rab. 1: 1). According to this view the Torah is not simply Law that came into existence at a certain period of historic development. It is a Divine blueprint pointing to the secret formulae and principles underlying nature. And similarly with primordial light. First God dreamt of a Menorah and then He created the light of sun and moon.

This notion of a preexisting idea or quintessence or an elemental light is entirely consonant with Greek Platonic theory. It is slightly paradoxial in view of this and in view of the fact that the Greeks more than any other culture have been lovers of light and reason, that the Jewish festival which mythologically celebrates the triumph of Jewish spirit over Hellenic form should be that of *Hanukkah*, the Jewish Festival of Lights. In 165 B.C.E. the Jews succeeded in winning back Jerusalem and the Temple from the Hellenised Syrians. The story goes that they discovered an uncontaminated vial of oil with which to keep the 7-branched Temple Menorah alight for a single day, but that this supply lasted for 8 days until fresh rations could be brought in. In time, this festival of victory over Greek culture came to be celebrated by the kindling of the 8-branched Hanukkah Menorah.

What is the hidden vial, in this context, but the elemental light, and what the miracle of the oil but a reenaction of the miracle of creation seen as the emanation of light from an original first principle.

Although both the Greeks and the Jews were very preoccupied with Ideal Light and with its various manifestations in aesthetics, while in the Greek legend Prometheus had to "steal" fire from the gods, in the Jewish story God did not begrudge man knowledge or eternal life or even divinity; it was man who cut himself off from all that while God, in a compassionate effort to give him some kind of substitute means for survival, made him the gift of fire and the power to kindle artificial means of illumination. The fire He gave him, however, contained within it the germs of absolute evil and of total self-annihilation as we see in the capacities brought within human reach by the fission of the atomic structure.

Samuel said: Why do we recite a blessing over a lamp (fire) at the termination of the Sabbath? Because then it (manmade lamps) was created for the first time). (Ber. Rab. 11:2)

Here "fire" is taken in the sense of human creativity, desire, and even evil. In commemoration of these two events, the withdrawal of "first light" and the possibility for the kindling of lamps, every week at the end of Shabbat, Jews make a ritual separation between "light and darkness," "good and evil," while also thanking God for creating the "brands of the fire", meager external compensation for man's loss of the rays of his own inner light.

To understand the tension that exists between art and spirituality it is useful to look at the series of stories that relate to Moses' difficulty in reproducing and bringing down to earth the vision of the celestial Sanctuary and the celestial Menorah-Lamp revealed to him in the transcendental spheres.

Seeing that he found it difficult, the Holy One Blessed be He, said to Moses: "Take a talent of gold, cast it into the furnace and take it out again, and the candlestick will assume shape of its own accord, as it says, "its" cups, its knops, and its flowers shall emerge out of it." (Ex. 25:31).

Moshe smote with a hammer and the candlestick took shape of its own accord. He took the talent and cast it into the fire and said: "Sovereign of the Universe! Behold, the talent is in the fire. Do Thou as Thou wilt!"

Thereupon the candlestick came out completely formed . . . Who then made it? The Holy One Blessed be He. (Num Rabba, 15:4)

According to this midrash (legend), because Moses did not like copies, counterfeits, or residual traces, God let him have the original.

According to another version, when Moses experienced great difficulty in reproducing his direct and all-transcendent vision, the Holy One, blessed be He, took Him up on high, and showed him (the) red fire, green fire, white fire, and black fire (of the Menorah), and said to him, "Make Me something resembling this."

He said before Him: "Sovereign of the Universe, and whence shall I get black or red or green or white fire?"

He said to him, "After their pattern, which is being shown thee in the mount" (Ex. 25: 40) (That is to say, according to the pattern of a celestial original.)

Moses' difficulty in these series of Midrashim is that he was so obsessed by the burning reality of the original that no copy or substitute would do. So according to the various solutions, God finally intervened and created the Menorah Himself; He let Moses have the original; and, like a *Deus ex machina*, an artist intervened.

With Bezalel the master craftsman, there enters the larger question of the place of art and the imagination in the religious life. With Moses art and images did not play any role. His situation has been compared in the Midrash to a king "who possessed a beautiful appearance, and gave instructions to a member of his household to make a bust exactly like him."

"But your majesty," — exclaimed the other — "How can I possibly make one exactly like you?"

The king replied: "You do the best with the colors at your disposal, and then I shall complete the picture with My Glory."

This is what God said to Moses: "And see that thou make them after their pattern," etc. (*ib.* 25: 40)

Moshe expostulated: "Lord of the Universe! Am I a god that I should be able to make one exactly like it?"

The divine reply was: "Make it after their pattern in blue, purple and scarlet; as thou hast seen above, copy the pattern below," for it says, *OF ACACIA-WOOD, STANDING UP*, that is, just as it appears in the heavenly precincts., "If thou wilt make below a replica of that which is above, I will desert My heavenly assembly and will cause My Shekhinah (Presence) to dwell among you below." (Exod. Rab. xxxv, 5—6)

Just because Moses enjoyed the most direct encounter with God that has ever been given to a human being, he had no use for dreams, images, visions by night. No wonder he found it impossible to translate what he saw into the form of an earthly Menorah.

And no wonder he was totally taken aback when Bezalel could. "How could you do it?" he marvels at Bezalel. "God showed it to me so clearly again and again and I couldn't reproduce it. And you . . . you weren't even there? What did you see?"

"Twice he (Moses) ascended Mount Sinai to receive instructions from God, and twice he forgot the instructions on his descent. The third time, God took a Menorah of fire and showed him every detail of it and yet Moses found it hard to form a clear conception of the Menorah.

So he told Bezalel, and the latter immediately constructed it.

When Bezalel had no difficulty in executing it, Moses cried out in amazement: "To me it was shown ever so many times by the Holy One, blessed be He, yet I found it hard to make, and you who did not see it constructed it out of your own intelligence. Bezalel! Surely you must have been standing in the shadow of God (*bezel el*) when the Holy One, . . . showed me how to make it!" (Num. Rab. 10)

So much do the Rabbis read into a name that they say Bezalel was given the task of being the Architect of God's Temple because be was called Bezalel, which means "in the shadow of God." God prescribed and he was the mechanical shadow who executed.

Moses's was the highest vision of the Divine. But not everyone can express what he sees; according to Aristotle, it lies within the special province of art, through the act of mimesis, to go beyond the limits of rational human intelligence and immediately connect with a higher source. A vision to which the lonely saint can only aspire at moments can be handed down to a people through means of the plastic arts.

Already in the world of the Midrash, Bezalel's artistic skill was seen as linked to his gifts as a magician and an exponent of Kabbalah (the Jewish spiritual tradition) as well as to certain moral qualities.

Said R. Yehudah, said Rav: "Bezalel knew how to smelt (or permutate) the letters with which heaven and earth were created." (B. T., *Berakhot*, 55a based on Exod. 35: 30)

Through his skill in Kabbalah, he was able to tap into the forces that brought the world into being. With these he built the tabernacle in form of a microcosm, and with these he was able to fashion a Menorah that piped energies of light and blessing to the outermost corners of the entire world.

According to The Zohar, human art overlaps dramatically with the realm of magic and that of divine creativity. It seems that the proscription against creation of images, especially of human images in the second commandment also stems from an extension of the first prohibition in the Garden of Eden. Prohibition against making images of god or man and the prohibition against eating of the fruit of forbidden knowledge are extensions both of them of human presumption into the sphere of divine creativity. The kind of magical secret knowledge in question is the art of usurping the function of God by creating life. It is interesting to note that Rabbi Loewe of Prague is alleged to have succeeded at this task, with the one defect that his Golem lacked a soul.

However, such commands as "Build Me a sanctuary." "Let light shine from the lampstand" do a great deal to compensate for that restriction on human creativity and thirst for knowledge. It has been said that the kindling of the Menorah-lamp is the "fixing" of the prohibition against eating the fruit of the tree of knowledge. The Menorah, image of human potential realised to its fullest capacity in which light meets lamp and God meets man on man's homeground, is God's apology for the claustrophobic barriers of Eden.

There is a midrash that has Israel ask God concerning the "commandment to kindle": "Master of the world, how can You ask us to give light to You. You surely are the Light of the world and Brightness abides with You, Yet You say: "The lamp shall give light . . . " (Num. Rab. 15)

To the ever-repeated question as to why God, the "Light of all worlds" should require the kindling of the Menorah, the answer is given that it is the duty of the Community of Israel (the Beloved) to "give light back to God, as a blind man was asked to kindle a lamp in a house for a man who guided him to it."

What the Midrash is suggesting is that, though God certainly does not need anything man can do, yet He looks for certain forms of reciprocal behavior, "in order that you may give Me light as I give you light."

The Midrash says that "from the beginning of the world's creation, the Holy One longed to enter into partnership with flesh and blood. (Ber. Rab. 3: 9)

God gives light to the world, for it is written, And the earth did shine with His glory (Ezek. xliii, 2) yet did He command Israel THAT THEY BRING UNTO THEE PURE OLIVE OIL BEATEN FOR THE LIGHT — Why? So that "Thou wouldest have a desire for the work of Thy hands." (Job 14: 15) (Ex. Rab. 36: 4)

Here God desires Israel to do what He actually does Himself. One might think that since He is perfectly capable of doing these things, such as illuminating the world, why ask another to do them for Him. The answer is desire itself. God desires to create, not an object, but a relationship with a being who himself creates and kindles. . . .

The border line between the realms of man and of the gods in the ancient world was not clearcut. And the Serpent's reading of Genesis is very Greek, painting the portrait of a Creator who does not want to share such divine prerogatives as knowledge of good and evil, the ability to create life, and immortality with any of His creatures. All the

Serpent's arguments to Eve produce a black case against God rather than against man that has not entirely been dispelled by subsequent events. Unless one is reminded that God was generous enough to create man in His image in the first place!

On the one hand man is forbidden to make images; on the other hand, he is commanded to make images and kindle Menorot. But there is another kind of artistry that man is invited to undertake which shows that far from resenting human pretensions to creativity, in the appropriate context God welcomes and even requires them. Essentially, the internal work upon the soul is the real "work of the sanctuary," "work of the Menorah." Although it may be taboo to make a full physical image of the human being because he is an imitation of the Divine, this is only so because God actually wants him to fashion that image in its truest sense. God does not begrudge man the creativity of the gods but on the contrary to fashion the Divine image is actually what He requires him to do. God does not want man to make a "fixed" image of God, that is to say an idol, because He wants man's "image of God" to keep pace with his own spiritual progression. For what is the "image of God" after all, but man's gradually dawning awareness of Him! And that must be continually made and remade. God is not only inviting man to "remake" his own soul; he is also begging Him to "make" God's as well:

"If you walk in My statutes and keep My commands . . . then you will create with them. . . ."

"Whoever performs the commandments of the Torah and walks in its ways is regarded as if he makes Him above." The Holy One Blessed be He says: "(It is) as if he had made Me." (Lev. Rab. 35: 6)

Precisely the image that it is forbidden to make in one context (outside the Temple) it is God's supreme desire that we fashion within it. The very language that is used for the prohibition against imagemaking ("Thou shalt not make with Me" (Ex. 20: 23), which the Talmud said referred to "God's attendants," the sun and the moon in the heavens and the Menorah in the Temple) the Midrash employs in urgently recommending a particular style of imagemaking. Really the whole purpose of the creation is that man should "create with them" (the commandments standing for the divine attendants); the goal is for man to be creative also to the utmost of his ability, and that he should make the grandest image of all, the Image of God (that is the soul) out of the physical substance of reality. So, although it may be forbidden to make plastic images of God this is only because to carve out God Himself into the bedrock of creation is the very purpose of life.

One meaning of the Hebrew word *mitzva* (commandment) is "link"; yet another is "to sculpt" or "to hew"; It is as if the commandments themselves are so many chisels with which man will perfect not only his own soul, but God's image or "statue" in the world; with each practical commandment that is kept by each physical organ, the "image of God" is hewn and chipped out of the bedrock of the physical. By using his organs in God's service the individual is carving out at once the "Human Form Divine" of mankind, the "image of God," and he is also, as it were carving out the various dimensions and facets of God's spiritual body of light. By carrying out the Torah with his physical organs (allegedly numbering 613 to correspond with the 613 *Mitzvot*), man reintegrates these facets or *Parzufin* of Primordial Light and helps bring about a *Tikkun* or reintegration of the various faces of the Divine.[2]

Here God is visualised as having 613 faces and not, as in Ezekiel, a mere four. On the one hand He is one; on the other, in His relationship with the rich and diverse creation He has produced, He is infinitely versatile in His manifestations:

R. Levi said: The Holy One appeared to them as though He were a statue with faces on every side, so that though a thousand men might be looking at the statue, they would be led to believe that it was looking at each one of them. So, too, when the Holy One spoke, each and every person in Israel could say, "The Divine Word is speaking to me."

Note that Scripture does not say,, "I am your God," but "I am the Lord your God," (your very own God). Moreover, said R. Jose bar R. Hanina, the Divine Word spoke to each and every person according to his particular capacity. And do not wonder at this. For when manna came down for Israel, each and every person tasted it in keeping with his own capacity — infants in keeping with their capacity, young men in keeping with their capacity, and old men in keeping with their capacity. . . . (Pesikta de-Rav Kahane, Piska 12: 25)

Here the "Face" of God and the "Divine Word," that is to say, the Torah are interchangeable as the way God addresses and appears to man. And this "way" is manifold. Images for this unity-in-multiplicity of God and His manifestations or of the Torah and Her many inter-pretations is that of a jewel with many facets and rays, a burning coal, with many scintillations, the Menorah, with many individual lights and eyes, and the statue with a thousand faces.

Each irradiation or facet of this jewel or this figure is the limited perspective of an individual human being. Although where actual sculpture is concerned it is forbidden to make a multi-dimensional image of a man or a complete image of God (if that were possible!) in the spiritual realm this is precisely the aim — to transcend one's own limited perspective and achieve as complete a vision of the celestial Menorah as possible.

New York

NOTES

[1] Avodah Zara: 42c
[2] See Aryeh Kaplan, *Meditations and Kabbalah* (New York: 1982) pp. 210—11.

MARLIES KRONEGGER

REASON AND LAUGHTER: *JEANNE D'ARC AU BÛCHER* AND *LA DANSE DES MORTS*

> L'ordre est le plaisir de la raison,
> le désordre le délice de l'imagination.
> (Paul Claudel)[1]

I. CHAOS AND ORDER,
HISTORY AND CREATIVE IMAGINATION

While *Jeanne d'Arc au Bûcher* and *La Danse des Morts* do not give any objectifying explication which would make creation amenable to history and psychology, and while Claudel firmly holds that all his works unfold his creative imagination and not facts, there is the appeal of a poignant subtext, impossible to ignore in any performance and which has moved the audience to both tears and laughter. Both the historical division of countries into North and South and the emergence of an exceptional individual with a unique vocation were points of departure in the unfolding of Claudel's creative imagination. In *La Danse des Morts*, he refers to the division of Biblical Israel, in *Jeanne d'Arc au Bûcher*, to the antagonistic religious views which opposed North and South after the schism of Bâle in 1361 and to the voices of dissent when in 1429 an English King reigned in Paris; English forces occupied all the land from the Channel to the Loire, as well as the Duchy of Aquitaine. The powerful and autonomous Duke of Burgundy tolerated the invaders. Pestilence and famine, dissent, chaos, civil strife and warfare inspired painters and poets. Villon's obsessive visions of death and decay and frescoes of *danses macabres* on the walls of churches and cemeteries recorded the human condition of despair. In this period of bitterness there emerged Jeanne d'Arc. In the entire history of France there is no more stirring figure than the young peasant girl from Lorraine who became the soul of national resistance. She met with Charles VII at Chinon and informed him of her mission to save Orléans and to drive the English from the kingdom. She persuaded the hesitant king to be crowned and anointed at Reims on July 18, 1429. His support grew in the provinces of Champagne and Picardy. In May 1430

351

A-T. Tymieniecka (ed.), Analecta Husserliana, Vol. XXXVIII, 351—361.
© 1992 *Kluwer Academic Publishers. Printed in the Netherlands.*

Jeanne d'Arc went to Compiègne which was under the siege of the
Burgundians. There she was taken prisoner, later delivered to the
English, and convicted of witchcraft and heresy, burned at the stake in
Rouen, a city in hostile Normandy on May 30, 1431 without a gesture
of Charles VII to rescue her. The English were assisted by Bishop
Cauchon of Beauvais, a man divided within himself and completely
loyal to the Anglo-Burgundian party, not only in condemning Jeanne
d'Arc, but also in silencing the great wave of French patriotism against
foreign domination. Claudel's creative imagination has transfigured
these specific historic moments into eternal truth. He believes in the
life significance of his oratorios. Both sacred oratorios were performed
in 1938. Claudel and Honegger here stood in for politicians as the
conscience of the nation, awakening the national conscience and interpreting the national will. With them, theater is a vanishing point where
all the lines of force of the age meet, a seismograph of the times.
Dissent, treason and denunciation, the unjust hypocritically meticulous
trial, death and devastation put on stage in dissonant tonalities foreshadow and anticipate a chaotic human condition to come. France will
soon be amidst both material and spiritual disintegration and disaster.

II. EMOTION AGAINST REASON:
FROM TEXT TO PERFORMANCE

Claudel feels, sees, understands through antitheses. In both oratorios,
the scenes confronting each other are sometimes mischievously cheerful, maliciously gay or tender, elevating and spiritual. Each scene
evokes another kind of smile, grin or laughter which is sometimes
refreshing, sometimes destructive, but always an inner truth shows
forth. Laughter is the best instrument of liberation and for knowing the
truth.

Claudel and Honegger realize that the poles of theatrical text and
audience, together with the musical interaction which occurs between
them, and form the ground plan on which they have to build their
expectations of theatrical effect and response. No art exists only to
justify intelligence. Claudel's numerous essays on drama and music, on
Richard Wagner's *Gesamtkunstwerk* or on the Japanese Bunraku,
Bugaku, and the Noh theater focus on the immediacy of sound itself, on
a complete tonal and rhythmical reality, a totality of musical experiences. Music amplifies emotions. The Claudel-Honegger version of

Jeanne d'Arc au Bûcher expresses the continual rebirth of existence out of silence. Silence is not the opposite of speech, but the surrounding and therefore the setting-off element or climate of speech, which surges from, and returns to silence. Silence and language are as closely related as obscurity and light. Honegger confirms Claudel's musical directions: "Il me suffit d'écouter Claudel lire et relire son texte. Il le fait avec une telle force plastique que tout le relief musical s'en dégage, clair et précis, pour quiconque possède un peu d'imagination musicale . . . ."[2] The melodic line of the chorus, the spoken parts (of Jeanne d'Arc and Brother Dominique), the parts sung (by Marguerite and Catherine), the orchestra with traditional and modern instruments (including electronic soundwaves) is, in a polyphonic assemblage, capable of producing dynamic and affective relations of speed or slowness, of delay or anticipation which are very complex. In both oratorios there seem to be nothing but *intermezzi* composed of variable speeds of voices and floating effects.

The breath of life and its associations with music, rhythm, dance, and motion are central to Claudel and Honegger. Two considerations are fundamental to the understanding of rhythm. One is the force of gravity, and the other, the upward impulse in living beings: in *Jeanne d'Arc au Bûcher*, a sublime ascension, and in *La Danse des Morts*, a grotesque, carnavalesque and joyful resurrection leading to a renewal of faith. The audience listens to murmur, shouts, psalmody, crystalline heavenly voices, jazz and parodic atonalities, bells loud and soft, mocking ballet music and electronic sound waves. According to Claudel, words and feelings merge in "une tapisserie sonore . . . elle est pour l'oreillece que la toile de fond est pour le regard."[3] The rhythm of each scene precedes language and creates a spirtual tension with the color and flavor of sounds. The rhythm and orchestration of voices take more time than psychological instances. Claudel and Honegger refuse to set alexandrines to music: they are monotonous and as sterile as reason. With them, the iambic verse expresses the protagonists' breath of life, the movements of the soul and emotions which stir the imagination and sensibility of the audience. And the actor Jean-Louis Barrault confirms Claudel's conviction: "nous devons nous adresser à la poitrine du public plutôt qu'à sa tête."[4] Language, supported by music, is linked with Claudel and Honegger to breath, gesture, and attitudes rather than abstract thought.

III. THE INDIVIDUAL VOCATION

Amidst the chaos of dissonant noises and voices, Jeanne awakens at the summit of her life. The best way to understand life is from a summit. This summit is the stake on which Jeanne d'Arc, chained to a pillar, will be burned (scene 1). She relives essential experiences of her life in examination of her past, trying to understand how her inner forces and conviction guided her out of darkness to light. Claudel explains his interest in her vocation: "Chaque âme porte en elle des forces inconnues qui ont besoin de se manifester."[5]

The prologue creates the ambiance and anticipates both her earthly condemnation, heavenly ascension and redemption. Antagonistic voices rise from an undistinguished murmur: Yblis' desperate voice from hell, rendered in electronic sounds, penetrates the darkness of night, counterbalanced by a nightingale, the voice of hope. Jeanne's silence opens questions: why? wherefore? whereby? where? how? She emerges out of darkness, when a voice is calling her: Jeanne, Jeanne, Jeanne. This call of her name consecrates her. Her solemn gesture, the sign of the cross, sanctifies her mission which she is going to relive in retrospect. Her gesture holds a spiritual meaning and moves with solemnity. One feels that a mysterious and formidable power stirs and pushes her. The gesture is grandiose and majestic because it is the fulfillment of a divine mission. For Claudel, Jeanne's symbolic gesture of the cross moves across East and West, South and North, following her itinerary from Domrémy, Arras to Orléans, from Orléans to Compiègne and Rouen, or if we transpose Tymieniecka's words into Jeanne's context to understand her mission and to explain an exceptional vocation, "she set out from nowhere like the sun in the twilight zone, advanced to her zenith" in Orléans and Reims, "and finally lost the absorbing force of that luminosity in the flames of her own body" in Rouen.[6] Claudel isolates the vocation of Jeanne d'Arc on purpose. Elsewhere he compares her call to the creative poetic sparkle and freshness of both Rimbaud and Péguy.[7] Each of them had listened to inner voices in resistence to exterior pressures — to opaque materialism in the case of Rimbaud, and to a foreign intruder in the case of Péguy who, born in Orléans, the city where Jeanne defeated the English, also like Jeanne d'Arc gave his life for his country — at the Marne.

To unite, rather than to divide, is also the mission of other protagonists such as of Christopher Colombus as Claudel explains: "Une vie, une vocation, une destinée, la plus sublime qui soit, celle de l'inventeur d'un nouveau monde et du réunisseur de la Terre de Dieu se déploie sur la scène . . ."[8] The unification of France, the unification of the visible and invisible worlds link Jeanne's vocation to Christ's divine mission in Israel, a theme of *La Danse des morts*: "Afin que Je sois Un en vous et que vous soyez Un en Moi, comme Mon père et Moi, Nous sommes Un, parce que Un est nécessaire. Prends un morceau de bois et écris dessus: Éphraïm! Et cela fait une croix et Je m'étendrai dessus, car Je ne suis pas venu dissoudre et résoudre et diviser, mais remplir!"[9] The children of Israel will become one nation thanks to Christ's acceptance of the cross.

In a radical self-examination, Jeanne realizes that her vocation was to confront the world and transform it in climbing the cross herself. Invincible, inalienable and irreplaceable, she has collaborated with the Creator in her will to consecrate the unity of France and to accomplish the highest hope of life — love of the other and the sacrifice of life for the other. She has become the mediator between the natural and the supernatural as she stands at the fringe of two worlds (scene 2), out of one of which she originated and which she has surpassed with the greatest exertion of the spirit. The new, world presaged by Brother Dominique, a witness of her accomplishments, is as alien to her as the worlds from which she has come. While the world of earthly voices is polluted, Jeanne knows how to conquer pollution.

In the following scenes, the voices of Heaven and Hell confront each other. Brother Dominique comes down from Heaven to claim justice for Jeanne whose life is the book she has written, even though she does not know how to read. In later scenes, she is all at once the play-wright, heroine, actress, and spectator of her accomplishments when she reconstructs the meaning of her life. Her transnatural destiny and her messianic mission confirm that suffering lies at the roots of life. Through her sacrifice, encouraged by hope, faith and love, harmony will be restored. She knows how to listen to her vocation, and like a stained glass window, she becomes a prism of light and color, and like a cathedral, the receiver of the direct intervention of the Divine which speaks to her and whose echo she becomes. Her faith, hope, love and charity are privileged states. Her spiritual world, echoed in a chorus of innocent children, and in the soprano and alto voices of Catherine and

Marguerite, open the infinite harmony, the triumphant restoration and realization of the values of good and beauty, wherein the rules of Logos are overwhelmed by music in a hymn to joy, faith and love.

IV. MODALITIES OF REASON, MODALITIES OF LAUGHTER:
A PARODY WITHIN A PARODY

With mockery and affection Claudel has recreated the trial and judgment of Jeanne d'Arc as a living present. He clothes his most heartfelt concerns and reverence for justice in irony. He evokes truth in contradiction, since contradiction is the most soberly logical element in human reasoning. Jeanne relives in a flashback the beginning of the trial (scene 3). The voices of Earth, in sarcastic outbursts, sustained by malicious, dissonant, musical atonalities demand vengeance, calling Jeanne a heretic, witch, sorceress and relapse. From now on, official seriousness constitutes a field of immanence putting the war machine at work against Jeanne. The supporters of order and law are theologians of the Sorbonne and accomplices of the English. A parody within a parody reveals Claudel's deep appreciation of laughter. Why do people laugh? At what do they laugh? Why don't the so-called serious rational defenders of justice never laugh? How can the audience grasp the deepest meaning of Claudel's parody?

Trumpets announce the arrival of the court of justice. Soon, Cochon or *porcus* in latin (referring to the historical Archbishop Cauchon of Beauvais) will be appointed chief justice, Praeses. Sheep are his jury and Ass his scribe or secretary-witness. Notorious Lion, Fox and Snake refuse their participation and as such naturally eliminate their essential qualities: powerful, sly, and poisonous attributes. These qualities are not needed any more at the trial. Spokesmen of both the Sorbonne and the English occupation have asses pull the people's cart. The chorus bursts into a malicious grin, when Porcus-Cochon, the authoritarian and despotic Praeses opens the trial. Cochon's inductive reasoning can only provide repetition of data postulated by reason. He is the voice of sclerosed intellect, armed with Latin rhetorics and a fossilized, self-sufficient, brutal language. His task is to demonstrate axiomatic principles for burning Jeanne d'Arc at the stake, declaring her a heretic, sorceress, and relapse, all in defense of his own narrow, dogmatic, fanatic and political views. Appealing to the Sheep, in this case the public, he easily wins them over: a scapegoat offers an opportunity for festivities

which will saturate some of their appetites and lust for sensation. Even
though Praeses is nothing but a trickster, this hypochondriac is awarded
the applause and appreciation of the cheerful Sheep when he reads in
Latin his accusations of Jeanne d'Arc who does not understand Latin.
Praeses works like a machine operator. Being the center of gravity, he is
a force which develops by circular irradiation in all directions, committing himself to his routine. Jeanne admits to having defeated the English,
but without the help of the devil. Scribe Ass, on the contrary, writes
down that she says "yes." The punishment of Jeanne d'Arc is what
revenge and political justice demand. Monomaniac Praeses Porcus,
Scribe Ass and Sheep rely on the same postulate or concise formula.
They all feign a good conscience with a lie, again accusing Jeanne of
heresy, sorcery and relapse. They impose the rational constitutive system
of moral codes and prejudices of the period, based on objective and
preestablished structures, codes and prejudices putting it at the service
of their innate nature (egoism, stupidity, and sheepishness). Egoism,
envy, jealousy, hatred dominating the greater part of human deeds, be
they individual, social or national, they revert, without deliverance, back
to their cruel animality. Self-centered desires are a substitute for mind.
Cochon's ideology insinuates itself readily for the public, in this case
the chorus of sheep, is ready to swallow the ideological pill in order to
kill time and enjoy themselves. The mob is unhappy without immediate
results. The actualization of their greed and appetites makes them
happy for they are captive to their peculiar attraction to any diversion,
such as seeing Jeanne d'Arc burned alive at the stake.

   The atmosphere of this parody of justice, the justice of the victors
over Jeanne d'Arc, is suffused by the cheerful folkloristic tunes of
the market square and modern jazz, interspersed with spoken words
in both Latin and the vulgar French of the Sheep. Once again we
hear Yblis screaming in despair in hell, in a deep abyss, in anticipation of Jeanne's torments and suffering. The dehumanized confusion
which this mixture of musical elements suggests, is an image of both
contradiction and intoxicating joy which emanate from Praeses Porcus,
Scribe Ass, and the jury of Sheep. Dazzling and dizzying, this particular
scene has left many spectators on the floor bewildered and infected
with a contagious laughter at the trial. Theirs is a laughter of relief with
the sudden showing forth of an inner truth when the audience recognizes the corruption of human reason and will, the fallibility and deceptive nature of what passes for official truth. All this shows that Claudel

was a great humorist, when he created on stage the mock reality of the juridical system. Laughable are those who take themselves too seriously, and who like Praeses Porcus, appoint themselves supreme judges: his "moi, moi, moi" sounds like a lit torch, a torch that reflects his relaxed conscience and makes itself the center of attention. Irreverent, caricaturing and parodying tunes and mocking ballet music, a raucous interlude, introduces the "Play of Cards." The cardplay is a hedonistic interruption, a kind of pleasure discharge for Jeanne's opponents who reveal the truth of their essential characteristics in this particular game. The players are solemnly introduced: the four Kings with the attributes of stupidity, ambition, avarice and death. They change their positions, but not their queens whose natural inclinations of Lust remain immanent and dissonant as the music underscores their generalized coded narcissism. Their servants who committed high treason against France play chords in allegro, in a mocking, don't care attitude in enjoyment of the players distraction from boredom. In the vicious deformity of these player-puppets and in the light music which surrounds them, their inner truth shows forth: grinning and arrogant, we see their passions flare up in a weird sort of debauchery and paraxysms of mirth. The game of cards signifies politics in miniature: Kings, queens and their valets play their game as did the historical traitors of Jeanne d'Arc. For Jeanne things are moving irrevocably in the direction ordained by the card players for whom she has "lost"; nothing can forestall her doom.

V. LAUGHTER AND HAPPINESS

The following scene introduces us to the innocent happiness of simple peasants, Heurtebise and Mother Tonneaux, who symbolically renew, rejuvenate and restore the unity of France on a very sensuous level. Laughter is the best medication against sclerosed dogmatism, didactic, authoritarian and intimidating reason. Laughter is the organizing principle of Claudel's vision of the world. It is laughter which introduces expressivity in the audience, which is not the same as intelligibility. Heurtebise, from the North of France, and Mother Tonneaux, from the South, regenerate the vitality and happiness of the people who enjoy the material abundance of wine and corn in folkloristic dance and song. Their joviality breaks down social barriers and their *joie de vivre* is a source of life. Their respective dialects speak their hearts: whether from North or South, they speak and sing in a free, frank, and familiar language; in affirmation of simple life, they enjoy bread and wine for immediate consumption. Their wholehearted laughter and *joie de vivre* relieves the audience who joins in their happiness. With them, the mask of seriousness, hypocrisy and dogmatism, worn by Jeanne's accusers, has been replaced by what Claudel calls the heroic expression of the joy of life. For him, "la farce est la forme exaspéerée du lyrisme et de l'expression héroïque de la joie de vivre."[10] Rebirth and joy, the sensuous relief of carefree happiness anticipated another level of harmony, when Jeanne d'Arc has finally accepted without hesitation her sacrifice and converts the entire chorus of voices from antagonistic enemies into her joyful supporters, who finally join her in a hymn to joy, hope and love, while her body is consumed in flames and dissolved in ashes. While her reality wastes away, her flesh agonizing in the flames, the unification of France that she has accomplished moves the audience to tears. She remains the inspiration of her people, as she gave her life for those who made her suffer.

In *La Danse des morts*, Claudel's sense of humour transforms the macabre dances of death into a joyful, liberating, and regenerating occasion. The opening scene in the desert, inspired by Ezekiel, is filled with the convulsions of apparently skinless bones without flesh, nerves or spirit. Creative artists from Callot, Holbein to Dürer and Bosch, and composers from Bach to Hindemith and Stravinsky were fascinated by the theme.

The atmosphere is charged with a thunderstorm at the opening of this oratorio in anticipation of a carnavalesque and grotesque resurrection of the dead. The music evokes a hilarious challenge, when the announcer convokes the army of the dead to start to march. There are disharmonious whistles among the chorus' murmuring voices while all of a sudden the well-known tune "Sur le pont d'Avignon" is heard in a distorted version: "Sur le pont de la tombe, on y danse." Well-known personalities, King, Pope, Bishop, Knight, Philosophers pass by in a lighthearted whirlwind of tonalities from which emerges the Carmagnole and a frantic ballet overshadowed by the piercing sound of a trumpet.

The lament, the plaintive voice of the violin introduces the twisted, tortured voice of a baritone who sings that Our Lord should remember him, that as he comes from dust he will return to dust. The chorus then enforces a lamentation of despair. A dialogue of soprano and alto voices evokes Christ's Passion. A mounmental truth, supported by the orchestra refers to the divine promise to Peter that the future church will be built on him who is a rock. The following rhythms are falling, then rising to the soprano's tears of ecstacy when she assures the Christian that our Redeemer lives. While social distinctions have disappeared, Claudel proposes to laugh — why should we take death so seriously? With vitality he enforces a recovery from fear and anxiety and rejects any prefabricated perceptive code. Claudel invites us to recover the vitality which *La Danse des morts* radiates.

Thus, the aesthetic law of contrast, of negative and positive reactions which show forth in a smile, a grin, and laughter at or laughter with somebody, attains a state of equilibrium and ultimate poise in both oratorios when the conflict of elemental forces, the discordant manifoldness of aggression, hatred, and death wishes for the other are transcended in hymns to joy, love, and hope. Modern dramatists from Claudel to Genet assert that the Catholic rituals are the greatest theater. On the eve of the outbreak of World War II, the words and music of both oratorios return theater to the community. Burgeoning nationalism marked a renewed interest in Jeanne d'Arc and of the dances of death. Claudel and Honegger realized that something terrible was going to happen, though it was still an undercurrent as yet rather than something visible. Their creations brought subtle pressure to bear on the powers that will soon govern the North and South of divided France. Amidst death and destruction one kept waiting for an exceptional individual to emerge whose pristine spontaneity, burst of energy, and exalted pursuit of absolute values could transfigure the spiritual wasteland into a land of hope, love, harmony and equilibrium.

Michigan State University

NOTES

[1] Paul Claudel. *Théâtre*, II (Pleïade, 1965), p. 154. *Jeanne d'Arc au Bûcher* was first performed in Bâle on May 6, 1939, and later in Orléans and in Bruxelles in 1940 and 1946, in Paris in 1942 and 1951. Claudel visited Bâle in January 1938 in preparation of the stage production of *Jeanne d'Arc*. In the museum there, paintings of Holbein's *Danses macabres* inspired him to write the oratorio which was to be set to music by Honegger and completed on May 23, 1938.

[2] Pierre Meylan. *Honegger, son oeuvre et son message* (Frauenfeld: Verlag Huber, 1970); French translation 1982, p. 77, Pierre Brunel. "Théâtre et musique: *Jeanne*

d'Arc au Bûcher", *La Dramaturgie claudélienne* (Paris: Klincksieck, 1988), pp. 159–167.

[3] *Oeuvres en prose* (Pleïade, 1965), p. 150.

[4] Jean-Louis Barrault, *Souvenirs pour demain* (Paris: Seuil, 1972), p. 193.

[5] *Oeuvres en prose*, p. 65.

[6] A-T. Tymieniecka. *Logos and Life*. Book III: *The Passions of the Soul and the Elements in the Onto-Poiesis of Culture* (Dordrecht: Kluwer Academic Publishers, 1990).

[7] *Oeuvres en prose*, p. 149.

[8] *Théâtre*, II, p. 1266.

[9] *Ibid.*

[10] *Oeuvres en prose*, p. 203.

CARMEN BALZER

CREATIVE IMAGINATION AND DREAM

INTRODUCTION

A deepened analysis of the creative process in man discovers the necessary link between creative imagination and dream. But we can never deny the intervention of two other elements — play and chance. These three dimensions of creative imagination make up its production mechanism. Such peculiar "mechanics", however, are not contrary to the inner freedom arising spontaneously in the spirit of every human creator, no matter if he is an artist, an inventor or a common man, provided he manages to transcribe what is aesthetic to the field of life.

The freedom we are putting forward here offers analogies to that of Immanuel Kant's in his "Critique of Judgement". For the German philosopher, the interplay between the mental functionality of the representative understanding — excluding what is conceptual — and the imaginative schemes eventually leads to the agreement of the imagination with the understanding, i.e., to the agreement of the object with the imagination and the understanding. Art understood in this way impresses on us the effect of nature and at the same time frees us from it. At issue here is not only the freedom "to" — we should understand "to" reach the aesthetical judgement and "to" produce the work of art — but also the freedom "from", since it abolishes spiritual and psychical slaveries which constrain the unhindered development of the artistic and aesthetic personality, either the creator-artist's or the contemplator-spectator's. Such a spontaneity of play between the psychic powers, from whence the aesthetic enjoyment at the agreement springs, establishes — following Kant's thought — the link between nature and freedom, which before were divorced between the *Critique of Pure Reason* and the *Critique of Practical Reason*. For that very reason and always in the aesthetic field, the mind enjoys itself and creates for itself a world over nature. Thus, nature's beauty is ultimately reducible to the aesthetic and artistic one, since its harmony with the free play of our faculties, i.e., its harmony with the free play of our faculties of knowing, "seems to us" an objective purpose of nature; nevertheless, that inten-

363

A-T. Tymieniecka (ed.), Analecta Husserliana, Vol. XXXVIII, 363–375.
© 1992 *Kluwer Academic Publishers. Printed in the Netherlands.*

tional purpose we assign to nature is just the work of the subject contemplating it; it then corresponds to the aesthetic contemplation of it, "creatively" exercised by a contemplator.

Freedom understood as "free play", as we have just seen in Kant, also plays a role in dream. Rather than relating dream to imagination, we shall relate it to fantasy, since it is suitable to invert the link imagination-fantasy, as conceived by Coleridge, into the link fantasy-imagination. We believe, in fact, that fantasy is the properly creative psychic force, since it is fantasy which makes use of the resources of metaphoric associations, oppositions, intensification or attenuation, applying them to the materials in the memory, where they have been stored, and from where they are in time retrieved, at the gestation of the poetic innovation. Fantasy handles that unclaimed property, trans-forming it until a new creature is formed — a work of art. At the same time, fantasy also plays a part in the work of art that man is for himself, when at the ethical level he becomes the author of his own personality; or in the crystallization of scientific inventions. Indeed, fantasy is needed to do any truly creative work. In all these cases, it goes beyond the beaten paths and the stereotyped schemes.

Dream as the factor giving momentum to creativity not only marks the limits of a domain favorable to fantasy, which in it frees itself from the hindrances imposed by the logic and rational laws of the state of wakefulness, but is also co-gestator of the new creature — the work of art.

The oneiric fantasy, even though not yet perfectly conscious of itself and moving in timelessness, ultimately represents the starting point of all consciousness, of all temporality and, for that very reason, also of all history and vital argument — this latter, of course, inserted in the destiny of human existence. María Zambrano says: "For man, every-thing around him is the face of an argument that is gradually outlined or that in a moment becomes visible".[1] Thus, following the Spanish philosopher's thought, that true argument which is always accompanied by birth and by death, takes form in a figuration which needs to be constantly actualized, even in dreams, primarily in dreams. Such a figurative function appears spontaneously in history. But the creative mode as such is revealed in arguments where this history shows its sense and is transformed in salutory poetry: tragedy, novel or pure poetry.

When Zambrano refers to "the person's dreams", she shows how the action put forward in them "is an awakening of the person's intimate depth, that ungraspable depth from which the person is, if not a mask, a figure which may be undone and redone . . ."[2] Indeed, the action put forward is a poetic action, creative, of a work and of the person himself, who in that way gradually reveals his own face. That is why she concludes that the person's dream is in principle a creative dream, "which announces and requires that transcendent awakening and which may even contain it at the highest level of the dream scale".[3]

DREAM'S TWO SPRINGS

If we conceive dream as Jacques Vidal does,[4] we must stress its relationship to symbol, i.e., we must discover it as the symbol's domain. This approach discloses dream's double spring: as dream in sleep and as dream in wakefulness, when daylight does not turn out the imagination's light. In this case, the imagination, freed from the coactions of the thinking and working spirit, tries communication. Its living images, then, become characters at the mercy of history's vicissitudes. That is Vidal; Zambrano, instead, referring to nighttime or sleeper's dreams, completes the preceding reasoning, saying: "Dreams express as theorems the person's places, his personal life's environs, from where the person must come out, through time, in the exercise of freedom".[5] The same author, as regards wakefulness, points out that only during it "the subject trails behind him his own character, the one which has been unconsciously formed with its corresponding conflict . . . Under it, and accompanied by it, the subject acts. But his action shall only be true action if it manages to modify the conflict which in dreams is ordered to him".[6] That is why the communication by oneiric imagination through the characters necessarily leads from the person's sleeping state to his wakeful state. What here appears as highly significant is that in this intermediate state between dreaming and awakening the vicissitudes of man's history, inseparable from his destiny, are indeed played out.

Usually dream unites materials having deep origins, in a primordial image, with materials coming from images and remembrances of conscious life. On the other side, it seems to condense, distribute or transfer unused energy. From this there results a composition which the wakeful spirit is unable to understand except through an anamnesis and an interpretation. That is the reason why dream's domain involves the preliminaries of an understanding of images and symbols, i.e., the exercise of a memory which brings together the primordial time of a genesis and the present time of an accomplishment.

In the second place, it is pertinent to underline the contribution of the words involved in dreams; indeed, what is oneiric makes up an audiovisual mental universe. It not only has eyes to see the invisible, but also ears to hear the inaudible, the soul's eyes and ears just where it merges with the spirit. Dream, so conceived, is then not merely the inner spiritual domain of repressed wishes, which are symbolically expressed there according to Freud's thesis, but is also and perhaps mainly the antechamber of the spirit, even though this may happen in a hidden and not explicit way, more as an announcement than as a reality. This light which usually appears in the middle of the night and of bodily spaces and which emerges from there in the glory of the image, passes in dream to the word that is the spirit itself. But it is a different word for a different spirit, its sense can not be reduced to discourse. It may be a silent word, the dynamics of a secret and inner word that does not yet reach the visionary level.

DREAM'S PHENOMENOLOGY

A greater clarity and better characterization of dreams arises from the phenomenological analysis Jean Paul Sartre does in *l'Imaginaire* (Paris: Gallimard, 1940). The French existentialist's radical thesis lies in the categorical opposition between the perceptive attitude of the affirmation of reality and the timeless domain, lacking freedom, of dreams, where the dreamer is trapped in the endless chain of images launched in a frantic race, which are generated by the fascinating oneiric object. From the start, there is for Sartre no possible transition from the oneiric state to the state of perceptive wakefulness which hosts the sensible reality. They are two different intentional attitudes. He further rejects any linkage between irreality, concentrated in the oneiric world, and reality, corresponding to the state of perceptive-wakefulness which is expressed in man's conscious attitude before the world. The oneiric cosmos, then, does not build any bridges toward spatio-temporal outwardness; it is, moreover, deprived of any substantial hold and for that very reason is trapped in the sphere of the "as if", of pure fiction, which draws it somehow nearer — as is very suggestively shown by the famous author of "La Nausée" — to the detective novel, par excellence a fascinating literary genre, since it captivates the reader with chase advantures which give him no respite. This, at the oneiric level, is translated into the chase without respite of the sleeper by the dreamed images. Unlike Sartre, María Zambrano admits the transition from the timeless sleeping state to the temporal state of wakefulness, without rejecting the possibility of this latter's hosting a dream: the wakeful dream, either the "doze" before falling into true sleep or the "reverie", a type of daytime wandering. For the Spanish thinker, in fact, it is impossible to separate dreaming sleep from "awakening" to temporal and ontologic reality. Indeed, this predisposition of dreaming to awakening is dialectically linked, by means of a play of oppositions, to Parmenides' equation "being = immobility = plenitude", as opposed to "time = freedom = reality"; but the passage from one reality (that of dream) to the other (that of the perceptible and temporal world) in fact always takes place. The same can be said of the inverse process. The feasibility of that passage involves at the same time a being "oriented to", "that foreseeable purpose of History" — an oneiric destiny, in which from an original condition of the enclosure of being in the motherly womb, one tends to the exit, to emerging from the bowels, to one's own manifestation. From here comes the action, the doing and accomplishing. Such a thing is particularly evident about dreams or visions appearing during wakefulness, since they make up a repertoire, a true "hieroglyphic alphabet", according to Zambrano.[7] This is what she calls "real dreams".

When we look at dreams, at their beginning or at their nighttime character, we inevitably discover their timelessness and their lack of freedom, especially for the dreamer involved in them. Timelessness, Zambrano thinks, is the a priori of dreams separating them from the state of wakefulness. However, through the already mentioned "real dreams", "it becomes clear that in timelessness itself there somehow takes place the 'transcendency' which is its sign of what is specifically human".[8] Now, this "transcending" arising from real dreams, in order to accomplish itself, finds the way to creation through the word. This fact, in turn, does not exclude the possibility of the "transcendentality" of dreaming's taking place in other creative genres that do not become actual through the word, for instance, painting. But we think that only the word, the essential feature of man, since it is the perfect actualization of freedom, can give this poetic legitimacy to dreaming. And this is so — always in our own thinking — because although the word is not the only human expressive mode in art and even in other cultural domains,

it is nevertheless the foundation of them all. For example, what is pure
gesture — the mime's facial sign, the dancer's bodily or kinematic sign,
the painter's or singer's or sculptor's manual or vocal sign, the musician's
pure sound sign, all that is based in the mute and silent gesture or the
auditive-expressive one — does not have sense in itself and is incommu-
nicable, unless it is in some way translated into language, into words.
That is why Zambrano thinks that in poetic creation and its archetypal
genres may be the genesis of a kind of the poetic categories of human
living. In such genres — the Spaniard's thinking goes on — is enclosed
and accomplished the identification of the spontaneous transcending of
the human being in life with a work created by him.

Such an identification, in its whole, shows itself only if the content of
some kind of dreams is admitted — Zambrano's real dreams — and
dreaming itself is seen as the primary form in which the human being's
essential situations manifest it to him, i.e., as the first form of consciousness.

Once again we are urged to recognize the intimate connection
between dreaming and awakening, which is, however, inadmissible for
Sartre since in his phenomenology awakening would mean an overwhelming break with what is oneiric, a destruction of the dream's world
or atmosphere, and for that very reason, a positioning of the subject in
what is real, in what is perceptive.

According to Zambrano, instead, "dreams come from awakening;
they are already an awakening, and if it were not so, wakefulness would
have no place for them".[9] But undoubtedly, even this kind of creative
dreams — those carrying in themselves a germ of the poetic word giving
them legitimacy — do not fail to have an obsessing character. They trail
a "being so". A conflict without apparent exit, an aporia. The Spanish
thinker then remarks that the subject remains enclosed by a magic
circle, similar to the circle found in life as a whole, one which also
encloses beings in its interiority. That is why life itself appears to be a
magical circle to be transcended. This is a transcendency which is only
accomplished by living.

Simultaneously and gradually, symbols shall take form in dreams,
and this takes place just when the oneiric images enter reason. In fact,
"symbol is already reason" within this perspective.[10] But only when an
image loaded with meaning enters reason does it acquire the plenitude
of its symbolic character; only then is its meaning fully accepted by

consciousness. If it were not so, Zambrano points out, it would be, "just a fetish, a magical figure reluctant to enter reason".

When we embark under these conditions on the task of deciphering the oneiric image, we lead it to the light of consciousness and reason, "accompanying it from the dark place, from the 'atemporal' hell where it lies".[11] But, undoubtedly, this kind of reason welcoming the oneiric image, translating it to symbol, is a very special reason. It is wide and total, it is poetic reason and at the same time metaphysical and religious. Only in this way can it reach an understanding with the dark side of dreams which are the dawn of consciousness.

There is, then, a very close link between creative dreaming and the poetic accomplishment which involves man in his essence. Consequently, "poetically accomplishing oneself is entering the realm of freedom and time, without violence. When dreams accomplish themselves, 'emerging from the bowels' — according to Zambrano's widely commented on expression[12] — then the human being recognizes himself and rescues himself, leaving, in transforming himself, the darkness of the bowels and keeping his secret already felt in light".[13]

It is then evident that from dream comes out not only a movement towards consciousness and daytime reality, but that there is also a reverse movement from reality or from real dreams back to dreaming. Only from this latter movement do we become familiar with dreams' true nature, both in their symbolic and creative value. Dynamism runs between both oneiric ends: that of nighttime dream and that of daytime dream, real and creative. The former, the sleeper's dream thus appears as an omen, a herald of reality, of conscious life, and as a place for the concentration of a material precious for daytime dreaming. The latter, in turn, at the opposite end of the oneiric land, points to the nighttime or sleeper's dream, since it is capable of enlightening it in retrospect and explaining symbolically — though not rationally — its meaningful contents.

Thus we confirm the interpenetration of dreaming and wakefulness — one emerges inside the other and this latter in turn points to the former. On the one hand, reality calls upon dreams, awakening the sleeper; on the other, dream itself penetrates through the "pores" of reality, making the being in man explicit. "Dream, dreams, are not the presentation of a certain argument above all, but its means, its form, the content of which may be made up of images corresponding to wakefulness's perceptions . . . , and thus dreaming takes place not only when one sleeps, it appears in wakefulness, dotting it, piercing it. Its ways of presenting itself in sleeping and in wakefulness are, to a certain extent, opposite".[14]

Zambrano highlights still other features of what is oneiric. Thus, for instance, in the nighttime or sleeper's dream, dreams appear as an awakening, as a form of vision and of consciousness, where the subject feels as if he had been touched and even called by an arriving visitor. Unlike wakefulness, the dreaming state takes place imperceptibly for the subject. The effects of wakeful dreaming may be double: on the one hand, its contents may become a germ of obsession and alteration of reality; on the other, as soon as the contents of wakeful dreaming are transferred to the right place in consciousness, where consciousness and soul symbolically join, they come to be germs of creation in the process of personal life, or detaching themselves from it, in a creative work.

Moreover, parallel to dreaming, man reveals his being, a being suffering his own transcendency like the being transcending its initial dream.

Man, indeed, on this oneiric level, expresses in an evident way the existence in him of what has been called freedom. He has it not when he has already woken up, but in awakening itself. Freedom awakens him.

Consequently, we may perhaps accept with Sartre that in dreams man lives in timelessness and is then prisoner of the need of oneiric determinism; nevertheless, it can not be denied that as a transcendency towards awakening — since according to Zambrano "the initial dream is awakened along the successive awakenings" — he is pushed towards daytime reality, fluid and historic, where he makes himself freely, this time supported by wakefulness's creative dream. In this way the germ of freedom sprouts from the fertile earth of dreams, which on its opposite ends — the initial or original and the wakeful or creative — touch one another and merge into one another. This climate of dream impregnates a novel like *Don Quixote*. Cervantes, its author, in his work obeys his dream, and does so basically — according to the Iberian thinker's thesis — by seeing himself in his creatures, dreaming himself, recreating himself in his characters. But these characters suffer and actualize the dream of freedom. That is why Don Quixote starts his journey at dawn; he is indeed a character suffering in an exemplary way the dream of freedom, that dream which at a certain time, so uncertain, breaks loose in man.

DREAM AND HOPE

María Zambrano, Ernst Bloch, the philosopher of "what is not yet", to characterize him in a few words, defends daytime dreaming — *der Traum nach vorwärts* — as a truly creative dream. But what Bloch does not accept is the relationship the Spaniard establishes between "initial dream" and "creative dream", since for him only the second one is anticipatory, i.e., a "forward dream", while the other is paralyzed in an archaic past. The German philosopher holds on to only the daytime dreams, since only in them do advancements take place and only in them "the future land is trodden", the land of what-has-not-yet-been-conformed, what-has-not-yet-come-to-be, only they promote being and actualization. Bloch uses metaphysical images highly accurate and moving. One of them, for instance, is the "castle in the air". This should not be understood as a preliminary state of the nighttime labyrinths; rather, nighttime labyrinths are found to be cellars under the "castles in the air", as we read in *The Principle of Hope*, his capital work.[15] This means that we truly dream only in the daytime, only then are the "castles in the air" built, art created, utopias thought; nighttime dreaming, in contrast, is something secondary, never primary, labyrinthic and deprived of light. The same opposition, both terms of which oppose the positive in daytime-oneiric to the nighttime-oneiric, emerges in the following passage: "The presumed equality of the fantastic happiness, both here and there, is it not to be understood as the reestablishment of independence in the derivation of pleasure as regards assent in reality? More than once, given enough energy and experience, daytime dreaming has managed to rebuild reality in accord with this consent; while Morpheus has no arms but those on which he rests".[16]

For all the above mentioned reasons, Bloch demands a specific valuation of "daytime dreaming", since only it can enter a wholly different domain and open it up. This kind of dream comprises a wide range of types: from daydreaming, which is puerile, comfortable, coarse, escapist, equivocal and paralyzing, to responsible dreaming, which penetrates sharply and actively the thing and reaches artistic embodiment; thus dreaming may contain an untiring impulse oriented to the accomplishment of what fantasy has painted.

In contrast, in "nighttime dreams" nothing new happens, their contents are hidden and distorted. In "daytime fantasy", instead, "the contents are open, fabulating, anticipatory and what is latent in them is to be found ahead ... it comes from the widening of itself and of the world, it is a wish to have the best, a wish to know more".[17]

Even if daytime fantasy starts as a nighttime dream, out of wishes, unlike this latter, it "brings them dramatically to the end, tends to the place where they reach satisfaction".[18] Bloch's antithesis could be summarized in the binomial: nighttime dream — childish dream, turned to the past and merely repetitive as regards hallucinatory images, and daytime dreaming or daydreaming — adult dream, which does not recover a forgotten past, but transcends the present in search of an ideal future. It is in this "daydreaming", the second term of the binomial, that a "not-yet-conscious" becomes evident, something that has not existed nor been consciously held in the past, a drawning towards the future, towards what is "new". Also underlined in this approach is the importance given by Bloch to utopia, one form taken by "the will to reach a good end", by means of which consciousness is penetrated by unforgettable fabulous creatures in literature, and dreams are worked out in the outline of a better future; but also — and this should be understood once and for all — *suo modo*, in works of art. The world-perfecting fantasy appears in them, and not carrying men and things to the limits of their possibilities, exhausting and giving consumate form to all their situations. In fact, according to Bloch: "Every work of art, rather rests not only on its manifest essence, but also on a latency within the face of things to come, i.e., on the contents of a future which had not yet appeared at the time".[19] The creative sense of imagination or fantasy, as revealed in daytime dreaming, then, points at a "going towards", at a hope of accomplishment, rather than at a reality. This Blochian hope stays, then, in the pure process of the accomplishment of man in the world and the accomplishment of the world in man. That is why the "daytime dream", as a preliminary state of art, tends all the more clearly to the perfecting of the world; this is indeed its real and active nucleus: "Ahead, eyes down and the pain of the earth/intertwined with the joy of daydreaming". We quote Gottfried Keller together with Bloch in these verses that, in the former's "Poetentod", describing the poet's companions, with their fantasy and their genius. Art receives from daytime dreaming this utopian character, not as something lightly ornamented, but as something involving also renunciations, which eventually are engulfed by the joy of a future configuration.

BETWEEN DREAM AND WAKEFULNESS

What is creative in dream is thus closely linked to the gestation of the work of art, be it literary, plastic or musical, since the oneiric domain represents the crucible from which the outline of the artistic creation gradually emerges. But is is above all in daytime dreaming that the anticipatory fantasy which is always ahead of circumstancial reality plays a role. Thanks to it, creation assimilates its circumstances and its epochal moment, transforming them in the imaginary entity. From this approach and taking into account the anticipatory fantasy's orientation towards the future, there appear the guiding lines of an "art eschatology", a theory supported by some specialists in aesthetics such as Maurice Nédoncelle and also somehow implicit in Bloch's notion of hope. Such an eschatologic trend in fact coincides with the aspiration to absolute perfection, which lives inside every outline or scheme of a future work. This absolute, also accepted by Bloch, certainly refers to a peculiar "must be" of aesthetic character. Here the analogy with what is ethical can be seen at first sight. Even though man is embarked upon a perfectioning guided always by an ideal "must be" primarily at the ethical level, this demand for perfection also appears at the aesthetic level, but in the latter case it is related to the perfection of the work to be done, considering it both in its formal and material aspects. Undoubtedly, as happens in ethics, here the tendency to the ideal — the absolute — plays a role, and since such an ideal is never wholly accomplished, there is in the domain of art always a melancholy inspired by unreachable but coveted beauty, linked to the "not yet" of what is not wholly accomplished.

Thus the creative process in art before being objectively put into effect has been "dreamed" in anticipation. We essentially agree with Bloch's thesis on the creation of art as an expression of human hope, but disagree with his rejection of the nighttime dream as a real generating force of fantasy. In fact, for Bloch the sleeper's dream should be understood in the context of what Freud's disciples call "the pre-conscious" — *das Umbewusste*. In turn, the sense which such a psychic level may have is reduced to what-is-no-longer-conscious, to what is below consciousness, sunk in the cellar. Thus nighttime dreaming, as what-is-no-longer-conscious, is just at the antipodes of the not-yet-conscious, which defines the hope impulse oriented to the future, and is then the dawning of what is conscious. More in consonance with the oneiric facts, María Zambrano's thought values both daytime dreaming and nighttime or initial dreaming, since for her both play a positive role in the creative process. Undoubtedly this role has singular importance in daytime or real dreaming — which is properly creative — since it enlightens what is not conscious in nighttime dreaming, even though this latter in turn also represents a trial for those trying to understand what happens in "wakeful dreaming", illuminating its symbols and metaphors. In this approach, daytime, creative dreaming refers us to its origin in nighttime dreaming, an origin denied by Bloch. In this dreaming, everything that appears is pure outline and transitivity; in daytime dreaming, in contrast, there is more clearly outlined an organized configuration of the work which drives the individual to accomplish it. Indeed, we could then identify daytime dreaming, creative daydreaming, with the inspiration or creative intuition of the work.

We certainly can not deny that nighttime dreaming implies a descent from conscious and the wakeful state to the endothymic level — a level of internal affective states, of emotions and impulses where the subject "suffers" his psychic states, but neither is it possible to deny that in it arises a drive to the state of wakefulness, where the subject, even though still forced to a certain passivity, already tries the creative act of effectivity and freedom, through which he comes to artistic gestation. For all these reasons, we may say that the dreaming subject's passivity is not complete in any kind of dream and that oneiric timelessness does not wholly exclude time and history. The former, in fact, is alluded to in a succession such as takes place in reality; the latter, is to be seen in a certain oneiric "record", a certain provisional argument which "prefigures" creative freedom, and which in human existence is expressed by the destiny ruling the span between birth and death. It is not then feasible to separate dreams — daytime or nighttime — from man's life itself. Neither can we ignore the meaning of dreaming as an important element in man's psychic development; we can not then separate it from the retrospective and prospective elements of consciousness's dynamism. Only from this perspective can we also understand human creativity, as something essential to the human being. It too emerges from a past rich in archaic symbols and tends to the future of wished for, new and dazzling accomplishment.

Buenos Aires

NOTES

[1] *El sueño creador,* in *Obras reunidas* (Madrid: Aguilar, 1971), p. 34.
[2] *Ibid.,* p. 40.
[3] *Ibid.,* pp. 40—41.
[4] *Diccionario de las Religiones* by Paul Poupard, Barcelona: Herder (1987); original: "*Dictionnaire des Religions*" (Paris: PUF, 1985).
[5] *El sueño creador, op. cit.,* p. 39.
[6] *Ibid.*
[7] *Ibid.,* p. 47.
[8] *Ibid.,* p. 48.
[9] *Ibid.*
[10] *Ibid.,* p. 49.
[11] *Ibid.,* p. 50.
[12] Zambrano uses the Spanish verb "desentrañarse" in its double meaning: to come out of the bowels and also to be deciphered or understood.
[13] *Ibid.,* p. 51.
[14] *Ibid.,* p. 21.
[15] Spanish translation (Madrid: Aguilar, 1977), p. 74. Original: *Das Prinzip Hoffnung* (Frankfurt am Main: Suhrkamp Verlag, 1959).
[16] *Op. cit.,* p. 74.
[17] *Ibid.,* p. 86.
[18] *Ibid.,* p. 83.
[19] *Ibid.,* p. 86.

INDEX OF NAMES

Analecta Husserliana

The Yearbook of Phenomenological Research

Editor-in-Chief

Anna-Teresa Tymieniecka

The World Institute for Advanced Phenomenological Research and Learning,
Belmont, Massachusetts, U.S.A.

1. Tymieniecka, A-T. (ed.), *Volume 1 of Analecta Husserliana.* 1971
   ISBN 90-277-0171-7

2. Tymieniecka, A-T. (ed.), *The Later Husserl and the Idea of Phenomenology.*
   Idealism – Realism, Historicity and Nature. 1972   ISBN 90-277-0223-3

3. Tymieniecka, A-T. (ed.), *The Phenomenological Realism of the Possible
   Worlds.* The 'A Priori', Activity and Passivity of Consciousness, Phenomenology and Nature. 1974   ISBN 90-277-0426-0

4. Tymieniecka, A-T. (ed.), *Ingardeniana.* A Spectrum of Specialised Studies
   Establishing the Field of Research. 1976   ISBN 90-277-0628-X

5. Tymieniecka, A-T. (ed.), *The Crisis of Culture.* Steps to Reopen the
   Phenomenological Investigation of Man. 1976   ISBN 90-277-0632-8

6. Tymieniecka, A-T. (ed.), *The Self and the Other.* The Irreducible Element in
   Man, Part I. 1977   ISBN 90-277-0759-6

7. Tymieniecka, A-T. (ed.), *The Human Being in Action.* The Irreducible Element
   in Man, Part II. 1978   ISBN 90-277-0884-3

8. Nitta, Y. and Hirotaka Tatematsu (eds.), *Japanese Phenomenology.*
   Phenomenology as the Trans-cultural Philosophical Approach. 1979
   ISBN 90-277-0924-6

9. Tymieniecka, A-T. (ed.), *The Teleologies in Husserlian Phenomenology.* The
   Irreducible Element in Man, Part III. 1979   ISBN 90-277-0981-5

10. Wojtyła, K., *The Acting Person.* Translated from Polish by A. Potocki. 1979
    ISBN Hb 90-277-0969-6; Pb 90-277-0985-8

11. Ales Bello, A. (ed.), *The Great Chain of Being* and *Italian Phenomenology.*
    1981   ISBN 90-277-1071-6

12. Tymieniecka, A-T. (ed.), *The Philosophical Reflection of Man in Literature.*
    Selected Papers from Several Conferences held by the International Society for
    Phenomenology and Literature in Cambridge, Massachusetts. Includes the
    essay by A-T. Tymieniecka, *Poetica Nova.* 1982   ISBN 90-277-1312-X

13. Kaelin, E. F., *The Unhappy Consciousness.* The Poetic Plight of Samuel
    Beckett. An Inquiry at the Intersection of Phenomenology and literature. 1981
    ISBN 90-277-1313-8

14. Tymieniecka, A-T. (ed.), *The Phenomenology of Man and of the Human
    Condition.* Individualisation of Nature and the Human Being. (Part I:) Plotting

Analecta Husserliana

the Territory for Interdisciplinary Communication. 1983
Part II see below under Volume 21.   ISBN 90-277-1447-9

15. Tymieniecka, A-T. and Calvin O. Schrag (eds.), *Foundations of Morality, Human Rights, and the Human Sciences.* Phenomenology in a Foundational Dialogue with Human Sciences. 1983   ISBN 90-277-1453-3

16. Tymieniecka, A-T. (ed.), *Soul and Body in Husserlian Phenomenology.* Man and Nature. 1983   ISBN 90-277-1518-1

17. Tymieniecka, A-T. (ed.), *Phenomenology of Life in a Dialogue Between Chinese and Occidental Philosophy.* 1984   ISBN 90-277-1620-X

18. Tymieniecka, A-T. (ed.), *The Existential Coordinates of the Human Condition: Poetic – Epic – Tragic.* The Literary Genre. 1984   ISBN 90-277-1702-8

19. Tymieniecka, A-T. (ed.), *Poetics of the Elements in the Human Condition.* (Part 1:) The Sea. From Elemental Stirrings to Symbolic Inspiration, Language, and Life-Significance in Literary Interpretation and Theory. 1985
For Part 2 and 3 *see below* under Volumes 23 and 28.   ISBN 90-277-1906-3

20. Tymieniecka, A-T. (ed.), *The Moral Sense in the Communal Significance of Life.* Investigations in Phenomenological Praxeology: Psychiatric Therapeutics, Medical Ethics and Social Praxis within the Life- and Communal World. 1986
                    ISBN 90-277-2085-1

21. Tymieniecka, A-T. (ed.), *The Phenomenology of Man and of the Human Condition.* Part II: The Meeting Point Between Occidental and Oriental Philosophies. 1986   ISBN 90-277-2185-8

22. Tymieniecka, A-T. (ed.), *Morality within the Life- and Social World.* Interdisciplinary Phenomenology of the Authentic Life in the 'Moral Sense'. 1987
Sequel to Volumes 15 and 20.   ISBN 90-277-2411-3

23. Tymieniecka, A-T. (ed.), *Poetics of the Elements in the Human Condition.* Part 2: The Airy Elements in Poetic Imagination. Breath, Breeze, Wind, Tempest, Thunder, Snow, Flame, Fire, Volcano... 1988   ISBN 90-277-2569-1

24. Tymieniecka, A-T., *Logos and Life.* Book I: Creative Experience and the Critique of Reason. 1988   ISBN Hb 90-277-2539-X; Pb 90-247-2540-3

25. Tymieniecka, A-T., *Logos and Life.* Book II: The Three Movements of the Soul. 1988   ISBN Hb 90-277-2556-X; Pb 90-247-2557-8

26. Kaelin, E. F. and Calvin O. Schrag (eds.), *American Phenomenology.* Origins and Developments. 1989   ISBN 90-277-2690-6

27. Tymieniecka, A-T. (ed.), *Man within his Life-World.* Contributions to Phenomenology by Scholars from East-Central Europe. 1989
                    ISBN 90-277-2767-8

28. Tymieniecka, A-T. (ed.), *The Elemental Passions of the Soul.* Poetics of the Elements in the Human Condition, Part 3. 1990   ISBN 0-7923-0180-3

Analecta Husserliana

29. Tymieniecka, A-T. (ed.), *Man's Self-Interpretation-in-Existence*. Phenomenology and Philosophy of Life. – Introducing the Spanish Perspective. 1990
ISBN 0-7923-0324-5

30. Rudnick, H. H. (ed.), *Ingardeniana II*. New Studies in the Philosophy of Roman Ingarden. With a New International Ingarden Bibliography. 1990
ISBN 0-7923-0627-9

31. Tymieniecka, A-T. (ed.), *The Moral Sense and Its Foundational Significance: Self, Person, Historicity, Community*. Phenomenological Praxeology and Psychiatry. 1990   ISBN 0-7923-0678-3

32. Kronegger, M. (ed.), *Phenomenology and Aesthetics*. Approaches to Comparative Literature and Other Arts. Homages to A-T. Tymieniecka. 1991
ISBN 0-7923-0738-0

33. Tymieniecka, A-T. (ed.), *Ingardeniana III*. Roman Ingarden's Aesthetics in a New Key and the Independent Approaches of Others: The Performing Arts, the Fine Arts, and Literature. 1991
Sequel to Volumes 4 and 30   ISBN 0-7923-1014-4

34. Tymieniecka, A-T. (ed.), *The Turning Points of the New Phenomenological Era*. Husserl Research – Drawing upon the Full Extent of His Development. 1991   ISBN 0-7923-1134-5

35. Tymieniecka, A-T. (ed.), *Husserlian Phenomenology in a New Key*. Intersubjectivity, Ethos, the Societal Sphere, Human Encounter, Pathos. 1991
ISBN 0-7923-1146-9

36. Tymieniecka, A-T. (ed.), *Husserl's Legacy in Phenomenological Philosophies*. New Approaches to Reason, Language, Hermeneutics, the Human Condition. 1991   ISBN 0-7923-1178-7

37. Tymieniecka, A-T. (ed.), *New Queries in Aesthetics and Metaphysics*. Time, Historicity, Art, Culture, Metaphysics, the Transnatural. 1991
ISBN 0-7923-1195-7

38. Tymieniecka, A-T. (ed.), *The Elemental Dialectic of Light and Darkness*. The Passions of the Soul in the Onto-Poiesis of Life. 1992   ISBN 0-7923-1601-0

Kluwer Academic Publishers – Dordrecht / Boston / London